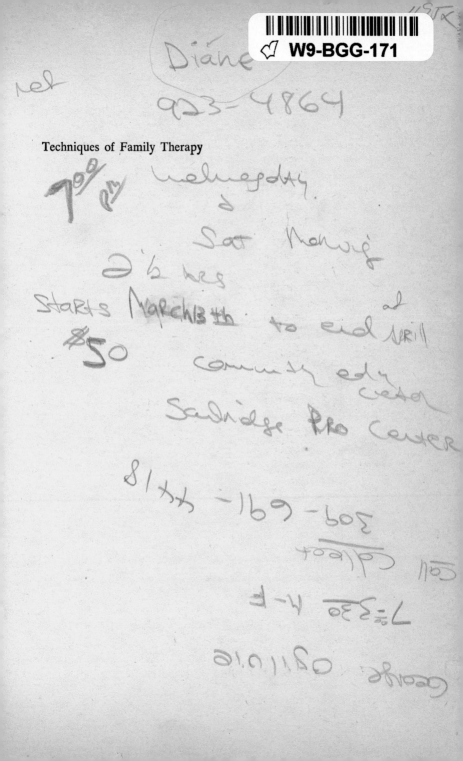

net

Diane
923-4864

Techniques of Family Therapy

7ºº PM wednesday

Sat morning

2½ hrs

Starts March 13th to end April

$50

community edu center

Sandridge Pro Center

8177 - 169 - 609

309-691-7718

call Gilreat

7:30 M-F

George 0211016

Techniques of Family Therapy

JAY HALEY
AND LYNN HOFFMAN

———

Basic Books, Inc., Publishers

NEW YORK

Introduction

In both form and content this book is designed to capture the excitement of family therapy for people who have not yet set out upon this adventure and for others who have begun to perform therapy with families and seek experienced guides. Family therapy has existed as a distinct type of treatment for about fifteen years and a considerable literature has developed about it. Yet the subject poses special problems for anyone who wishes to describe what happens in family therapy. A book by a particular therapist or his group tends to be parochial; it is confined to one method and does not express the variety of approaches to family treatment which have emerged. Yet no one has sufficient knowledge of the many family-therapy approaches to offer a concise work which summarizes both practice and theory. Even defining family therapy and distinguishing it from other therapeutic approaches can be difficult. Some family therapists regularly interview whole families together, but other family therapists will focus on parts of families or even work regularly with only one family member to bring about a change in the entire family. Because of the variety of ways families are treated, one cannot call family therapy simply a new method of treatment; it is a new way of conceptualizing the cause and cure of psychiatric problems. Family therapists are distinct as a group largely because of a common assumption: if the individual is to change, the context in which he lives must change. The unit of treatment is no longer the person, even if only a single person is interviewed; it is the set of relationships in which the person is imbedded. Out of family therapy has come what is, perhaps, one of the major questions of this century:

whether deviant and violent behavior by individuals is adaptive to the intimate social systems in which they currently live.

At this time in this rapidly emerging field, family therapy is best defined as what a number of family therapists are doing. To learn what it is they do, one must watch them at work and inquire about their actions. This book was designed to offer the reader an approximation of the experience of talking with skillful family therapists about their work.

The form of this book is unusual; it is a series of conversations with family therapists about specific family-therapy interviews. The content of the work deals with several mysteries: what happens in the human family, what happens among the intimates of social deviants and psychiatric patients, and how a skillful therapist intervenes in a family to produce a change.

The form of presentation here was designed to meet a special need. Psychotherapists who write about treatment tend to offer theoretical discussions which can be far removed from what actually occurs in therapy. Yet an observer who merely watches a therapist at work and writes about what he sees can misunderstand what is happening. The conversational form offered here provides a compromise between those extremes. The therapist describes what he does and the observer offers his own views within the framework of a discussion about the actual operations in the therapeutic interview.

Five experienced family therapists were asked to cooperate in this endeavor. Each was chosen because he had a style of working with families which was sufficiently distinctive to be a method in itself. Four of the therapists have worked with families for many years. The one exception is a therapeutic team which has begun to practice family therapy relatively recently but is both skillful and offers an original approach.

The selection of these particular family therapists is not meant in any way to be a reflection upon the many other family therapists who are making their contributions to the field. Concerns about availability, time, geography, and the space limitations of this work have made the selection rather arbitrary. Many other family therapists who are equally experienced and skillful and who have unique styles of their own would have been appropriate for this type of presentation.

All of the family therapists were asked to choose an initial interview with a family which they felt represented their usual approach to family treatment. The interview had to have taken place before the therapist knew that it would be used for this type of exploration, and it had to be tape-recorded. A further requirement was that this must not be an isolated demonstration or diagnostic interview, but an interview with a family which the therapist planned to continue with in treatment. The final outcome of the treatment was not considered in the selection of an interview; the focus was upon how a therapist starts off family treatment. In two cases, there had been a preliminary contact with the family prior to the interview which is presented. In one case the initial interview proved to be the only interview, at least to date, since the family did not continue. These exceptions are discussed in the text.

When a therapist had several initial interviews which might be suitable, an attempt was made to choose one which would give more variety to the total collection. Different types of problems as well as "patients" of varying sex and age were sought. Part of the value of this work is that it offers verbatim transcripts of the conversations of five contrasting types of families. The transcripts are as accurate as possible, with only necessary changes to protect the anonymity of the families. These five family interviews are set apart in the text so that the reader can examine them separately from the conversation about them. The verbal transcript can, of course, only suggest the complexity of the interchange between the family members as they talk with the therapist. The body communication of the participants is necessarily omitted and so is the range of vocal intonations which qualify whatever is said and done. Yet the verbal exchange is rich enough to offer a portrait of the family.

When an initial interview had been selected, the authors sat down with the therapist and played the tape recording of the family treatment session. As they listened, they talked to the therapist about the family and probed into why he did what he did step by step throughout the interview. This conversation was also recorded. Many hours of discussion were reduced to the conversation published here. The therapists were each given the opportunity to review the draft and change or edit what they said so that the final product would express fairly their approaches to family therapy. The final responsibility for what is presented resides, however, with the authors.

It should be emphasized that the family-therapy interview is presented verbatim, but the conversation with the therapist about that interview is a creation put together from a vast amount of recorded conversation.

All the family therapists were interviewed in their own offices, where they could be at ease. The interviews were conducted in a free manner, with little attempt to cover systematically scheduled points of information. However, many comparative questions were asked to bring out the variety of points of view on such matters as how many family members to have in the room, how to handle secrecy, whether sex should be discussed in front of children, whether to take a history, and so on.

What was sought in these interviews was not a collection of facts obtained on an interview schedule. Instead, the intention was to lure out of a therapist his ways of thinking about his operations, and to let ideas develop which might not have been previously considered by either therapist or interviewers. Because of this approach, there was an excitement and an uncertainty about the inquiry as it proceeded which was felt to be as integral a value as any information which could be brought out. This type of interview, when successful, makes explicit that which was previously only implicit in a therapist's work. It gets at a level which is often hidden when one takes a more direct and rational route. In this sense, these interviews can be seen more as an art form than as a scientific endeavor, just as therapy itself can be considered more art than science.

The organizing factor in each conversation was the particular therapy interview being discussed. The tape recording of the interview has somewhat the same usefulness as a script for a play when one is trying to talk about the entire theatrical production. The interview became a reference point for refreshing the therapist's memory, a base camp for forays into unmapped territory, and a concrete focus for bringing the conversation back to earth.

Two interviewers talked with the therapist, but in the text they have been reduced to a single interviewer. Although this "interviewer" at times speaks in different styles, it was felt that the reading would be simplified if the dialogue was between one interviewer and a therapist. Similarly, when a therapeutic team was interviewed, many of the statements of the group were put in the mouth of a single spokesman.

One of the interviewers was experienced in family therapy, while the other was new to the field. This arrangement was essential to cover questions of interest to practicing family therapists as well as other points which might be raised by readers inexperienced in family work. In addition, when experienced family therapists talk together, they tend to speak a jargon of their own, leaving many points unexpressed because they believe they share a common view when indeed they may not. Such a collusion, as well as moments of spurious debate, can be broken up when a participant who has less background in psychiatry requires more explicit statements of issues.

The views of these therapists about their work are, necessarily, only partially presented in this work. Each therapist must express his general style of family therapy when talking about a single opening interview for a relatively short period of time. What the therapist says is also influenced by his particular mood and the context within which he is talking. It is possible to argue that what the therapist offers here is a set of rationalizations, or explanations after the fact, rather than the "real" reasons for his behavior with a particular family. Not only would he prefer to show his work in the best light, but many of these therapy sessions had taken place some time earlier and he could not be expected to recall precisely why he said one thing to a family rather than something else.

However, it is doubtful whether one can ever really know why someone does what he does, and to ask him for his reasons does not necessarily disclose the "truth." From such queries we learn what a therapist's beliefs are about his work. If these be rationalizations, that is what all clinical writing is. This rationale is what he teaches others and becomes the foundation of a therapeutic method. This book makes an effort to get beyond the rationale, but by using a dialectical approach, not by offering an interpretation of its own. The conversations are a product of what the therapist brought, what the interviewers brought, and what was contained in the interview material. This not only has the advantage of a multiple view, but it gives the reader the freedom to make his own interpretations of the interview and to accept or reject the various explanations with which he is presented.

Hopefully, the transcript of the interview provides the reader with an approximation of the experience of joining a family in a treatment session. Therapists who have not yet sat down with whole families and observed them do not understand this new view of psychopathology. Only by observing a deviant individual, such as the schizophrenic, in conversation with his intimates can one discover that his strange and bizarre behavior is meaningful and adaptive to his natural setting. It is like seeing a fish in the water for the first time when one has previously only seen him stranded on the shore, gasping, and trying to fly with inadequate finlike wings.

The authors wish to express their indebtedness to the therapists who cooperated in this venture. Particular gratitude is expressed to the families who allowed this presentation of their experience.

JAY HALEY

LYNN HOFFMAN

August 1967

Contents

AUTHORS' NOTE

The tape recordings of the family interviews included in this book have been transcribed as accurately as possible and are presented in their entirety, with only names changed and places omitted.

Techniques of Family Therapy

1]

No Man's Land

An interview with Charles R. Fulweiler, Ph.D.

INT.: How did you come to see the Kane family?

DR. F.: The thirteen-year-old son, Mike, had broken into a store and had stolen some cigarettes and some loose change that was lying around. He was arrested, and since the investigating probation officer felt that this was a neurotic delinquent act and suspected some family involvement, he referred the family to me. I was working with the Guidance Clinic of the Alameda County Probation Department at the time.

INT.: Had the boy been in trouble before?

DR. F.: Never. This was a bolt out of the blue. The only hints the family had of anything that might have led up to this were the boy's rebelliousness about smoking and his general evasiveness at home. He had also been cited a couple of times for truancy.

INT.: What was the family like?

DR. F.: It was a run-of-the-mill lower-middle-class family. The parents were in their late thirties and they had a younger daughter, though I never saw her in therapy. These were the sort of naïve, churchgoing people who are convinced that they are living a good life and doing good works. The father had worked for years as an accountant for a finance company. He was made for a rut and he found it. Not a bad guy, but there was nothing about him that was spontaneous and free. The mother had more to her; she could have come out of a soap

Charles R. Fulweiler, Ph.D., is Consultant in Family-Centered Psychotherapy at the Department of Psychology, University of California at Berkeley, and is also in private practice.

opera. She had a lot of unexpressed flamboyance, hints of black-lace underwear and sheer nightgowns, which didn't fit with a husband like that. He was about as romantic as mashed potatoes. This couple's idea of a big evening was to go with the children to a restaurant in the suburb where they lived and have the blue-plate special.

INT.: What was the boy like?

DR. F.: Not a delinquent type at all. He was a good student, took pride in himself, tried very hard to convey the appearance of being a good boy, was polite to his elders, and so on. He never stepped out of line, really, except when he committed the burglary.

INT.: Had you seen the family or spoken to them before this session?

DR. F.: No. All they knew was that they were going to come into therapy with me. They had no idea of what family therapy was, but since the probation officer urged it, they were very anxious to comply. The fact that the boy was to have therapy influenced the court to put him on probation rather than sending him to a correctional institution.

INT.: So they were, in a sense, coming in under duress. Did this make them more resistant to the idea of therapy?

DR. F.: No, not these people. I've had families who literally had to be ordered into therapy by the judge. They come in with a politeness that is overwhelming, but they block and resist in every way they know how. This family was different. They weren't used to the idea of anybody in their family being in jail, and they were ready to do anything to reinstate themselves in the eyes of the community and prove themselves good, proper people. They were falling all over themselves to cooperate with me.

INT.: I noticed that this tape was divided into two sessions, one short one where you introduce your method to the family, and another later one where actual therapy begins. Is this routine for you?

DR. F.: No. I usually tell people about my method and go into therapy right away. I had some tests I wanted them to take, or I wouldn't have broken off here.

Introductory interview with the Kane family

> DR. F. (*referring to tests the family members have just taken*): Awful, aren't they?
>
> MRS. K.: Horrible. (*Laughs.*)
>
> DR. F.: I somehow have guilt feelings (*Mr. and Mrs. K. laugh*) about giving these. Has Mr. Williams [*the tester*] explained to you what the purpose of the testing is?
>
> MR. K.: Ah, to a certain extent, yes. He didn't go into it in any, any great detail.
>
> DR. F.: Well, a major reason for this is that I'm engaged on a research into the, ah, nature and functioning of this family. . . .
>
> MR. K.: Mmm, yeah, yeah.
>
> DR. F.: . . . that's what I'm doing. It's part of my work and I, at this point I'm taking only cases where I can have a research function as well as the therapy itself. . . .
>
> MRS. K. Mmm.
>
> MR. K. Mmm.
>
> DR. F.: . . . so the tests don't influence your work with me at all, but they are of great value to me, and I will ask you to, at the conclusion when we're through, to wind up by taking the same series again, as bad as that sounds.
>
> MRS. K.: (*Laughs.*)

INT.: What were these tests for?

DR. F.: They were part of the research I was doing at the time for my Ph.D. thesis. I don't ordinarily test people. But there was another reason for bringing up the tests in this way. By being friendly with the family and empathizing with their problems in the tests, I was trying to establish the fact that my role as an authority didn't make me automatically superior as a person. Whenever I can underline a symmetrical relationship, a relationship in which each party is valued for his unique contribution, I do so. I insist on my role as an authority where it's appropriate, but when the father or mother or child has a richer experience or authority than I have, I don't hesitate to sit at his feet.

INT.: You start out here by implying, "You are going to help me," not "I am going to help you."

DR. F.: That's right. I put us on an equal plane by pointing out that although they are coming to see me as a professional, there is something important they can do for me too.

INT.: It must surprise them, when you consider that they're in there because their kid has done something wrong and the law is involved and you're part of all that. But it's probably more necessary in that framework than it might be otherwise.

DR. F.: Yes, although there are some frameworks where you can't work this way, where you must establish your hierarchical superiority right off. There are people who won't respond to therapy in any other context, very authoritarian people like Nazis—I've worked with them too. But these are only a small minority.

INT.: In other words, you adapt your approach to what you think will work with the particular patient.

DR. F.: Yes. A problem, I've found, is that many people feel that any therapy that isn't psychoanalytic therapy is second best and they'd be in analysis if only they could afford it. That's partly why I make it clear from the start that I'm not going to act like a classical analyst; I'm going to enter into therapy in a direct, personal way.

INT.: By presenting family therapy as something very different, you prevent possible objections along that line.

DR. F.: That's right.

INT.: Does it make a difference for you if the family has no knowledge of psychotherapy at all?

DR. F.: Yes. I'd much rather work with a naïve family like this one than, say, a psychiatrist and his family. They can be the most dreadful patients that ever came down the trail, and the most resistant.

> DR. F.: Ah, it isn't that bad really. There's one more test for you to take today, which will take you just a few more minutes. It's not a hard one to take. But, ah, as I say, these don't influence what goes on here.

DR. F.: Now this last one was the Semantic Differential Test, really a weird test to take. You had to rank all these concepts as to whether they were hot or cold, weak or strong. Mother, for example, was she hot or cold? I didn't know how these people would react to some of these things. I was being evasive, trying to put them on the spot, so they couldn't just take one look at the test and reject it.

INT.: This wasn't an effort to make them feel like equals?

DR. F.: Not this part. Here I was manipulating like mad, because I knew the test would puzzle them. I was trying to get them to feel that if I thought this was simple and easy to do, why of course they ought to.

INT.: Did any of these tests give you useful diagnostic information?

DR. F.: No. They were a waste of time, especially the Minnesota Multiphasic Personality Inventory. I had MMPIs done on all my dissertation families, both before and after treatment, and I couldn't use the material. Nothing helpful came out at all. The only useful test was the Family Unity Scale which I developed myself, in the Interpersonal Check List.

> DR. F.: Now, I, as I understand it, Mike has been into a good deal of trouble, recently, and all of you are concerned with what is the cause of this, what are the things that have led up to it and so on.

INT.: When you mention this "trouble" Mike has been in, did you know exactly what he had done?

DR. F.: I don't remember whether I knew it or not.

INT.: Ordinarily, would you name the crime instead of leaving it general like this? It's such a gentle way of putting it.

DR. F.: It would depend on the case. If the family seemed to be trying to avoid talking about it or facing up to it, I would probably come out much more coldly. As long as they're not, there's no need to say, "Mike did this and this and this. What are you going to do about it?"

INT.: When you say that they are all concerned with the cause of Mike's difficulty, did you have some knowledge that they were concerned, or did you just assume it?

DR. F.: I assumed it. I expected them to be concerned. This is a very powerful tool in therapy, to expect your patient to behave in the way you wish he would behave. By riding into it this way, you can exert a great deal of influence. It would take a socially blind person, an authority-blind person, to say to a therapist in Juvenile Hall, or to a therapist anywhere, "I'm not concerned about my son's behavior. I don't care what made him get into this." You can pull for a lot of cooperation by doing this, even force it.

> DR. F.: The purpose of my work here is to try to remedy the things that lead up to a youngster like Mike getting into diff-, serious

difficulty. I take it as a starting point that when a child is in trouble, that the parents are not to blame, nor is the child to blame in any kind of, ah, right or wrong sense, but that the relationships within the home are confused or disturbed in some ways.

INT.: Why do you immediately bring up the question of blame?

DR. F.: There's a specific reason why I phrased it this way with this family. When these people came in, they looked like frightened rabbits. They were all ready to be blamed. They had already heard, "There are no delinquent children, there are just delinquent parents." They were ready to swallow this whole hog, say *mea culpa,* and put on sackcloth and ashes. But this was not what I wanted. So I started out by trying to get rid of the blame.

INT.: Do you do this routinely?

DR. F.: No, I usually begin by pointing out that the child has grown up in the family and its various social experiences, and that however the parents may feel about it, the family shares some responsibility for the behavior of the child. Here I felt it wise to start out by expunging the idea of blame, because the parents were just bleeding. Otherwise, I didn't think they'd stay in therapy.

INT.: You start out by relieving the parents of any specific responsibility. At the same time, you define the problem as something they've participated in. They can't really refuse to deal with that, because you're taking the blame off them by the way you're putting it.

DR. F.: That's the whole point. You hook them on this without affronting them.

INT.: I notice that you don't start out with "The child is not to blame," and then shift to the parents; you start with "The parents are not to blame," and shift to the child.

DR. F.: I do that because it's easier for the parents to forgive the child if they've been cleared first.

INT.: It would have been very different if you'd begun by saying the boy was not to blame.

DR. F.: Yes. I could tell they were religious, God-fearing people the minute they walked in the door. If I'd said that first, it would have stirred up all their moralistic principles.

INT.: You're trying not to get stuck on a moral issue. But by saying the boy can't be criticized on moral grounds, you're implying that the parents don't have to criticize themselves either.

DR. F.: I'm trying to tell the parents, "It's not that you're right or wrong. You've made mistakes, but you didn't intend them, even though the effects of these mistakes are to some extent bound up in what your child is doing now." I sometimes explicitly say to parents, "If you had known what you were doing with your child, you would have done differently with him, and the results would have been different. Therefore, I assume that if you can find out what causes your child's difficulties, you'll want to change it.

INT.: That's quite an assumption.

DR. F.: Yes. I make them responsible, but under a different set of rules than morality usually implies. I believe that we can characterize our actions as partly determined. To the extent that they are, we can free ourselves from moral judgments and go on to look at the whys and do something about it. But there's another reason I want to take the blame off the parents. I feel very strongly that one of the therapist's primary jobs in the first session is to seduce the patient into therapy.

INT.: Seduce?

DR. F.: Just that, seduce him. Create attitudes or feelings or relationships which will encourage him to come into therapy and continue it. Any therapist who thinks he isn't playing this game is going to have a sad lack of patients. You have to sell the therapy to your patient, win him over to a relationship with you. If you don't, you lose him, and then he has had a failure experience and becomes less open to help of any kind.

> DR. F. (*cont.*): And I think that, ah, probably during the course of this you will try to blame people, at times.
>
> MR. K.: Mm.
>
> DR. F. (*to Mr. K.*): You will try to blame Mike or your wife, and your wife will try to blame you or Mike, but as far as I'm concerned, neither one of you is to blame, both of you have contributed to the— (*Sentence breaks off.*)

INT.: That's a slippery phrasing, when you say, "Neither one of you is to blame, but both of you have contributed." It's again this mixture of absolving them and yet, in the act of absolving them, including them.

DR. F.: I'm trying to present it so that they can see that they are responsible for, or have contributed to, the situation, without having to accept the burden of having done this intentionally.

INT.: It's an interesting technique. If I want to get over a premise to you, I can present it wrapped up with another one which is less acceptable. Then you won't refuse the premise I want you to take, because you're being cleared of the unacceptable one.

DR. F.: This is exactly what I'm doing, and it comes up many times, in many guises. I do this with love, when I point out that people love each other and fight and hurt each other at the same time. I phrase it as though all people who love each other hurt each other.

INT.: Why do you point out so explicitly that there's going to be all this blaming?

DR. F.: I'm saying to the father that I know that he and Mike will be ganging up against his wife, and that his wife and Mike will be ganging up against him. I am exonerating the father beforehand for doing this, so that it will be easier for him to forgive his wife when she does it to him, which I knew was going to happen very quickly.

INT.: It's the same thing you did when you forgave the parents first, so that they would then have to join you in forgiving the boy.

DR. F.: Yes. The boy was the one who could do the really dreadful things that hurt, so I put him second. And the same way here. The one I expected to have a dramatic problem with was the wife. She was carrying a load of guilt and anger and she was going to cut loose as soon as she found a safe place to do so. She looked to me as if she were already feeling safe, and I thought I'd better do a little preparing.

INT.: When you announce that people in the family are going to blame each other, is that also to make it seem less terrible?

DR. F.: Yes. Everybody was feeling so guilt-ridden and anxious, especially sitting there in front of me, that I knew they weren't going to want to criticize each other. They'd do it outside the therapy session and outside my knowledge.

INT.: They've probably already done it.

DR. F.: Repeatedly. So I am trying to provide some kind of acceptance or some kind of framework within which it can happen without their panicking or without its disrupting therapy.

INT.: It's a way of giving permission for it to happen.

DR. F.: Yes. I'm saying, "You can talk about it. You can bring it up here, where we can deal with it." It's a reassurance. This family was so particularly sensitive to blame that I felt it wise to desensitize them a little.

DR. F. (*cont.*): In the course of a, of marriage, ah, for various reasons, for the pressures of building a career, the pressures of earning a living, the pressures of having kids needling at you and pushing at you all the time, you build up, or tend to build up, patterns of defense against each other.

MR. K.: Mm-hm.

DR. F.: Both of you probably know each other's problems better than I do, at this point certainly, even after extensive diagnosis you both know each other's problems much better than I.

INT.: When you say that the parents have built up defenses against each other, you are both excusing them because they are only acting in self-defense, and implicating them because there has to be something they are defending themselves against. It's that same trick of putting an acceptable and an unacceptable idea in the same package.

DR. F.: That's right. When I say, "the pressures of building a career and earning a living," I'm assuming the other part of the sentence: "which would cause conflict between you and your wife." I don't think they miss it.

INT.: And the phrasing, "You know more about these problems than I do," not only assumes that there are problems but makes it unlikely that they will deny it, because you are giving them credit for being the authorities.

DR. F.: Well, they are. They know more about the specifics. Of course, if somebody backed me to the wall and said, "If you know so little about their problems, what are you doing treating these people?" I would be forced to admit that I did know more about their problems. Not what exactly caused the difficulties, but what kind of difficulties they were.

INT.: It's a way of slipping out from a position which they could hang you on, of knowing more than you really know.

DR. F.: I hadn't thought of it that way, but it's true.

INT.: It's a little like playing a fish. You pull and then let go, pull and let go. Was this particular shift part of a routine introduction, or were you responding to the reaction you were getting at the moment?

DR. F.: I was responding to the reaction. It's the kind of thing I do with everybody, standard operating procedure, but I phrase it differently with each group, to fit the people I'm working with.

INT.: I'm curious to know why you go into this discussion of marriage.

DR. F.: Part of it is that I sincerely believe that marriage is a difficult task, that it isn't all beer and skittles. It's hard to earn a living, keep bread on the table, feed and clothe kids. The other part is this business of showing respect for your patients. If you treat raising a family as something any fool can do, that doesn't make the patient feel very good. It's this symmetrical idea again. Everyone hasn't the good fortune to be a psychotherapist and sit back and earn a lot of money. I point out that I know marriage is a tough job and I try to show that I have some respect for how the job is being done, even though there may be some difficulties with it now.

INT.: By suggesting that everyone has these difficulties, you're also giving them a way out, so they won't feel on the spot.

DR. F.: I would say that I am presenting them with a reality confrontation rather than a way out, because I believe that any man who has been married fifteen or eighteen years and has brought up a couple of kids and kept his family economically sound has done well. Even if his child is all loused up, he still deserves credit for trying.

INT.: That's a comforting way to look at it.

DR. F.: Suppose your client is a forty-year-old operating engineer who has run a crane all his life and has raised four or five kids and is getting them going in the world. After all, that man has done a real job of work. If you, a scientist, a researcher, a psychotherapist, sit back in your fancy office in your fancy chair and look down your nose at him, how much therapy can you do for him? This comes up with young therapists all the time. They're nervous and inexperienced and when they get some hardheaded guy like this, they don't know how to handle him. They've been taught to insist on keeping their professional distance. Twelve or fifteen years ago, it was considered inappropriate to laugh and joke with your patients, to be friendly with them, to show them respect as human beings. I don't hold with that.

DR. F. (cont.): But you protect each other too. You don't, unless you're angry and unless you're in difficulty, you don't deliberately attack each other, nor do you deliberately attack Mike where he is weakest or most sensitive, nor does he attack you unless he's angry and, ah, there's a blowup of some kind.

MRS. K.: Mmm.

DR. F.: You see, I'm describing marital fights for them. I'm reading their minds, in a sense, by pointing out that they have fights in which they use every dirty trick they can. When they're angry, they undermine each other, they find each other's weak spots and hurt each other viciously. But when they're not angry they tend to gloss over and avoid these sore spots.

INT.: I notice you say that they don't hurt each other unless they're angry, which establishes the premise that they do hurt each other. It's almost hypnotic technique: "Would you rather go into a trance now or later?" And you put it in the nice frame of protecting each other.

DR. F.: This is to encourage them to talk about it and be able to deal with it without being embarrassed or ashamed. By labeling it and recognizing it, I encourage them to bring it into therapy.

INT.: The way you put it implies, "You don't attack each other without due provocation." You almost justify them. Then you slip in another exonerating phrase: "Nor do you *deliberately* attack Mike where he is weakest or most sensitive."

DR. F.: I am trying to tell them that I know they won't set out on purpose to attack each other where they know they might destroy each other. Of course, they are probably in a covert way attacking each other's weak places all the time. That's in there too. But if I put it as "not deliberate," it makes it more acceptable.

DR. F.: For the most part you learn, or tend to learn, in the course of marriage, to respect these sensitive areas for each other, and kind of shy away from them. The difficulty arises, a lot of it, in that these sensitive areas get to be somewhat bigger and bigger as time goes on, and there tends to develop a pattern of, not of shared communication, but of disrupted, or slanted, or biased, communication.

INT.: I take it that this is partly to persuade them to talk about the things they're sensitive about and so on, but it's also an interesting way to describe how a marriage develops.

DR. F.: Yes. These silent areas get bigger and bigger. The more suppressed feelings of resentment there are in a marriage, the more caustic and critical the eyes of the married partners become toward each other, which means that even larger areas develop which they don't want to tread upon.

INT.: Would you say, then, that a marriage in which there is open anger is better off than one in which there isn't?

DR. F.: It would be very difficult to state this categorically. In general, yes. But there are some marriages in which there is a pathological degree of directly expressed anger substituting for things under the surface that aren't talked about.

INT.: In other words, this anger is still not open communication.

DR. F.: Right. But in the majority of cases, if the couple can meet a problem and have an honest, angry fight about it at the time, they are far better off.

INT.: An interest is beginning to develop in how to get a couple to start a fight with each other. There isn't much written about it, but it's becoming more talked about.

DR. F.: This is a touchy area. In the case of two or three families I've had, if you permit it to happen too soon, it becomes the dominant thing and you lose the family entirely. But if you can get them to fight about the appropriate thing at the appropriate time and in the appropriate place, that kind of fighting can be most beneficial.

INT.: Do you encourage that kind of fighting in your therapy?

DR. F.: Sure. I was never so pleased as when a woman patient of mine, who had been taking it and taking it from her husband, finally responded to an insulting remark of his by lighting into him and physically assaulting him. Then she ran sobbing to her bedroom and tried to call me. I wasn't available, so she worked it out with her husband and they had a wonderful weekend, the best sexual relationship they'd had in years.

DR. F. (cont.): Ah, the real things that are happening emotionally to people within a family group are very seldom discussed or brought out, and this is part of my job, to, ah, literally pry into or explore the pattern of relationship between all three of you, so that perhaps in improving communication generally, including each person's understanding of the other, there will be *real* therapy for all of you . . .

MR. K.: Mm-hm.

DR. F.: . . . and I consider it something of benefit to all, all three of you. It's not, I'm not just working on Mike.

INT.: This is the first time you've been so explicit about your role as a therapist. I gather you're trying to help the family anticipate what you're going to be doing with them.

DR. F.: I do this with all my patients, in differing degrees and depending on the kind of people they are, and the circumstances. With this family, it was obvious that if I began to pry into their sexual relationships, they were going to panic. So I was warning them in advance that I was going to do this. I've also tried to frame it so that it will be more acceptable when it comes.

INT.: How have you done that?

DR. F.: We've gone through the process of recognizing that they do fight, that they have problems, and I've been relieving them of feelings of guilt and anxiety all along, as much as I can. Now I'm making a demand which I think they're better prepared for. I've deliberately said that I will pry and be nosy. This is an attempt to disarm them. If I tell them my job is to be nosy and to pry, they can't get mad at me for doing it.

INT.: The word "pry" has an unpleasant connotation. It would be very different if you had used the word "explore."

DR. F.: My assumption was that this father would use these words in defending himself against me if I didn't use them first. He would say, "He's prying into our business."

INT.: Why do you point out that therapy is going to be for all three of them? This is your second attempt to include the whole family as patients without saying that they're all patients.

DR. F.: This is designed to emphasize specifically that they are all three in therapy, not just the boy.

INT.: Again, you label it as something beneficial. What's curious is the way you stress "real" therapy. What would "unreal" therapy be?

DR. F.: I don't know whether I was trying to dislodge the idea that the boy was the only problem and that the parents were only pretending to be in therapy to help him, or whether I was telling them that they were in actual treatment, that they weren't just being counseled or talked with. I did want to force upon them the understanding that they as well as the boy were in therapy. This is one of the hardest things to accomplish when the child is the presenting problem. Sometimes it takes months before the parents accept it, no matter how directly you put it.

INT.: Do you usually put it that directly?

DR. F.: At some early point, I generally do. But once in a while you get a case in which you have to encourage and preserve the myth that all of us adults are helping this poor little child. In one instance, it was about a year before I got around to pointing out to the parents that they were in treatment too.

INT.: But you assumed, just from the look of this family, that you could come out this flatly?

DR. F.: They labeled themselves as patients when they walked in the door. But that didn't mean I had carte blanche to say anything. If I had affronted them in any way, I would have lost them completely. For instance, it would have been terribly inept of me to attack their religious principles or to use vulgar language. They were that sensitive. But by this time I'm feeling that most of the seduction has been accomplished. The mother's in, the father's in, and their eagerness for help and willingness to cooperate are quite apparent.

DR. F. (*addressing Mike*): Boy, are you a sad-looking case today! (*The son has poison oak.*)

MRS. K.: (*Laughs.*)

MR. K.: He sure is.

MRS. K.: (*Laughs.*)

DR. F.: You really did it up brown.

MR. K.: He looks just about as bad today as he did the day I took the picture of him (*inaudible phrase*).

DR. F. (*overlapping, to Mike*): You look like you need treatment of a different kind . . .

MRS. K.: Yes.

DR. F.: . . . at this point.

MRS. K.: Yes, doesn't he though, goodness sakes!

DR. F.: I'll be very anxious to know what you look like when you're (*inaudible words*).

MRS. K. (*laughing*): When he looks normal. (*Laughs.*)

DR. F.: That's right.

MR. K.: He sure is roughed up.

INT.: Why did you suddenly shift to the boy?

DR. F.: It was quite deliberate. I had just labeled them all as patients in psychotherapy, and before they had a chance to object, I took them immediately off the topic and simultaneously brought Mike into the discussion in a friendly way. He had to be seduced too. The timing was very important from my point of view; I find those abrupt shifts of mood very helpful. The laughter relieves the tension and jumps us up to a level where things can be a bit more *bon vivant*. You notice that the father and mother came right in immediately.

INT.: Do you often take that tone with the child?

DR. F.: Of camaraderie?

INT.: Camaraderie, but you also insult him.

DR. F.: This is a technique of mine. I tend to call my good friends bastards.

INT.: You apparently knew about the poison oak before they came in.

DR. F.: Yes, because they were delayed in coming to see me because of it.

INT.: Why do you say to Mike, "You need treatment of a different kind"?

DR. F.: It's a play on words. I'm bringing in the idea of treatment again, but in a comfortable, easy way. It's part of the seduction.

INT.: Again, you slip in the premise that they need treatment, by saying that he needs a different kind.

> DR. F.: Anyhow, this is, ah, where I start. Now, as far as I'm concerned, the responsibility for this rests with you folks. It's your job to, ah, open these areas up, to discuss, to talk, and so on.

INT.: Is that a way of keeping them from pushing the responsibility for therapy onto you or is it a philosophy about therapy?

DR. F.: It's a philosophy about therapy as much as anything else. My contention is that therapy is not a scientific tool you use to cure people with. It's an interaction between people and you play your role as best you can. If they want to lie, or dissemble, or evade, they can make a monkey out of me or any other therapist. I try to win my patients' acceptance of the fact that the responsibility for progress in treatment is theirs, not mine.

INT.: I think it's unusual for someone to state it that directly to a family.

DR. F.: Well, if you accept the sole responsibility, even implicitly, for treating them, in the sense of curing them, then they are going to foist it off on you at every opportunity, in ways that can be highly unpleasant because you won't know what to do. They come in with a whole background and understanding of their roles, the things they have done together, their interactions over the years. Anyway, it would be presumptuous of you to assume that you understand everything they say or do. Ninety percent of it, you don't.

INT.: If a family does badly in therapy, would you suggest to them that it's because they haven't taken enough responsibility?

DR. F.: If I thought they weren't doing what they could, I would tell them so. Of course, it might also be that I'm not the kind of person that could work with them, or I might just be grossly inept.

INT.: This responsibility thing is complex. You say that they have to help themselves, but they are then helping themselves in the context of your helping them to do so.

DR. F.: This runs through the whole warp and woof of therapy. It has to do with the relationship between equals which you are trying to establish. If you are the curer, the healer, and they come to you for your ministrations, it puts you hierarchically above them, and I don't think this is a valuable kind of relationship.

INT.: A lot of the process of therapy seems to amount to making it possible for the patient to get out from under that.

DR. F.: Sure. As soon as they are able to tell you to go to hell, they are on the way to getting well.

INT.: There's a suggestion of a time line here. Up to now, you've been clearing these people of responsibility for past mistakes. Here you imply, "Now that you are in therapy it's different, I expect you to take responsibility."

DR. F.: Exactly. I expect them to take responsibility for working in treatment. It's also a way of defining "treatment" with respect. If I don't respect the treatment process and feel that it's of value, no one else is going to.

INT.: It's another of these assumptions that lead people where you want them to go.

DR. F.: There's one other hook I don't want to get onto. If you accept responsibility for curing your patients, you not only get the credit for their successes, but you get the blame for their failures. I, personally, don't want that responsibility.

INT.: That's understandable.

DR. F.: There are many instances in which you have to play yourself down as the authority. However, there are other times when, based on your information about the family, your knowledge of what goes on in people, your training, and so forth, you can say, "You have to do this, *now*." A therapist shouldn't hesitate to say this when it's called for. He can't make people do what he says, but he can come out with an authoritative statement about what he thinks they should do.

INT.: Do you ever make that kind of authoritative statement, knowing that the patient will do something else, or even ignore it, but will do what you think he ought to do as a by-product?

DR. F.: I worked with a couple some years ago to whom I recommended divorce twenty-five or thirty times, very strongly. Every time there was a serious fight I told them to call a lawyer and get proceedings started. And every time they rejected my advice I said, "Well, there obviously is something more to your marriage than you're willing to admit. Something must be keeping you together."

INT.: Did you do this because you knew they wouldn't get divorced and it was safe, or because you really thought they should get divorced?

DR. F.: I had a dual motivation. I would have been very pleased if the wife had taken action, because it would have meant that whatever the problem was that was holding them together had been resolved. At the same time I knew she wouldn't, and that her not having done so would give me a lever to get at whatever was cooking with her. I've done the same thing with parents. I've said, "You're not able to handle your child, he's obviously beyond your control, you'll have to institutionalize him." And they don't. So we go on and on in the same pattern until they finally understand what's happening and why.

INT.: In other words, you give them an unacceptable alternative to facing up to the problem and dealing with it directly.

DR. F.: Yes. I carry it to the extreme end result.

DR. F.: There will be times when I will ask each of you individually to come out of the room with me and we'll talk over some aspect of it that I think is unclear or that needs talking in another office . . .

MR. K.: Mm.

DR. F.: . . . independently.

INT.: Were you laying the groundwork here in case you wanted to talk with them individually?

DR. F.: Yes. This is something I often do during the course of therapy, and I did it with this family.

INT.: Do you ever treat family members individually?

DR. F.: Oh yes. Right now, I have about ten cases where I've split the families up and am seeing the various members separately. At this point they can't work together.

INT.: I take it you would disagree with the opinion that it isn't family therapy unless you take the whole family as a unit.

DR. F.: I would disagree with any rule about how you treat a family. The needs of the particular case dictate what you do. When a child is the problem, I have found it more productive to treat the child with his parents as a triad, rather than bring all the other siblings in, though I like to see the others at least once. That's why, in this family, I didn't include the younger girl in treatment. I've worked through several families by taking each child in a threesome with the parents as he gets old enough to participate. When I'm working with a couple who have small children, I'll ask them to bring the kids in once, but this is only to observe the way they handle the children, as a help to understanding their own problems. I would never see a family of more than three all through therapy. The number of interactions is too great.

INT.: Is there any other reason why you single out the triad to work with?

DR. F.: Well, if you accept the idea of family homeostasis, of a family system, it doesn't matter which section of it you're dealing with. If you change the interpersonal balance of one triad, you will affect the whole system.

INT.: Some therapists concentrate mainly on the parents. They feel that if there is a problem child, he is merely a cover-up for the marital conflict.

DR. F.: I agree with this to some extent, but I feel that the child can get something out of therapy, at least in the first sessions. Later, when he is no longer the focus of the struggle between the parents, I let him drop out. But again, I don't have a hard and fast rule for this.

INT.: When it comes to taking people out of the session and talking to them privately, how do you handle the other people who are being left out?

DR. F.: It's not supposed to be secret. People are welcome to ask questions or to tell each other about what went on. It's a different matter when I schedule separate individual sessions for husband or wife or child. There they are guaranteed privileged communication. I just started working with a husband and a wife with the agreement that what goes on between each of them and me will never be communicated to the other, unless they themselves choose to tell about it. These individual sessions are tremendously useful to me in working with a marriage unit. I know what is going on, I don't have to guess, and I can work with the family in a much more fruitful way.

INT.: I take it that you don't carry the ideal of open communication too far.

DR. F.: I've learned the hard way that one of the very important things in marriage is for the partners to respect each other's privacy, that there are some things that it's better not to talk about. When a husband or wife is having an affair, it is usually hostility that prompts a "confession." I've never seen a situation in which I wouldn't rather they said nothing and learned to bind their own tensions long enough to let the thing dissipate. This doesn't imply that I think infidelity is any answer to marriage problems. I've never known it to bring anything but confusion and misery to all concerned. In the past, many psychiatrists operated on the premise that the patient ought to free his repressed impulses, and would even encourage people to have affairs. I think this was an extremely misguided interpretation of Freudian theory.

INT.: To get back to the issue of privacy, I take it that you feel that one of your jobs is to protect people from each other.

DR. F.: Yes, and this applies to the child as well. I don't encourage the child to talk about everything. If the parents really knew everything their children were thinking, it would scare them to death.

INT.: Some therapists use the child as a way of getting out information about the family. Do you?

DR. F.: No. I will listen if the child has something he wants to say about his family, but I don't use the child to pry with. This is what has happened to him all his life. But that's a technical point. A more skilled therapist might be able to do this with a child in such a way that it would benefit the whole family.

DR. F. (cont.): There'll be other times when I'll have—Mike, for example, will leave the room and, ah, wait while I discuss something that is much more pertinent to your relationship, and it isn't any of his business or concern. When these kind of areas come up, Mike will not be included in the, the whole picture.

INT.: I gather you don't think the children should be involved in these discussions.

DR. F.: That's right. I recognize that I'm at variance with many of my colleagues, but I don't think it does the child any good, particularly between the ages of ten and eighteen, to be involved in the complexities of his parents' sexual relationship.

INT.: What reasons do you give the child for his going out?

DR. F.: I tell him that some of the problems his parents are having are none of his business, that they're adult problems and he can stay out of it.

INT.: You're drawing a generation line, too. Giving him the comfort of being a child.

DR. F.: And giving his parents the respect and comfort of being adults. They should have some secrets from their children.

INT.: Do you think that in so doing you are making sex a special area that children shouldn't know about?

DR. F.: I don't really deal with it that way. I deal with it as an adult problem that they are not privy to yet. It's not a taboo subject, because we talk about sex in therapy, but we don't talk about the parents' explicit sexuality. If I bring up the child's sexuality, I don't try to pry out the actual thoughts he has while masturbating, or something of this sort, in front of his parents, unless there's some pathology that really necessitates it.

DR. F. (*cont.*): But I stay most of the time behind that, that screen, that is, a mirror—a one-, a two-way mirror—I can never really remember whether it's a two-way mirror or a one-way mirror, it's, whatever it is, I can see through from the other side (*Mrs. K. laughs*) and the microphone is hooked up to a tape recorder. There's a reason for tape recording these. Ah, sometimes I'll have something to say where I put the finger on one of you as having an attitude or a feeling that is not clearly expressed but is certainly there, and in interpreting this I will want to play back to you what you've said, so you can hear and then judge for yourselves what you've said and what you, what has gone on . . .

INT.: Here we get into your method, so let's take some time and go into that in detail. I take it that you've got one room where the family sits and an adjoining room with a one-way screen and a tape recorder, from which you can observe. And that you alternate going into the observation room and watching with going back into the room with the family. How did you come to develop this method?

DR. F.: The way I came to it—and it was the way I started working with families too—was a total accident. In 1953 or 1954, when I was still working at the Alameda County Guidance Clinic, a girl was sent to me because she kept getting into sexual-type delinquencies. She was in the habit of running away from home and turning up in strange places, valley towns, migratory workers' camps, honky-tonks, and so on. And here she was, sweet, pretty, intelligent, blond, blue-eyed, and well-to-do, the perfect stereotype of the 100 percent American girl. Her father had lots of money, and her parents repeatedly expressed nothing but love and concern for her. I gave her a whole raft of tests, which showed no pathology at all, so I patted her on the shoulder and said, "Go forth, child, and sin no more." Three weeks later, back she came, in trouble again, and I gave her a lot more tests and again she breezed through all of them. It still seemed like such a lovely test picture that I sent her back home and told her parents to be nice to her and everything would turn out right. Then she was sent to me a third time, and at this point she was in Juvenile Hall. She had been picked up in one of the central valley towns living with a bunch of migratory workers and had been in jail down there for about a week before being sent up here. By this time I was pretty mystified, since the tests showed nothing of interest, and apart from her odd behavior, nothing else seemed wrong. So I asked the parents to permit me to observe them—we had a one-way mirror in an observation room for training in testing—while they had their first meeting with the girl after her latest scrape. I arranged to have the parents sitting in the room, and then I brought the girl over from Juvenile Hall and left her there while I went behind the screen to watch. The girl had no knowledge of this. Well, after fifteen or twenty minutes of observing the family as they got together at this rather crucial time, I began at last to see why the girl was behaving the way she was. The father was sitting off to one side of the room with a disapproving frown on his face, saying nothing. The mother and daughter were sitting very close together, having an animated discussion about the price of cigarettes in Juvenile Hall in Fresno and whether she liked this kind of candy or that, and how the institution clothes were cut here compared to Fresno. It was completely banal, completely lacking in any warmth or feeling. I listened for about ten minutes and finally, more out of exasperation than anything else, I went out of my observing section, tapped on the door, and called the father out of the room. Just standing in the hall, I said, "Say, do you love your daughter?" He said, "Of course I do." I said, "Well, for Christ's sake, go in there and tell her so," and I sent him back in the room. As I say, I was simply exasperated. My feeling was, "That idiot, his daughter is in trouble, why doesn't he do something about it, say something meaningful to her?" Well, he did. It took him ten or fifteen minutes to say "I love you," but when he finally managed to get it out, the whole character of the meeting changed. The girl began to cry, the mother began to cry, and they all began to talk about the things that were really bothering her and what had led up to her running away. I went in and called the mother out and asked some question of her and sent her back in, and I noticed again that this produced a change in the character of the meeting. They began to talk about what possible reasons the girl might have for wanting to do what she had done, and what importance it had for her. It struck me suddenly that nothing I had done in individual therapy with a child had ever approximated the degree of change—and change potential—that I saw right there in front of me. It seemed a highly desirable way of working with people, so I went on in the same manner for about an hour and a half during that first session, and then set up another appointment. In the meantime, I went to the court and asked permission to keep the girl's case off the court calendar for a couple of weeks while I continued working with the family

INT.: In that first session, did the girl ever know that you were observing?

DR. F.: No. I had a very strong feeling that if she did know, it would distort the relationships and make it impossible for her to behave normally or naturally. That didn't change until I described the technique to a colleague a year later, and he asked me why I didn't tell the child that I was observing. I had no answer; there didn't seem to be any legitimate reason for not telling the child, and from then on I did. Of course, once everybody knew what was going on, it then became possible to play the tape back to the family, which also turned out to be very useful. Since then, I've tried working in the room with the family continuously, to see how it compares with going in and out of the room, and my strong impression is that the second method is the more effective. The more the therapist can be absent from the room, certainly in the initial stages of therapy, the more information of a direct sort he can gain about how the family interacts. The more he is in the room, the more he distorts the very phenomena he is trying to observe. To the extent that you can remain outside of the thing, you get a closer approximation of a real life view of the patient and his family. I treated that particular family for sixteen or eighteen sessions and the girl's problems cleared up very nicely. No one at the clinic objected, but no one was particularly impressed either. The girl had, I think, four interviews with the psychiatric consultant for the clinic, and I am pretty well convinced that to this day he thinks it was these four meetings that did the trick. I had close to thirty hours with the family, compressed into six to eight weeks, and I have the delusion that this is what did it.

INT.: Had you ever, for any purpose, seen the whole family together before that?

DR. F.: Only to prepare for individual testing. This was the first time, to my knowledge, that the principle of psychotherapy had been applied to treating the family unit in this country.

INT.: To get back to your technique, granted that you have objective reasons for using the separate rooms, I gather that you find it more comfortable for personal reasons too.

DR. F.: That's true. But I can't really distinguish one from the other because I started this way, and it always seemed right for me. I have found that staying in with the family is extremely tiring. My trainees too comment on how much easier it is for them when they can go in and out freely. Also, I don't think that I pick up as much information if I remain with the family.

INT.: Do you find that you talk more than you feel you should when you are in the room?

DR. F.: That's a hard question to answer, because I talk more than I should under any circumstances. This is one of my faults as a therapist.

INT.: Developing a method of getting out of the room sounds as if it could also be a way of dealing with that.

DR. F.: It probably is. It's a useful way of keeping me from inter-
acting all the time and continuously. It really shouldn't be Fulweiler
therapy, it should be therapy for the family.

INT.: So when you say to them that the responsibility for treatment rests with them, your method is a way of helping them to realize
that ideal.

DR. F.: It's also a protection for me. If the therapist is in the
room with the family, and someone starts to say something, that person
will look to get a reaction from the therapist and then qualify differently
what he says. With three people all focusing on the therapist at the
same time, it can be pretty exhausting. I usually describe this by drawing a diagram of the three family members and the therapist and putting a line between the therapist and the family. I point out that when
the therapist is in the room, communication is always from family
member A through the therapist to family member B, and the same with
all the exchanges between the family.

INT.: You're like a filter.

DR. F.: Yes. Every communication goes through the therapist,
every single one. Even if people turn and look at each other, which they
don't usually do, they will be glancing out of the corner of their eyes at
the therapist. It's as though they were constantly saying, "You see, Mr.
Therapist, when I try to do this and such, what he does to me." If the
therapist so much as wiggles his ears, he's responding to this. When you
have three people in the room with you and this is going on at both
verbal and nonverbal levels, the number of interactional combinations
is tremendous. Another thing is the control of the countertransference,
which is much easier to handle if you're behind the screen.

INT.: Are you using "countertransference" in the psychoanalytic
sense?

DR. F.: No, I'm using it loosely to signify directing inappropriate
feelings toward your patients. If you have ever been married, or have
ever been a child in a family, or have had any kind of family experience
at all, these people will catch your problems and demonstrate them for
you and to you and through you. If you are constantly in the room, it's
hard for you not to react as if these really were your problems. If you
are out of the room, you don't have this constant necessity for controlling your responses. I don't know how many times a kid has gotten
fresh with his parents and I've had the strong desire to turn him over

my knee. Behind the screen I can mutter, "The little stinker," so that when I go back into the room I don't have to carry that with me; it's worked out, it's done. If I'm in the room, it's going to take some time for me to be able to handle it.

INT.: I should think this would be particularly true of a therapist who is trying to seem human. Being behind the screen relieves you from being human all the time.

DR. F.: It gets you out of a lot of traps, too. This is particularly true in a marital interaction. Most of us, whether we know it or not, are thoroughly biased in this area. We take sides very quickly. I think it takes a lot of maturity in the therapist, and a lot of time, to get to the point of recognizing that the labeled patient isn't always the victim, that it's sometimes quite the other way round.

INT.: Do you find that you tend to take sides with one sex?

DR. F.: I think that the biggest trap for a male therapist is sympathizing with the woman for being married to such a clod. We tend to think, "If she were just married to a man like me, what a wonderful life she'd have." But there are other factors too. Therapists have diurnal variations between being God one minute and the Devil the next. With the first family in the morning I feel fresh and great, and it's a shame that all the people who are sick in this area can't be referred to me so that I can cure them. Then around two o'clock in the afternoon I'm a charlatan who is taking money under false pretenses. You can be victimized by this sort of thing very easily.

INT.: To shift to the family, what effect does your being out of the room have on them?

DR. F.: For one thing, as a colleague pointed out to me, it's an implicit command to them to talk, work, do something. After all, they're just left there. They know your beady little eyes are behind the screen, watching them. Your hallucinated presence is there, urging them on. My students also react to the pressure of being observed and taped. They feel very much under the gun. When they are in the room with the family, they feel that they've got to produce while they're in there, and there's even a pressure of time. It's a rare student who has sufficient poise to be silent if he can't think of anything to say, or just to stop what he's saying and get out. But the advantage is that my students, while they are out of the room, can consult with me about what they're doing. It's an ideal setup for supervising treatment.

INT.: It occurs to me that when you started using this method you were working with people who were more or less forced to come to see you because their children were in trouble with the law. Getting out of the room would be one way for you to counteract this framework. It would make it hard for them to see you as a continuation of a law-enforcement officer, as somebody who is going to tell them what to do.

DR. F.: That may have been a good reason for it initially, but it isn't confined to families with delinquents. People come to a doctor's office expecting to be treated and cured. I ask them to do something different from what they would do in a doctor's office. They usually live up to it.

INT.: This method also keeps the family dealing with each other, and I should think that they would tend to carry the therapy home with them more than they might with methods which make them feel that they can't talk to each other unless the therapist is there.

DR. F.: That's true. A family will frequently reestablish the therapy situation at home, the seating arrangements around the dining room table, and so on. But this isn't true of a couple. In marital therapy, people will store things up that irritate them and save them for the therapy hour. The therapist becomes symbolic of their being able to talk together. This may also be because I don't go in and out of the room with couples, and they tend to depend on my presence for talking together.

INT.: Why don't you use this method with couples?

DR. F.: Because the number of interactions is small enough so that I can usually follow them without strain. And it's not so hard to get a couple to talk together while you're there. Whatever the reason, I'm more comfortable working with a two-person family in the room than I am with a three-person family. With a four-person family, I'm not even comfortable in the other room.

INT.: There's another way this method must be useful. Beginners in family therapy find that one of the first problems they face is just making themselves heard. The "infernal machine" of the family grinds on and drowns them out. Your method provides a dramatic way of intervening. It signals the family and arrests them.

DR. F.: At first, yes. In the beginning, when you come into the room, it's like a pistol shot. Everybody stops, freezes where they are, and waits for the great man to say something. Dead silence. This can be quite disconcerting to the therapist. "What I have to say, can it really be that important?" As therapy goes along and the families feel more comfortable, you have to bang on the table or do something startling to interrupt them. But by this time you have already established your right to come in, and though you may have to do something to call attention to yourself, they are not going to override you.

INT.: This is quite a staging device; it weaves together a whole complex of powerful positions. First, you are going to come in on the family unexpectedly and they never know when that will be. Second, you're behind the one-way mirror watching them, which makes you an objective authority on their problems and gives you an advantage they don't have. Third, you have the tape recorder going and you can play back to them what they have just said. So when you first come out, you must seem like some kind of *deus ex machina.*

DR. F.: Yes. But this machine idea could also apply to the tape recorder in the other room. The whole setup could make me a *deus ex machina* in an extremely negative sense. In fact, the family could be thinking of me not as a god but as a devil. That's why I try to minimize this business of my being a great person. When I come back into the room, this humanizes me.

INT.: Humanizes you after dehumanizing you. There's a double effect there. On the one hand, you take the position of one who is not going to sit with the family and run everything. At the same time, behind that screen, you see everything and know everything. There's a framework of great power and a humbleness within it, an inhuman situation and a human one when you come in.

DR. F.: It's a situation that can easily get out of balance. That's why I try to counteract the fact that they are not always able to observe me. I make a strong effort to be wholly observed as a person.

INT.: In the tape, just now, you called the screen "a two-way mirror" and then said, "I can never remember whether it's a two-way mirror or a one-way mirror." You may not have meant it, but that slip brings in the idea that they might be able to see you as clearly as you see them.

DR. F.: This again is part of my philosophy of treatment. If you pretend to be a person without problems, without feelings, just a purely objective scientist practicing a scientific method, you won't be a very valuable therapist. I believe that the patient has a right to a real experience with a real person in therapy. That means I get mad, I laugh, I have problems.

INT.: Except when you are behind the screen.

DR. F.: Even when I'm there, the family will sometimes do something that will break them up, and I'll break up too. I don't make any effort to hide it.

INT.: Can they hear you laugh?

DR. F.: Yes, but I'll generally go out and join them laughing rather than stay in the observation room.

INT.: That's a pleasant sort of intervention.

DR. F.: No, it's just sharing with them. Or if I'm angry, I'll sometimes do the same thing.

INT.: It's interesting that you use a physical setup to divide this double aspect of the therapist, the human person and the objective person.

DR. F.: It changes during therapy too. Toward the end of treatment, I tend to spend more time in the room with the family. This would tie in with what we've been saying about symmetricality. As the patient progresses, there is a movement toward a more equal relationship between him and the therapist.

INT.: I should think that the method would require more time in the room toward the end. There's a parallel here with analysis. Analysts start being more human toward the end of treatment, when they come out from behind the couch. You do the same thing by coming out from behind the mirror. It's a shift in the relationship between you and the patient.

DR. F.: I think most of the process of therapy lies in achieving that shift.

INT.: What effect have you found it has on people when you tell them that what they say may be played back to them?

DR. F.: Originally I thought it would inhibit them terribly, that it would be a stricture on openness and freedom of communication. But I haven't found that to be true in any way. The natural patterns of interaction between family members are so strong that once they start talking, the patterns take over. As they play their roles, almost against their own wills, they get so involved that they forget all about being taped and act the way they would at home. Now there are exceptions to that.

In one family I had, the father was one of these sententious, wise men who had some deep comment about anything that happened. This wasn't because he was being recorded; it was simply his response to any situation in which he was being observed. With a family like this, the therapeutic problem becomes to get the father off the profound bit.

INT.: Did playing back what he'd been saying accomplish this?

DR. F.: Somewhat. After a while, when he started off on one of his profundities, he would get halfway through, break out laughing, and say, "There I go again." So it did work, but it was slow.

INT.: Playing back the tape sounds like a way to help the family to be as objective about themselves as you can be from behind the screen.

DR. F.: This is again part of my philosophy of treatment, to help people see themselves more clearly. I don't turn my back on introspection, either. I think that a personal report is a perfectly useful technique for getting information, and it shows respect for your patient to lend credence to what he's saying. Always with the proviso that there may be in the background a problem which he isn't aware of at all.

> DR. F. (*cont.*): Ah, but the work of it, other than my facilitating this and, ah, acting as a kind of gadfly and a, an external conscience maybe, ah, other than this, I will stay out of the room and you all will work with each other, ah, in this room here, and I'll be glad to show you the interior of that room, if you have any concerns about it. I can't talk to you from there, ah, I can hear you and see you but to talk to you I have to come in the door and talk with you, there's a reason for that too, this isn't (*inaudible phrase*) but because I want you to keep some kind of idea that I do have a body.
>
> MR. K.: Mm-hm.
> DR. F.: I become a disembodied voice too quickly.
> MRS. K.: (*Laughs.*)

DR. F.: That's another attempt to reduce the mystery about being behind the screen. I like to show them the tape recorder and let them observe each other from behind the screen. To get them to empathize more strongly with the therapist's role, so that they have a feeling of where I am and what I'm doing.

INT.: At the same time, saying that you're going to act as a "gadfly" and an "external conscience," certainly points up the disagreeable aspects of your role.

DR. F.: Where I can, I like to reinforce the idea that therapy isn't all roses. I will frequently point out to people that if it doesn't hurt, it isn't working. I do this when I know very well that it is going to hurt, when people have the kind of problems it will upset them to have uncovered.

INT.: Was it your feeling that this was a pious, God-fearing family that led you to use the term "external conscience" here? From the way it sounds, this family is sitting, hands folded in prayer: "Lord, what shall we do?"

DR. F.: I use it with other families too. Part of it is that I find the role of therapist much too seductive. It's so easy for the therapist to get an overwhelming sense of his own power. It may be that the reason for getting out of the room, making myself "external," is in my own personality.

INT.: You do seem to make more of an issue of trying not to be omnipotent than most therapists.

DR. F.: It's because I know how easy it would be for me to take an authoritarian role. I'm not what you'd call a shy, retiring person.

INT.: You sound so when you are dealing with this family. You say that you are going to do your best, that you will try, but that it's really up to them. At the same time you suggest that you are going to be an unpleasant brute who will stick pins in them.

DR. F.: That's quite a trick, isn't it?

INT.: It's this double framework that runs all though this. It almost has to. Patients, as a class, are very skillful at leading you on. They can be so helpless and so innocent and so naïve and build you up so easily.

DR. F.: And then cut you down easily.

INT.: Why do you go on to tell this family that you aren't going to become a disembodied voice?

DR. F.: It's because I've been asked so many times why I don't just set up a microphone and talk to the family from the observation room. I frankly don't have the guts to do this. With some very simple people I've worked with, if I am silent for too long a period and someone says something to me while I'm in the other room, instead of looking at the window they look up, and I have a feeling that maybe I really am disembodied and floating around.

DR. F.: Now does this meet with your understanding or . . .

MR. K.: Yes.

DR. F.: . . . your interpretation of what we're facing here?

MRS. K.: Mm-hm.

DR. F. (to Mr. K.): How do you feel about it?

MR. K.: We are, we are most anxious to cooperate in this and I'm quite sure you are too, are you not, Mike?

MIKE: Mm-hm.

MR. K.: (Inaudible words) try and work this thing out as a three-way deal because we realize there must be something wrong, it's not, ah, in keeping with Mike's normal activities and so forth, nor is it in keeping with the things that we know. I realize it must be some combination of circumstances that has created this situation and caused him to do these things but Mike is, since, ah, August, everything as far as we are concerned in the, our home life with Mike and so forth has been fine. He started high school this year, and is most interested in his work, so, ah, it's one of those situations where we're just up against a stone wall and we must have help from someone.

INT.: Why did you bring the family in at that point?

DR. F.: I was breaking up the lecture. The reference to disembodied voices was a somewhat humorous one, a kind of signal that I'm through.

INT.: What does the father mean when he says that everything has been going so well since August? When was the boy arrested?

DR. F.: Sometime around November, December. He's saying that the arrest was totally unexpected.

INT.: The father brings in the three of them so quickly. Granted that you have been emphasizing this, it's still quite an explicit triangular statement that he makes.

DR. F.: This is a middle-class father who wants to do what is right, and in a sense I have defined what is right as "all of you taking responsibility." So he follows along with this immediately. If I had said, "Something is wrong with your child and you've got to help him," he would have taken the opposite tack just as quickly. It's his immediate response to any kind of authority situation.

INT.: Would you have done differently with a different type of family?

DR. F.: With a different type of family, I might have had to reiterate the problem as a three-way affair many times. But with this man, you have him committed right from the start, and if he drifts off, you can simply nudge him gently and he will come right back.

INT.: Was his readiness to accept it a help to therapy?

DR. F.: It was lip service only, as I found out later in the therapy. But it helped me to seduce him into the therapy process, and it gave me a lever, later on, for pointing out the discrepancy between this commitment and his actual behavior. At the time he said this, he hadn't taken any steps except the minor one of coming in to therapy.

> DR. F.: Good. I'd like to point out then at the start . . .
>
> MR. K. (*to Mrs. K.*): Cigarette?
>
> MRS. K.: No, thank you.
>
> DR. F.: . . . that, ah, this process is not always pleasant. There are times when it gets . . .
>
> MR. K.: We realize that.
>
> DR. F.: . . . there'll be times when you will feel that I'm being nosy, ah, and kind of nasty about my nosiness, and this is my job. I re—
>
> MRS. K.: Huh?
>
> DR. F.: . . . reserve the right to be nosy and impolite if I feel this is necessary.
>
> MR. K.: Mm-hm.
>
> DR. F.: Ah, if you really want to, I think there is an awful lot to gain.

INT.: When you say it's going to be hard, are you responding to the father's inordinate agreeableness, or is this just routine?

DR. F.: I'm responding to what I sense as the brittleness of the relationship between the father and mother. It is going to be fine so long as it's kept on a very superficial level, but as soon as I begin to probe, I know they're going to hate it. I'm setting the stage for it so that they won't then pull out of therapy.

INT.: When you anticipate how difficult everything is going to be, this would make it hard for them to blame you for hurting them, because you've already said you're going to.

DR. F.: Yes, because this is the kind of family that would turn all this against the therapist. They'd say, "You're not being a good therapist, you're making this unpleasant and there's no necessity for it," and ease themselves out of therapy on these grounds. This way I can refer back to the initial framing and say, "You remember, I suggested this would happen."

INT.: Do you always stress the disagreeableness of the process?

DR. F.: No. There are times when, in order to keep a family in treatment, you can't refer to it as family therapy, you can't even indicate that it may be unpleasant. But I thought this family could take a lot, as precious as they were.

INT.: Are you more comfortable with a family with whom you feel free to point out the unpleasant aspects?

DR. F.: No, I only feel comfortable in doing this when it's appropriate. If a family is so fragile or lacking in resources that they can't take any threat at all, I don't feel the slightest discomfort in dissimulating completely. Not only am I willing to hide that this is going to be a painful process, I am even willing to keep it from being painful. In a few cases I might say it's going to be painful and not mean it at all. There are families to whom you have to say this, in order to give them the feeling that they are about to embark on a very dangerous task that only people with courage and maturity could achieve. Then you'd better not do it or you'll lose them.

INT.: You exaggerate the whole thing so that they won't be unpleasantly shocked.

DR. F.: No, so that they will feel a certain amount of demand. They will have committed themselves to a dangerous enterprise, and they'll be cowards if they back out.

INT.: They can't leave without conceding that they're not up to it.

DR. F.: That's right. Regardless of the fact that I'm making it as gentle as I possibly can. And there are other times when I point out the glorious aspects of therapy, how wonderful, sweet, charming it is all going to be, how they are going to get to love each other so much, understand each other so well.

INT.: In this speech you tell the family that therapy is going to be an ordeal, but then you quickly switch and say how much they can benefit from it.

DR. F.: My own feelings about therapy are that it's helpful and useful, and I try to communicate this to people. But this has little to do with the actual operation of therapy. I'd be a charlatan if I applied the same techniques to every family.

INT.: A therapist who uses the same method, no matter who comes in the door, might feel that it was dishonest to change the method for whoever comes in the door.

DR. F.: I would consider such a therapist dishonest himself. It would be strange if a therapist were to treat every family in the same, unvarying way, as though they were all alike. Or if he were to set up his own ideal and try to force it on people. He has to be open enough and flexible enough to go along with whatever comes and work with that. It's a question of effectiveness, too. If I presented myself as authoritatively and directively as I'd often like to, I might accomplish immediate results with a tremendous number of patients, but a two-year follow-up would probably show that not all the changes had lasted.

INT.: Do you feel, then, that a directive approach is less effective because it only produces a surface change?

DR. F.: Not at all. I think I would have the same results if I were nondirective all the time. And this is true of the sessions too. If I vary my approach from session to session, according to what I feel is appropriate, I'll have a higher ratio of success than if I use the same approach throughout.

DR. F.: I, I've worked with families a great deal. As far as I can tell, ah, no marriage goes on for, ah, ten, twenty years without there developing real blank spots on the map, real unexplored areas where communication can be improved, where relationships can be improved, where people can understand each other and their roles better, where resentment could be lifted and, ah, eased out, eased off at any rate, and people could get along better together. I take it as a fundamental premise that, well, it's not an easy job marrying and raising a family, it's a hard job in my opinion, and I take it as a kind of basic premise that people who do this and stay together love each other, that on this kind of a basis, regardless of how much unpleasantness may have transpired, regardless of the defensiveness of the people, regardless of how sensitive the areas are, with this kind of a basis, things can work out, positively and well, if we agree or assume it's so, and I assume this with you all. And I think it's, ah, the one valid assumption. With this and my desire to help Mike and yourselves, I think there's no barrier whatsoever.

INT.: It must have quite an effect to bring in this positive statement that people who stay together love each other, when all you've been talking about so far has been the unpleasantness of therapy, the problems they have, and so forth. Do you use this phrasing with other families?

DR. F.: Yes, I do. It's a way of saying that there's a bond which will persist, no matter what happens in this room.

INT.: Are you easing the parents' minds about the possibility of a separation?

DR. F.: Not at all. These people were bound by much too strong ties for such a possibility even to come up. Of course, the therapist has to be able to recognize when people would be better off divorced or separated. But this is only true in a small percentage of cases. And if the therapist makes such a suggestion too quickly, the people don't get divorced, they get right back together again and change therapists. Also, if you make yourself the judge on whether a marriage should or shouldn't continue, it's equivalent to making an ex-post-facto judgment that these people should never have gotten married in the first place. I think you have to have a lot of evidence before you can do that. For the purposes of this family or any other, it does less damage to assume a love relationship, even though that may be assuming a great deal. If that assumption is proven wrong later, that's fine.

INT.: They're innocent until they're proven guilty.

DR. F.: Right. But with this particular couple I knew we were going to have trouble. You could sense the strong feelings within the wife and the iron defenses of the husband. I was trying to cushion against the bitterness I knew would come out by stressing my faith in their relationship.

INT.: You put them in a bind by taking the lowest common denominator you could think of for love. Your assumption that they love one another because they've stayed together is a positive one and pressures them to agree with you. But if they disagree and say, "No, we don't love each other," you can always say, "The fact that you've stayed together proves it."

DR. F.: In my marriage cases, I frequently say, "I don't care how much you hate each other and fight each other, you've been living together for fifteen, eighteen years, and the probability is that if you work at it, you can find a better love relationship with each other than you could with anybody else." I think that's a strong statistical probability.

INT.: When you say that people who stay together love each other, you give them implicit permission to love each other, without requiring any responsibility from them. It just happened because they lived together so long.

DR. F.: It also relieves them of the responsibility for having hated each other.

INT.: In a context in which they probably are accusing each other of not loving each other, on the premise that love is a voluntary thing. You make love something involuntary that comes with living together.

DR. F.: I hadn't thought of it that way.

INT.: You're really creating a climate to work in. Instead of assuming that they hate each other and the problem is to work out the difficulties, you give them a basis on which to get together.

DR. F.: Exactly. It's a useful kind of ground rule.

DR. F. (*cont.*): So what you can call on me for, you have, I have certain responsibilities to you folks, the one is to, ah, be as honest as I can, not to pull any, pull punches . . .

MRS. K.: Mm-hm.

DR. F.: . . . or to evade the issues that come up, to be an, a, as nearly as possible an objective mirror to re-, reflect back to you the kinds of things you seem to be saying, really. If you're rationalizing or, ah, evading the truth, or trying to put things in a good light, then it's my responsibility not to be fooled by this . . .

MR. K.: Mm-hm.

DR. F.: . . . to, to see through this and to help to structure it in a different way. And I'll try to fulfill that, as much as I can.

INT.: Where does the phrase "objective mirror" come from?

DR. F.: I picked it up from Carl Rogers. But my criticism of Rogers, after seeing him work, is that he is about as nondirective as a sledgehammer. What he reflects back to the patient is not what the patient has said but what Rogers wants the patient to think he has said. And of course I do the same thing.

INT.: You're a selective mirror.

DR. F.: Yes. I'm the one who's deciding what's objective.

INT.: In your next statement you say that your job is not to let them evade the truth. I think it's unusual for a therapist to come right out and say that. It's usually put in terms of "I'm going to help you understand," not "I'm going to make you face the truth."

DR. F.: I came to this as a result of an experience with one of my private patients. He was really conning me, leading me down the garden path, and I was going along with it. When it finally went too far, I called him on it and made a rather cruel summary, point by point, of all the chicaneries that had been going on. The patient was so grateful and took such a turn for the better that it taught me something. People want to be free to try to trick you, but they don't want to succeed. This kind of remark, "It's my job not to be fooled," is intended as reassurance. I'm really saying, "I know what you really are like before you even start, so you don't have to worry about it. At the same time, I'm not going to let you get away with it." I free them from feeling guilty if they try to con me and also prepare them for being exposed.

INT.: This gives you the freedom to say whatever you like from then on, because you've established the premise that it's your job to call them on anything you think you ought to call them on.

DR. F.: That's right.

INT.: Your tone here is not an accusing one. You're simply accepting the fact that they're going to behave this way.

DR. F.: You know, in teaching young therapists, one of the things that's hard to get across is the difference between condoning a person's behavior and understanding it. You are sitting across the table from a young thief. It does him no good to pretend that he is in the vanguard of social change and making a protest against social inequities by stealing hubcaps from cars, or that he is just an innocent victim of his environment. People who deal with delinquents generally go to great lengths to avoid making the kid feel he's done anything bad. But there's a difference between accusing a kid: "You're a thief!" and saying, "In other words, you're a thief."

INT.: You call the kid a thief but don't bring in the emotional judgment.

DR. F.: I treat it as something he can change if he wants to. I don't imply that he is labeled and pigeonholed and that's all he'll ever be. But I don't ignore it.

INT.: This remark about evading and cheating sounds like the sort of thing you'd direct to the delinquent member of the family. Yet you're directing it to the family as a whole, as if it were itself delinquent.

DR. F.: It is. I don't think there's any difference between the boy and his parents on that.

INT.: Do you think this is true only of a family with a delinquent or would you say the same thing to any family?

DR. F.: I would say it to any family.

INT.: When you tell the family that it's your job not to let people get away with things, is this for some reason of expediency or because you believe in sharing with the family what you feel your function is?

DR. F.: Well, both. I try to share my beliefs about therapy with the family as much as possible. If they ask me if I'm a Freudian or a Jungian, I'll tell them no, I'm not a Freudian or a Jungian. But part of it is that if a therapist makes a big secret of himself, or plays the wise old man, it puts too heavy a burden on him. In a sense, expediency governs all my therapy. I have no set beliefs or theories.

> DR. F. (*cont.*): And again, a part of my bias is that I kind of like
> families. I live in one.
> MRS. K.: (*Laughs.*)

INT.: When you say that you like families, is this because you feel you've gone too far in pointing out the uncomfortable aspects of therapy?

DR. F.: It's the usual switch I make when I've gone in a negative direction, to undo some of it. But it's also part of the seduction.

INT.: You use "bias" in an odd way. In talking about the dreadful things the family is going to do, you present yourself as an "objective mirror" which will reflect these things back to them. Now, when you say how much you like families, you add, "But I'm biased."

DR. F.: I almost always say to a family that I have a bias in regard to wanting to preserve families. That I will go perhaps further than would be objectively desirable in trying to keep a family together.

INT.: Is this another way of creating a positive base to work from?

DR. F.: It's really intended for families in which there might be a deeper-rooted pathology than I am picking up. I am guarding against the fact that there may be something in this relationship that I'm not seeing which will make it mandatory for the family to separate.

INT.: If it turns out that way, you can say, "I told you I was biased in the first place." They can't get you on being wrong.

DR. F.: Yes. It's calculated.

> DR. F.: I think that, ah, again, that you folks are probably the best
> therapists in the world for Mike, better than any other therapist
> that could ever be dredged up for him, you folks are. So long as

Mike, as things are confused or there's difficulty, I don't think you can be, but I think you can function in the best way as therapists for him, so that this is what we're working toward. When this point has been reached, then we have had the answer.

INT.: Why do you say to parents who obviously are falling on their noses with their kid that they are the best therapists in the world for him?

DR. F.: Because I feel very strongly that no outside person is an effective substitute for enlightened, well-intentioned, capable parents. When I was working with adolescent delinquents, I found that I could win them over, even help them a little, but I did very little in the way of bringing about any lasting change. If you can help parents to be better parents, this is the best way to help the child.

INT.: This is a reason you give to somebody else. Why do you tell the parents this?

DR. F.: I'm disclaiming any intention of substituting for them. I'm saying to the mother and father, "I'm not trying to take over your function and tell you that *I* know what's best for Mike. I'm going to try to help you to do what *you* know is best for Mike." There's another part to this, too. Each family has a different cultural background, a different ethos, and it's not my job to change that. I have no intention of coming in and training their child to be like me, and I want the family to know this. I also want the parents to feel that I have some respect for them as parents.

INT.: Is this move of giving the parents respect partly tactical? They must come in feeling like miserable failures because their boy is in difficulty, and the man who's going to solve all this tells them they are better therapists than he is.

DR. F.: For the reasons I just gave, I do believe this. But I am also trying to bolster their self-confidence. In that sense, it's tactical.

INT.: You take that back a little bit when you go on to say that as long as things are confused they can't be the best therapists for Mike.

DR. F.: I'm pointing out that they are part of the process that got Mike where he is, and if things are confused, they are obviously part of this confusion. Until this is clarified, they are not going to be able to function maximally.

INT.: You put an umbrella over their heads and at the same time dig a hole under their feet.

DR. F.: That's right.

INT.: You also give yourself more rein, because you're cutting off the possible objections they might raise along the line of "You don't know my child as well as I do." If you anticipate them by saying that they are in a better therapeutic position than you are, they can't resist you as easily.

DR. F.: This is deliberate. And it caters to this delusion that people have about their children. If anyone started to tell me about my daughter, my immediate reaction would be, "Go jump in the lake, Jack. I've lived with her for fourteen years, and who are you to tell me?" I try to get around this with a family by saying, "Sure you know her better. Things are mixed up and communication is distorted, but if we straighten that out, you'll obviously be in a much better position than I."

INT.: I notice that you often refer to distorted or disrupted communication to avoid coming out with something that might not be acceptable in plain words.

DR. F.: That's more of my expediency.

INT.: To go back to your point about the relative ineffectiveness of individual work with children, is it also because you feel that a therapist has a better chance to help the child to change if he can help the family to change?

DR. F.: It's more than that. If you work five hours a day, five days a week, with an adolescent, you still are only working about one fortieth of the time with him. He is exposed to other people who are exerting a continuous influence on him, and if the child is in trouble, I assume this influence is a negative one. No therapist is powerful enough, with the techniques and tools he has, to counteract the influence of a family.

> DR. F. (*cont.*): Do you have any questions or . . .
> MR. K.: No, I don't have.
> DR. F.: . . . of any sort?
> MRS. K.: No, I don't think I have anything.
> DR. F.: If you have, well, of course then we can bring them up at any time. If you have questions or you want to fight with me about something (*Mrs. K. laughs*) feel free to, anything at all.

INT.: Here again you put in the assumption that you might be wrong.

Dr. F.: That's because I would find it very difficult to be in a position in which I had to uphold some ideal continuously.

Int.: It seems to be a continuing enlargement of your range of future behavior. If you allow them to be free to comment against you, because you have already anticipated them, you have a lot more room for footwork. All through this I notice that you're enlarging, at a variety of levels, everything possible that you can do.

Dr. F.: I'm also being self-protective. In the initial stages of therapy, all the patient sees of you is a tremendous image of power, but when that image begins to crumble and you become a plain human being, watch out.

Int.: So you step one down to begin with by telling them they can criticize you.

Dr. F.: This is also showing respect for them, saying, "You will have perceptions, ways of looking at things that will be better than mine." But the main point is that if I *care* whether I'm one down or not, I'm hung. I don't think a therapist would stay in the business if he couldn't accept a one-down position, because he is too often in that position by virtue of his patients' progress or lack of progress alone. They have come to you for help and you haven't helped them. That's the biggest one-down the therapist gets.

Int.: You mean you're one-downed if after five minutes you still haven't helped them?

Dr. F.: Or five years. It can be just that. In two or three families, I've worked with every kid in serial order as they come up. Sometimes three or four of them. As to how effective my role has been, I think it's averted some tragedies, but I don't think it has produced any miraculous results. These families would have every right to say, "What are we spending our money for?"

Int.: Perhaps if they felt that way, they wouldn't keep coming.

mrs. k.: Mike, do you have anything . . .

dr. f.: Any questions, Mike?

mike: Mm-mm.

dr. f.: No? How do you feel about it?

mike: Fine. (*Pause.*)

dr. f.: Well, I will get the other test and ask you folks to—I'm sorry we have to use a session to do this, but I think it's as well to get that out of the way before we start entirely . . .

MR. K.: Mm.

DR. F.: . . . ah, to complete this first, this last of the tests, in this pretesting period.

(*Session ends with family arranging to meet after the New Year holiday instead of the following week.*)

INT.: Why did you turn to Mike so particularly?

DR. F.: Because he had been left out for a long period of time.

INT.: You get a response from the mother and father too.

DR. F.: Their response is a kind of acceptance of the ground rules.

INT.: The ground rules?

DR. F.: What we had been talking about. And I want something from Mike, too.

INT.: What you get from him is the nicest of all possible statements. Now I gather that if it weren't for the testing, you would go right from this introduction into therapy.

DR. F.: Yes. I'd start them off, ask them to discuss their problems or something general like that, and then get out of the room.

Second interview with the Kane family*

DR. F.: Well, do you recall our last meeting? What we talked about then?

MR. K.: Mm-hm.

DR. F.: Remember that, as, essentially we talked about the need to develop adequate or improved means of communication between all three of you. And my role in this as that of kind of needling you or acting as a kind of gadfly. And the fact that my interest is in your discussing the *real* problems that are going on in your family, ah, that's what you've given some thought to. One of the major things that's going to be needed here is that you folks are going to have to help Mike to express himself to a great extent. It's kind of a difficult situation for him. We'll be counting a great deal on your approach and your attitude as you express it. I'm sure that maybe kind of bugs you, so I'm going to get out of here and we can get started then.

(*Fulweiler starts to go out.*)

---

* This session takes place three weeks later than the introductory session and is presented in its entirety. Names have been changed and places omitted.

INT.: When you ask them if they recall what went on during the last meeting, how much do you assume they will remember?

DR. F.: I don't assume they'll remember it in any specific detail. And the way they remember it will be completely different from the way I do. What I do assume is that the session was important to them, that it was a unique event in their lives. This is especially true of a family with a first-offender delinquent because the event that brought them in stands out from the routine of their ordinary life.

INT.: When you tell the parents that you want them to help their boy to express himself, is this routine or did something about the boy give you a lead?

DR. F.: This is more of a routine thing. Actually, it leads to the first good reason for coming in and making an interpretation. Most youngsters, in the presence of their families, are going to be dummied up. And most parents, to help the child express himself, will beg him to say something. Then as soon as he gets a word out, they will argue him down. I'm setting up the situation so that I can come in and point out what they are doing. I'm asking them to fall into the trap I'm setting for them.

INT.: In other words, you are more free to point this out if you've anticipated it.

DR. F.: It isn't a matter of anticipating it, it's a matter of encouraging them to do it. Of asking them to start out by making this mistake. I try to get my students to structure this at the beginning of therapy, because if they don't and the parents start to argue the child down, they're stuck. They can't go in and say, "Now, we've talked about how you can facilitate your child to communicate. What happened?" and play the tape back and point out what actually occurred.

INT.: If you didn't set this up, would the family possibly do something different?

DR. F.: No, they'd do exactly the same thing, though maybe not right away. I want them to do it right away.

INT.: Is part of it the setting they're in? After all, they're there because the child has done something wrong, and you're watching them.

DR. F.: That's part of it.

INT.: What you're doing is encouraging them to do what they're going to do anyway, as a way of arranging a situation which you are then free to comment on.

DR. F.: That's right. It's a relatively good, neutral, dramatic instance of family therapy, to bring home to them the process of therapy.

INT.: By setting it up this way, you arrange your first intervention.

DR. F.: But you also *want* the family to help the child communicate, you want the atmosphere to be one in which the child feels free to talk. The only way to do this is to encourage the family to help the child express himself, so that you can show them how they are actually doing the reverse.

> MRS. K.: Ah, ah, Mr. Fulweiler, we just start up a conversation, or what?
> DR. F.: Well, you know the areas that, ah, we have, we discussed last time and the things that have led to some of the difficulties. If you'll try to start on them, I'll help you out as you go along.
> (*Fulweiler goes out.*)

INT.: If the mother hadn't come in there, would you have gone right out?

DR. F.: Yes.

INT.: Is that as little framing as you generally give them on what they're supposed to do after you leave?

DR. F.: I honestly don't think you can structure it for them too much without destroying what you're after, which is a relatively spontaneous interaction. That's why I try to get away with as ambiguous a comment as possible.

INT.: The mother isn't about to let you.

DR. F.: No. She's uneasy. Most people are, when you leave them sitting in the room staring at each other. I made that remark about the things that have led up to some of the difficulties just as I was opening the door and getting out. I wanted to prevent them from trapping me and using me, so I was getting out fast. I had one student who never succeeded in doing this. As soon as somebody said, "What shall we do?" he would get caught in an interaction with the family. For two years, he never got out of the room.

> MRS. K.: (*Laughs.*) Well? (*Laughs, long pause.*) Hm.
> MR. K.: (*Inaudible phrase to Mike.*)
> MIKE: I don't know. (*Long pause.*)
> (*Fulweiler knocks, enters.*)

INT.: Why did you come back in so soon?

DR. F.: Because it was obvious that they weren't going to move very far if I didn't give them a push.

INT.: You didn't assume that if you waited longer they'd ultimately get around to doing something?

DR. F.: No, I felt that if I waited too long with this family—there was an optimum waiting period—it would leave them with a very bad feeling. They would have felt like failures and they would have become critical of therapy. I didn't want to let this kind of negative feeling get started.

INT.: How long do you sometimes let a family sit and wait?

DR. F.: I've let them sit without saying a word for as long as twenty-five minutes.

INT.: On opening? What kind of a family would you do that with?

DR. F.: It's hard to say. You just feel whether you can or you can't. I think I might do it with people who are ordinarily very verbal and are quite aware of their blocking. If a family's silence is a real bewilderment, as it was here, I tend to help them out. If their silence is a hostile one, I don't.

INT.: You must have to know how to read silences.

DR. F.: It's not hard to do. Their nonverbal behavior can tell me very quickly. Or they'll say, "I wish he were in the room. Why doesn't he come back in?" Then there will be a long, dead quiet in which they're obviously waiting for me to come back in. I would frustrate this.

INT.: Even if it creates a negative reaction?

DR. F.: Yes, with a family that is deliberately resisting. But the first time they break the silence, I'll come back in and give a further structuring. As a reward.

INT.: It's a way of establishing the premise that you come in when you want, not when they want.

DR. F.: Yes. Except that there are times when the family calls me in with such humor that I can't help laughing and I'll come in and laugh with them and then go out again. But I make it quite clear that I'm coming in on my own terms.

DR. F.: Suppose you start then with what led up to Mike's difficulty, which is the reason for your being here—mainly. What do you think, Mike, are the things that led to your getting into trouble? What kind of feelings you had or attitudes you had.

MIKE: I can't think of anything that, any feelings that I had.

DR. F.: Well, can you think of any criticisms or, or gripes you have? There's plenty of gripes you have at home. (*Pause.*)

MIKE: I don't, I don't think so.

DR. F.: Do you have any insight into this, Mr. Kane?

MR. K.: Well, there's one thing that has come up fairly recently as far as Mike is concerned and that's his smoking. He's told me that, ah, he wants to smoke and he's going to smoke whether I want him to or not. I have forbidden it at times, previously, but apparently it didn't do any good.

DR. F.: This is a good starting point then, or at least a problem. What are your feelings about it, Mrs. Kane?

(*Fulweiler goes out.*)

INT.: Did the father turn and speak to the boy when you first went out?

DR. F.: Yes. They look immediately to the child to bail them out.

INT.: By turning to the child when you come in, you are doing the same thing they would do.

DR. F.: I'm recognizing what they are doing, and also emphasizing that, in point of fact, they wouldn't be there if it weren't for the child. To evade this would be hypocritical, to the boy as well as to the parents. By joining them for this moment, I am also winning them over.

INT.: When you ask Mike about what got him into difficulty, is this a way of saying, "I know you're a thief," and getting that over with?

DR. F.: Yes.

INT.: An acknowledgment that he's the problem.

DR. F.: No, that he's the precipitating factor. I've already framed it so that he isn't the whole problem.

INT.: It's in that phrasing when you say, "He's the reason for your being here—*mainly*."

DR. F.: It's the hesitation that's meaningful. I'm putting the emphasis on their being in the office rather than on the boy's being in trouble.

INT.: When you then ask about any gripes he might have, you turn the tables on the parents.

DR. F.: Yes. I've joined them and now I'm backing the boy, but from a safer vantage point, I think.

INT.: What you've done is to side with the parents by bringing up the boy's problem, then you side with the boy by asking for any criticism he might have, then you turn and ask for insight from the father. It's a rapid alternation, in a matter of seconds.

DR. F.: I'm saying to the father, "Mike's criticisms of you are important and they're going to come up." Then I ask the father about them. I'm setting the stage for complaints. Even if they had brought up some different matter, I would probably sooner or later have come in and asked for the complaints.

INT.: You put the father on the defensive by bringing in the idea that his son is going to complain about him. You almost insure that he's going to counter it by jumping on Mike.

DR. F.: Yes, but I give him the chance to put it as what Mike, not he, complains about. Of course, he brings up a complaint of Mike's which he feels is indefensible. When he mentions the smoking, he thinks it's a matter on which I, or anyone, will unquestionably support him, the sort of thing which will easily prove that he is a good parent and Mike is a bad boy.

INT.: So after setting that up, you go out again. I take it that you don't care what problem they discuss, so long as it's a problem.

DR. F.: Part of my position is that whatever problem they choose to talk about will contain within it the difficulties in the parent-child relationship.

INT.: It's like kicking a system on, or priming it a little to get it started.

DR. F.: Sometimes you have to do a lot of priming.

INT.: Why did you choose gripes to prime this one with? You might just as well have said, "What's nice about your family?"

DR. F.: That's not why they're here. I will frequently point out to people that they are in the therapy room because of what's wrong, not what's right. Therapists have to be kind of carrion birds, psychologically.

INT.: I have a suspicion that if you had started with what's nice about the family, they'd go right to something like smoking, anyhow.

DR. F.: Sure.

MRS. K.: Well, I think Mike knows that I would prefer that he didn't smoke.

MR. K.: I can't understand Mike's feeling that, he's going to do it whether we want him to or not. (*Pause.*)

MRS. K.: Well, I feel that if he's going to smoke I'd rather have him smoke at home than out on the street some place.

MR. K.: Well, that's good. I agree with you there but I think he, I don't think he should smoke at all. And I think that he realizes that it's not only that he can't ["*stop*" *implied*]. Certainly as much as he has been smoking, it's not, it's not habit. How do you feel about it, Mike?

DR. F.: You notice the way the mother comes in there. Her tone, everything about it, tells you immediately that she has encouraged the boy to smoke. That she is in conflict with the father about it.

INT.: She starts out with a defense before the accusation has been made.

DR. F.: That's what you tag immediately. That this gal has done exactly what she's defending herself against. When she says she'd rather the boy smoked at home than out in the street, you know that's where she has undermined her husband. The old man has been ranting and raving and she has quietly undermined him.

INT.: He seems to be trying not to pick up the cues in her remarks. When she disagrees with him, he ignores her and turns to the boy.

DR. F.: Sure. Any husband who heard that first speech of the wife's and didn't reply with, "Then why do you let him smoke?" is obtuse.

INT.: It also sounds as if the last thing he wants to do is face up to his wife. Even when he interrogates the boy, he's pretty indirect.

DR. F.: That's partly because his feelings of powerlessness have no external cues to hang on. No obvious ones. He feels undermined, he feels powerless, but he doesn't know why.

INT.: Do you think that his question, "How do you feel about it?" to Mike is something he might ordinarily say, or did he pick it up from you?

DR. F.: I think he picked it up from me. I told him to help Mike express himself and he's doing what is expected of him. In ten years, I bet he's never asked his wife or his son what they thought about anything.

MIKE: Well, how much do you have, how much do you have to smoke before it's a habit then? In your opinion?

MR. K.: Oh I'd say, half a pack to a pack a day. Are there any, any certain times during the day when you smoke?

MIKE: No, not especially.

MR. K.: Just when you happen to think of it.

MIKE: Uh-huh.

MR. K.: And you have the opportunity.

MIKE: Uh-huh.

MR. K.: Do you have cigarettes with you now?

MIKE: Yes.

MR. K.: Do you smoke at school?

MIKE: No.

MR. K.: Do you smoke on the bus on the way home from school?

MIKE: No.

MR. K.: Are you allowed to smoke on the bus?

MIKE: No.

MR. K.: I don't know, I'm just asking, I don't know. Have you had any cigarettes today?

MIKE: I had one this morning.

MR. K.: What time?

MIKE: Before, while I was riding to school with Mom.

MR. K. (*to Mrs. K.*): Did he smoke in the car with you?

MRS. K.: Yep. (*Pause.*)

MR. K.: Well, I don't, I just don't think the idea of a thirteen-year-old boy smoking is proper either at home or anywhere else. It's just one of those things that I've been defied on completely. And I can feel about it any way I want to, or anything else, but he's still gonna do it. As far as he's concerned, he doesn't care about my feelings on the subject at all. And he's expressed himself that way. Very openly and above board about it.

INT.: I gather you wouldn't come in on that interchange between father and son. Not this early.

DR. F.: I don't think so. Nothing has really happened. The father is acting like an interrogator but it hasn't gone far enough nor is it destructive enough yet to warrant an intervention. When the father says, "I don't know, I'm just asking," he's backing away. If he had kept it up as though he were a trial lawyer, I would have come in, but I wanted to let it go on at this point and listen. What's interesting is the way the father disengages the mother from responsibility. He comes up and touches it and gets away from it.

INT.: She comes in almost cockily, almost daring him. That "Yep."

DR. F.: Sure. It's defiance. And he backs right off.

MIKE: Well I, I, I said, I said something and you, whenever I say something, you take it . . .

MR. K.: Well . . .

MIKE: . . . for what *you* think it was . . .

MR. K.: Well . . .

MIKE: . . . you, you asked me if I was gonna smoke and then you said, ah, that then you're doing it just, just to spite me. And I'm not.

MR. K.: Well, I've told you not to smoke, haven't I?

MIKE: Yes.

MR. K.: That was a direct order.

MIKE: Uh-huh.

MR. K.: And you have, and you say you are going to smoke.

MIKE: Yes.

MR. K.: In other words, it, it's, in one sense . . .

MIKE (*overlapping*): I'm not doing it to spite you.

MR. K.: . . . in one sense of the word, it's, ah, because I have told you not to, it's just sheer disobedience, isn't it?

MIKE: Yes, but it isn't spite. I'm not doing it just because you s-, you don't want me to.

MR. K.: Okay, I'll, I'll accept that. Nevertheless, I told you not to.

MIKE: Yes. (*Pause.*)

MR. K.: And, no matter what I want, along those lines, you're still gonna do it.

MIKE: Yes, I guess I am. (*Pause.*)

MR. K.: You know it's not good for you, don't you?

MIKE: Yes.

DR. F.: I think that's a delightful interchange. It's so typical of many families. Parents will put words and ideas into their children's mouths and then react according to their own interpretations. The father is saying here that the boy is being spiteful, when the boy really isn't. If kids are doing something destructive or malicious, then this is true, but if they are doing something which pleases them, like drinking or smoking or going to a movie, in opposition to their parents' wishes, this isn't spite. It's rebelling, testing the limits of their parents' control. They are really saying, "Look, control me if you can."

INT.: So the father is really lost, because spite isn't the issue.

DR. F.: He's lost because he's never taken any effective action. Whether he could have, with the mother standing in the background, is another matter. But he's put himself in a very difficult situation. Once he's laid down a flat rule, or thinks he has: "No smoking," and the boy goes on smoking, he's made a fool of himself. All he can do is protest it in a futile way.

INT.: The son sits there calmly and says, "Yes, I guess I am going to go on smoking."

DR. F.: What makes it even more peculiar is that this insolence is coming from a boy whose superficial appearance is that of a goody-good. He really is a nice-talking, nice-acting, sweet-looking kid. What he's doing is making a demand that his father take authoritative, direct action. And the father can't. This reminds me of another family I worked with where the father complained that his boy wouldn't go to bed when he was told. In the particular instance he was referring to, the mother was in bed already and the father started to go to bed and on his way through the dining room he noticed that the boy was still studying. He said, "Don't you think it's time to go to bed now?" and the boy said, "No." The father said, "Don't you think it's getting pretty late?" and the boy said, "Yep." So the father went to bed. About fifteen minutes later he still hadn't heard the boy move, so he came out and again said something like, "Don't you think it's getting late?" and got the same response. This scene was repeated about five times and finally the father went to the mother and said, "You've got to do something about that boy, he refuses to go to bed." Yet all that time he had never directly asked the boy to go to bed, just made asinine statements about how late it was. The mother was quite incensed; all she did was to get up and go into the room and say, "Damn it, get to bed." The kid picked up his things and went to bed.

MR. K.: I don't know what the answer to it is. I can't follow you around twenty-four hours a day. Where are you getting the money to buy cigarettes?

MIKE: From my allowance.

MR. K.: What?

MIKE: From my allowance.

MR. K.: I didn't give you any allowance in over a month.

MIKE: Yes I know, and I was sick, and I had some money left.

MR. K.: How much, how much did you have left?

MIKE: About a dollar and a half.

MR. K.: What are you going to do when that money runs out?

MIKE: I don't know. (*Pause.*)

MR. K.: Well, I don't feel that I'm going to give you any allowances to go out and buy cigarettes with.

MRS. K.: Well, I don't think cutting his money off is the answer.

MIKE: Well, I do work around the house and I should think I should get paid for it. Whether I'm going to buy cigarettes with it or not. It's just if . . .

MR. K. (*overlapping*): If I don't approve . . .

MIKE: . . . if Mr. Carter [*father's boss*] didn't want you to do something, what would you say if he cut off your pay?

MR. K.: If Mr. Carter didn't want me to do something, he'd fire me.

MIKE: Well, I mean if he was your father or something. You work and so do I.

INT.: Again, I gather this isn't something you would come in on.

DR. F.: Not yet. I'm not entirely sure why, because listening to it again, I can think of a dozen places where I could have come in and made a comment. I think I stayed out because it seemed to me that the interaction wasn't complete, the little play hadn't been acted out yet. I didn't have the kinds of things I would need in order to intervene.

INT.: Is there some kind of unit that has to take place before you come in?

DR. F.: Yes. Something that has some completion, some action that has been rounded out. Sometimes I would intervene before it got a chance to round out, if I thought it would end up in a way that would be bad or unhelpful to the family. Here, if I had thought the father's interrogation was going to hurt the boy, I would have come in and showed that he wasn't really helping Mike to express himself, the way I set up for in the beginning. But it rapidly began to look like something else entirely. Now, right at this point, the problem has become the parents' problem, not the child's. Nothing they can come up with from now on is going to change that.

INT.: At what specific point here does it become their problem?

DR. F.: Where the mother says, "Well, I don't think cutting his money off is the answer." This is where she is battling her husband and using Mike as the weapon. At this point, if smoking were really the problem, there should have been a united front on the parents' part. The mother, by disagreeing with her husband, gave the son the chance to argue effectively against his father.

INT.: Do you feel that there is any family situation in which the child's problem is not the parents' problem?

DR. F.: That's a hard question to answer, because there are levels of causation. If a child has been reared in a family, you can't completely disentangle the parents from the child's problem. But I have a feeling that children can have their own problems. There are a lot of influences besides the parents, differences in physiological make-up and neurological responsiveness, different experiences with school, friends, and so forth. But in some families the child gets a kind of social neurosis that is tied in directly with the parents. In this family, the parents are fighting each other through the boy, instead of fighting each other directly. Aside from that, there's not too much wrong with him.

> MR. K.: Well, part of that money, Mike, I mean, it, ah, the thing that Mother and I, you are thirteen years old, we do still have some control, although I sometimes doubt if you think we do. As to your comings and goings and what you do and what you don't do. You still have certain obligations to us, as a thirteen-year-old. And if you don't care any more about this—I, do I get paid for doing things around home? Does Mother get paid for doing things?

INT.: This speech of the father's is peculiar. To argue that you should have power over somebody because he's only a thirteen-year-old is a self-refuting statement. If he's only thirteen, you wouldn't argue about it anyway.

DR. F.: Exactly. The minute you put it that way, you're lost.

INT.: He's treating the boy as if he were an adult with whom this could be discussed. It's as if he said, "You're a responsible person with whom I can discuss the fact that you're thirteen and still irresponsible."

DR. F.: He's also encouraging him to get further out of control. The boy probably feels quite panicky at this point, because the father has told him, "I can't control you, you're on your own, thirteen or not." He's also depriving him of what all adolescents need, the security of knowing someone is around who can keep him from killing himself. It would have been far better if the father had said, "Look, I'm going to the mat with you, right now, unless you stop."

INT.: It's interesting the way the father tenaciously sticks in that "we," trying to make it a united front with the mother when he knows it isn't.

DR. F.: You notice how he indirectly maneuvers without ever facing the issue head-on. At the end of that speech, where he says, "Do I get paid for doing things around home?" he's shifting ground and going back to a point the boy has made, but it's a complete non sequitur. What he's trying to do is arouse a feeling of guilt in the child so the child will do what he wants.

MIKE: No, but do I, do I work any place?

DR. F.: Do you consider that, ah, you're doing those things and y-, you're receiving pay for them, is that the way you consider it?

MIKE: Yes.

MR. K.: You don't consider it just helping around, around home?

MIKE: Well I, I should think I should get *some* money. (*Pause.*)

MR. K.: Well, Mike, I'm, I'm very much afraid that I, I don't agree with you on that score.

MIKE: Well, I guess you don't.

MR. K.: But if you're going to spend your money for something that I don't approve of, I, I don't see any reason that I should be obligated to give you money. If you're going against my wishes and against my orders. That's one way I know of for at least a, an approach to the solution that, ah, would satisfy me.

(*Fulweiler knocks, enters.*)

DR. F.: You haven't expressed any opinion on this, Mrs. Kane, but you look kind of disapproving. What, what is your idea?

MRS. K.: I've just said that I don't think, ah, cutting his money off is the answer.

DR. F.: What do you think is the answer? I think your opinion might be helpful.

(*Fulweiler goes out.*)

INT.: Why did you come in and ask the mother for an opinion here?

DR. F.: Well, the mother knows, and the boy knows, that the allowance is the tool the father is going to use to try to coerce the boy into giving up smoking without ever dealing with the smoking directly.

The mother was sitting there swelled up like a poisoned toad. I was giving her the chance to express herself before she burst.

INT.: Had the father already stopped the boy's allowance?

DR. F.: Yes, and that's what made the boy's burglary such an apt gesture. He was carrying the battle with his father over smoking to its logical conclusion: "Even if you stop my allowance, you'll still pay for my cigarettes."

INT.: He's also bringing the community in against the parents.

DR. F.: Sure. You can read his stealing as a cry for help, not just for himself but for the whole family. When I see a neurotic delinquent like this, I assume that he knows perfectly well what he's doing, knows right from wrong, but that he's desperate to create some kind of crisis that will require a change at home and bring him closer to his parents. I've often asked kids, "How did you feel when you were caught?" and they've answered, "I felt glad because I thought that at last somebody would talk to me."

(*Fulweiler has just gone out.*)

MRS. K.: Well, I don't really know what the answer is, but I don't think that, I think that he's entitled to some money to spend. And I . . .

MR. K.: (*Inaudible phrase*) any way that he sees fit.

MRS. K.: Well, I think that if he's going to be given an allowance, I don't think he should have to, ah, put down every cent that he spends. If he's gonna, if you're gonna give it to him, then he should spend it, and if you're not going to give it to him, then, okay.

MR. K.: Would you approve of him going out and spending it for something that you didn't, ah, approve of?

MRS. K.: Well, I mean within reason, I don't think he's going . . .

MR. K.: Well, now, within reason, le-, let's analyze that a little bit. What do you mean by within reason?

MRS. K.: Well . . .

MR. K.: Something you've forbidden him to do?

MRS. K.: Pardon me?

MR. K.: Something you have forbidden him to do? (*Pause.*)

MRS. K.: No.

MR. K.: Well, I, I have forbidden him to smoke, should I give him money to go out and buy cigarettes? That's what he's going to do with it.

MRS. K.: Well, I don't think we're going after any, ah, ah, I think we're teaching him to be deceitful. By cutting off his money—he's gonna smoke, and I would rather—I, I know that you, when I say this, you kind of, you say I'm evading the issue. But I would rather have him smoke, in front of me, and in front of you, and have his confidence, than know that he's out on a street corner someplace smoking a cigarette.

MR. K.: I agree with you on that point. I would rather have him smoke in front of us.

MRS. K. (*overlapping*): And I think that, ah, that, ah, it's, too much of an issue is being made of the smoking. I would much prefer that he didn't smoke now, because I think he's too young. And I think it's gonna impair his health, to a certain extent. However, I don't think it's something that we can control so that, ah, by cutting off his money.

MR. K.: (*Long pause.*) The look on his face the other day when I walked into his bedroom and he was lying there in bed smoking a cigarette. Just as much as to say, "Well, what are you going to do about it?"

MRS. K.: I heard you tell him that if, that if you wanted, that if he was gonna smoke he was to smoke, at home, in front of you. Then . . .

MR. K.: Well . . .

MRS. K.: . . . when he did it, you flew off, you had a fit.

MR. K.: I agree with you.

MRS. K.: Now make up your mind . . .

MR. K.: I agree with you . . .

MRS. K.: . . . you want him to smoke at home or don't you?

MR. K.: I realize that. I don't, I'm completely confused about the whole thing, I guess. I just wish that his, his wants and desires and so forth would change to the point where he wouldn't want to smoke yet. Because I don't think he's old enough. And I certainly do agree with you that I don't like to see him, to see boys out on the street corner smoking. I've seen an awful lot of it down in [*nearby town*] while I've been working.

MRS. K.: I do . . .

MR. K.: . . . and it just doesn't look nice at all.

MRS. K. (*overlapping*): I have asked him if he has been smoking at school and he has told me no, and I have asked him please don't.

MR. K.: Are there any places down there where you are allowed to smoke, Mike?

MIKE: No, not exactly allowed.
(*Fulweiler knocks, enters.*)

INT.: What brought you in? The father being confronted by the mother?

DR. F.: No, that wouldn't have brought me in. It was the father saying, "I wish his wants and desires would change to where he wouldn't want to smoke." This is a variation on the theme of the parent who questions the child who has lied. He says, "Why did you lie?" The child says, "I lied because I knew I'd get punished if I didn't." And the parent says, "Why did you *want* to lie?" That question always implies that there must be something awful in the boy's character for him to want to. It's a horrible bind for the child. The father here is using this device to try to arouse enough guilt in the boy so that the boy will make the choice the father wants him to make.

INT.: Was the father also responding to the mother's defense of the boy?

DR. F.: No, I think he's responding to his own insecurities. He isn't the kind of man who can say, "You won't do this, period," and then back it up. So instead he leaves it open for the boy to decide whether or not he's going to smoke. I'm quite sure that when he put it to the boy he structured it something like this: "If you do smoke, you are no good, despicable, and vile. If you don't, you are a wonderful boy. But you're perfectly free to make the choice." So the child is in the position where if he smokes he's no good in the father's eyes, and that is exactly how the father controls it. Except that the father ends up in an impossible situation. Here he's given the boy free choice, but when the boy chooses what's most appealing to him, as children usually do, there's no way in the world for the father not to end up looking ridiculous. As the mother points out, the father has set it up himself, has given the boy permission to smoke, and then when he does, tries to punish him for it.

INT.: Where the father says, "I'm confused about the whole thing," would that be a point where you might conceivably have come in?

DR. F.: Not unless he genuinely wanted some clarification. But the father isn't really confused. It's just a ploy. The mother has thrown down the gauntlet, saying, "Make up your mind," and when he says he's confused, this only means that he's not going to give a direct answer. He's going to come around Robin Hood's barn and give a devious, subtle answer. And that's exactly what he does. He says, "I want him not to *want* to smoke."

INT.: The father talks as though he doesn't want to make an issue of it between him and the boy, as if he wishes the whole business would go away without his having to do anything about it.

DR. F.: Yes, but this is deceptive. He's the one who repeatedly ignores the boy's plea that he isn't smoking out of spite and keeps bringing it back to a personal issue between them.

(*Fulweiler has just entered.*)

DR. F.: That's, ah, an important point in the session there, a part, rather. As I gather it, what you did originally then was to tell or put Mike more or less on his own, say, "Okay, you, ah, if you're going to smoke, I want you to smoke in front of me." Then when he did it, why you . . .

MR. K.: Well, he's only done it once.

DR. F.: He'd only done it once then.

MRS. K.: And that w-, that was quite by accident.

MR. K.: I found out—oh, it was?

MRS. K.: Well, I mean, ah, wasn't it?

MR. K.: No, he . . .

MRS. K. (*overlapping*): Are you speaking of Sunday?

MR. K.: Well, his, his bedroom door was open and I just, ah, he wasn't hiding it at all, were you, Mike?

MIKE: Well, I just figured that you wouldn't walk into the room at that time, you were doing some work.

MRS. K.: But he wasn't being, he wa-, didn't have the cl-, the door closed or, or locked or anything.

DR. F.: He wasn't hiding it.

MRS. K.: He wasn't hiding it.

MR. K.: No, he was just in his room, when he was smoking . . .

DR. F. (*overlapping*): This was according to your instructions about that.

MR. K.: What?

DR. F.: This was according to your original instructions.

MR. K.: Why, yes. See, we didn't, ah, we didn't know apparently for quite some time that he was smoking, he, he'd been smoking for about a year.

DR. F.: What do you think of your wife's point that perhaps, ah, there's much ado about too little on this particular point?

MR. K.: It's possible.

DR. F.: How do you feel about it?

MR. K.: Well, I . . .

DR. F.: See, here's a point that has gone on here where Mike has more or less, um, takes the, ah, gets a bad time out of it but doesn't get much help out of it . . .

MR. K.: Yeah.

DR. F.: That is, you and your wife are in conflict about what to do here, and I gather—is this the first time you've discussed this this way?

MR. K.: Oh, yes.

DR. F.: Ah, and, and compared notes? What has happened . . .

MR. K.: This . . .

DR. F.: . . . what happens, then, when you do compare in this fashion?

MRS. K.: Oh, we end up the same way. (*Laughs.*)

MR. K.: We end up with no solution. (*Mrs. K. laughs.*)

MRS. K. (*overlapping*): (*Inaudible phrase*) the same thing. (*Laughs.*)

DR. F.: No solution.

MR. K.: That's right. As I say, this has been one thing that I thought of discussing down here.

DR. F.: What? The conflict of discipline and . . .

MR. K.: No, the, ah, the idea of this, of this smoking and how, our feelings about it, and . . .

DR. F.: Well, when you then, when you discuss it this far, then end up with no solution, I'd like to know how each of you feel about it.

MRS. K.: Well, it just stays up in the air, I mean I still have my opinion and he has his things go on. (*Pause.*)

DR. F.: And who gets the short end?

MR. K.: Mike.

DR. F.: Exactly. (*Mrs. K. laughs.*) Suppose you continue, then, a little beyond this point this time. (*Mrs. K. laughs.*)

(*Fulweiler goes out.*)

INT.: You do a curious thing here. First you start to take up the father's inconsistency about the boy's smoking. Then you suddenly switch and say that the real trouble is that he can't get together with his wife over it. I wondered whether you did this in response to the conflict between them. It came out so evidently in that little bit: "That was by accident." "Oh, it was?" "Well, wasn't it?"

Dr. F.: I don't know. I think I shifted in response to something about the mother. What prompts me to go in when I am observing will sometimes change quite rapidly during the time it takes me to get in the room. The father's inconsistency would inevitably cue me off, because it stands out in the early part of this session as the first issue we could really deal with. And I do go back to it. But here, when I started to talk to the father, the mother was looking as if she were thinking, "Well, here it goes again. I'll get snowed under by this verbal barrage and then I'm dead." She had an emotional point that was quite valid in dealing with Mike, but she was a voice crying in the wilderness. I think I was simply trying to take her side against the husband at a point where she was emotionally right and he was logically right, and yet she was right. The father always managed to argue her down rationally, but he was usually dead wrong. You often see this in families where the men are frightened of their emotions and erect these logical structures to safeguard and isolate themselves. A lot of engineers are like that, physicists, or accountants, as this man was.

Int.: Is that why you asked the father how he *felt* about the mother's point?

Dr. F.: Yes. But I know beforehand that if you ask most engineers or accountants what they *feel* about anything, they will tell you what they *think*.

Int.: I notice you didn't give him the chance to tell you.

Dr. F.: I knew he was going to give some kind of complex verbal rationalization, so I cut him off.

Int.: There are a lot of rapid switches here. After taking sides with the mother, you bring in the idea of a conflict which is hurting Mike, and so take his side against the parents. Then, instead of going on about the conflict, you ask about the rules they have for dealing with the conflict. It puts them on another level of discourse.

Dr. F.: I hadn't thought of it like that, but it's true.

Int.: It's partly in the nature of your method, too. It puts the emphasis not on what the problem is but on what they are going to do about it. When you ask the father, "Do you and your wife ever discuss this?" the implication is that he and his wife never have any meaningful talks.

Dr. F.: That's right, nothing ever comes to a solution. And I already have an idea that the father is not going to let it come to a solution.

INT.: What are you doing at this point to make them talk more meaningfully?

DR. F.: I'm trying to arouse their guilt by asking, "Who gets the short end?" And the father says, "Mike," and the mother laughs and indicates that she is supporting my position.

INT.: When the father mentions what he's thought of talking about in these sessions, and you come in with, "What, the conflict of discipline?" was that really what you thought he had in mind?

DR. F.: Heavens, no. I wanted to open the door a little further to the matter of the conflict, but I knew perfectly well this wasn't what he was thinking. This is just nondirective therapy; you tell the patient what you would like him to think he thinks, and hope that he'll begin to think it.

INT.: Why do you go out at this point? Do you assume you've done as much as you can in getting them going?

DR. F.: I leave because I've given them something to work on, and rather than sit around, I get out and let them take over. It would be easy for me to stay and go on talking about the conflict of discipline, but what is important to me is what they make out of the interaction I've engaged them in. When I get back to the observation room, I can see what they do with it.

(*Fulweiler has just gone out.*)

MR. K. (*to Mike*): Would it please you, I presume it would, it would please you if I said that it was all right with me for you to smoke? Would that make you feel better?

MIKE: Yes, I guess it would.

MR. K.: Well, for your sake, Mike, I wish I could, but I honestly and truly can't. I still don't think it's the right thing for you to do. (*Pause.*) I really don't.

MIKE: Well, by taking my allowance away, you're, you're both, not being, I'm not able to buy cigarettes, or I'm not being, I'm not able to do anything. I can't go to the show, I can't . . .

MR. K.: Now, Mike, whenever you have come to me, in the last two or three weeks, and asked me for money for some specific thing, I have given it to you.

MIKE: Those things I had to do. (*Pause.*)

MR. K.: You're right. You're right.

(Fulweiler knocks, enters.)

DR. F.: I think what Mike is saying would invariably make a big difference to a kid, between the things he has to do and has to have money for anyhow, and things he might want to do and having a little bit of money to just goof with. You asked a question a few minutes ago, and here I'll take Mike's, ah, side here that, yeah, there is, there is a time when a kid needs money just to spend, period. Not to save, or to put into something worthwhile for some specific purpose, but just to spend and to have, you know . . .

MRS. K. *(overlapping)*: Now that's, those are my feelings.

DR. F.: . . . some ready cash, jingling in his own pocket. But there's a point that we can't avoid here too, Mike, and that is that your father is, ah, as he points out, is in control of this situation. If he says you will not smoke, you will not smoke. The court will back him up, everyone will back him up. He has the say about this. It still remains, ah, a legal offense for you to be caught smoking outside. This could result in your getting picked up or anything, quite a number of things. Remember that when your dad lays that kind of a law down, you can work it out between each other. If you, *(to parents)* he can smoke around you in the home, it's another matter. If Mike, *(to son)* you're at liberty to do that. Ah, there's a good deal of license in your own home, but outside that isn't so. And the, ah, anyone, everyone will back your dad up in this. He's, he's the boss for when it comes to this. What we're talking about now are mainly, ah, the idea of, how to, not only how to get this over to you, but what really is wanted, what your family really wants, and right now it's a conflict, isn't it? *(To Mrs. K.)* You want him to smoke, not that you want him to smoke, but you don't want to make an issue of it. *(To Mr. K.)* And you want to make an issue of it, or do you?

MR. K.: I'd rather not . . .

DR. F.: All right.

MR. K.: . . . but I will if it's necessary. *(Laughs.)*

DR. F.: Um, now what does that mean?

MR. K.: Well, what I mean is I don't want to make an issue . . .

DR. F. *(overlapping)*: You don't want to make an issue of it as long as he stops smoking? *(Mr. K. laughs.)*

MRS. K.: I mean . . .

MR. K.: I can't honestly say. I, I mean I can't bring myself to, ah, agree, with Mike and, and to condone his smoking. I just can't do it, I mean I could go ahead and tell him, "Sure, go ahead."

DR. F.: Did you, did you, did you condone it, at first?

MR. K.: Well, when, when he actually, flatly de-, defied me and said, "I'm going to smoke," which he did, then I told him I'd rather have him do it around home. Now he, he did, absolutely, flatly say, "I am going to smoke, whether you want me to or not."

MIKE: I didn't say that, "whether you want me to or not."

MR. K.: Well, you said you were going to smoke.

MIKE: Yes.

MR. K.: Well, the, the rest of it was inferred, though.

MIKE: All right, but I didn't *say* that.

DR. F. (*interrupting Mr. K., who starts to speak*): Ah, this came up before, Mike's, Mike's complaint, and this may be a complaint that Mike has more frequently, that you take what he says and kind of twist it into something more extreme or more, or nastier than he intends it. He doesn't really intend to do this.

MR. K. (*overlapping*): Ah, I have, I have, ah, I believe it is probably true, because Mrs. Kane has told me that before.

DR. F.: This may have some roots too . . .

MR. K.: Sure.

DR. F.: . . . in the past. (*Mrs. K. laughs.*)

(*Fulweiler goes out.*)

INT.: What were you after when you came in?

DR. F.: My plan on coming in was to reinforce the father's role as the father, as the head of the household, and to point out that he has the right to make demands he should be making but isn't.

INT.: Then why do you start by criticizing his position on the boy's pocket money?

DR. F.: Because the first person I want to support is Mike. He is perfectly right in saying that he should have pocket money. But I also want to prepare for building the father up. If I support the father first, I run the risk of turning the boy off, of giving him the impression that I have betrayed him.

INT.: The way you support the father is to say that all of society will support him in the strong stand he isn't taking.

DR. F.: I'm really saying, "If you'd stop acting like a jellyfish and be a real father, you'd have everyone's support." I say he's wrong to cut off Mike's allowance but that he has the right to lay down the law to the boy if he will only do it directly.

INT.: You've managed to take sides with both simultaneously.

DR. F.: That's right.

INT.: It's such a complex thing when you say to Mike, "Remember when your dad lays down this kind of law, you can work it out between you." You imply that the father is in control, and at the same time you suggest that the son has a share in determining what the law shall be. You're not building up an authoritarian image of this father.

DR. F.: No, it's an authoritative one, which gives the boy fair play as well as the security of knowing what the restrictions are, and I do this in the context of supporting the father's image in the family.

INT.: You might alternatively have said to the father, "Stop acting like a jellyfish."

DR. F.: If I did that, I'd be undermining the father in his wife's and son's eyes, and also trying to substitute for him. He's got to retain a degree of respect from them, and if he doesn't have it when he comes in, it should be built up. If I were dealing with him individually I might tell him, "You're an ineffective weakling in your own home." But this would be done in a context where I have given him many indications of my appreciation of him as a person, so that he would know I wasn't attacking his character but what he was doing.

INT.: There's a big difference between talking to someone face to face and in the presence of his family. You have to consider what effect anything you say to him will have on the others.

DR. F.: This is what makes family therapy so delicate. You proceed by a kind of condensed, synoptic interaction, in which, by the by, the actual content is relatively unimportant. It wouldn't make any difference whether we were talking about smoking or something else. You don't want anyone to leave the session feeling down because you've undercut him, or anyone else feeling down because you've built the other person up. That's why, when I come in and make an interpretation like this, I can be exhausted after a few minutes. I'm building up, knocking down, forestalling, in many different directions at once, to keep it relatively even.

INT.: Why do you go on to say that the real problem is what the family wants?

DR. F.: For "family" you can read "father" there. I'm saying to Mike, "What you really want to know is what your father wants." I go on to point out that Mike is in a bind because he doesn't know which way to go. One way affronts mother and pleases father; the other way affronts father and pleases mother.

INT.: When you say to the mother, "You want him to smoke, not that you want him to smoke but you don't want to make an issue of it," is that to bring out the idea that she is supporting the boy in his smoking?

DR. F.: No. That was a slip. If I'd left it as, "You want him to smoke," the father could then light into her and say, "You see, you're an evil person, you want him to smoke and smoking is bad and the church says it's bad." I was simply recouping my mistake, or trying to.

INT.: Why do you leave them on the issue of the father's twisting what the boy says?

DR. F.: This refers back to where the father was insisting that the boy smokes to spite him. This is something that just enrages the boy, he gets tied up in a knot when the father makes this accusation. I was opening that one up.

INT.: And siding with the boy.

DR. F.: More than that. The mother had apparently made the same objection to the father many times, as the father admits. And I suspected that he had twisted the mother's words many times too. That was why I said, "This may have some roots in the past." The mother's knowing laugh tells me that she got right off what I was getting at.

INT.: This time, when you leave, you don't give any instructions as to what they are to do. I take it you assume they are sufficiently trained.

DR. F.: Yes, and I figure that they have plenty to work on now. But it's become apparent that the father is going to come back to the smoking regardless, no matter what I do, just as a compass needle comes back to the north. These interpretations are making little nicks at him, but they are not getting through.

INT.: Do you take this steadfastness of the father's as discouraging?

DR. F.: Heavens, no. Not in the first session. He's got a right to his defenses. As long as he's still at it, still working.

(*Fulweiler has just gone out.*)

MRS. K.: I don't, I think that, if you recall you doubted him on Sunday as to where he was getting the money, and you, you asked him where he was getting the money, and he told you, and you said you didn't believe that he had spent what he had for Christmas.

MR. K.: I didn't say I didn't *believe* that he had spent what he, I just wanted . . .

MIKE: Then why did you ask me before that?

MR. K. (*overlapping*): Well, I, I wanted to verify it, Mike.

MIKE: In other words, you didn't believe that I spent that much for Christmas presents.

MRS. K. (*overlapping*): (*Inaudible phrase*) if you had to verify it, you *inferred* . . .

MR. K.: All right.

MRS. K.: . . . that you didn't believe he spent that much for Christmas.

DR. F.: You see, here she's following the line that I've been taking, by saying to the father, "You're trying to prove your boy a liar." That's just what he's done. Instead of accepting the kid's Christmas gift, he went back and questioned it and tried to find out how much he had spent and in the process tore up the whole idea of Christmas.

INT.: So when you brought up the father's twisting what the boy says, it was a deliberate effort to support the mother into taking it further.

DR. F.: The mother and the boy both. I also want the father to have to pay some attention to her. Did you catch her emphasis on the word "inferred"? She's repeating the father's word of a short time before, when he was speaking to the son. She's hoisting him on the same petard.

MR. K. (*overlapping*): All right, I didn't believe he spent that much for Christmas, now wh-, now where do we go from here? (*Pause.*) Let's put it this way, I didn't *realize* that he had spent that much for Christmas. But when he told me, as we went down the list item by item, then I, I could see how he had. But it didn't seem to me, I had forgotten about Betty and Al. (*Long pause.*)

MIKE: Well, I know I don't have as much authority, but I, I don't see why I should ask you what you spent for everybody's Christmas presents.

MR. K.: Well, Mike, that is, ah, that's another point. I realize that that was, perhaps, in some ways was the wrong thing to do. Nevertheless there's one thing that you've got to remember, and I am very much afraid that there are times when you forget it, and that is that I am your father and when I ask you something, you are to tell me.

MIKE: Yes, but it . . .

MR. K.: And when I—you blow off the handle, nine times out of ten, you get mad and pop off and everything else, when somebody asks you to do something at a time when you aren't ready to do it. I think you'll agree with me on that, won't you?

MIKE: Yes, I guess so. But I don't see, I don't see why you should (*wavering voice*), whether you're my, whether you're my father or not, why you should ask me what I spent for your Christmas presents.

MR. K.: Forgive me, I've, I've . . .

MIKE: All right.

MR. K.: All right. I, we've been over that before. I shouldn't have done it. I'm wrong. In your eyes. (*Pause.*)

MRS. K.: Well, I feel sometimes that I, of course I have been . . . (*Fulweiler knocks, enters.*)

MRS. K.: . . . caught up . . .

DR. F.: Sorry, I missed that. (*To Mr. K.*) What were you wrong about?

MR. K.: Well, he, ah, he says I shouldn't have—oh, one minute—he, ah, claims that he spent some twelve or thirteen dollars for Christmas presents. I didn't realize that he had spent that much and it didn't seem to me as though he had. So he itemized the things that he had, ah, that he had bought. And among the things of course that he bought was my Christmas present, and he doesn't like the idea of my knowing how much he spent.

DR. F.: Yeah. That's kind of legitimate, isn't it?

MR. K.: Sure it is. Sure it is. I agreed with him on that. There wasn't any way that I could find out. But I have asked him in the past, many many months ago, in trying to teach him to take, ah, care of his money and so forth, I have asked him to itemize what he has spent his money for, and he has yet to do it, in any, any detail. He did it for a couple of weeks. And then, he just doesn't like the idea of having to account for his money. It's been a habit of mine for many, many years. Maybe it's, it's a, ah, foolish habit to have. Nevertheless, it's a habit that I do have and I keep track of every single penny that I spend. Every penny.

DR. F.: This is very useful, for you. And it's my question just how intensely Mike would feel pushed to do the same thing.

MR. K.: He's apparently, from, from, ah, his past actions and his little green book that he was given and so forth, he doesn't think anything of it at all.

DR. F.: Mike, it was you brought up the question of your dad misinterpreting what you said to him, taking things one way that you meant in another.

MIKE: Mm-hm.

DR. F.: What else, what other things do you have to, do you feel cause unhappiness to the family other than this?

(*Fulweiler goes out.*)

INT.: What cued you to come in there?

DR. F.: Nothing very profound, I'm afraid. I would guess that I simply didn't hear what was going on. I may have been talking on the phone or not paying attention. This is sometimes one of the reasons why I enter the room.

INT.: Do you ever ask them to repeat something as a tactic?

DR. F.: Yes, sure. But this time I don't think I did. The fact that I brought them back to the father misinterpreting what Mike says shows that I didn't have anything new to offer at that point. I wasn't coming in for a therapy purpose.

INT.: You still used your entrance to turn things a bit. You don't ask about the father misinterpreting Mike, you ask, "What other things cause unhappiness?" It's a much broader question.

DR. F.: I'm trying to get Mike to put into words what other things he sees going on in the family, since he seems to be opening up a bit. I'm also trying to see how the parents will deal with this, whether they will encourage him or shut him up.

(*Fulweiler has just gone out.*)

MR. K.: (*Pause.*) You know what Mr. Fulweiler said last time, Mike, this is, this is no man's land here, you can bring out anything you want.*

MIKE: I know it. (*Pause.*) I don't want . . . (*Long pause.*) I guess this smoking has been most of the trouble. Um, you know, I, I kept my budget for more than two weeks . . .

MR. K.: All right, how long did you do it?

MIKE: . . . and I was keeping it in the bank, too, but I didn't want to write down (*wavering voice*) how much I spent for *your* presents.

MR. K.: All right, Mike, now le-, let's forget about what you . . .

* The father is referring to a conversation not included in the tape recording of the previous session.

MIKE: You said . . .

MR. K.: . . . . spent for my Christmas presents. You didn't keep track of the others in, as, ah, in as much detail as the list that I had started for you on your, in your bank.

MIKE: Well, I thought Christmas presents would be enough. I didn't think you'd have to know exactly what I spent it for.

MR. K.: Well, let's forget that particular item. Remember the green book I gave you?

MIKE: Yes.

MR. K.: How long did you keep that?

MIKE: I (*wavering voice*) kept it for, a lot longer than two weeks.

MR. K.: Well, tell me, would you tell me something very honestly, were there any times when you put down on there that you spent money for a phone call, or magazines, or something like that, when actually you spent it for cigarettes?

MIKE: Yes.

MR. K.: Sure there was. So that, as far as, ah, as that sort of thing is concerned, there was no point in keeping it, 'cause you didn't.

MRS. K. (*overlapping*): Well, I (*Mr. K. trying to continue*) can't see that it's so important for him to keep track of it. Of course, there's where you and I disagree again.

MR. K.: That's right.

MRS. K.: And if he's going to be given an allowance, I don't see why he should have to account for it.

MR. K.: Is he going to follow . . .

MRS. K.: (*Talking simultaneously, inaudible phrase.*)

MR. K.: . . . is he going to follow that practice all his life? The only reason that I had him, I started him on . . .

MRS. K.: Now I'm—simply because you've, have always kept track of it . . .

MR. K.: All right. It was just, it was merely to try and, and ah, to give him a little training in the handling of money, that was all. It wasn't that I wanted to know exactly what he spent his money for. (*Mrs. K. and Mike start speaking simultaneously, inaudible words.*)

MRS. K.: You made him present that before you gave him his next allowance. I would resent it . . .

MR. K.: I didn't care . . .

MRS. K.: . . . *bitterly.*

MR. K.: I, the thing is, Evvie, I didn't, it wasn't that I wanted to know what it was that he was buying. It was just the mere fact that he was keeping the record. Do you see, do you see what I'm trying to get at?

MRS. K. (*overlapping*): I see what you mean, but you . . .

MR. K.: That. . . .

MRS. K.: . . . made him, nevertheless he knew he was gonna turn that, that itemized account in to you before he got his next allowance.

MR. K.: That's right.

MRS. K.: Now I would resent it bitterly if I were made to do that.

MR. K.: Well, I didn't know any other way to, ah, get him to do it.

MIKE: You told me once that, that you want, that—twice, I think, you told me the reason for me keeping that is because you wanted to know if I was buying cigarettes or not.

MR. K.: And you falsified it anyway.

MIKE: Falsified what?

MR. K.: The fact that you d-do—there never was an entry on there for cigarettes.

MIKE: Yes, I know. But you said to me that you just wanted to train me in the handling of money. You admitted, twice, at least, when, when you asked, found me out before, that you wanted to know whether I *was* buying cigarettes or not. In other words, you want to know exactly what I spend my money for.

MR. K.: I think that, that's right, Mike. (*Pause.*)

(*Fulweiler knocks, enters.*)

INT.: This "no man's land" the father quotes, is this a phrase you often use?

DR. F.: Yes. It's to try and encourage people to let the bars down and communicate freely about what's on their minds.

INT.: It makes therapy a special place which doesn't have the same rules as other places.

DR. F.: The corollary of this is to ask the family to respect the situation enough not to carry over into outside life the results engendered by the therapy. If a child confesses in the therapy session that he's done something wrong, he is not to be punished afterward. Or if a wife says something nasty to her husband, he is not to get back at her when they leave.

INT.: I should think this would be a problem as soon as you got the family in therapy together.

DR. F.: That's why I use this phrase. It's pretty much a myth to expect the family to forgive and forget entirely, but you can hope to lay down some ground rules so that they won't be explicitly difficult with each other later on.

INT.: There's another thing which could happen. If you tell them this is a "no man's land" where they can say things they might not ordinarily say, one of their impulses would be to test it out. And for that reason alone they might come out with things that otherwise would be kept hidden.

DR. F.: They test it not only in the first session but repeatedly during therapy. Of course, as this father shows, they can also use it against each other. Here he is copying me and saying to the boy, "Go ahead, you can say anything," in the most helpful and considerate tone. Then when the boy brings up the father's unfairness over the Christmas list, the father dismisses the topic and attacks the boy for falsifying his accounts. It stands out very clearly that the father is using the list to spy on the boy. It's a tribute to the fact that most of the time people don't know when they are lying. The father accuses the boy of falsifying his accounts, and yet he himself is being completely dishonest.

INT.: When the mother comes in to take the boy's part, and the mother and father start to quarrel, I take it that you wouldn't break in.

DR. F.: No. The mother is doing very well, she's holding her own. And the father isn't in a very secure position. Any intervention I made now would serve either to flatten him or to flatten her. He's backing a little, giving a little.

INT.: On your entrance here, was it the pause after the father says, "I think that's right," that decided you to come in?

DR. F.: I think so. Apparently the father has been trying to induce guilt again.

INT.: It's that same scene in which the father attacks the boy unfairly, the boy protests, and the father backs down and says, "I'm wrong, you're right." Each of your entrances so far has come at the end of a version of this scene. Do you often find patterns like that in the families you are treating?

DR. F.: Yes. But I wasn't seeing this as a pattern. I knew what the father was doing, but I'm not sure that this was necessarily motivating me to come in. I don't think it was the type of interaction that was bringing me in so much as the sense that the interaction had reached a terminal point. I tend to come in when a scene gets rounded out. Anything that came after this scene could have a bad result. That's why I intervene.

INT.: What do you think could have happened here?

DR. F.: I would anticipate a complete change. I would expect that the boy would become terribly frustrated or blocked because the father had tied things up the way he did, and that they would shift to something else and come back to this later. The father would then act as though he had never said or heard any of these things before.

INT.: I take it that you see this as the kind of destructive cycle that perpetuates the family's difficulties.

DR. F.: Yes.

INT.: Are your entrances designed to break up this cycle, to block it?

DR. F.: To block it and also to try to make some sense out of it which will be of benefit to all of them.

(Fulweiler has just entered.)

DR. F.: Ah, again, this is something, as a training device, I think you have a good point there. It's an excellent way of training someone to learn how to handle their money, in order to know what they're spending their money for and keep them aware of it. But training a kid is something, ah, perceived in a somewhat different fashion. That is, you've made a mark on Mike, as far as—I doubt if he'll ever be, at the end, as free and easy with money as he might have been, if you hadn't trained him. It sounds kind of as though your own goals got mixed up in the process, and that in addition to the training, it began to be sort of a, a, almost a spying technique . . .

MR. K.: Um-hm.

DR. F.: . . . to be darn sure he wasn't stepping out of line.

MR. K.: Um-hm.

DR. F.: I think from this standpoint I can understand your wife's objection, and Mike's objection.

MR. K.: Um-hm.

DR. F.: As far as objecting to it as a training device, no, it's a very good one.

MRS. K.: I don't object to it as a training device.

DR. F. (*overlapping*): Even if it hurts, I think, even if it hurts and makes him squawk like a wounded banshee, it's still good. But when you do get con-, you get the two mixed up, you know, when you, it sounds a lot as though—and this has come up two or three times today, that's the kind of feeling that I get—that you have to establish control, in some way, you have to be sure yourself that you're in control, in Mike, in, in Mike's situation. And I wonder whether this is really necessary. I think I know some of the reasons why. (*To Mrs. K.*) I think that you can answer that one, too, as to why Mr. Kane feels a little out of it, at times, and needs, it seems to me, to reach out and establish a firmer or stricter control. I think this relates much more closely to the, this business of one of you championing one side and the other the other, and conflicting, than it does to anything Mike is actually doing. He's doing pretty well. Pretty good. And I think between the two of you there's this feeling that Mr. Kane has, and I think he's pretty well justified, that he's, ah, sometimes he's fighting both of you and not just one (*tape recording skips*) and, and I think this may be very disheartening for Mike, too, that he, that you and he are teamed up against his dad, in a way, and that puts his dad out in the cold.

MRS. K.: Yeah.

DR. F.: The good things, the valuable things that Mr. Kane could teach are kind of lost in the family.

MRS. K.: Yeah.

(*Fulweiler goes out.*)

INT.: Can you elucidate that? There's a lot in that speech.

DR. F.: I'm going after the father, but first I want to give him some points. So I compliment him on using the list as a training device.

INT.: It sounds as if you were straining for that compliment.

DR. F.: Actually, at the time I thought that I'd like to be able to do the same thing with my own kids, to train them to use money. It's impossible, because I don't know how to use it myself.

INT.: Are you using this genuine admiration on your part to support the father for tactical reasons?

DR. F.: Yes. To set him up so I can lay him low.

INT.: You certainly do lay him low. You accuse him of spying. But then you turn it into why he needs to spy.

DR. F.: He's been making such a fool of himself that I want to restore some of his dignity. I do this by pointing out to the mother that she is playing a part in his loss of dignity.

INT.: This is the first time you've gone after the mother.

DR. F.: Yes. Up to this time, everything I've said has been very supportive of Mrs. Kane. I've been coaxing her and encouraging her and hacking away at these techniques the father uses against her and the boy. But here, at the end of this speech, I turn and really give her the business. I point out that by teaming up with Mike she is undermining her husband's authority. I'm also implying a destruction of their sexual relationship.

INT.: You don't say, "You're undermining your husband," but "Your husband is acting the way he is because he has to fight both of you." It's still not a direct attack.

DR. F.: It's not meant to be.

INT.: This is the first time you've come out and identified the mother-son coalition. What made you feel this was the proper time to do it?

DR. F.: I think it has to do with the rhythm of the family, the rhythm of the session, more than anything else. I've been hinting at the conflict between the parents, bringing it up, dropping it, coming back to it again, and they seem to be taking it well. I've indicated the way this conflict is related to the smoking issue and now I want to round out the picture further and say, "Here's another line that's tied up with the conflict between the two of you that you may not have been aware of." Also, the way the father terminated that last interchange was so hopeless and resigned. It suggested that they were ready to move on. When I point out the mother-son coalition, I am building on all the interactions that have gone before. It's a merger and a step to a new stage. I think that every family has its own rhythm and that this rhythm determines the way you work with it. Some families are rapid and staccato, some move in a kind of gentle rise and fall, and some go through long periods of nothing till all of a sudden there's an explosion.

INT.: How would you characterize the rhythm of this family?

DR. F.: I think oscillating up and down rather rapidly. There have been four or five different things brought up in the space of this first session, all of them very profound, tough things that you would work a long time to get at in individual therapy.

INT.: Does it surprise you when a family can bring up this much?

DR. F.: Even for a family, this one is pretty rapid. They take the interventions with less disruption of their ties than many families do, and with less disruption of the session. I could work quite fast with them.

INT.: About this interpretation, it's a very complicated one and you do a great many things in it. There are several ways of looking at it. One is that you are providing some new information for Mrs. Kane. By showing her how she is siding with her son against her husband, you are giving her an understanding which will make her behave differently. This is how it would often be interpreted.

DR. F.: It would be delightful if this were true.

INT.: You could also say that it would be very hard for the mother to go on siding with her son and leaving her husband out, after you have told her she is doing this. It would be equally hard for the husband to keep on staying out after you have showed that he is contributing too. But there's one other way to look at it. Running through the whole interview, but extremely evident here, is the way you manage to side with all three of them at once. You side with the father by saying that getting his boy to keep track of the money he spends is good training. Then you side with the boy by suggesting that the father has used this as a spying technique. Then you side with the mother by supporting her objection to the spying. Then you side with the father again by saying that the reason why he feels compelled to use such devices is that the mother and son are getting together and leaving him out. At the same time, you say this to the mother in such a nice, helpful way that it gives the impression that you are siding with her in this difficult problem of dealing with her husband and child.

DR. F.: Sounds pretty good, doesn't it?

INT.: Well, it gets better. You also side with the parents by saying that this arrangement is really hardest on them; the boy is in pretty good shape. You then side with the boy by saying that the situation is disheartening for him too. I suspect that you've sided with and against each individual and each pair, all within a one-minute speech.

DR. F.: There's one point I think should be brought out. In a way, I'm siding against each person or pair, because if I side with any one element in a side-taking situation, I will inevitably be siding against other elements. If I support one coalition, I disrupt another. But I think I am trying to suggest that I am siding with all of them against the pattern they are caught in, which makes all of them the losers.

INT.: I should also think that putting everybody in the right and in the wrong at the same time would tend to cancel out the benefits of taking sides, for the moment at least.

DR. F.: I'm also trying to build my therapeutic relationship with these people in an effort to achieve a status from which I can work. I join with each of them, so that each will feel that I am on his or her side, without overly blaming the others. In my own mind, I see it as the four of us working together.

INT.: The four of you against the world.

DR. F.: At least against this abstract entity, "the mess you're caught in."

INT.: What's interesting is that if one reads your interpretation swiftly, it sounds like a rational, causal explanation for the mess. As if you were trying to help them "understand."

DR. F.: I try to stay away from this simple, causal frame: "Because you did this, your son does that." I think all it does is upset people, unbalance the picture even further. I try to let a meaning grow in the context of the interaction.

INT.: When you were introducing your method to these people, you said, "All of you have contributed, but none of you is to blame." There it stood as a mere verbal statement. Here it's translated into the actual relationships.

DR. F.: It would be foolish to say that what I did here was a conscious and deliberate act, but as a matter of technique, it's devoutly to be wished for.

> (*Fulweiler has just gone out.*)
> MRS. K.: (*Long pause.*) I, I can see Mr. Fulweiler's point, in that I've— (*Pause.*) It's unfair to him and I shouldn't have. (*Pause.*) How do you feel about that, son? (*Pause.*)
> MIKE: I don't understand.

INT.: The mother is making the first admission that she is part of the problem. Do you think she has already had this thought?

DR. F.: I think she has been quite aware that she gets together with her son, but I suspect she has never thought of it as being unfair to the boy. One reason I brought the boy in was to arouse enough guilt in her so that she would have to acknowledge the statement I was making. Take the boy out of it, take this hook out of it, and she might well have turned on the father and fought or denied it.

INT.: It's a way of preventing them from getting into a fight about it?

DR. F.: Yes. If they discuss it the wrong way this first session, it can do more harm than good.

INT.: Would you say that this difference in the mother signals some kind of shift? The whole character of the session seems to change from now on.

DR. F.: Yes. The mother starts working to relate the boy's behavior to the conflict between herself and her husband.

INT.: She doesn't sound antagonistic toward him at all, though earlier she was ready to throw the book at him. In the beginning of this conversation, you said that you expected trouble with the wife. Now she not only has failed to become a problem, but she is extremely conciliatory. How did you prevent her from blowing up?

DR. F.: I didn't prevent her, I merely slowed her down. I didn't want her to come out with everything she's got against her husband in one fell swoop, before he's got his bearings in the new situation. There are a thousand little ways you can do this. One way is to turn the responsibility on her, turn it away from the husband, as I just did. Or you can calm her down by giving her emotional support, as I also did. She has given many indications of how she feels about her husband during this session, and another way to forestall her is not to hear her until you are ready to. Later on in the sessions, I gave her plenty of chance to let off steam, and she did. She could be an extremely vigorous antagonist.

(*Fulweiler still out.*)

MR. K.: Well, if Mother were anywhere as adamant about your smoking as I am, it's probably a difficult question for you to answer, I realize, but if, if Mother were as adamant about smoking as I was, as I *am,* would you quit?

MIKE: I don't know.

MR. K.: It's something I'm afraid of with Mike, and it's—I don't know, really, what the reason is, or—but part of the problem, I think, is that Mike has, for a long while, I think, has had a, a sense of independence, far beyond his years. How do you feel about that, Mike? Do you . . .

MIKE: Well, what do you expect me to do?

MR. K.: Well, ah, haven't you, ah, haven't you resented our wanting to know where you were and what you did, many times . . .

MIKE: Yes.

(*Fulweiler knocks, enters.*)

MR. K.: . . . almost feeling it was none of our business?

MIKE: Yes, I guess so.

MR. K.: Well, it definitely is, I think.

DR. F. (*to Mr. K.*): Ah, a feeling like this? What do you think causes this, Mike?

MIKE: Well, I think the smoking has to do with it too.

DR. F.: How do you mean?

MIKE: Because I wanted to and they didn't, they didn't want me to, so I had to do it some place where they couldn't find out about it.

DR. F.: This is probably true of other things. Have you any idea why it is, you think, that you feel this independent that you'd be able to get away with things?

MIKE: No.

DR. F.: You don't suppose, ah, that you've learned how to get away with things, do you? A little bit?

MIKE: No, I don't think so.

DR. F.: Well, what happens if you want to do something, and you know it's something that, that your dad won't approve of? Probably won't, or you, you're afraid to ask him anyhow.

MIKE: I don't know, I guess I either just do it and not tell him about it . . .

DR. F.: Or, what else could you do, what could happen? (*Long pause. To Mr. K.*) Do you know what he does? Do you have a good guess?

MR. K.: No, I don't.

DR. F.: Do you suppose he might have, ah, learned how to play both ends against the middle? How to play each of you off against each other?

MRS. K.: Well, that could be.

DR. F.: It kind of sounds like he might be able to, a little bit, you know, by working the angles correctly. It's, ah, something kids learn awful fast, and once they learn it, it's probably the saddest lesson they ever learn. It gets so successful, so fast, maybe, at any rate so easy. Does that sound right to you, Mike?

MIKE: No, I hadn't intended to do that, I don't think.

DR. F.: Well, without even thinking about it, do you suppose that it entered into (*inaudible phrase*).

MIKE (*overlapping*): Well, it might be, but . . .
(*Fulweiler goes out.*)

DR. F.: This is a relatively simple intervention. I'm just bringing the boy into the act, pointing out something he's responsible for.

INT.: I notice that this time when you come in they go right on talking, they don't stop.

DR. F.: Yes. I'm just part of the family now. This is very early in the game for this to happen.

INT.: Do you take this as a good prognostic sign?

DR. F.: Yes. It means they're caught up in the therapy process.

INT.: Why did you come in so quickly this time?

DR. F.: I didn't like the direction the father was going in. He was saying, "My boy has too much authority at home and this makes me feel childish."

INT.: This same scene has occurred several times, and each time you've waited until it came to a completion before you came in. This time you don't even give it a chance.

DR. F.: Because he's just going to increase the boy's feeling that he can't control him and demean himself in the eyes of his wife and son again. He's done it over and over and there isn't any sense in letting him do it again. I've pointed out the ways the father and mother enter into the picture, and now it's the boy's turn to be brought in. He's playing mother off against father. They've set the stage for that, but I want to get the boy to recognize or admit his part. This will also make him share a certain amount of responsibility for therapy. I want him to feel that he has done some work too.

INT.: I notice that your phrasing doesn't implicate the parents very heavily. This playing off both ends against the middle is an unfortunate happenstance that the boy has engineered.

DR. F.: Well, I'm really pointing out to the parents that the split between them has played hand in glove with this. I'm weakening the mother's coalition with the boy, because if she recognizes that he is playing them off against each other, she's going to be a little more hesitant about falling for it.

INT.: So you're not only trying to get the boy to acknowledge his share, but you're using this to pull the parents together.

DR. F.: However, if you notice, when I try to get the boy to agree with me on this, he denies it. This is an example of an interpretation that fell flat on its face. I had to go ahead and force it.

INT.: It wasn't something he had done in the room there, so you couldn't point it out or play back the tape.

DR. F.: Exactly. But I felt it was important to get a concession out of him, so I forced it, and when he got out that "Well, it might be, but," I backed quickly out of the room. I wasn't going to stay and let him get that "but" out in contradiction.

INT.: When you use the phrase "without thinking about it," are you suggesting that his behavior is something he might not have been aware of?

DR. F.: Yes. So that he can't very well refute me.

(*Fulweiler has just gone out.*)

MR. K.: (*Pause.*) Well, do you suppose that this might stem clear back to [*city*] in any way?

MRS. K.: (*Pause.*) It could.

MR. K.: Back to the seventeen or eighteen months or so that I was away, when Mike was so small? And in those very early months, when you were so completely in charge of him? That there might be, ah, both in Mike and in you, to a greater or lesser degree, a feeling of, you might say resentment, at my coming into the picture?

MRS. K.: Well, I wonder if that doesn't have something to do with it.

MR. K.: And that was many years ago, I realize, but I've often wondered about that. There've been a few times when I, I can't think of any specific cases, but I seem to recall that there have been a few times when Mike has asked me if he could do something and I have said no, and then he has gone and asked you. There are times when perhaps you might say yes, without stopping to think that he might have already asked me.

MRS. K.: I don't remember, ah—was that I am aware of one time that he did that, and—but it stopped, and that . . .

MR. K.: Do you, ah, do you ever recall any times like that, Mike?

MRS. K.: That time was when we lived in [*city*], he was very small.

MR. K.: I'm not, I'm, I'm not trying to, to pin it down to any particular incident, but, ah, just in, in general, do you think that you've ever had that idea . . .

MIKE (*overlapping*): Well, yeah . . .

MR. K.: . . . that Dad won't, if Dad won't . . .

MIKE: . . . but I can't think of when.

MR. K.: . . . that, ah, Dad, ah, won't let me, but, ah, maybe Mother will? I know [*daughter*] has done it, hasn't she?

MIKE: Well, I've probably done it, but I can't think of anything.

MR. K.: I just wonder if that has ever happened when he has gotten away with it, which would implant that idea in his mind that perhaps he could. (*Pause.*)

INT.: Two interventions back you propose the idea that the mother is getting together with the boy against the father. Then you go out, and the father turns the topic back to the boy's defiance, or "independence." When you come in again, you relate the boy's independence to his playing both ends against the middle. This time when you leave, the father turns it back to the mother getting together with the boy against him. Is this a way of pushing the father in the direction you want him to go by giving him a new alternative he likes less than the first?

DR. F.: I wasn't consciously working at it in the way you suggest, though it did have the effect of turning him back to the mother. If I'd let him go on about the boy's independence long enough, he might eventually have gotten around to hinting that this stemmed from the mother's independence and so forth. This way I got him to deal with the mother more quickly. However, it's not much of a victory. You notice how deviously he goes about confronting her. For instance, that phrase: "in those very early months when you were so completely in charge of him." It hangs her. No matter what has happened since then, she has to take the rap for the genesis of the boy's problems. And it's all done in the spirit of earnest and intelligent investigation. This kind of attack is probably a daily occurrence in their house, always under the guise of making a helpful suggestion: "Why don't you put a little more oil on the dust mop, doesn't it sometimes help to pick up the lint?"

INT.: In other words, he has taken your attempt to include both of them in the problem of the boy and put all the blame on her.

DR. F.: That's right. And she can't even accuse him of attacking her, because he doesn't make her entirely responsible, the war was responsible, since that's why he was away for those eighteen months. She has no way to defend herself. It's a beautifully done thing.

INT.: The mother answers in such a doubtful way.

Dr. F.: Yes. She knows there are hidden traps, but she doesn't see them until it's too late.

Int.: What he does next is to come back to the boy's playing them off against each other. He's going in the stages you suggest.

Dr. F.: Yes, but again he gets her. He's saying, "Mike is playing one of us off against the other, but it's your fault, because you never stop to think that when he asks you for something, he might already have asked me."

Int.: He's still declining to admit his part in the situation.

Dr. F.: Sure. He could sit in the living room and hear Mike go into the kitchen and ask his mother the question and never intervene at all. This is partly why I don't go along with the usual business of blaming the mothers. Many people have said I am a lot rougher on the fathers than most therapists, and the reason is that there's been a kind of I-hate-mothers cult among psychotherapists for years. My contention is that the fathers are far more adroit manipulators in the home than the mothers have ever thought of being. In most cases, when you find a mother who is being bitchy, contriving, nasty, you name it, you find behind her a coldly manipulating father who is keeping himself emotionally isolated from his family and making them pay for everything they get.

Int.: I think the mothers of schizophrenics are partly responsible for this emphasis on mothers. These women have a range; they can weep, they can fall apart, they can be helpless, they can be sarcastic, they can join you, they can unjoin you. Once a therapist has dealt with one of these mothers, I don't think he ever forgets it.

Dr. F.: I think the mothers only seem more extended, more versatile. Watch the father while the mother is going through her gymnastics. He doesn't appear touched at all, but whenever he wants to produce any of these behaviors in her, he pushes the right button and turns it on. The father in this family isn't as worthy an antagonist as some I've met; he's much too childish and sensitive and brittle. You can shatter him very quickly. But even at that, he's still putting the knife into his wife and son at every opportunity and with everything he's got.

(*Fulweiler still out.*)

mrs. k.: Well, I think as far as I—I have bent over backwards, ah, not to take the authority on which I've, have, since come to the conclusion it wasn't right either, because I think he's entitled to an answer from, either yes or no, from either one of us. (*To Mike.*) But that I'm, am, I've, in doing, in so doing, I have been possibly unfair to you—but I wasn't aware of it, I was doing it for you, at the time. Or that you would come ask me, I would say, "Well,"—my answer would quite often be, "It's all right with me but you'll have to ask your father." (*To Mr. K.*) And of course I realize now that if you said no, then you were the stinker who said no.

MR. K.: Well, that, that's true.

MRS. K.: But I was not doing it with any, I didn't realize how, how it would sound at the time.

MR. K.: You had no impression . . .

MRS. K. (*overlapping*): What impression it was making on him. I was trying not, not to take the authority away from you.

(*Fulweiler knocks, enters.*)

DR. F.: That's very good. Ah, the point, ah, being that most of these things that occur are not intentionally done. And this is what I meant, in the very beginning session, about not blaming people. Ah, if you slipped into this kind of a trap, you didn't do it with your eyes wide open.

MRS. K.: No, I didn't.

DR. F. (*overlapping*): You did it by accident.

MRS. K.: I'm aware of it now.

DR. F.: Yeah. And you can see this side of it. There's another part of this that I thought might, we might as well bring in to round out this particular picture (*to Mr. K.*) and this is *your* feelings, ah, perceiving this and feeling kind of left out with Mike and (*inaudible phrase*).

MRS. K. (*overlapping*): I, ah, Mr. Fulweiler, I think that's where I started. I think he, I've felt that, that my husband felt that he was not having, that I had too much authority.

DR. F.: Yeah. (*To Mr. K.*) You left him at how old? How old was he when you came back?

MRS. K. (*simultaneously*): And Mike would come to me before he would go to him.

MR. K.: He was about twenty months when I came home.

DR. F.: He was twenty months when you came home.

MR. K.: Three months when I left.

DR. F.: And three months when you left.

MR. K.: Well, he . . .

DR. F.: You came home to find him a, pretty much of a kid . . .

MR. K.: Yeah.

MRS. K.: That's right.

DR. F.: . . . and not just a little infant.

MRS. K.: And he was, ah . . .

DR. F. (*simultaneously, to Mr. K.*): And I wondered to what extent you developed feelings of being out of it, just from having that . . .

MR. K.: Oh, yes.

DR. F.: . . . long absence.

MR. K.: Sure.

MRS. K.: Because he would be . . .

DR. F. (*simultaneously*): This just might be the root of that need to reach out and control him in some ways that, that hurt him.

MRS. K.: Of course when he came home, he wouldn't let his father even play with him, something or other had to be, something had to be done, he would come to me. And Mike and I have always had a very close relationship. Of course I think it's not on-, only true with us, but I think it's very true with, ah, mothers and sons. And also I think that he and his father are *very* much alike, and they're inclined to be a little antagonistic because of this.

DR. F.: Yeah, I, I think we've seen them both use the same arguments against each other quite directly, ah (*inaudible phrase*).

MRS. K. (*overlapping*): But, um, what I started was, as I said, I did it trying to, to put the responsibility on . . .

MR. K.: *Shift* the . . .

MRS. K.: . . . for, on him.

DR. F.: Yeah.

MRS. K.: For, to bring you ba-, to make him feel that he was being in, to being brought into the whole thing, and in the course of it (*Mr. K. talking in background*) I did more harm than good.

DR. F.: Yeah, this happens sometimes.

(*Fulweiler goes out.*)

INT.: Let's see what brings you in there.

DR. F.: Ex post facto reasoning, I think it was because the mother had taken so much on herself, said *mea culpa,* and the next minute she would have begun to pour ashes on her head. It was toward the end of the session and I wanted to get her off that guilt and ease her up, so that we could end more evenly.

INT.: Is this the time you usually end a session?

DR. F.: I think this one had already gone on longer than usual.

INT.: Why did you say to her, "That's very good"?

DR. F.: To give her some support and shut her off at the same time. But I was really pleased, too, not that she took the blame from the father, but that she went one better on him. She points out that her trying not to take the authority made him into the "stinker." It's her own contribution.

INT.: She doesn't just agree with him. She says, "I can find an even better reason for blaming myself than you can."

DR. F.: But she was already feeling guilty enough so that I was beginning to be a bit uneasy about it.

INT.: There's something about the way you use the word "guilt." You seem to see it, not as something that sits inside a person, like an emotion, but as a way people influence other people, usually not for the better. Here I take it that you are concerned with the effect on other people if the mother feels too much guilt.

DR. F.: Yes. If she feels guilty enough, she will become angry and resentful and will begin to undermine therapy, her husband, her son. It could be very disruptive.

INT.: The way you relieve her of guilt is by suggesting that these actions are not intentional.

DR. F.: That's right. That they slip into habitual patterns.

INT.: This is what you set up for in the introductory session. Now all you have to do is say, "I told you this would happen." It would give you greater weight in dealing with her, I should think.

DR. F.: Exactly.

INT.: This "It was unintentional" is interesting. It's something so many therapists use. Somebody starts to blame himself and then the therapist comes in and says, "But it wasn't intentional." It's always in the intransitive; not "*You* didn't do it intentionally," but "Most of these things are not intentionally done." It was a happening which took place outside her awareness all by itself. I was wondering whether there might be another way you could go about relieving someone's guilt.

DR. F.: If I didn't want to give the mother an out by making it unconscious, I might praise her for her insight, make her feel pleased that she had discovered something about herself. But that wouldn't be nearly as effective.

INT.: No, that would still leave her to blame for the past. And it would put the other people down. The "unintentional" phrasing is a way to support one person without putting the others down. It's a mixture of relieving guilt and taking away credit. If you make the mother that responsible for having caused whatever it is, you are also making her that powerful. By suggesting that she did it inadvertently, you take away the credit.

DR. F.: Credit for having too much influence, you mean?

INT.: Yes. That undermines the father's position too, because what he is saying to the mother is, "You set all this up."

DR. F.: An indirect way of dealing with her guilt would be to turn it on the father, show how he is letting himself be the stinker. I believe that people ask for what they get, that there are no victims in the ordinary sense. I do turn to the father and point out that when he came home and found his wife occupied with the baby and not paying attention to him, he got his nose out of joint and as a result tried to control the boy too strictly.

INT.: That's right. You don't let him get away with being an innocent bystander. But again the implication is that it wasn't intentional.

DR. F.: You notice that the mother then points out that the father and son have a coalition too, where she says that they are extremely alike.

INT.: That's the first time this coalition has been mentioned.

DR. F.: That's why I emphasize it. I bring out a specific way I have observed that they are alike, rather than taking it back to their antagonism, as she does.

INT.: What is beginning to be impressive here is the amount of balancing that goes on. You balance one coalition against another, one side against another. If someone starts blaming himself, you suggest that somebody else is to blame; if someone is attacked, you support him; if somebody takes credit, you give credit to somebody else. There's an emphasis on equal participation, whatever the content. If you take a mother, father, and child in a situation in which the mother and child are getting together and the father is being left out, and you keep bringing the father in as a participant, you're changing the balance they had in the direction of making it a more equal one.

DR. F.: Yes, but that doesn't mean there's a real change, not at this point at least. To use a metaphor, the therapist is like an operator that is added in different proportions to each side of an equation, so that it ends up being balanced. At this stage, if you took the therapist away, the original order would still be there. Hopefully, at some point the merit value of the operator, the therapist participation, will decline and the equation will still remain in balance.

INT.: That's quite an image. The therapist going from one side to another, adding weights.

DR. F.: Literally throwing his weight around. The intent is to have the family experience an entirely different quality of relationships for this period of time and leave the session feeling good about what they have achieved.

INT.: When it's really been the added factor of the therapist that did it.

DR. F.: But that's invisible, or you hope it is. They never have to identify it at all.

INT.: I should think that giving people a different experience of balance would be a more effective kind of therapy than just handing them a verbal interpretation. They can't toss it back as something you've imposed on them, and they can't escape being in it.

DR. F.: Neither can the therapist. When I am engaged in therapy, I am totally involved, I am *in* the family, emotionally, physically, behaviorally. That's what I mean when I sometimes say I "join" the family.

INT.: You join them when you set up this more equal balance, but you're attacking the balance that exists.

DR. F.: I don't really feel that I'm attacking them when I do this. I feel that I am supporting their healthy impulses.

INT.: What do you mean by "supporting their healthy impulses"?

DR. F.: I'm supporting everything that will make them feel that they are good, responsible, intelligent people.

INT.: You could also say that when each is able to concede his appropriate share in the total operation, this is healthy.

DR. F.: That's right. Without overdoing it or taking too much of the burden.

INT.: It wouldn't be healthy if they did it like that. It's exactly this sort of skew that you constantly correct. Until they can correct it for themselves, you use your own weight to do it for them.

DR. F.: Yes. I use the therapeutic relationship itself to simulate the kind of family interaction I want.

(*Fulweiler has just gone out.*)

MR. K.: Well, it's a complex thing.

MRS. K.: But I, I didn't realize that in, in making you make the decision—if I had said, "Well, I don't know, ask your father," it would have been a little different than if, than my saying, "Well it's all right with me, but ask your father."

MR. K.: Yes.

MRS. K. (*to Mr. K.*): And then when you said no, then you were the stinker. "Well, Mother would have let me, but Dad won't."

MR. K.: Yes. Well, then there have been times when you have come to me after Mike has asked you and it's been all right with you and I have said no, there have been times when you have come to me and talked me into it. Do you realize that, too?

MRS. K.: Well, I suppose there have been. But I, I think now that we each ought to have the authority to say either yes or no and give him a direct, a direct answer. (*Pause.*)

MR. K.: And the other one ought to back it up.

MRS. K.: And the other one ought to back it up.

DR. F.: The mother does something quite admirable here. The father is driving it in, how she has "forced" him into a position of never having any authority with the boy, and she replies, "We ought to get together and give him a direct answer, yes or no." Again, she takes what the father says and goes further. This time she implicates him squarely.

INT.: This is the first time during the whole interview that the parents have shown any sign of unity. When the father says, "And the other one ought to back it up," the mother comes right back and repeats the phrase.

DR. F.: This is what she always wanted, and it wasn't the last time she made this point. She came out several other times, very strongly, and indicated that they should get together.

INT.: What importance did you place on the fact that this couple was able to agree, for the first time ever according to their previous admission, on how to handle their son?

DR. F.: I was pleased that they were able to formulate this agreement in the initial session. I knew it was a matter of making promises they weren't going to be able to keep, but once they had said it, it meant that I could then refer back to it in later sessions and show them how much they were departing from their eminently reasonable conclusion. The important thing was that they had said it, not me. But here, of course, the father turns it right back to the boy.

INT.: That's strange. You could see how he would want to avoid his wife earlier in the session, when she was acting so defiant. But there's none of that quality in her voice now; she sounds quite supportive. Why would he turn away from her at this point?

DR. F.: Because he's very frightened of the relationship with his wife. He feels that she runs rings around him, not intellectually but in sophistication. This has to do with their sexual and social relationships. He's bright enough to recognize that he is an awkward, obtuse person, sexually shy and untutored, where she is a warm, attractive person who wouldn't have any trouble forming relationships with men much more capable than he. She has needs that he can't meet.

INT.: She was making an advance here, and this worried him as much as her defiance.

DR. F.: That's right. If she ever got turned on, he would probably become sexually impotent in the same way that men sometimes do when their wives reach that period, right around the menopause, when they are no longer constantly frightened of pregnancy and always refusing their husbands. Instead, they are tripping the old man up and beating him to the floor. Then the husband isn't the ever rutting stag any more, and he suffers a very real impotence. It takes a lot of patient work to get over that hurdle in marriage. This man was about forty, and he was well aware that if his wife ever got uncorked, he was not going to be able to satisfy her. He knew when he married her that he was getting someone who was better than he could have hoped for, because he was the kind of bumbling guy who never had much to do with women. The way he made up for being this kind of inadequate man and kept his wife in line was to control the finances and the order of the home and adjudicate on moral issues. This way he kept his wife within very narrow limits of behavior and himself from being proved inadequate.

(*Fulweiler still out.*)
MR. K.: Does that seem reasonable to you, Mike?
MIKE: Umm.
MR. K.: Does that seem more fair?

MIKE: Yeah, I can see that, yeah . . .

MR. K.: Can you see how, perhaps, that's one reason why there's been, to a certain extent, greater or lesser extent, a resentment against me because I've always been the one to stick pins in your balloons, you might say, and your ideas, the ideas that you've had, and the things you've wanted to do, that Mother's passed the buck to me and I've been the one to say no?

MIKE: Um-hm.

MR. K.: I think over a period of time . . .

MRS. K.: But I've, as I say, Mickie-boy, I was not doing it with any, *any* thought of hurting your father.

MIKE: I know it.

MR. K.: You don't remember I don't think, Mike, but, but, I don't know how many weeks it was, or how many days it was, but it was quite a long time, back there in the apartment in [*city*] you'd kiss that picture good night rather than kiss me good night.

MRS. K.: Oh, now, you might as well have been the garbage man as far as he was concerned, he didn't know you, the fact that you were his father didn't mean a darn thing to him.

MR. K.: I realize that. I realize that.

MRS. K.: I mean, Daddy was more of a father to him than you were, at that point.

MR. K.: Yeah. That's right. (*Pause.*)

DR. F.: See how the father changes the subject here to the bad behavior of the boy and begins rubbing it in, how the boy wouldn't kiss him good night when he was small. Making him feel guilty again. The mother quite sensibly calls him on this. I like the way she puts it: "You might as well have been the garbage man."

INT.: And then the father slumps down and says, "That's right." It's the same put-upon tone he's used with the boy, the same phrase even.

DR. F.: He's quite an artist.

MR. K. (*cont.*): As I've told you so many times, Mike, if Mother and I didn't care, didn't care about you, didn't love you as we do, we wouldn't be one tenth concerned as much as we are. And after all, you are old enough now to carry, you might say, some of the family reputation. Your share of it. And certainly you know this and we . . .

MRS. K. (*overlapping*): Well, now, you can do it this way, you can do things that are gonna ruin your life for yourself, regardless of, of any, ah, feelings toward Daddy and me. You have your, you have your own reputation to consider, and, and the people with whom you, you associate and y-, you, and you should be particular and, and, ah . . .

(*Fulweiler knocks, enters.*)

DR. F.: You've done a very good job. All three of you. I think this is about enough for this afternoon. You look pretty tired to me now

MRS. K.: (*Laughs.*)

MR. K.: I'm enjoying it, frankly. (*Mrs. K. laughs.*)

DR. F.: Well, good, ah . . .

MR. K.: I mean if we can, if, well as I say, if, whatever we can do to help the family situation that in turn is going to help Mike—as Evvie said, he's got his life ahead of him. If, by golly, if, if it's . . .

DR. F.: Well, let's not forget one important point, ah, you haven't got one foot in the grave and the other on a banana peel yet yourself.

MR. K. (*laughing*): Oh, I realize that . . .

DR. F.: There's a possible chance that this . . .

MRS. K. (*overlapping*): I think, I think today he thinks he has. (*Mr. and Mrs. K. laugh.*)

DR. F.: Well, as I pointed out last time, this is as much for you folks as it is for Mike, and I think there's something for you to gain. Obviously there has been this conflict, under the surface . . .

MR. K.: Mm-hm.

DR. F.: . . . and implied, whether expressed or not, for years, and getting at the root of this and finding out what causes this is very important for your life, as well as for Mike.

MR. K.: Sure.

DR. F.: So this is not only, ah, good for Mike, it's good for you too.

MR. K.: Oh, we love him dearly.

DR. F.: In fact, it may hurt him. In some aspects, you two might find it a little harder to get along. (*Mr. and Mrs. K. laugh.*) Let's adjourn then until, ah, next Tuesday at three-thirty.

MR. K. (*simultaneously*): Three-thirty?

DR. F.: The same time.

MR. K.: Fine.

DR. F.: Same station.

MRS. K.: (*Laughs.*)

DR. F.: Thanks very much, you've done a very good job. (*Noise of people moving about.*) See you, Mike.

MIKE: Goodbye.

DR. F.: You look a lot better without poison oak, old man.

MRS. K. (*laughing*): I was going to say, what do you think of him now?

DR. F.: Much, much better. (*Voices fade away, tape recording ends.*)

INT.: What brought you in there to terminate?

DR. F.: They'd had a reasonably positive interchange. It was late and I was tired and they were tired. It seemed a good time to end the session.

INT.: Do you generally try to end on a positive note?

DR. F.: Yes. Especially in the first session.

INT.: Would you have let it go on longer if you hadn't got this?

DR. F.: Probably so. If my schedule was at all flexible, I wouldn't end a session where feelings are running high. I'd work it out if it took another hour. There have been times when I have gone out and told my next patient that I couldn't see him that day. In family therapy you can't always plan to end within a pre-set time the way you can with individual therapy. You have to work a lot longer sometimes to weave things into a relatively even state. If the family goes out feeling up in the air, this could be detrimental to the therapy.

INT.: At this point, the parents were joining together and speaking to the boy as a united front for the first time.

DR. F.: Yes. They were handling themselves and the boy very well. I like to end on a note that will make people pleased to come back the next time.

INT.: On the other hand, when the father says so brightly, "I'm enjoying it," you turn it into something a little different.

DR. F.: I simply took the opportunity in a reasonably positive emotional context to reinforce the idea that they were all in treatment and to get them off the idea that they were just coming in for Mike. I wanted Mike to hear this, too. At the same time, I am serving warning on the parents that I am going to deal with their relationship more directly and in greater depth in the future.

INT.: And when the father says, "I love him dearly," you counter this with a little implication of some difficulties that may arise.

DR. F.: Yes. That was an obtuse and banal remark. Up to the end of the session, he hadn't shown the slightest bit of affection for the boy.

INT.: How did the course of therapy go, as you remember it?

DR. F.: We had about twenty-two or twenty-three sessions. Mike dropped out of therapy after eight or nine sessions. This initial session illustrates that old comment that's been made so often about therapy, that the patient will show you all his problems in the first hour. Well, this family did too; they laid all their problems out on the table. My biggest difficulty was to get the father to accept even the tiniest bit of responsibility for what was going on. He kept ducking out from under, just as he does all through this session. It was a rugged course of therapy, and it got more difficult as it went on. I locked horns with him time after time. When he finally did get to the point of acknowledging his share, he broke down completely, sobbed, cried. He confessed his total inability to deal with the major problem that was facing him, which he admitted was the relationship between him and his wife.

INT.: How far along was that?

DR. F.: About midway. The wife had a very close woman friend, and the husband objected to this friendship strongly. He went over this issue again and again.

INT.: Was he suggesting that there was something homosexual going on?

DR. F.: He never quite said it explicitly, but there were a lot of dark implications. In a sense he was right, not that there was a physical relationship between the two women, but there was this tremendous involvement that kept the wife emotionally and intellectually occupied. As soon as this woman called up on the phone, the wife was full of fun and pleasure, and she never gave any of it to him. She couldn't have fun with this guy; whenever she made an advance, he flattened her. This was the point. He was facing two threats: one, that she would become sexually demanding in a way that he couldn't possibly match, and two, that he might lose her entirely. He couldn't accept what she wanted to give him and he couldn't stand her giving it anyplace else.

INT.: How did you try to improve their relationship?

DR. F.: Well, one specific thing I suggested was that he take her out to dinner. It turned out that they had never been out together as husband and wife, they had always gone out as a family. There was entirely too much togetherness. Just at the end, an amusing thing happened. The father came into the terminating session and declared that there had been an enormous change in the family and that things were great. The reason he gave for this change was not the therapy but their going to hear Billy Graham.

INT.: How did you take this?

DR. F.: I felt it was really an accolade, because I was completely out of it. He had taken all the responsibility and all the credit and pinned it on Billy Graham. I wasn't offended. The father put it quite simply and naïvely, and it pleased me, because I felt that I'd gotten out of the way very successfully. When the therapist gets the credit, it means that he is taking too much on his own shoulders; the wheels are showing. If I put my weight into the family equation, I try to do so as a neutral person, not as an authority from on high.

INT.: If you're an authority from on high, you put too much weight in whatever you do.

DR. F.: That's right. The goal is to have the equation stay in balance without you. Then the job of the therapist is over.

A Family of Angels

An interview with Virginia Satir, M.A., A.C.S.W.

INT.: What was it that brought the Pope family in to see you?

MRS. SATIR: They had been on a trip to Europe to visit relatives, and while they were traveling, Gary, the seventeen-year-old son, began to talk and act strangely. They took him to a European psychiatrist who labeled him psychotic and recommended that he be institutionalized, so they came back to this country and put him in a hospital here. He had been in the hospital a week when I saw them.

INT.: Did you know anything about the previous history of the family before this interview?

MRS. S.: No, and I rarely do.

INT.: How did they happen to come to you?

MRS. S.: A psychiatrist who had been in one of my training groups had seen the boy and his parents, and he told them that one of the best ways they could be helped was to be seen all together as a family. He referred them to me. They were very cooperative about the idea from the beginning. I took them as a demonstration family for my trainees.

INT.: How long were they in treatment?

MRS. S.: I treated them as a demonstration family for five or six weeks. Then I saw them privately for about two years.

INT.: What kind of people were they?

MRS. S.: They were quiet, nicely dressed, middle-class people.

Virginia Satir, M.A., A.C.S.W., has taught family therapy at many institutes throughout the country, has published several articles on family work, and is the author of *Conjoint Family Therapy* (1964).

The parents were in their forties. The father was co-owner of a small industrial-parts business; he was rather tall, soft-spoken, physically handsome. The mother was pretty in a delicate way, or could have been pretty, but there was a feeling of constriction about her. Both of them had an air of caution, as if they were walking on eggs.

INT.: Did all the children come to that first session?

MRS. S.: Yes. There was Gail, twenty-two; Gary, the labeled patient; Lois, twelve; and Tim, five. They were nice kids, but pale in spirit, as if they weren't sure what they could or couldn't do. The whole family conveyed an obvious eagerness and willingness to learn, but there was a lack of spontaneity at the same time.

INT.: Did you see them or talk to them on the phone before this session begins?

MRS. S.: No, but I had already introduced myself to them in the waiting room downstairs and explained the setup, the one-way observation mirror, the tape recorder, the teaching setting, and so forth.

INT.: Did you continue to see the family as a unit through treatment?

MRS. S.: Yes. To understand the meaning of the symptom, I have to see how it fits into the family system. I believe that every piece of behavior in a family is logical to that system. That's why I tend to see the whole family during the first meetings. Later on, I may take out different units and see them separately, but I always make it clear that I am doing this within the framework of the family as a whole, and I never pull out any unit in terms of which is the "sickest." I usually see the parents alone fairly early, because I believe that where there is a disturbed child, the marital relationship has been displaced onto the parent-child relationship.

INT.: If the child with the symptom gets better, do you leave him out of treatment and concentrate on the parents?

MRS. S.: No, I don't. I have ambitious goals for therapy. I don't want simply to repair the family. I want to focus on prevention and also to accomplish an expansion of possibilities for each person.

Initial interview with the Pope family

> (*Background noises, people entering room.*)
> MRS. S.: Let's see if we'll have enough chairs.

GAIL (*laughing*): We're kind of a large family.

MRS. S.: No. That's not unusual. Let's see . . .

GAIL: Well, Tim can sit on my lap. That's all right.

MRS. S.: Well, I'll get another chair. This will be my chair. The others . . .

GARY: Well, I took the one out here. This (*inaudible phrase*) now, and Timmie up here.

(*Everyone talking together about seating. Voices jumbled.*)

MRS. S.: Now, everybody has a place to sit. It looked for a minute like Tim wouldn't . . .

MRS. P.: Yes.

MRS. S.: . . . and all of a sudden he had two places to sit . . .

MRS. P.: Yes.

MRS. S.: . . . he had Gail's lap and Gary's lap. (*Pause.*)

INT.: Do you have a reason for saying that the little boy has two places to sit?

MRS. S.: I begin to give out, right at the outset, a message that there is a place for everybody. So I always start in on either name or place, the chair, the place to sit. I do this because one of the things I often notice is that people in dysfunctional families are lacking in individuation. I want to show that I see each person as an individual, with a timing and a thought that fits him.

MRS. S.: I wonder what, as you're all sitting here, as you're thinking about it, what is it that you expect? (*Pause.*) As you came here?

GARY: I didn't think about it. I knew I was going to come down here. But I, ah, I was kind of dubious of, that it would do any good. To be frank.

MRS. S.: Well, we have your contribution. Everybody else has ideas, 'cause you're all here.

INT.: Do you usually start with a formal question?

MRS. S.: Yes. This is to show that I'm in charge. I try to give out the idea that I have some kind of structure, something that will lead some place, so that they can immediately begin to feel some kind of hope.

INT.: Why do you direct this question to all of them?

MRS. S.: I want to firm them up in a contract in which they will commit themselves to coming not in the interests of the patient but in the interests of themselves. When they come in, they naturally see themselves as coming on behalf of the patient. I want to begin to break this up and to get them to see that we're working with a family system in which each person is making a contribution.

INT.: And you do this by asking them all what they expect.

MRS. S.: Yes. This is also a way to get into the communication analysis. One of the other things I've found is that people in dysfunctional families are unaware that somebody else might think differently than they do. They operate on the idea, "If I think it, then naturally you must." They talk on behalf of other people and behave as though this is the way this has to be. So I ask about the expectations, to give everyone an immediate opportunity to see that each person sees things differently.

INT.: I notice the patient speaks up first. Were you looking at him, or did he volunteer?

MRS. S.: He volunteered. I would have been looking round at everybody, to show that they were all included. Gary jumped in first, but I didn't let him go on because I wanted to give a chance to the others.

INT.: You say, "Everybody else has ideas, because you're all here," but that doesn't really follow. They might be all there, but they might not all have ideas.

MRS. S.: Oh, yes, everybody has ideas. There may be a question about whether the idea fits the occasion, or whether they can comment on it, but everybody has an idea, because you cannot *not* have an idea.

INT.: You're saying that in this situation you expect them not only to have ideas but to express them, because they've come for this purpose.

MRS. S.: That's right. This is how I make the family system obvious, by having everybody take part.

GARY: Funny, today I had this, this, this, ah, now at the time we had this ward meeting up at the hospital, and I'm immediately controlling it, unfortunately.

MRS. S.: You were doing what? I didn't hear.

GARY: Controlling the meeting. Because this, I sit there and try to draw people out.

MRS. S.: I see.

GARY: 'Cause this doctor . . .

MRS. S.: Well, that will be my job here. (*Female laughter.*)

GARY: That's right.

INT.: How did you receive that exchange?

MRS. S.: I saw that Gary was a spokesman for the family. He was saying, "I have both the burden and the joy of having to manage this family." As long as he sits in that role, he's got to be sick. So what I say to him is, "You don't have to take the burden, I'll be directing this ship."

INT.: Would you take this remark of his as a challenge or as an invitation to restrain him, or as a warning to you, or what?

MRS. S.: I took it as his perception of himself. And a message to me, telling me what the situation is in this family: "These people, my father and mother, can't manage for themselves. I have to manage for them. But I'm only a child and I can't do it."

INT.: Gary is also saying, "I control situations like this one."

MRS. S.: But this tells me what I have to do. I have to be in the driver's seat. Now, a therapist would get into trouble here if he received this as a threat rather than as a comment on the perception of the person's self in relation to the others. Such a therapist would be reacting to the control rather than to the way the self sees the self.

INT.: You prefer to go along with it.

MRS. S.: Yes. I'm also indicating to Gary what sort of person I'm going to be. At this point he doesn't know whether I'm going to be an authoritative person who will say, "Do what I tell you to do!" or whether I'm just going to be a leader. One of the things that's all mixed up in these families is how to react to a head-sorter. Is this an authoritative person or is this somebody who just leads? My structure is that of administration, sorting, rather than telling you how you ought to be.

MRS. S.: So let's hear about the rest of you. Gary has spoken. Now let's hear about the rest of you. 'Cause you're all here and you have something that you expect.

MR. P.: Well, we hope that, ah, Gary can find his place with the rest of the family here.

MRS. S.: When I heard that "we" from the father, I immediately knew that in this family there is very little differentiation between "I" and "you." Very often the children would be hearing "we," but the behavior they saw would obviously have to be of different sorts, because it belonged to different people.

GARY (*interrupting*): Here's, here's part of the trouble already . . .

MRS. S.: Excuse me just a minute. I'm not finished. Ah, anything else?

MR. P.: That was, ah, that was the main, ah, thing, to find the homogen-homogeneity that we, ah, that, ah, hoped for before, that, ah, existed before, and find some foundation for that now.

MRS. S.: O.K. Let's hear about the rest of you. (*To Lois.*) What about you? Since you're next to Dad?

LOIS: (*Laughs.*) I don't know. Well, I don't know, what was going— (*Gary talking in background.*) Well, I don't know what to expect, really.

GARY: I think it's something new to us. We didn't really, well . . .

MRS. S. (*to Lois*): Well, why do you think you came?

LOIS: 'Cause I'm part of the family. (*Laughing.*)

MRS. S.: And if the family has a wish, you want to go along with it. (*Pause.*)

INT.: That's a pretty careful rephrasing of what the daughter said.

MRS. S.: That, you'll notice, is something I do in my interventions. I take what is said and I put it into a frame which will enable us to go some place with it. Lois said, "I just came, I'm part of the family." That tells me that this is a child who will not openly announce what she's thinking and feeling. It's another form of "Somebody can be a spokesman for me." So I translate it: "What you're saying, then, is that if you know about the family's wish, you go along with it." I give her an active function.

INT.: You phrase it as something she wants.

MRS. S.: That, you'll see, is the way my interventions work. I do this kind of rephrasing all the time. Because I also want to give a message to these people that whether they see it this way or not, whatever they are doing represents a decision.

INT.: Why did you turn to Lois? Do you have a particular order you usually go in?

MRS. S.: I don't have a predetermined order, but whatever order I choose, I label it. In this instance, I took it by position.

INT.: She was next to the father and so next in line?

MRS. S.: Yes. Or sometimes I will say, "Well, let's see, let me take the adult male first, now you're the adult female. You're the number-one child, you're the number-two child." I point out the order that I'm going in because I want to make clear that there is no universal formula for picking anything.

MRS. S.: What about you, Mother?

MRS. P.: Well, I think this is just, I'm just looking for the answer to a prayer. I feel like this is perhaps our, our answer over here.

MRS. S.: Tim?

TIM: Well, I guess the same as Mother.

INT.: I gather that since you're going round the circle, you don't want to go further into what each one says.

MRS. S.: I want to avoid bringing out facts haphazardly. If I stopped and followed through on every lead, it would be a mishmash.

INT.: Did it require a little restraint for you to keep silent there?

MRS. S.: It always does. But I feel that more is accomplished by working on the structure, the structure in this case being that each is to comment, never mind about what. It's very easy for the therapist to pick up somebody's comment, get interested in the content, and bypass the process.

INT.: You might have said, in some fashion, "I'm not the answer to your prayers."

MRS. S.: I wouldn't do that, because it is more important for me to get everybody to comment. In a family with a schizophrenic, it is as though there were rules that people cannot comment. I want to break into that.

INT.: Well, there are these rules that people cannot comment, and yet you yourself are not commenting. Are you going along with their rule in that sense?

MRS. S.: No, my rule breaks theirs, which is that *nobody* is to comment. I want them all to comment close enough together so that it will be an experience of everybody speaking out.

INT.: That's why you break in so quickly on everybody's speeches.

MRS. S.: That's right.

INT.: You're also indicating you're not going to let yourself be provoked. I don't think I could have turned to the next person without a quality in my voice that showed that I was reacting to what the mother had just said. That statement might provoke some therapists to decline the omnipotent position she seems to be putting you in.

MRS. S.: I don't have to react to anything unless I have some use for it. I try to discipline myself so that I hear everybody's production as something about themselves, and if I'm not ready to use it, it's merely a production about themselves. You could sing gobbledygook, and if I just wanted you to report, I would thank you and move on to the next person. That tricky little statement of Mother's: "We're going to church, God's going to take care of everything" just said to me: If God has something to do with this, then how can man do anything? In my language, it's a way of giving charge of self over to someone else. But I don't pick that up until I'm ready to deal with how you handle taking charge of yourself, which is another thing.

> MRS. S.: What about you, Gail?
> GAIL: Well, I hope that we can work together to find a solution so that we can all become a real family again.
> MRS. S.: All right. So what you were talking about—you are aware that in some way Gary has been hurting, and you don't understand why, that there was a time when Gary didn't hurt and the family— (*Gary interrupts.*)

MRS. S.: There's one other thing I get from this conversation. When I hear these people responding, I look to see whether the person brings out something that is unique to him or whether he follows along with somebody else. You notice that Lois doesn't comment for herself, and Tim goes along with Mother. That "we" of the father's tells me that he goes along with Mother, too. Now Gail takes the same line as the father.

INT.: It's a remarkably ambiguous statement. When she says, "Well, I hope we can work together to find the solution," she doesn't say the solution to what. I couldn't tell at that point whether you were commenting on what she said or using what she said to review what had been said.

MRS. S.: I used what she said to review it.

INT.: You used what she said to reverse it, too. Everybody has been implying that the family was a real family until the thing they can't mention happened. It is Gary who has hurt them. You turn that by saying that it is Gary who has been hurting. By shifting the focus onto his hurt, you put him back in as a member of the human community.

MRS. S.: This is something I always try to do as quickly as possible. I call it "taking the label off the identified patient."

INT.: An idea of causality is being introduced here. If Gary is hurt, it's possibly because something happened to hurt him. His craziness didn't come out of the air, as the family likes to think.

MRS. S.: You can't do very much, you know, with conclusions about "God did it," or with the "sick," "bad," "stupid," or "crazy" formulation, because that usually ends right where it begins. You've got to put it into some kind of a frame which allows people to envision change. If something caused Gary to hurt, something can be done to cause him not to hurt.

INT.: This is also the first time that the idea that there is a problem has been introduced. You ask the family why they're here. Gary says he's doubtful about the value of coming, since he usually controls these situations. The father says he hopes Gary can find a place with the rest of the family, which is the only approximate statement in here that something is wrong. The mother says coming here is the answer to a prayer; Lois and Tim go along with her; and Gail says they're going to work together to find the solution so that they can become a real family again. What you do is to summarize their comments in such a way that you introduce Gary as the problem when nobody has been admitting he's the problem. Furthermore, you say the problem is that he's been hurting, which isn't the way they see it at all.

MRS. S.: I always translate these things. I call their approach the morality play. You can't do anything with a morality play.

GARY: I don't understand. What do you mean by the word "hurt"?
MRS. S.: Hurt. Hurt.
GARY: Pain? Physical, mental, anguish?
MRS. S.: Mental, maybe physical. I don't know.
GARY: Are you saying that I am hurting?
MRS. S.: This is what I'm saying the family is saying. There was a time when you didn't hurt. I'm checking this out. And you want to now have a family in which things are again, where people aren't hurting.

INT.: That's pretty complicated, too. First you said that Gary was hurting, and now you shift to everybody in the family hurting.

MRS. S.: I try to do that as quickly as possible, to get it into a frame of family process.

INT.: It's like saying, "You poor flood victims," instead of, "You poor family with a schizophrenic."

MRS. S.: You see, I know that I really can't begin to do anything about changing behavior until I take the focus off the patient and put it onto the family.

GARY: You see, it's . . .

MRS. P. (*simultaneously*): I don't feel that, we don't feel *you* have inflicted the hurt, Gary. That isn't what we mean. We just mean that whatever it is that— (*Gary interrupts.*)

INT.: There's a flurry here and Mother and Gary talk at once. The mother is behaving as though you said that they were accusing him, when you haven't said this at all.

MRS. S.: Yes, but the fact that one member of the family is suffering any kind of trouble, particularly craziness, is a strange phenomenon to the others. It's very hard to make an identification with the sick one. The mother is doing two things. It's her self-esteem that's operating when she attempts to say, "I am a good mother, I didn't do this." At the same time she tries to signal the idea of strangeness.

INT.: The tone of her voice when she says that Gary hasn't inflicted the hurt labels him very clearly as the cause.

MRS. S.: She's also the first to agree that there is a hurt.

INT.: But she does it by bringing the focus back to Gary. She's really bypassing your statement that the family is the problem, and going back to where you presented the problem in terms of Gary.

MRS. S.: Well, she picked up that first part of it. Sometimes you have to say A, then push it to C, in order to get the person to say B.

INT.: It sounds as though you've made a remark that they're not quite ready for and they go into a flurry to try to handle it. The mother then goes back and accepts the thing you previously wanted them to accept, in preference to this worse thing.

MRS. S.: I do that in many of my interviews. I lead ahead and lead ahead, and people often use my expeditions as a basis for going further themselves, but they usually keep a couple of sentences or sometimes even a paragraph behind. It's as if I were a pioneer and I were moving the brush, and the few behind me couldn't see for the brush, but after I'd already gone by, they could come up and say, "Oh, the place is really cleared."

INT.: Some therapists would maintain that in dealing with defenses you shouldn't go further than the person's ready to go. You would maintain that you should, because then people will go further than they otherwise would.

MRS. S.: That's right. Sometimes I will move *way* over. I did it later in this interview when I said, "Who's going to drop dead?" Their fears are about keeping safe, but I don't talk about how awful it is to be going in the dark; I say, "Who's going to drop dead?" By the time I get *there,* the other fear, by comparison with dropping dead, has already been reduced. It's a way of reducing differences. In another family I had, the father was talking about his daughter wearing lipstick. I turned to the girl and said, "What your father's really saying is that he's scared that you're going to get in bed with some guy."

INT.: This may be the function of the whole *reductio ad absurdum* technique in therapy. When you carry something that far, going a moderate way doesn't seem very far at all.

MRS. S.: I've found that it's much easier for people to accept something if I can carry it much further than they in their fantasies ever dreamed of.

> GARY: Well, that isn't, it's not the idea. It's the word. I can't seem to get to what you mean. At [*university*] we're taught to, to be able to communicate with others, and to try not to let the words get in the way. The word "hurt" sort of befuddles me. I don't actually understand what you meant by that word. See, if I don't understand what you meant by the word, I don't know what you mean.

INT.: You've said that in this kind of family nobody can make a comment about anything puzzling that they find in anybody else, but this boy seems able to do it.

MRS. S.: You can do it if you're an identified patient. If you're not, you have to be careful.

INT.: He catches you on the word "hurt." One of your aims in therapy seems to be to get these people to drop their double talk and learn how to report clearly. Yet you yourself use the word "hurt" in an ambiguous way.

MRS. S.: I think I do a different kind of double talk from the family. In the double talk I give out, one of the messages corresponds to "life out there," and the other part of it burlesques the double talk in the family. That was double talk the mother was using when she told Gary that he wasn't to blame for the hurt, while her tone said he was. I double talk with "hurt" too, but it's to get them to acknowledge the real meaning of their situation: that they all hurt and that the thing that is hurting them is their relationships together.

INT.: You have them in a bind. They can't deny that there is hurt, because you've already defined that as the reason why they are there. You also know that they won't want to come out and point to Gary directly, so they'll probably want to accept your version that it's everybody.

MRS. S.: Yes. The way the family uses this kind of double talk is a bind for sickness. The way I use it is a bind for health.

> MRS. S.: Of course, and I'm glad that you are bringing this out. Because one of the first things that we will try to do in family therapy is to be sure we're all talking about the same thing. And Gary asked me what do I mean by "hurt," and I will tell him what I mean by "hurt." Hurt in feelings, hurt in body, hurt in emotions. This is what I mean.
>
> GARY: Yes, but you, you still use the word "hurt" to define hurt and —hurt in feelings, for instance. What would this be? Sadness, or . . .
>
> MRS. S.: It could be sadness, or it could be anger. It could be . . .
>
> GARY: Now that's good. Now keep going along that line.
>
> MRS. S.: . . . it could be disappointment. It could be frustration. It could be any of these things.

INT.: This exchange about the word "hurt" seems to have some of the effect of what has been called a "confusion technique" in hypnosis. The idea is that if you baffle someone sufficiently and then come out with a clear statement about what you mean, they will be so relieved that they'll fall right in with you.

MRS. S.: I see what you mean, but what I was most pleased about was that Gary was going to be able to insist on getting clarity from me.

Some therapists would have picked this up as Gary resisting. But I don't pick up that kind of thing in that way.

INT.: You took his question very seriously.

MRS. S.: I wanted to give a message to the family that whatever a communication sounds like on the outside, you can get some sense out of it if you look at it. The biggest thing to do, you know, is to keep people from giving up in their negotiations for meaning.

INT.: It's a rapid move to a more abstract level. You've shifted from talking about the hurt in the family to discussing what you mean by "hurt." And the way you do it almost makes it seem like a classroom problem in semantics.

MRS. S.: I do this to invite the cognitive aspect of the person to function. I want to show people how to clarify the messages they give out. For instance, I will help people to separate a message into its directions about content and its directions about relationships. Take roast beef. Someone says, "This is terrible roast beef," but really means, "You don't love me." If it was terrible roast beef, all right. That's a comment on roast beef and what it does to your stomach and your teeth. That's content. But it is also a comment on "my idea of what you think of me." One of the things I want to do is separate these two things, so that the person can distinguish between them. If the roast beef is being used symbolically, I want to straighten this out.

INT.: You do another thing here. When you say, "It could be sadness or it could be anger," Gary says, "Now that's good, keep going along that line." But you don't go along that line.

MRS. S.: No. I go along my line.

INT.: You shift at this point to disappointment, rather than keep to the subject of anger. Is this because you don't want to get into the question of whether Gary is angry or not?

MRS. S.: No, it's because I always see anger as a secondary emotion, as a cover-up for hurt and as protection for the self. There are two ways of handling hurt; one is the carpet way and the other is the bull way. I can crawl under the carpet: "I'm terribly hurt, you've stepped on me." Or I can act like a bull and attempt to annihilate you. That's when you see the anger.

INT.: Then you would consider disappointment more basic than anger?

MRS. S.: Oh, yes. Much more so.

MRS. S. (*cont.*): And these are—you didn't say this. This is what different members of your family were, I think, talking about. And I'd like to find out a little bit more.

GARY: You mean, what we've said so far?

MRS. S.: Um-hm. Somewhere at some point the family didn't feel as they're feeling now. This is what I gather.

INT.: You don't say this time that they are feeling hurt, it's just that they are feeling different. Is that to make it less threatening?

MRS. S.: Yes, but I'm also attempting to help them to measure the past by the present. Another thing I've noticed about these families is that they behave as though change doesn't occur. They like to feel that everything is as it always was, even though yesterday it was quite different.

INT.: By slipping in the premise that things have changed, you're slipping in the premise that change is possible.

MRS. S.: Right.

GARY: I, ah, I, in my being with the family, just because I was at [*university*], I don't feel any different toward the family than I have felt, at this moment, than I have felt, pretty much, at least underneath, I have felt pretty much the same since ever I was born.

MRS. S.: I think you have.

MRS. S.: Here I get some confirmation of the fact that he has not been able to stop feeling like a little boy. Because one of the messages in this family is that to grow is to threaten.

INT.: He is disagreeing with the family when they say, "Things are different now that Gary is so strange." He's saying, "No, I'm just as I always have been, it's just that you are noticing it now." Which is probably true.

MRS. S.: That's right. He's also commenting on the fact that the family has always hurt, but they haven't recognized that either.

MRS. S. (*cont.*): And what we're talking about are the family's, the other members of the family's feelings. Not your feelings toward them.

GARY: Well, it has to be all together. I mean, all—his feeling toward mine, my feeling toward Mother. I mean . . .

MRS. S.: You want to know what they are.

GARY: No. Well—O.K., go on.

MRS. S.: Now that's lovely. He said an unequivocal no. Now I'm waiting to see whether he's going to disqualify it. That's another thing I watch for in these families. To see who gives a no or a yes, and they practically never do. At this point, when he came out "No" right away, I was wondering when he'd disqualify it. Can this stand by itself?

INT.: He does disqualify it, almost in the same breath.

MRS. S.: The very fact that he could say no was already something. Another patient might not have commented at all, or he might have come out with a psychotic symptom. Gary could say no. But then he had to disqualify it.

INT.: Again, you're doing a transposition. First you were talking about Gary's hurting, then you talked about the way the whole family hurt. But this is a third shift, because it's not all of them hurting, it's the family excluding Gary. Why do you do this?

MRS. S.: The identified patient always tends to try to keep the focus on himself. See, he starts out again: "*my* feelings." If I go along with this, then I don't get the other family members to make it clear that they hurt too. This is a subtle point. If you ever get off on this tack, particularly in the first interview, it takes forever to get back. The patient feels this as a validation of the fact that he is the identified patient, and there's always this sparring going on with him. If I let the patient keep on with the label, he can get crazy very quickly. Because then he feels there's no hope.

INT.: It's a slippery sequence. You say, "We're talking about what the other members of the family feel." He says, "It has to be all together." Then you say, "You want to know what they all feel." And that's when he says no.

MRS. S.: I think I may have been putting those words in his mouth. I wanted to get something explicit in relation to the other family members and so I may not have been hearing him quite.

INT.: What was it you were trying to get from them?

MRS. S.: I hadn't been able to pin down the other family members. You're always vulnerable if you don't get them committed. You must get each family member to confirm the fact that he makes a contribution, never mind whether it's for good or for bad. Then you've got everybody committed to treatment. A lot of therapists, it seems to me, try to get a confession from people that their productions are destructive. Then there are other therapists who try to show that the opposite is true. I don't hold with either approach. What you have to do is get each person to validate the fact that he *can* make a production. How he uses it is something else again.

> MRS. S.: O.K. All right. (*To Mrs. P.*) So, now let's see how it was, as you think about it, when the family was all happy together. When you felt that the family was all happy together, how was it, then?
>
> MRS. P.: Well, we were all, we were all working together, and, ah, whenever anyone had anything nice happen to them, they'd come home with it and there would be enthusiasm. Ah, this, ah, this hurt, that begins, I think when we were in [*city abroad*] and Gary first said he wanted to leave us.

INT.: Gary must have begun to enjoy himself independently over there. It sounds as though he got involved outside the family.

MRS. S.: He did. In this family the gratifications were so nebulous that when any of the children had any joy outside the home, that was already a threat. Here's a situation in which the husband and wife are really saying, "Everything's perfectly beautiful and wonderful," when everybody who lives in the family knows that isn't so. When the kids have some nice experience outside, they don't bring it back in, because it's an affront. It's an affront because there's such emotional poverty between the parents.

INT.: I notice you phrase it to the mother, "How was it *when you felt* that the family was all happy together," as if there could be some doubt about that.

MRS. S.: I put it this way because I want to give a signal to Gary that I hear him.

> GARY: I never said that.
>
> MRS. P.: Well, yes, you did.
>
> GARY: No, now, wait a minute. I have to tell you my side of the story. I brought you fruit, I brought you roses as gifts . . .
>
> MRS. P.: Yes.
>
> GARY: But, then . . .

MRS. P.: But then you wanted to take yourself away. What good are roses . . .

GARY: Well, now, no, no, no, no—O.K.

MRS. P.: . . . and fruit, without you?

GARY: When I had gone just for one night, to have a little fun.

MRS. S.: With this kind of an interchange, even if I hadn't known that Gary had been in the hospital, I'd have known right now that this was a schizophrenogenic family. The mother criticizes Gary for not bringing joy home, by implication, and he says, "Look, I tried to give you flowers and everything in the hope that maybe I could get out." She rejects his presents, so that she's really saying, "It doesn't matter what you would give in return, you may not grow up." This I know would be the message of the schizophrenic's family. She is also saying, "There is no way for you to do anything except give *me* validation." It's a total invalidation of growth for the child. It's so obvious that the boy can't get anything except messages of "You can only grow in my image."

INT.: Her voice is that of a woman injured in love. "What good are roses and fruit without you?"

MRS. S.: Yes, but this isn't love, it's a matter of self-esteem. You can't talk about love with people who need this kind of thing just to get a feeling that they're alive. This is where a lot of therapists make a mistake. They get all involved in incest long before the people have even developed to that point. This is particularly true with schizophrenics. The ones I have observed, at least, haven't reached the point where they're making integrations at a male-female level.

INT.: It's basically assumed here that if Gary left, it would be a betrayal. He doesn't debate whether he has a right to leave, he debates whether he would really be leaving. He knows he isn't supposed to leave.

MRS. S.: That's exactly how it was. When he started to leave, they locked him up.

GARY: I didn't do anything bad in my mind. You would have probably approved of everything I did. I came back in the morning with two friends who had been drinking. I had not been drinking. And suddenly I'm locked in my room for over twenty-four hours, it was well over twenty-four hours, and I could not understand this reason to be locked up. I became frustrated. I became mad. And this, to be locked in this room, I felt, was unjust, unfair. And so this, I didn't do anything about it until we got to [*city abroad*]. I couldn't stand to be locked up like that. And then I ran, because I don't like to be locked up. If you'll understand what I mean.

INT.: One thing you don't get from the transcript is the very phony acting quality of what he says here. It's an oration.

MRS. S.: That's right.

MRS. P.: Well, prior to this business at [*city abroad*], you would never have picked up two absolute strangers on the street and brought them into our home, and that's the same thing when (*Gary is trying to talk*) you brought them into our hotel room.

GARY: I brought some of my school friends. I felt it was about the same thing.

MRS. P.: School friends and strangers in a strange city are two different things, Gary.

GARY: Well, I . . .

MRS. S.: Could I stop you now?

MRS. P.: Yes.

INT.: Why did you interrupt them? Why didn't you let this go on?

MRS. S.: Because I saw it becoming a useless interchange. Also, I had uncovered another rule in the family: strangers are not allowed. I was putting this together in my head with the rule that growth for the self is penalized.

INT.: By "growth for the self" you mean independent activity, don't you?

MRS. S.: Yes. I think his bringing strangers home had two functions. One was an attempt to make a substitute for himself so that he could get out, as in the matter of the fruit and the flowers. And the other was to break the rule about strangers not being welcome. You see, these people were on their way to a foreign country to visit relatives, and the message was, "We want to show our folks there that we don't have monsters for children." The mother and father were cousins and there had been dire predictions about the consequences when they married. Also, this was supposed to be a fun trip. What I didn't know until later was that Lois attempted suicide just before Gary broke down. She attempted suicide the day before, while they were on shipboard. But Lois was never labeled.

INT.: You mean Lois attempted suicide on shipboard, and the next day Gary brought these strangers home?

MRS. S.: Yes. Then his craziness followed. Since the identified patient soaks up all the pains in the family, and since nobody had paid much attention to Lois, it was almost as though he was testing out for Lois' sake. Lois was growing up to be quite a tomboy. And she was in a terrible bind, too.

INT.: Why aren't strangers welcome in this house?

MRS. S.: I got subsequent data on this. Strangers are wanted but at the same time they are dangerous. Now why are they dangerous? Because this family was a tiny, closed kind of place. The mother had two sisters who were several years older. They were like extensions of her to the children, but to her they were mother figures. The family never did anything except go back and forth to the sisters' house and to the father's mother—it was such a tightly closed unit. The strangers are an attempt to alleviate this. One of the things the mother talked about later was all her dreams for becoming acquainted with different people. So the boy was bringing something for his mother as well.

INT.: He was trying to free her with his roses and his strangers.

MRS. S.: Sure.

INT.: You wouldn't think it would be much appreciated, his bringing in two strangers the day after his sister's attempted suicide, and acting kind of crazy as well.

MRS. S.: Of course not. But it doesn't seem very different from an incident I remember when a mother was distraught over something that had happened, and her little child came in with an old ragged doll. It was so obvious that the child was trying to divert the mother's attention: "Don't feel so bad." There's never just one thing going on, there are several things going on.

MRS. S. (*to Mrs. P.*): Because you obviously are coming here to get all the help I can offer, and I think—let's say that Gary is trying to say something about *his* feeling, and you are trying to say something about *your* feeling, and, as Gary pointed out with me, the two of you weren't communicating. And he was asking you a question which you somehow didn't see an answer to, because I think it was hard for you to figure out why Gary was saying what he was saying. Just as hard as it was for him to figure out why you were saying and doing what you were doing. All right. These are some of the things, I think, that may occur with other members of the family, and not only with Gary and yourself. How does this happen between you and Dad? How does it go when you and Dad are trying to figure out something that seems strange that one or the other of you do? Suppose you go and spend some money that maybe Dad didn't expect you to spend, and he thinks this maybe might be kind of odd? I don't know about it, but let's suppose. (*Mr. and Mrs. P. laugh.*)

MR. P.: I don't think we've had this situation. (*Laughing.*)

MRS. S.: Well, what kind of situations have you had where it might turn out that Dad did something that you didn't expect him to do, or you did something that he didn't expect you to do? How would that go?

MRS. P.: Well, I'm the type that blows up, you know, and then I get over it, and am sorry. And Father is the quiet type. I mean, he just takes it, and that's the way it is. But we haven't had too many blowups (*laughing*) fortunately, so we're very happy.

INT.: When you ask the mother, "How does it go when you and Dad are trying to figure out something that seems strange?" it sounds as if you really mean, "something that makes you angry." But instead of "angry," you use the word "strange," which is close to "crazy." Are you trying to make a parallel to Gary's craziness?

MRS. S.: Yes. This, you see, is how you translate all behavior into the family system. You try to get the family to use a different vocabulary. You start with, "You're crazy, insane," and you translate that into "unexpected" or "different" or "strange," and then you get some evidence in some other family member about "strange," and then you can work back to the first "strange" again.

INT.: You make a calculated use of "strange" to shift the symptom onto the family relationships.

MRS. S.: That's right.

INT.: The mother then offers something that sounds pretty strange; she says she's the type that blows up.

MRS. S.: You see, if at this particular point I had been trying to get the family to talk about how they get angry, I wouldn't have gotten that from her. It would have been too threatening. But when I put it in terms of "What do you do in the case of something strange or unexpected?" then she is able to acknowledge it. I found out something else here when she said, *"I'm* the one that blows up and he's the one that just takes it." This tells me that the father has given out very little about what he himself thinks and feels, and that the woman will have to be, by the nature of things in the family, the spokesman for the husband. So there is a great deal that the husband thinks and feels that the boys in the family just have to guess at, as does everybody else, but particularly the boys. The husband is labeled as good because of this, but if the boys puzzle people, they are labeled as being crazy.

INT.: A while back, you explained how you use exaggeration to lead people ahead. Here you rephrase anger as something milder, but the process seems to be the same in that it allows people to explore themselves more than they might ordinarily wish to.

MRS. S.: I think that's the function of it. Here I was trying to cut into this impression that all of them are angels except the identified patient, particularly the parents.

> MRS. S. (*to Mrs. P.*): Do you know whether your husband disapproves of something that you do?
>
> MRS. P.: Yes, he's, he's much more quiet then (*inaudible phrase*).
>
> MRS. S.: Well, then, do you ever know then what he disapproves of?
>
> MRS. P.: Yes, I think I can tell. I mean, it's, it's mostly facial expression. (*Tim talking in background.*)
>
> GARY: That's a good question. That's a good question Timmie just picked out. He said, "How come you went out of the car when we opened the door? How come?" Now see, here he picks up something that he remembered himself.
>
> MRS. P.: He's thinking of [*city abroad*], when you tried to run away from us.
>
> MRS. S.: Well, I don't know if he is. I don't know. We'd have to be sure to find out.
>
> GARY: I think the reason that I ran . . .
>
> MRS. P.: I think this was the only occasion.
>
> MRS. S. (*simultaneously*): Well, you don't know. You don't know.

INT.: Here you don't say, "Does your husband ever disapprove of something that you do?" You simply assume it.

MRS. S.: I do that a lot. There's no point in getting somebody to admit things if they're paining. I don't make them get down on their knees.

INT.: That was a quick switch Gary makes from how the mother and father show disapproval to how he ran away. I notice that Gary did it through the other boy.

MRS. S.: That's right, through Tim. Tim started, almost on cue, to make noises then. I think Tim might have been under the table.

INT.: What does that question of Tim's refer to?

MRS. S.: I don't know what that was. I chose to let it go by because I wanted to pick up the mother's claim that she knew what Tim was talking about. She was speaking for Tim, and I wanted to disabuse her of the idea that she automatically knew what he meant. By doing that, I was also saying to the patient that I knew that whatever was said about him might or might not fit.

GARY: I think the reason I ran was that Daddy did something that I did not expect of him, by locking me up. He locked me up because I did something that he didn't expect of me, and the reason may have been that he didn't have a full understanding of my personality, of my n-, of my naïve, gullible personality [*inaudible phrase*]. This is something we have to discuss, because I, I, I'm not overly friendly in that I have a glad hand, but then, I trust people, perhaps more than I should. I mean, I, I trust people and I should trust God and believe in people, and let them prove my belief.

MRS. S.: Why? Why should you openly trust, without reason?

GARY: Trust God?

MRS. P.: People.

MRS. S.: Anybody.

GARY: There is no reason to. But this is my personality ever since I was born. I tend to, let's say believe in people, believe they'll turn out good, when I, I don't know for sure. Sometimes.

INT.: Did you take Gary's remark to be in reference to people?

MRS. S.: Yes, because I translated God into people. When God is used like this, I don't go along with the displacement.

INT.: You wouldn't worry about any religious objections that might be raised?

MRS. S.: No. I have a thing about that; I say, "Well, any religion can be used neurotically."

INT.: Gary is telling you that he doesn't trust people at the same time that he's telling you he does. Your saying, "Why should you openly trust, without reason?" sounds like a way to give him the chance to deny his statement that he trusts.

MRS. S.: I'm saying to him, "You don't have to mouth anything; you can talk about what you feel and think." This was a church-going family, but I learned later that none of them really wanted to go to church, they just didn't want to hurt the feelings of the mother's older sisters.

MRS. S.: All right. Then these are some of the things that we will learn about. Let's come back. Gail, how do you know when your father disapproves of something you do? Mother says she knows by his facial expression. What do you know?

GAIL: Oh, he'll just tell me.

MRS. S.: Well, what will he say? "Gail, you know that I don't think that you should have done this or that"?

GAIL: Oh, in, in a way, yes. He, he'll say it and we'll discuss it, and I, I don't think (*laughing*) I've done too many (*inaudible phrase*). Lately.

MRS. S.: Do you know that you ever did anything to get Dad's disapproval?

GARY: At least that he knew of. (*Laughing.*)

GAIL: Once in a while. And he'd tell me.

MRS. S.: He'd tell you.

GAIL: And then I'd tell him my reasons why, and then we'd discuss it, and then . . .

MRS. S.: How about you, Lois? Do you know when Dad disapproves of something you do?

LOIS: Well, yes. I think that we just talk about this, and, well . . .

GARY: But what have you, do you think, Lois, you ever remember anything you've done that Dad really did disapprove of?

LOIS: Well, ah . . .

GARY: I think that when we do something bad, we know that we've done it. And we know it. We know ourselves, to ourselves, that it's something that nobody would disapprove of, perhaps.

MRS. S.: It might. Let's see how Lois decides that Dad has disapproved of something she's done.

LOIS: Well . . . (*Pause.*)

MRS. S.: Does he frown? You see, Mother says she knows this by the way his face looks. Now, does he frown, or does he say, "No," or what?

LOIS: He te-, he tells me that, well, that, well, well, he doesn't exactly go along with what I've done, and we sort of, well, I say why I did it, and he says what reasons he has for disapproving of it, and we usually come to agreement.

MRS. S.: Tim, how do you know when you've done something that Dad disapproves of, he doesn't like?

TIM: Nothing. (*Female laughter.*)

INT.: Once again, you're going around the family circle on this without dealing with the content of what they say.

MRS. S.: That's right.

INT.: You can hardly tell whether the girls are saying that Dad ever does disapprove, or if they know it, or anything.

MRS. S.: I felt quite certain that the father never disapproved of anything openly. Never gave any clues as to what he disapproved of. He's already been labeled as the quiet one. The message is that he doesn't show what he thinks and feels, so then he can be taken for the stupe, or he can be taken for the reluctant one. Mostly he was taken for the stupe. Later on, we had a very interesting interview about father's messages of being a stupe.

INT.: You used that word?

MRS. S.: Sure.

GARY: I don't think he's done anything. I think that actually we're (*inaudible phrase*), we're actually working on sort of a, on a superficial, superficial— (*Lois talking in background*) I think if we worked on how we relate to our parents, I think how we, how we relate between any human being, then we could find perhaps how we relate to ourselves, as, in the family group. I mean w-, I treat the members of the family approximately how I would treat, well, with a different feeling, but in, in a similar manner that I might treat any group of individuals that raised me up from my very birth. You see, you see what I'm getting at. If I've learned to, to trust the family, then I've learned that it's good to trust other people too.

MRS. S.: I'm not so sure there's any reason why anybody should trust

anybody until they know exactly how to do it. And what we're
talking about here . ...

GARY: How do you trust?

MRS. S.: This is what we're going to talk about. And what we are just
now trying to figure out is what kind of signals does the family use
to find out when Dad disapproves of them.

INT.: You agree that what you're all going to talk about is trust,
and then you don't talk about trust.

MRS. S.: I say we're going to talk about it, but I don't say *when*.
This is a way of telling him, "What you have to say is useful; it gives us
some clues and we'll deal with it." But by not hamstringing myself,
since I don't say when, I don't have to pick up all the clues when I'm
not ready.

MRS. S. (*to Gary*): How do you know when your father disapproves
of you? What do you use?

GARY: I can't tell, really, a lot of times. I can't tell.

MRS. S.: You don't know, sometimes.

GARY: I know when, I know more when Mother disapproves. I can
tell because . . .

MRS. S.: Well, now what signs do you use?

GARY: Well, she tells me.

MRS. S.: Did you notice the change in Gary's voice when I asked
that? I felt that this was a surprise, that he would be looked upon as
though he, too, could be part of this whole process, that he could be
like everybody else. I think this was the first time he realized that
maybe he wasn't going to be treated like a patient.

INT.: You made him wait till last in this round of questioning.
Was this to keep him in his place?

MRS. S.: No, it was because if I went to him first, whatever he said
would be received as something crazy. He wears a label. This is why I
often leave the identified patient till the last, after I've got the process
out, so that his contribution is seen within that framework.

INT.: Twice at least he's tried to take you off the question of the
father's disapproval and you've come right back to it. I think he's also a
little surprised at your persistence.

MRS. S.: That, by the way, is something you'll find me doing all the time. I keep coming back to the thing. Later on I'll interpret: "What do you have to rescue your father for? He and I aren't going to drop dead." But I want to give the experience before the interpretation.

MRS. S.: She says words. She says, "You're doing something I don't like."

GARY: Well, I remember, I can only remember once when Dad has ever said anything. And at the time I didn't think that I had done anything wrong. No, well, twice, the time in [*city abroad*]—I'm thinking of another time. And then he told me. But, unless he tells me, I really, really, I do not know.

MRS. S.: See what he did there? I ask him about Mother disapproving, and he tells me about Father.

INT.: And before, when you asked about Father, he shifted to Mother. What a good boy!

MRS. S.: O.K. Now . . .

GARY: I do know what I can do in a situation like, and I know what I approve of myself, but I, I cannot tell, I do not know unless he tells me.

MRS. S.: What I am trying to get at here, because we have some very definite work that we need to accomplish, what I'm trying to find out here, and to help you all find out, is what do you use in the way of clues from each other to decide how the other one is feeling about you?

MRS. S.: At this point I was hearing him again take over and I was reminding him that we were here for a purpose, we had definite work to do. I often get the impression from this kind of speech that the patient thinks that what he's supposed to do is go on and on in terms of his inside self, because that's what the therapist wants. I'm saying to him, "All right, that may be what somebody else wanted, but it isn't what I want." I am really shutting him off.

INT.: He was apparently about to get wound up on what he disapproves of in himself and give you the breast-beating that so many therapists would prefer.

MRS. S.: That's right.

MRS. S. (*cont.*): Now you said, and Gary, we'll use you as an example here, you said that you didn't often, or rather, didn't always know

when Dad was disapproving. You knew more often when Mother
was disapproving.

GARY: And I told you the reasons.

MRS. S.: Yes, because she says so.

INT.: Why did you accept this boy's statement that his mother
tells him explicitly when she disapproves, when there is considerable
doubt about it?

MRS. S.: I left it so that I can come back and wind up the discrepancy later. It would be so easy in this first interview to have the whole
thing go on between Gary and myself. That's where a lot of therapists
go wrong, because they get involved in a war with the identified patient.
So I just leave it. I'm gathering information in a kind of relaxed way.

INT.: Of course.

MRS. S. (*cont.*): Now, let's find out from—Gail, for instance, how do
you know when you've displeased Mother?

GAIL: Oh, I think we talk it out. I mean, she'll tell me what, what I've
done, and I think the same way with my father.

MRS. S.: You mean, you see it's the same kind of thing. That is, they'll
tell you.

GAIL: Yes. That's the way I think that I like it. I mean, I like to know
when I've done something wrong, and then, again, we discuss it.

MRS. S.: What about you, Lois?

LOIS: Well, when I've done something definitely wrong, well, I usually,
well, sometimes, I can tell . . .

MRS. S.: We're talking about Mother, now.

LOIS: And, but then, sometimes there's something I've done that I don't
quite understand. And then we'll talk about it and then, well, I
usually see that Mother doesn't like it.

MRS. S.: Mother will tell you?

LOIS: We'll sit down and talk about it, and see why it's wrong, or I
say what I think and we sort of discuss it.

INT.: That's a remarkable series of statements. You don't get any
idea about what goes on between mother and daughter.

MRS. S.: No, you don't. What I was trying to do was take Father
first, because he isn't so dangerous to discuss. By the time I get to
Mother, everybody feels a little freer. By that process of taking the two
and getting out the data about first one, then the other, I learn that you
can't tell anything about Mother.

INT.: And rather than comment on it at this time, you just accept it and go on?

MRS. S.: That's right. If I comment at this point on these little pieces, I can't bring out the idea of a system. So often a family goes out of an interview feeling lost in all the little pieces. They don't get the Gestalt. That's what I'm gunning for. And that's what I mean when I talk about process. Say you spit in an interview. Well, that could look as if it was just you spitting, but in fact it has a relationship to what everybody sees and how everybody feels about it. Your spitting is a way of getting out some message about yourself that you can't get out any other way. So I ask, "How does each one here get out that which he can't say directly?" Then I've got a *system* interpretation rather than only an individual one. When I listen to my interviews, I notice that I often start off on some trivial thing, and then I build this into a meaning that may not be so comfortable for people to accept. But they don't know at first that I'm doing this. In a way, it's as if I were giving people very sweet-tasting sleeping pills without letting them know they're getting sleeping pills. But by the time they realize what's happening, they have some overall meaning they can use, and so they aren't left full of anxiety afterward, with no place to put it. I don't think that pain is so bad for people, but they've got to have some way of seeing how to integrate it.

MRS. S.: What about you, Tim? How do you know when you've done something to displease Mother?

TIM: Well, when I'm monkeying in the flour.

MRS. S.: When you monkey in the flowers?

TIM: The flour. (*General laughter and something that sounds like an explanation about a flour sack.*)

GARY: Monkeying in the flour. Oh, yeah. I used to do that when I was a boy, Timmie.

MRS. S.: Well, you're telling me what you did, but how do you know that your mother disapproves? 'Cause I don't know that everybody would disapprove of your playing in the flour. How do you know that Mother does? Does she frown at you? What does she do?

TIM: No. She tells me.

MRS. S.: She tells you. O.K. Now, I'd like to come back to Dad. What do you, how do you know what the family, let's say when Gail, when you've done something that makes Gail feel disapproving of you? (*Pause.*)

MR. P.: Oh, I don't know. (*Female laughter.*)

MRS. P.: Does that situation ever occur? (*Laughs.*) We have a pretty unusual daddy. (*Laughter.*)

GARY (*low voice*): Yes, we do.

MRS. P.: We really do. (*Laughing.*)

INT.: You shift here from how Dad expresses his disapproval to how he finds out that others disapprove of him.

MRS. S.: I do this because there's a rule here that you're not supposed to look at anybody's disapproval.

INT.: The women start to laugh and there's the remark about the unusual daddy. Again, you can't tell what they're saying about him. And Gary comes in very quietly with that "Yes, we do."

MRS. S.: When I heard Gary say this, I saw that in this family the guy who has to live up to the fact that he can't comment is the father. Then I immediately saw Gary and the father and Tim together, facing very definite ideas about what males could and couldn't do. I saw that another function of Gary's symptom was to show a better way to the males, particularly to the father. Do you remember, further back, how Gary used Tim as a front by picking up Tim's question? This shows the way the males here protect each other. They are all in a frame of "You can't comment," and the females are in the driver's seat.

MRS. S.: Well, I go on the principle that no humans are angels. And I just don't think that anybody is really an angel. But they can be fine people, that has nothing to do with that. But I'm sure there must have been times, Gail, when you have been disapproving of something your father did, or said, or looked, or acted.

GARY: I think the reason is 'cause I don't think there hardly ever is. That's why we're sunk.

MRS. S.: I think there is.

INT.: Is Gary saying, "One of the reasons I'm in trouble is that my father doesn't act out enough, so I have to do it for him"?

MRS. S.: That's a part of it.

INT.: The mother came in when Gail was queried, and now Gary comes in when the father's on the spot. It's an interesting rescue system.

MRS. S.: Rescue operations are going on a mile a minute here. The rationale for it is that they've got to protect each other, they don't want to hurt each other's feelings, and this all acts as a reinforcement for "Shut your mouth!" So you notice these pungent things I put in here like, "Nobody's an angel."

GAIL: I think the only time I could ever think of was one time when I had a flat tire, and that wasn't Daddy's fault. That was the fault of whoever used my car before. (*Laughing.*)

MRS. S.: It wasn't Daddy's fault.

GAIL: No.

MRS. S. (*to Mr. P.*): How do you know when Lois is disapproving of something of you?

MR. P. (*Gail laughing*): I don't know as I know. (*Female laughter.*) Maybe, maybe she's, ah, gone into her room and sulked a little bit, I think. It probably's possible . . .

GARY: I, I can remember when the . . .

MR. P. (*overlapping*): (*Inaudible phrase.*)

GARY (*to Lois*): Remember when you get mad and cry and go to your room? I remember those times. Remember those times? *I* remember those times, 'cause I remember them, they're very rare, but when they happen, it's quite a, an exper-, quite an event.

MR. P.: I think it's happened sometimes when (*name inaudible*) was in school.

GARY: I remember when I was five, or was I four, remember when I got mad at Daddy for not giving me a whole waffle, and I broke Gail's doll? Remember that. Now that's sort of a round-about way. And then in [*city abroad*] of course, I ran, 'cause I did disapprove of him locking me up. I thought he was going to put me in a mental hospital. I didn't want that, so I ran.

INT.: Why is everyone getting so excited?

MRS. S.: There's a rule that nobody can show disapproval to father. But Gary is beginning to think perhaps he can trust me a little. So he comes out with very definite evidence about Lois. What's shaping up here comes close to an explicit statement about the presence of anger and disagreement. That's the most explicit it's been and so everybody starts to talk.

MRS. S.: All right. Then, you see, if we start putting our thinking caps on, then we can begin to remember that this is not a family of angels, but a family of people in which people are going to be disapproving and disappointing as well as loving. Now, Mother, tell me —what do you think happens when Dad disapproves of something you do, and he doesn't tell you about it?

INT.: At first, when you started asking how people show disapproval, you put this same question to the mother. Tim and Gary deflected it and you went around to all the children before getting back to the parents. Why did you think it was all right to come back to them at this point?

MRS. S.: Because I've been around to everybody now. I got the message before that showing disapproval is dangerous. So I've made all these cushions. I've gotten everybody to talk about everybody else, and this is now a familiar kind of thing. I approach the husband and wife with this kind of cushioning so that I'll get the least defensive reaction.

INT.: You could have said, "Dad, how do you know that Mother disapproves of you?" That is, you could have done it the other way around.

MRS. S.: I deliberately picked the woman, because, as I'm seeing the family system now, you can pick on Dad, but never, never on Mother. By asking her to acknowledge her husband's disapproval—and I think I put this in an interesting way—I bound both of them. I said, "What do you know about your husband disapproving of you when he doesn't tell you he disapproves?" I'm saying that I know the messages of disapproval in this family get across but they aren't acknowledged. I put it into that frame, asking her to give evidence about when he disapproves, when he doesn't let her know.

INT.: You get in the assumption that she's got to do something wrong for him to disapprove of.

MRS. S.: Precisely. The way this is phrased is a subtle maneuver. She has to acknowledge, "I do something that he disapproves of," as well as, "He disapproves."

INT.: You also sound as if you were going to come in with something big. You say, "Now, Mother," then you pause, and then you go ahead. I'm sure she felt on the spot there.

MRS. S.: Well, I try to engineer a strategy like this so that there is a bind in it for both persons, but there is also a way out. Look what the mother could do. She could say, "I am always bad, and I'm always doing something he disapproves of." She could say, "He always disapproves of everything." Or she could say, "I never know when he disapproves, so I'm constantly worrying about it." There are all kinds of ways to go, you see, but she has to do something with it. The choice she makes helps me to get more information about the family system. But I try to set up every intervention so that it leaves the person a way out. This also helps me to see how people get out of a threat situation.

INT.: You set this up as if something were coming, and then it's quite mild. I'm sure she felt she was going to be blamed. There must be both a feeling of relief that that's all it is and an opening up because that's all it is.

MRS. S.: I'm sure that's right.

MRS. P.: I suppose I freeze up and I get quiet and . . .

GARY: Hmm.

MRS. P.: . . . and resentful. I don't think he ever . . .

MR. P.: I think you'll have to get the question rephrased again. I slipped a little bit, just exactly what you said.

MRS. S.: That is, when your wife knows that you disapprove of something, but you haven't said that you disapprove of it, but she knows it. Then what does she do?

MRS. P.: I think that's what I do. (*Loud laugh by Gary, humming sound from Tim.*)

GARY: Ha, ha—we've got a game!

MRS. P.: I would hurt him with my silence.

MRS. S.: You would hurt him with a silence.

INT.: Was Gary playing a game with Tim?

MRS. S.: No, he was saying, "This is a game. Games like this go on in our house."

INT.: The mother says very explicitly, "I would hurt him with *my* silence," and you say, "You would hurt him with *a* silence." Was this deliberate?

MRS. S.: Yes, it was. At this point I was only getting at the techniques; I didn't want to label them as belonging to anybody. Later on, I talk about the various ways in which people are operating.

INT.: You didn't want to identify this technique with the mother at this point? You wanted to make it a general one?

MRS. S.: Yes. Silence is used in this family, it's one of the rules. I'm still working toward the family homeostasis. I want to find out who else uses silence.

INT.: Did you also feel that the mother was provoking you, saying she was doing something bad to see what you would do with it? This is a pretty extreme statement, "I would hurt him with my silence."

MRS. S.: No, I felt that she had put something together. If I had asked her this question at the outset, she wouldn't have been able to answer this way. But we have removed a few things, so that she was able to see that silence is a way of hurting, a secret way, because you can't find out about it. It is also a discrepancy, because silence is not usually looked upon as something that hurts.

INT.: It's hard to tell whether she's saying that she is deliberately silent or whether she means that it's inadvertent.

MRS. S.: I think she means it's inadvertent.

INT.: You certainly lifted it off her by making it "a" silence instead of "her" silence.

MRS. S.: Well, in my effort to get at the rules, I'm trying to put in all the dimensions that I can get. For one thing, the possessive pronouns have to be redistributed, the "me's" and the "my's." I've found that there's a conviction in these people that whatever has been preceded by "my" is unique to that self. Or that whatever is preceded by "your" is unique to that self. I do my diagnosis in a lot of ways by the use of the pronouns, and I judge how far the treatment has gone by the use of the pronouns. As I said before, one of the things I have come to believe is that in dysfunctional families there's no room for any outside reality. All things and all people and all ideas, no matter where they come from, are a comment on "me." If the tomatoes are rotten, that means that I am not loved.

INT.: You're implying that everyone uses a kind of confused language in a family with a schizophrenic, not just the schizophrenic..

MRS. S.: That's right. That's what you find out when you get the family together.

MRS. S. (cont.): Well, what happens then? How does this get clear, when it happens?

MR. P.: I think, time.

MRS. S.: Well, would it be a minute or ten minutes or what?

MRS. P.: It depends on the degree of the (inaudible phrase).

MR. P. (simultaneously): Oh, maybe a few hours. Probably. Few hours, possibly.

MRS. P.: Yes.

MRS. S.: Have you ever noticed this, Gail? When Mother and Dad are somehow in a silent period?

GAIL: Oh! Oh, sure. But it's never for very long.

MRS. S.: At this point, I was remembering the statement at the beginning of the interview, "We were happy," which said, "The thing that has made us all unhappy is you, Gary." What I'm gradually building up here is a picture of the pain in the family. I learned later that these parents had sometimes not spoken to each other for two or three days. So what I am doing is to ask Gail for a validation of the pain.

INT.: Gail seems to be the model child in the family. It's interesting that you use her as the validation.

MRS. S.: How have you interpreted it? What did you think was going on?

GAIL: Oh, I interpreted it as they had a slight disagreement, or something, and they don't see eye to eye on the same thing. And so then they just, be quiet for, for a few minutes, depending on that. And then, oh, maybe a couple of hours later, it all blows over.

MRS. S.: Do you think they're angry?

GAIL: For a while. Everyone gets angry, I suppose.

MRS. S.: Well, maybe we'll find out something. I don't know. We'll have to check this out.

GARY: Some people would let out their anger in other ways.

MRS. S.: Have you ever seen this phenomenon between your parents?

GARY (*overlapping*): I was preoccupied with my . . .

MRS. S.: Yes, I noticed that you were.

GARY: Yes, I'll say it again. It was . . .

MRS. S.: Have you ever noticed when your father and mother are silent with each other? Have you ever noticed this?

GARY: To be frank, no.

MRS. S.: You've never noticed this?

GARY: No. I'm, I usually take people right on their face value, and, ah, like I said, naïve and gullible, so I don't notice that sort of thing, and I've always been busy with friends most of the time. Most of my life is spent with my peer group, but a very great portion is also spent with the family, so . . .

MRS. S.: Well, it's already been established that, at least by Gail, anyway, that Mother and Father have periods of silence once in a while, and they've established it, so I guess it's all right for you to look too, if you happen to see it.

MRS. S.: What I was working toward here was to get the silence between the parents validated by Gail so that Gary could get off the hook of having to deny what he saw and heard. What I heard him say was, "Don't trap me. I'm not sure that it's safe to say anything and I smell a trap here." But he's teetering with the possibility that maybe he can comment.

GARY (*overlapping*): I can't see—if I saw it, looked for it, I might see it, but then again, I might be like Freud, and he had a theory to test and so every time he got the people to say what he wanted them to, and he just discovered an exception will prove the rule, you know.

MRS. S.: Yes, well, all right. But just for the record, at the time being, you have not thought and recognized that Mother and Dad have periods of silence. They agree that they have it and Gail has seen it. (*To Lois.*) Have you ever seen this?

LOIS: Well, I think, well, once in a while. But I think this is caused by each one thinking, well, they think over what they have done, and they, well, they just think about it and usually, well, these silent periods don't last very long.

MRS. S.: I know they don't.

MRS. P.: And they happen very, very infrequently.

MRS. S.: But when they happen, when they would happen, it would mean that everybody would have to figure out what was going on. I'm going to ask Mother a question. When you're silent with Dad, is that because you're angry with him?

MRS. P. (*sighs*): Well, sometimes, I mean, it happens so stupidly. It's because I think something, and because I think it, I think he should follow the same line of thinking, and of course he doesn't, and then it's my disappointment in him that causes this. (*Inaudible phrase.*) And then after I analyze it and I get all through going through, everything's fine again.

MRS. S.: Then it isn't anger at all, is it?

MRS. P.: That, that's the thing. It's just stupidity, really.

MRS. S.: Well, let's— (*To Mr. P.*) Are you angry when you're silent with your wife?

INT.: You've got a special inflection in your voice when you talk to the father.

MRS. S.: How would you describe it?

INT.: It's almost a coyness. Was this because you felt this material was hot and you were trying to soften it?

MRS. S.: Yes, by my voice. The voice will protect while the words say, "Come out." One of the things in these families is that the self-esteem is so low in everybody that it's easy to turn them back. The minute you do that, you arouse defensiveness.

INT.: It's a little like herding sheep into a corral; they'll flee if you move them wrong.

MRS. S.: That's right. I go on the principle that to make changes I have to keep the lowest level of defensiveness.

> MR. P.: No. No, I think it's the more, I have a question of letting healing time take place.
>
> MRS. P.: Well, isn't it lack of communication, sometimes, that . . .
>
> MR. P.: Well, sometimes, yes, I think that's right. The lack of communication is right. But, I mean, ah, at that particular time I can't communicate, If I tried to—so then, the, ah, the way to do it is to let time lapse, and then you can— (*Gary interrupts.*)

INT.: I realize you think anger is a secondary emotion, but you seem reluctant to let people assume that anger is what's motivating them. First you bring out the idea that it isn't anger with Mother, then you turn to Father and ask, "Is it anger?" Finally it ends up as a lack of communication.

MRS. S.: Since I see anger as a secondary emotion, the way I treat it is to say that if a person shows anger, he's hiding his hurt and giving bum messages. If I put too much emphasis on anger, if I pick that up before I uncover the hurt, then I've got more work to do.

INT.: How do you mean, you've got more work to do?

MRS. S.: I have to go through this whole monkeyshine of anger. People who are giving out messages which look like anger messages can be either angry or hurt. If a person feels hurt and wants to say to somebody, "Come closer," but expresses it in an angry way, the other person goes away. What I want to do is to get that message of hurt out first. If I accuse the anger, the anger always comes out in relation to the attack on the other person, and I get into the business of blame. Then I have to spend more time on it than I want to.

INT.: I assume that you don't think it's important to bring out what they blame each other for.

MRS. S.: Yes, but that comes after I get at what I call the ego-enhancing part of the self.

INT.: Right here, why are you getting the question of anger out of their discussion?

MRS. S.: Because in this family nobody will acknowledge anger. I want to show that anger is basically each one's hurt and disappointment with the other.

INT.: In a sense, you're going along with the family by trying to get anger out of the picture.

MRS. S.: No, no. I want to put it in its right place.

INT.: Is part of it that by going along with the family's idea that they mustn't call anything anger, you enable them to speak more freely about their real feelings?

MRS. S.: That's right. Toward the end of the interview, when I came to the question of the mother-in-law, we could talk differently about anger. By then I had made it possible to do that. There's a timing element here.

INT.: That's one of the things I'm trying to get at.

MRS. S.: I would never talk about the anger at the outset, especially when it is seen by the individual as something so devastating that he can't acknowledge it. Later on, when he doesn't feel he'll drop dead, he can acknowledge it.

INT.: Is that the way you would treat every family?

MRS. S.: Oh, no. In other families, families with delinquents, for instance, I say, "It sounds to me as if you want to draw blood on that one." I've noticed that many therapists think there is something therapeutic about getting out anger, that there's something therapeutic about reporting what one's emotions are, never mind what. So you get patients pushing to get out anger even if they're not angry. You know: "Be angry!" Pretty soon you've got a countertransference situation in which the poor patient has to announce that he's angry, when he's only going along with the beliefs of the therapist. I don't think there's any particular growth in that.

INT.: There's another possibility for what is happening here. The mother says that the anger is a lack of communication, and the father agrees with this. It sounds like a comment you would make, it's in your language, only Mother makes it for you. The question is whether she picked it up from what you said previously, or whether she picked it up on the outside, or whether it's been engineered so that this would come out, which is what I begin to suspect.

MRS. S.: The way I heard her, she was not talking about communication but about isolation.

INT.: I'm sure she isn't using the word in quite the way you would, it's just that she's got the terminology. I wonder if another therapist working with this family would get the same terminology.

MRS. S.: This is something to look into. But I try not to give any messages that say, "Give me what I want," but rather, "How do you see it?"

INT.: As I remember, you said before that you take A and push it to C so that they will come up with B. Insofar as you do that, they're going to come up with ideas you're engineering them to have.

MRS. S.: It could be. All I know is that the families bring in their own pieces very nicely.

GARY (*to Mrs. S.*): May I say something about this subject?
MRS. S.: Yes.
GARY: I think it's difficult for, for—Daddy is quiet quite a lot of the time, and he's busy working and all, and so it's hard to find when he's a little more quiet than usual. (*Female laughter.*)

INT.: There's one thing here that is impressive. In this short time, you've got that boy asking your permission if he can speak.
MRS. S.: That's right, he does.

GARY (*cont.*): You know what I mean. He, it's not that, I don't know how well my daddy and mommy communicate together, 'cause this isn't my affair and I usually stick to my own business. But, but Mother may have trouble because Daddy talks, not, not too terribly much, and she maybe can't tell the difference, maybe, when he's angry at her.
MRS. S.: Well, we've had an illustration here of something. Gail has observed this phenomenon between Mother and Dad when they were silent sometimes, and she concluded it was because they were angry with each other. And Lois has seen this . . .
GARY: Could we ask Tim?

MRS. S.: Pardon me?

GARY: He may be the most observant of us all.

MRS. S.: Well, I will ask him.

GARY: Ask him simply, so—you know.

MRS. S.: And, Lois, you kind of concluded that, ah, things are going to get to be all right.

LOIS: Umm.

MRS. S.: You're not sure whether your mother and dad are angry with each other at that time or what.

LOIS: I don't think they are angry. I think they're just, well, it, it's hard to define angry, I think. I mean, it, it . . .

GARY: Yes, you're right.

LOIS: I mean, on various levels, angry can mean angry over maybe someone spilled a glass of milk, or something. But, ah, I think it's hard to define (*laughing*) angry.

MRS. S.: Yes, but you know, if people call someone else angry, then they expect that person who has angry feelings toward them to hit them or to reject them or something of this kind. So it's very important that we understand, because when anger is around, people fear there's going to be trouble. So we have to get this clear. Well, Tim, have you seen your mother and father when they seem not to be talking?

TIM: No.

MRS. S.: You never saw this?

GARY: (*Laughs.*)

MRS. S.: Well, so you and Gary haven't seen this.

GARY: We're the men and, you know, we're more, we're not so sensitive about things like this. Women are more sensitive on the whole about this sort of thing.

INT.: Gary says, "Tim may be the most observant of us all." But then he finds out that Tim hasn't noticed his mother and father not talking.

MR. S.: Well, the men can't acknowledge that.

INT.: Neither can Lois.

MRS. S.: She was classified as a tomboy at this point. There were only two females there, the mother and Gail. All the rest were labeled males.

MRS. S.: Well, we'll see. But what comes out is that whenever this happens, Mother has a feeling of disappointment, and I think Dad has a feeling that he doesn't know quite how to go until a little time goes by. Isn't that right?

MR. P.: That's right.

MRS. S.: You just kind of stop and wait to see what you can do. So that when this silence comes, it has nothing to do with anger, but it has to do with the fact that, for that moment, you haven't been able to find your way to each other. Isn't that right?

MR. P.: I think that's right.

MRS. S.: Go ahead.

MRS. P.: But it happens very seldom. I mean, this is the thing that is amazing. I mean, we really have had an amazing relationship.

MRS. S.: I know. Well, you see, this has a relationship now to the thing Gary was trying to get at, when he was talking about what was going on in his mind, and the behavior that he had, and then what he saw in the way in which you responded to it and his father responded to it. And he wanted a chance to clarify this. It looked to him something that I think you thought was different. Now—why did you lock him up in his room?

MR. P.: Well, it wasn't really, he wasn't really locked up in the room.

INT.: The mother is emphasizing—the whole family is, to some extent—that there are no negative feelings and that everybody is quite happy, except possibly Gary. Your approach goes along with what the family would like to think, that it isn't really anger, that they have positive feelings, and that they have amazingly happy relationships. Their desire to emphasize the positive coincides so well with your emphasizing the positive.

MRS. S.: I'm not saying there isn't any anger. I'm relabeling it as hurt and disappointment. To get people like this to comment even on disappointment takes a little art.

INT.: You said before that if you confronted the family with how angry they were and how miserable they were, and so on, you would silence them. So what you're doing is accepting the positive impression they're trying to give. You're encouraging them to go on the way they are within this framework you're changing.

MRS. S.: I have seen nothing that contradicts my idea that people want to grow and survive and get close to others. But I don't think anybody grows under a defense. So I build very clearly and cushion things.

INT.: What follows all this cushioning is a confrontation. You go suddenly into the question of why they locked Gary up.

MRS. S.: That's right. That's why I do this bridge-building.

INT.: It's also kind of leading them down the garden path. The way you emphasize the positive and the way they do appear to be the same. They're saying that it just somehow happens that things go badly, in spite of their positive intentions, and you seem to be agreeing with this. Then all of a sudden you ask, "Why did you lock him up?" You don't say, "How did it happen that he got locked up?"

MRS. S.: You notice how far along in the interview we are before I come to that. I feel I have to give enough ego-enhancement so that what is ego-assaultive can be tolerated.

INT.: Well, there's an acceptance which they're going along with, and all of a sudden there's a capper on this and the Gestalt changes. You're behaving as if you were still going along with them, when actually you're confronting them with something very different from anything they would accept.

GARY: Well, as far as, I mean, to me, I could not leave. Let's say that.

MRS. P. (*simultaneously*): We were (*inaudible phrase*), that was all.

MRS. S.: Were you literally locked in a room?

GARY: Yes.

MRS. S.: With the key in the door locking it?

GARY: No, there was no key in the door. It was just (*inaudible phrase*).

MR. P. (*overlapping*): No, we were watching Gary so that he wouldn't go out by himself.

GARY: Let's say I (*inaudible phrase*) "May I go down to get a drink of water?" I would have come back, but you grabbed me like this.

MRS. P.: We had water right in the room, Gary.

MRS. S.: O.K. Now just a minute. I'm trying to look at what the facts are. Now, the facts were, you were in a room and you couldn't get out. Now, my question was . . .

GARY (*overlapping*): (*Inaudible phrase*) in any way. I couldn't get out. I can't remember exactly whether it was locked or not.

MRS. S.: Now, the question was, "Why did Dad do it?" That's your question to him, so I'm asking him.

INT.: Gary didn't put it as, "Daddy locked me up."

MRS. S.: No, he put it as, "I couldn't get out."

INT.: You prefer to make it more active and to pin the credit on Dad.

MRS. S.: Right.

INT.: There's quite a flurry here. Perhaps it's because you've jumped so suddenly from everybody's good intentions to their locking Gary up.

MRS. S.: It's as though their good intentions carry them along, or at least they think so, never mind how they are manifested. I'm beginning to say, "All right, so you've got good intentions inside, but let's take a look at how they come out. Let's take a look at what kind of message this gives to somebody else."

MR. P.: Well, the question, the reason at that time was, ah, ah, we couldn't trust Gary to, ah, be sure that he was doing what we thought was right.

MRS. S.: Now, did you want to punish him?

MR. P.: No! No punishment.

MRS. P.: No.

MR. P.: No, we felt he was sick, that Gary was sick, and that he needed rest, terrifically.

MRS. S.: So this was a way you wanted to protect him?

MR. P.: Right.

INT.: You won't let the father off the hook on this. He's been saying, "Gary wasn't really locked up," and "We were just watching him so he wouldn't go off by himself," and you've been shifting it back to, "Why did Dad lock him up? Why did Dad do it?" Here you ask, "Was it punishment?" and that's not accepted, so you say, "Was it protection?" and finally he agrees. You come on strong, then slide into redefining what happened as a protective thing. There's a kind of coming out, giving off, and sliding back again.

MRS. S.: Yes, I try not to give too big a lump. It reminds me of a play in bowling. You hit first to the nearest pin, and if you're successful with that one, the next time you try for more. The therapist has to be a little farther ahead; these are really like flyers. I always watch for the stress reactions, and if it's too much, I come back, we rest a little, and then we go back again. There is a persistence in it, and one of the ways of persisting is to build the context, a specific context, which is, "We'll put this picture together."

INT.: There is also a considerable persistence about responsibility here. In that statement, *"We* couldn't trust Gary," the father is not taking responsibility himself, even though you almost drowned him with it. He doesn't say, *"I* couldn't trust Gary." He doesn't even say that he locked Gary up because Mother was so upset, though this was probably the case.

MRS. S.: The fact that he is the one who answers the question, "Why did Dad lock him up?" shows that he is indirectly accepting the responsibility. But you're right about that "we." I think if I were to do this again, I would say, "I don't understand 'we.' " I would have checked out that pronoun. But it would be within the context of "I don't understand." To Mother I would have said, "I don't understand how you people came to do that," and to Father, "Oh, you mean that this was something you did for your wife?"

INT.: He may be trying to give you a clue with that "we."

MRS. S.: Yes. "I'm just a pawn in this."

INT.: Why did you say, "Did you want to punish him?" You knew that they would deny it, or that he would.

MRS. S.: I wanted to make it explicit that punishment is part of what people do sometimes, and in this case I was saying, "We want to find out whether what you intended to do fit what Gary got out of this." I was again introducing the idea that people perceive things differently.

INT.: You knew that they were going to say "no punishment."

MRS. S.: I did know. But it had to be on the record because I knew that Gary perceived it as punishment.

INT.: This is again a way of getting the negative things out of the picture. You don't say, "Of course, you didn't want to punish him," you say, "Did you want to punish him?" You knew you were going to get a denial.

MRS. S.: This also paves the way for a discrepancy comment later on. I often say in such cases, "If you didn't want to punish him, how did your hand come to slap his face?" But first I want the discrepancy to come out loud and clear in front of everybody. Later I can pose the discrepancy and ask for the explanation.

> MRS. S.: But Gary didn't feel that way about it, but nevertheless that was your intention.
> MR. P.: Right.

MRS. S.: You see, I posed the discrepancy. "You didn't mean it that way, but Gary *perceived* it as punishment."

INT.: In view of the context of Gary's actions, it's possible that they may have been afraid he would try to kill himself. They might find it very hard to believe that he thought they were punishing him, since they were devoting themselves to protecting him.

MRS. S.: Well, let's suppose I want to shake your hand. Suppose you're kind of far away, and I put more weight on your hand than I intended. I may only be aware of my effort to try to reach you. You, however, can be quite aware of your broken finger. Now the facts are that you have a broken finger. You've got to do something about it, no matter how you interpret it. But how you interpret it is going to affect both how you feel about yourself and how you feel about the other person. I don't really believe that anybody starts out deliberately to do damage to another person. It's usually what I call "an accident in the interest of the self." As I see it, the parents' behavior with Gary was that kind of accident.

INT.: Your philosophy about it seems to fit so well with what the family would like to hear.

MRS. S.: I was raised on the notion that you catch more flies with honey than with vinegar. The problem is how to do this in the interests of growth. If I use my technique, the honey, to tell you what you must do in order to please me, I take away from you your opportunity to grow. If I use my honey technique to attract you to a place where you can learn something, then I have used my technique in the interests of growth. I don't think you hear much of the usual reassurance from me. The reassurance comes in making things obvious.

INT.: The way you make things obvious is often very reassuring.

MRS. S.: Yes, but I know therapists who tell people, "You're a good guy," and that sort of thing, which I don't believe in. I think one of the most reassuring things to say is, "You know, your nose is split wide open and bleeding." But I would never say, "Your nose is split wide open, and it's all your fault."

INT.: You don't tell this father that it's his fault. You don't say, "You were a bad person and did this bad thing." All you say is, "Your son *felt* this as a bad thing."

MRS. S.: That's right.

INT.: This is again a way of going along with what the family would like to think. The family is very busy indicating they're not responsible for what happened. You say, "Your son perceived that you punished him. Nevertheless, that was not your intention." The emphasis on how the son perceived it is a way of playing down the question of responsibility. What the father did, he didn't really intend, and what the son perceived, he had no control over, and it was all a misunderstanding. Nobody is responsible for what happened, which is what the family would like the phrasing to be. You accept the family's view of things, but in a way that can ultimately produce a change. There's a subtle way of going along with the typical pattern that is partly in the nature of your method, but partly in the nature of psychotherapy in general.

MRS. S.: Sometimes I have the feeling that I'm coming right in for the kill, and then suddenly, bang! Here's where the timing comes in. When I'm building up to a major discrepancy and moving in, that's where I'm convinced that the real change begins to take place.

GARY: Well, by that night they were worried because I hadn't been getting too much sleep. I had been doing, at the end of school, a lot of writing. At the end of final exams, and after school, I wrote quite a lot. And, ah, I was subtired, a little, but I was able, I got, slept some naps in the daytime, in the afternoon, and though I, I knew I was tired, I, after I had finally finished finals, when the final period was over, you feel a little excited, exhilarated, and this was, I think, the sense of being, perhaps, too much alive, or at least appearing too much alive, it was almost like a nervous breakdown, but it wasn't. Too much alive, that they thought perhaps, that I might be sick. And I think it was a misunderstanding. After all, I, I had been studying pretty hard the last four weeks, and I hadn't any communication *then* with the parents. I had to study hard 'cause I'd had mononucleosis and, and, ah, was, was not able to perform up to my capabilities at the beginning of the quarter. So it was just at the end that I started to get a little interested in some of the subjects, and to read them, and to get the knowledge I should have gained while I was sick. Physically. Then, I think that I was—finally I was out of this house where a boy had been very mean to me, and out of [*university*], so, so that I had nothing to do, and just to write and have fun, and I think that this great exhilaration was noticed by my parents, and I think perhaps they interpreted this as perhaps being sick. I didn't do . . .

MRS. S.: It could be. We can ask.

GARY: . . . wild things. I just . . .

MRS. P.: But you didn't sleep at all when you were home.

GARY: I slept enough.

MRS. P.: You didn't sleep, Gary.

GARY: I slept enough for then.

MRS. P.: Two hours?

GARY: You see—wait, wait. Another thing that you have to notice is that when I was getting over mononucleosis, I would sleep between ten, eleven, twelve, thirteen, fourteen hours a night.

TIM (*whispering*): Wow!

MRS. P.: That doesn't help you.

GARY: Well, yes it does, yes it does. I mean, up until this time I had been getting a lot of sleep, and I really didn't need it for (*inaudible phrase*).

MRS. S.: Well, what we are . . .

GARY: It's, ah, not important now. It's over. It's not important.

MRS. S.: All of this is important because of the fact that it again illustrates the fact that if you want to get over a message about something about yourself, and it doesn't come over in a way which you meant it, then you wonder why did it happen. And it's quite obvious that, in this instance, your being locked in the room, from everything you could see and everything you could feel, this felt like some kind of punishment to you.

GARY: No. No.

MRS. S.: As far as your parents were concerned, it felt like they were trying to do something to help, at least as far as Dad was concerned.

GARY: I didn't think of it as punishment. I felt that it was, they were doing something . . .

MRS. P. (*overlapping*): Overprotective.

GARY: . . . to me that seemed to be unjust, which I couldn't understand then. I did not ever think that I was being punished, which I (*inaudible phrase*) or being put in the hospital at the time.

INT.: Why did you let him go on at such length?

MRS. S.: I remember that he was under terrible pressure to comment, and I felt that I didn't have to respond so much to this. He was also beginning to look quite withdrawn, and I wasn't quite clear what was happening with him. I hoped that if he went on a little bit, I'd get some indication.

INT.: I wondered if you thought the question of why they locked him up was too distressing, and were letting him take the focus on himself.

MRS. S.: I don't know. I was trying to get some things clear at this point, because there was quite a change in the family. The tension level was rising very high. I wasn't sure where I was going to go with it, as I recall. And I remember having feelings of annoyance. Gary's voice becomes more clipped here and you can hear the agitation.

INT.: It's a pretty agitated speech.

MRS. S.: When I thought back on it later, I felt that I would have done better if I had continued to relabel their locking him up in terms of a misunderstanding, to show that he wasn't really so crazy. I could have asked something like, "What did you think your father and mother saw and heard that made *them* think that *you* thought that *they* thought you were crazy?"

> MRS. S.: Well, all right. Now, let's leave all of this now and go into another level of our material, which is what we need to do. And that is, how this whole family came to be in the first place. And where does that start? It starts out the first time that you and you (*to Mr. and Mrs. P.*) ever laid eyes on each other. When was that and how?

INT.: Why did you move to the family history at this point?

MRS. S.: It's as though I've examined the body and I find that the respiratory system is not in such good shape. Now I've decided to find out some more about the basis for the disorder. To go on as I was then would be wasting a lot of time that I could use better. Also, I want to make the parents be responsible. When I ask the question, "How did you two get together?" I'm implying that they have made a selection. One of the things I want to do is give the parents an experience of choosing. The power of this question is that it means that you select, that you have responsibility.

INT.: Did you make this shift to the past because you thought the topic you were on was getting too upsetting?

MRS. S.: I wanted to get into some of this material before. I find it very difficult to understand all the ways in which the people before me are behaving unless I know something about their development. That's one thing. The other is that in families with schizophrenics there's no idea of continuity. The past runs into the present, just as though it fell in out of the clear blue sky. So I bring out the continuity aspect. Also, a discussion of how the family came to be can give the children assembled an opportunity to get some new clues. There are many things that come out in a family life chronology. One of the critical factors here was the shadow of the first-cousins relationship of the parents. I want to find out about what I call the witches. What are the witches that are around? The shadows that are going to affect everybody.

INT.: Do you take a family history with every family you treat?

MRS. S.: I always regret it when I don't. It's like diagnosing an illness without doing all the appropriate tests. The therapist can always be wrong in his perceptions.

INT.: Does the point at which you start this vary from family to family?

MRS. S.: Yes. I find more and more that at the outset I tend to do rule analysis.

INT.: By "rule analysis," do you mean an analysis of what the rules are in the family?

MRS. S.: Well, I might ask about the rules for fighting or for pleasing. I might say, "Well, every family has rules about all kinds of things, and you may not have thought about these rules, but what can you do—and I pick out one person—that you know will make so and so angry," or "bring a smile on his or her face?" Then I ask this of everybody in the family.

INT.: As you did when you asked this family how they showed disapproval?

MRS. S.: That was a similar kind of thing. What I usually try to do in the first interview is ask about the hurt and anger, to try to get people to differentiate between them. I'll say, "What do you see that leads you to the conclusion that he or she is angry? How do you tell?" I do this also to focus people on the relationship between the other person and themselves. Then I usually go into the family life chronology, if I don't do some symptom reading first.

INT.: What do you mean by symptom reading?

MRS. S.: In one family I interviewed, the girl was not doing well at school. She was obviously a very bright girl, and I couldn't understand it, so I said to her, "What was it that you did that said to other people that you were stupid? You know, I don't understand that." Then I went into the messages about stupidity and brightness. I said, "Let's take a look and see how this whole business got started, because it's obvious that in this family people have a highly developed sensitivity to who's bright and who's stupid." That's what I call symptom reading— reading the messages that relate to symptoms.

MRS. P.: That was in 1934. Chicago.

MR. P.: Chicago.

MRS. S.: All right. We've got that. A lot of people in Chicago, so it must have been something more than that.

MRS. P.: Well, actually, I mean, ah, you have to know that we are first cousins, and so, ah, Henry and his mother came back to visit and . . .

MR. P.: We hadn't seen much of each other up until this time.

MRS. P.: . . . and I was nineteen and he was two—twenty-one—and the inevitable happened. First there was a lot of protest on his mother's part.

MRS. S.: Wait, wait before you get that far. All right. So, you're first cousins. We'll put that over here.

MRS. P.: Yes.

MRS. S.: This is a place where some therapists would have hung themselves up on this cousin business and gotten way off the track. I can see a therapist coming in with the terrible question, "How did you feel about that?" All right, it was a fact, and I knew it was loaded with affect, but what I was interested in was, "What did you really react to?" They didn't marry because they were cousins, they were reacting to something else, and the fact that they happened to be cousins was only a part of it.

INT.: Were you passing over their being cousins to try to minimize it?

MRS. S.: No, I deal with that later. The important thing I wanted to do here was to get at what they saw in each other.

INT.: You could have chosen not to pass over it. The way I hear you say this, it sounds as if you're trying to make it lighter.

MRS. S.: I am, because I already know this has much too much affect. When somebody tells me about a mixed marriage, I do the same thing. I relabel it by not treating it too importantly, and later on we can go back and look at its consequences.

INT.: I wondered, too, whether you were reacting as a representative of the scientific community, knowing that they were watching to see what you'd say about a marriage between first cousins.

MRS. S.: That was part of it. This can be a juicy kind of thing. A therapist can get sidetracked by it. I've noticed that what a therapist comments on can sometimes be much more related to what he finds juicy than to what he finds helpful.

INT.: Perhaps that's why so many therapists bring out sex, to liven up the sessions.

MRS. S.: I think I can get just as far with any process. The content can be about tying your shoes, or eating, or anything.

> MRS. S.: What made you think he was so nice? You know, after all, I'm sure plenty of people could meet each other and go right by, but you didn't.
>
> MRS. P.: Well, actually, I think that, ah, well, it's ridiculous to say such a thing, but I think I had worshipped him ever since I was a little girl. We had his picture. He was blond, and he was to me the most beautiful little boy in the world. (*Laughing.*) Of course, I don't think he felt that way about me.
>
> MRS. S.: Well, wait a minute. We'll find out about that. Is that so unusual? For a girl to have an ideal? And worship an ideal? Is that so unusual?
>
> MRS. P.: Ohhhh . . .
>
> GARY: (*Inaudible phrase.*) That's just the way it was.

MRS. S.: When I ask the mother what appealed to her in her husband, I'm posing another question that says, "You had a choice."

INT.: You challenge the idea of the "inevitable" by saying that there was a choice. But you also go along with it by implying that there was something special here, some form of destiny, perhaps. When she answers you, that's the part she picks up.

MRS. S.: That's in the same category with, "The wind blew and it came in." You are never going to get people involved in change unless you can get them to see themselves as agents of change.

INT.: When you try to make it more commonplace for a girl to have an ideal, in one sense you're making it less her choice, less individual. Is this because she's gone so far in having it be exceptional that she's making it a power beyond her?

MRS. S.: I'm playing on that. I'm trying to enhance the fact, "Look, kids, you choose these things," to get away from the idea of the inevitable. What I'm aiming for all the time is what I call "people taking charge of themselves." I know I can't get to first base unless I crack that one.

> MRS. P.: Ohhh, I don't know. There was this little boy lying on the, ah, bench, with a big wide belt on, and I just thought he was the cutest little boy in all the world. And of course, then, we visited

them when I was seven, and his father was the most wonderful man I ever knew in my life.

GARY: Smoked cigars.

MRS. P.: Well, he was completely different from my own father, though.

MRS. S.: How are you related? Brothers?

MRS. P.: Mothers are sisters.

MRS. S.: Your mothers are sisters.

MRS. P.: Yes. And he was affectionate and, ah— (*Tim interrupts.*)

MRS. S.: Later on, Gary came in smoking a cigar, and it turned out that the family had all kinds of prohibitions about drinking and smoking. The husband's mother couldn't stand her own husband smoking cigars, and she also put on this big WCTU act. The wife's mother, who was her younger sister, had to put on the WCTU act too. Everyone knew that the wife's mother was fun-loving, but she couldn't openly announce it. This was exactly the same bind the wife was in with her own two older sisters, as I found out later. Another interesting thing was that about five weeks after this session Gary had another breakdown, which began while he was eating out with his father. He took all the condiments on the table, Worcestershire sauce and ketchup and salt and sugar and pepper, mixed up a cocktail, and handed it to his father for a drink. Then he went out and urinated behind a signboard and got picked up by the police. It was an obvious protest against the family's Victorian ideas.

TIM (*whispering*): How old is Daddy?

MRS. S.: Ask him; he'll tell you. How old is Daddy? (*To Mr. P.*) Do you want to let him know?

GARY: Multiply your age times ten. You'll come out almost exactly.

INT.: Why did you pick up this child's whisper?

MRS. S.: It had been a long time since Tim had commented, and I was already aware that Gary was watching to see who I'd leave out. Besides, it was the kind of question that I felt never got answered in this family. I noticed when I listened back to the tape that he didn't really get an answer.

MRS. P.: And so I think all of this was built up, and so when he came he was handsome, and, ah, it just happened. I mean, it was love at first sight so far as I was concerned.

MRS. S.: No, I don't think it was love at first sight because you didn't know—there were all these years that you were looking at these pictures. (*Laughter.*) All right, so we see that. But as far as your contact with your husband was concerned, it was limited up until you were seven. Is that it?

MRS. P.: Yes.

MRS. S.: Mostly it was by picture.

MRS. P.: Yes, I saw him when I was seven. And then they went to [*abroad*] and came through and I saw them I guess when I was nine, ten? Was that it?

INT.: You seem to be more matter-of-fact in your tone than you usually are. Is this partly to cut through the cloud of love at first sight and idealism?

MRS. S.: There are some tears around. She's near tears, right at the moment.

MR. P.: '25.

MRS. P.: Yes, 1925. And, ah, of course, then he wasn't quite so sweet. He was kind of in that age where he was putting dirt on me and things like that.

MRS. S.: What age was he?

MR. P.: About twelve.

MRS. S.: About twelve.

MRS. P.: Then he was kind of pesky at that age. (*Everyone talking at once.*) But anyhow, when he came back, he just was everything that I had ever . . .

MRS. S.: And then when he came back . . .

MRS. P. (*overlapping*): (*Inaudible phrase*) hadn't found him any different.

MRS. S.: At what age?

MR. P.: Twenty-one.

MRS. P.: Twenty—it was in 1934 and I was born in '15 and he was born in '12.

MR. P. (*simultaneously*): Well, it was 1934, yes.

MRS. M.: So I had done a lot of dating, so I mean, it wasn't that I had never seen a boy before. But Henry was everything that I ever looked for in a husband.

MRS. S. (*to Mr. P.*): Well, now, how about you?

MR. P.: Well, I thought she was pretty great. (*Laughing.*)

MRS. S.: Well, did you have her picture? Was it the same kind of the development of an ideal?

GARY: No. A little boy wouldn't be that way.

INT.: Why does everybody talk at once when Mother tells about Father being pesky and throwing dirt?

MRS. S.: There are two rules. One is that you can't criticize Father, and the other is that you can't cast aspersions on a romantic ideal. It's as though they were trying to disguise the fact that Mother really makes more efforts toward Father than Father does toward Mother.

INT.: Why does Gary speak for the father here?

MRS. S.: I think he's making a burlesque of the father's position in the family.

INT.: He's saying that it would be better if Father weren't so accepting?

MRS. S.: That's right.

MRS. S.: Well, I don't know about that. Let's see.

MR. P.: No, I hadn't any, ah, thoughts along that line. (*Laughing.*)

MRS. P.: He was mechanical-minded. (*Laughs.*)

MR. P.: (*Inaudible phrase.*)

GARY: Ask Tim.

MRS. S.: I got lost there.

MR. P.: (*Inaudible phrase*) time in 1934. That really was the start of it as far as I was concerned.

MRS. S.: And then how long was the relationship before you married, one in which you were labelling yourselves as sweethearts?

MRS. P.: Well, I came out here to visit in 1936, and then in '37 we were married. So it was three years.

MRS. S.: And then people raised cain about this?

MRS. P.: We had been writing—my own mother, before she died, she said that (*pause, starting to cry*) as far as she was concerned, love was all that mattered. And my own family felt that way. But, ah, Henry's mother didn't approve. (*Weeping.*)

MRS. S.: They didn't. And so they made trouble for you?

MR. P.: No. No, not trouble, but, ah, disapproved.

MRS. P. (*simultaneously*): His father, his father died at fifty-seven.

MRS. S.: And then how did you handle that?

MRS. P. (*sighing*): Well, we came home to her the night that, ah, we were married, back East, we came home to her, and, ah, she wasn't very nice to me (*weeping*) and I was prepared to give, completely, because I just thought that Henry was my husband and I'd make every overture. But, ah, I mean, to this day, I really don't think she, she really cares.

INT.: Where the mother says, "I was prepared to give completely," she sounds like a bride rejected by her husband, even though she is talking about her mother-in-law.

MRS. S.: It's a matter of self-esteem again. The mother didn't feel that she counted for anything and wherever she could she tried to get some kind of validation of her worth, which is pushed onto Gary. What comes out here is that Gary sees that he can be useful to his parents in two ways: first, to make life worthwhile for his mother and give what the father didn't give; second, by his extreme behavior, to give his father clues about how he can live. If he can accomplish these two things, if he can get Father to be more interesting to Mother, then Mother perhaps can use Father instead of him. At the end of this tape, there is a problem about who is going to live with the mother-in-law. Again, symbolically, you'll see how Gary will be the rescue agent.

GARY: I, I think I see the outside of this, because I wasn't involved.

MRS. S.: You weren't even there. (*Female laughter.*)

GARY: I think that, I think that Grannie did it actually accidentally. I mean, she did not mean to hurt Mother. I don't think she really meant to.

MRS. P.: She loves the children. She adores the children.

GARY: I think it was sort of a, just a l-lack of communication th-that, you see, Grannie had, was born a long time, I mean, she was born many years before, and they had ideas then that this sort of thing was, they had taboos against it.

MRS. S.: You mean about cousins marrying?

MRS. P.: She had, ah, a sister who— (*Gary interrupts.*)

MRS. S.: There were a great number of relatives here. There were the mother's two older sisters, who never married, and the father's mother, who was also the mother's aunt. It was very complicated. Every day the mother would have at least three calls and maybe two visitors. She was still very much in a child relationship to all three women.

GARY: She probably had been pretty well isolated in her little Danish group, and this seemed so much out of the ordinary to her, that, that it might have been very difficult for her and she naturally would be . . .

MRS. P. (*simultaneously*): She told me that all the children would be born deformed.

GARY: You see, she made the comment—she may be naïve, herself, intellectually, and when she's told—there's kids at [*university*] that think they come out half feeble-minded. But actually, if you —I've read a book, a *book,* on it that says that if they come, if anything happens, the recessive genes are reinforced, and recessive genes may be good. They may be bad. As it is, we get our blond hair and blue eyes from this same reason.

INT.: Why did Gary come to Grannie's rescue here?

MRS. S.: The patient plays all kinds of roles, rescue roles, peacemaker roles, in trying to help the so-called healthy adults, which they don't notice, with their pains—and this is a very painful kind of thing. Gary was trying to give at least one reason why his mother wouldn't have to feel so bad. That was one part of it.

INT.: He's also the result of this marriage, so Grannie could be right about the monsters they created. He's protecting himself to some extent.

MRS. S.: There's that too.

MRS. S.: Let me stop you just a minute, Gary. (*To Mrs. P.*) What do you think about Gary's comment that this didn't have very much to do with whether or not you were acceptable in your mother-in-law's eyes, but that it had something to do with her fears because she was uninformed?

INT.: Is there a particular reason why you stopped Gary and interpreted his statement to the mother?

MRS. S.: I wanted to make it clear that Gary was trying to give the mother something to work on, something that was almost a straight message. Both the mother and the father still felt that what they had done was so terrible they had no way to look at it, and I thought that

Gary was giving them a clue. I wanted to rephrase it clearly to see what the mother could do with it, and I wanted to make explicit to Gary the fact that I knew he was making a contribution. I wanted to make Gary appear to be able to make contributions, to be taken seriously, not just to be thought crazy. One of the ways to remove the patient from the scapegoat position is to demonstrate whenever possible that he has a contribution to make. This is a good opportunity for me because I know what he's saying has some validity, that the fear about this kind of thing is not supported by scientific fact. But if I let Gary go on too long, he's going to disqualify himself, so I'm going to cut him off while the cutting's good.

MRS. P.: I think it was partly, and also the fact that her husband died when he was fifty . . .

MR. P. (*simultaneously*): I think it was partly that. '33, yes, that's . . .

MRS. P.: . . . and, ah, I think that almost any girl would have had a hard time. Because, I mean, she was the possessive type of mother who came down here, and took an apartment and lived with Henry when he was here at [*university*], and this, I mean to me, this is the kind of thing a mother just doesn't do.

MRS. S.: Well, here you were . . .

MRS. P.: I think she did have an overpossessiveness.

MRS. S.: Well, we can look. Now here is a problem here for you in feeling that you were unacceptable, and how did you try to handle this? 'Cause obviously the love for the two of you was strong enough to stick together, so how did you (*to Mr. P.*) try to handle this and help Mother communicate?

MR. P.: Well, I tried to tell her what we were doing, and, ah, she, ah, there really wasn't any, 'cause I think her main worry was the fact of, ah, children.

MRS. P. (*overlapping*): Children.

INT.: I take it you think this statement the wife makes about the mother-in-law's overpossessiveness is going to get the husband's back up. So when you say, "How did you handle this?" you're not just raising the question whether his mother was overpossessive, you're assuming it, so that he isn't quite in the position to deny or affirm it.

MRS. S.: That's right, I skip that problem. Trying to get somebody to what I call the "confessional" is just engaging in a power tactic, and if I engaged in this kind of tactic I would lose ground.

INT.: It's interesting that you wouldn't consider skipping the problem a power tactic.

MRS. S.: It's not the kind that brings out defensiveness.

INT.: I see what you mean about the difference, but it's a more powerful maneuver to slide through on these people.

MRS. S.: Yes, because it doesn't engage in active war. To assume trouble within this kind of situation is 'congruent with the situation. Then to assume that not only was there trouble but the husband did something with it is a comment to him that I see that he can cope. It's an ego-enhancing comment about a difficult situation.

INT.: There's a lot in that speech. It's not only, "How did you try to handle it?" It's also, "The love between the two of you was strong enough to keep you together."

MRS. S.: That's evidenced by the fact that they're in front of me and haven't been divorced.

INT.: You make a translation here. They haven't unitedly handled his mother, but you're implying this by saying, "The two of you have stuck together." You almost say, "stuck together *on this issue.*"

MRS. S.: But I didn't say that. What I'm doing here is to say, "The two of you had something with each other, but at the same time you had terrible problems with each other." I'm beginning to see that the woman doesn't talk very much, and when she does she double-talks, and he doesn't talk at all. So there are many implications when I then ask him directly how he helped his wife. Since this was his mother, he probably had ways of dealing with her, and he would be the one who would have to help his wife in relation to this.

INT.: You did mean the father's mother, when you said "help Mother communicate"?

MRS. S.: I meant "wife." I said it wrong.

INT.: Then he might have misunderstood you where he says, "I tried to tell her what *we* were doing."

MRS. S.: That's right. I hadn't caught that until now. He did misunderstand me.

INT.: This slow hesitation might have been because he was trying to figure out what way you meant that.

MRS. S.: That's right, and he couldn't ask me. I gave him a bum steer by saying "mother" when I meant "wife."

INT.: It's a nice problem for him about which side you're helping on.

MR. P.: And, ah, so that was, I tried to convince her that that was not founded. I had done some reading and so forth on it to check it up before we did anything, and, ah . . .

MRS. P.: You and your mother didn't even talk to each other before we were married, though. I mean, they were not even speaking to each other, although they were living in the house together.

MR. P. (*overlapping*): No—yes—yes.

MRS. S.: The thing is beginning to crack a little bit. The parents have been saying, "We're together on everything," and then the husband says, "I talked to my mother," and the wife says, "No, you didn't talk to her." The rift between them is beginning to come out.

INT.: Was the husband's mother still in the picture?

MRS. S.: Very much so. She lived almost next door.

INT.: Then this is why the wife would come in on this point.

MRS. S.: Oh, yes.

MRS. P.: It was a really (*inaudible phrase*) situation. It wasn't easy.

MRS. S.: No, of course it wasn't.

GARY: And then, there is the possibility that the fault was more with, with Grannie. It could be that. You can't say, but then, there's always that possibility.

MRS. S.: Of course there is.

INT.: Gary has just defended the grandmother and now he comes in to take his mother's side.

MRS. S.: This is the dilemma of the schizophrenic. He has to go around to everybody, that's why he comes out with so much double-talk.

INT.: He's got so many triangles to keep the peace in.

MRS. S.: That's right.

INT.: If I understand it, the husband's mother moved in with him while he was going to school and then they didn't talk to each other. Was it while he was going to school that he was married?

MRS. S.: He had finished school.

INT.: Was the mother still living with him after the marriage?

MRS. S.: Yes. When he went to college, his mother came to live with him, to keep house for him. Later in this interview it turns out that she wanted to do the same thing with Gary.

MRS. S. (*cont.*): You know, as you look at this— (*To Mr. P.*) Is your mother still living?

MR. AND MRS. P.: Yes.

MRS. S.: And what is she now? Does she live close to you?

MRS. P.: Yes.

MR. P.: She's close. She lives in [*next town*].

MRS. P.: Yes, and she's with us an awful lot of the time. I mean, more than most mothers-in-law.

INT.: At this point, did you know the father's mother was still very much a part of this?

MRS. S.: No, but I quickly try to find out where all the parents of the people involved are. I want to find out what may still be operating; you know, leftover homeostasis from other family organizations.

INT.: It's a very quick switch to the present. I take it that you aren't too strict about keeping to the family history if something you want to get at comes up.

MRS. S.: I try to use the family life chronology in as creative a fashion as possible. This is why it sometimes takes me five interviews to get one. First of all, the calendar is a wonderful vehicle by which you can keep things straight and give a sense of continuity. Also, what has happened in the past is residual in the present. So I'm doing several things, and here again it's a matter of clinical judgment. I saw, with the mother-in-law, all the ways in which she could still be used by the family as a scapegoating device to keep the husband and wife together. I have enough information now from the past to see some of the pieces for the present. So it will serve my treatment purposes better here to see what's going on in the present.

INT.: Is this partly because you see the end of the interview coming and think this is a problem that ought to be dealt with? At about this point, you must be realizing that there is a triangle between the husband and his mother and his wife, which you could either let go and take up another time, or take up right now.

MRS. S.: I felt I could bring it in and still have a unit feeling to my interview. I could see that Gary played a part as well in this triangle of the mother-in-law and the husband and the wife, and I wanted to get to that too. And I thought I could do it. Ordinarily, I hold interviews for an hour and a half; this one was only an hour.

INT.: It's always a problem of judgment when something like this comes up. A therapist has to decide whether to deal with it right away or to go on with the matter in hand and circle around back to it. In the earlier part of this interview, where you were going from person to person, if something critical came up you went right on to the next person. Here, when the question of the mother-in-law comes up, you go right to it.

MRS. S.: I almost never pick up anything like that at the beginning of an interview, certainly not in an initial interview. And I would never bring anything up if I knew I couldn't work it into a process before the end of the interview.

INT.: You tend to think of an interview in terms of a unit?

MRS. S.: Yes. Every interview should be like a well-done symphony, complete in and of itself. So that even if people never came back again, they would still have something from it. The job might not be finished, but the experience would be unitary. My interviews almost always have a kind of preparation period, like a prelude to a climax, but when I get to a climax, there's no letdown. I shape off, so that the interview has a whole lot of embracing parts to it. I want people to take with them something that's ego-enhancing. The wound has been sutured and you can see that it's going to heal. Next time we may take the stitches out and maybe make another cut. Maybe we'll even have to do this one over again. But you know you won't go home all full of morphine.

MRS. S.: Well, how does this come about that your (*to Mr. P.*) mother and your (*to Mrs. P.*) mother-in-law is in the house so much?

MRS. S.: Here I feel that I need to find ways to confront each person with the idea that he is more able than he thinks. I'm starting with Mother because she has indicated that she's hopeless, helpless, picked on. When I ask her, "How does this come about?" the question is itself an indication that I know she has made choices about the situation with her mother-in-law.

INT.: That's a complicated question.

MRS. S.: Sure it is. I rarely get someone who can't respond to a question like that, because it's an ego-enhancing question, not an attacking question. It puts an action within a frame that implies that things could be different.

INT.: I think that's partly the tone you give it. It could be an attacking question if you said, "Look here, why are you allowing this?"

MRS. S.: But that wouldn't be using the same words. I don't know how you can say, "How did this come about?" so that it sounds attacking. I have several questions like that.

INT.: This could be tactical, too. It's typical of all patients to say, "I don't know how this came about." By definition, nobody's responsible for his symptoms. By asking these people, "How did this come about?" you're giving them back what they ordinarily would say. So that they're not responsible, it just came about.

MRS. S.: But when they're saying it to me, they say, "It just came about." When I say to a person, "What's your idea about how it came about?" I'm already changing things by turning the statement into a question.

INT.: The fact that you're questioning the person about it implies that he's responsible to some extent, but the phrasing is such that he's not responsible. There's a double level there.

MRS. S.: I see what you mean.

INT.: It's very different from saying, "How could you let this happen?" or, "How did you bring this about?"

MRS. S.: I would avoid such a question. I pay special attention to the way I phrase my questions.

INT.: Can you give another example of that kind of question?

MRS. S.: All right. "As you think of it now, how do you suppose you got into that fix?" "As you think of it now"—that's the part that gives you freedom. If I just said, "Why did you let this happen?" that's a defense-producing question. If I preface it with, "As you think of it now," they can pick any point along the way to look back on whatever they did then. I'm always looking for that which makes it possible to create some distance from the self, so that the person can envision change. It's interesting how many of the responses to these questions are responses of "I see myself as a person who is responsible for what I do."

INT.: When you say, "As you think of it now," you're saying, implicitly, "Now that you're a responsible person who initiates what happens, how can you, as this person, see how you let such a thing get beyond your control?"

MRS. S.: That's exactly right. I want all my questions to have an escape hatch, but I also want to get across the idea that people tailor life for themselves.

INT.: You're leaving people no out. If they talk about how helpless they were at that time, they're still conceding responsibility from the point of view of the present. And if they say they were responsible at that time, they're taking the position that you'd like them to take anyway.

MRS. S.: But they come out with a feeling of ego-enhancement rather than assault.

INT.: I think what you mean by "ego-enhancement" is giving them some kind of freedom to take responsibility for what they do and to acknowledge their behavior openly.

MRS. S.: That's exactly right.

MRS. P.: I guess I'm just kind of weak.

MRS. S.: Well . . .

MRS. P.: I mean, I just, I just don't, I mean, I don't like it because I do think that it's too much, but I don't know what to do about it. She, she's a strong personality.

MRS. S.: What happens when you tell her no?

MRS. S.: Here she elaborates a little on this business of being weak and then says that the mother-in-law is really too much. So what I do is to reach way over here and take something functional and then pose it: "So what would happen if you said no?"

INT.: You don't say, "What *would*." You say, "What *does* happen?" You assume that she does say no.

MRS. S.: That phrasing marks over here the point we're aiming for. Then, instead of relating to how bad things are, she has to relate to why she can't stand up for herself.

INT.: You treat her as somebody who could, who does, tell her mother-in-law no. And you do another thing. You ally yourself with the mother against the mother-in-law. It's conceivable that you could take the other direction and say, "Perhaps you don't understand your mother-in-law well," or whatever.

MRS. S.: Those would be fighting words. I side with the mother, but in such a way that it doesn't turn out to be an alliance.

INT.: It's an odd form of alliance. At the same time, you're not exactly siding with the mother-in-law.

MRS. S.: This is what I would call siding with the interests of the healthy process. When I say, "What happens when you say no?" I am siding with a healthy process.

INT.: Thinking of alternatives, you could say, "Let's try to understand why your mother-in-law would get so involved." I take it you wouldn't do this either.

MRS. S.: That would be saying to them, "Look, you really are dopes, and you really are children." This is not the time for that. Later on I might put some such question: "As you think about it, how do you explain the fact that your mother is always dropping in?"

INT.: But at this point, with the information that you have, you simply assume that this is an intrusive mother-in-law and that the problem is to draw limits with her?

MRS. S.: Yes, and being able to say no in the interests of the self.

GARY: I, ah . . .

MRS. P.: I don't know as I've ever told her "No." I mean, she has told me, I mean, we had a real rousing battle once in her apartment, when we were first, when Gail was a baby. She told me never to step inside her door again. Maybe a lot of people never would have, but, of course, I have. (*Laughs.*)

MRS. S.: Why did you, as you think about it? Why did you step back?

MRS. P.: Because I couldn't take Henry's mother away from him, when it's all he had.

INT.: What did she mean by that? She was his wife, so how could his mother be all he had?

MRS. S.: My thought, as I listen to it now, is that since Henry's father died at such a young age, he has been perceived as a man without a father. And he was an only child. What she's also saying is, "I cannot stand my husband to be mad at me, and I see him valuing me to the degree that I don't make trouble between him and his mother." And she is saying, "I see my husband as somebody who cannot cope with his mother, so that I have to do the coping for him."

INT.: There's another less attractive side to the phrasing "it's all he had." There's an implication that if his mother weren't there, she'd have her husband entirely on her hands.

MRS. S.: I don't think that fits very well because he was practically never around. That's one of the reasons why she's always had his mother to entertain.

INT.: Yes, but this sounds a little like wives who encourage their husbands to have affairs because when they don't, they get all the attention of the husband.

MRS. S.: Well, perhaps.

MRS. S.: Well, let's find out from Henry whether he worried about that or not.

MR. P.: I wasn't worried about that, particularly. But, ah, of course she, she'd get very, ah, angry at situations like that, but, ah, she would always come back again. You know, come to visit.

MRS. P.: Well, she'd call up and ask if she could buy me a dress or something, which was ridiculous. I mean, I didn't want . . .

MRS. S.: That didn't fit her not liking you, did it?

MR. P.: Oh, I think she does, but, ah . . .

MRS. P.: You know, you can't *buy*—if just once she would be wholly loving, it would take away all of it. (*Starting to cry.*)

MRS. S.: I'm getting ready to do some fancy footwork here. I want to shake loose the idea in this family that people have to be victims. So I go into a real thing about how come this unloving woman would want to buy her daughter-in-law a dress.

MRS. S.: I wonder what—Gary I think has a comment that might be of help here.

GARY: I have been observing people, I think, of a certain type like Grannie. For instance, in *Anna Karenina*, reading this and reading a lot of books, that she has tried to be too loving. She has tried to be all-loving, and therefore stifled the rest of her emotions. She told me, I told h-, I told her once while she was rubbing my muscles that, oh, I had trouble communicating to Mother, and she said, "All it takes is love." And yet, if, if all we have is love, it stifles the rest of us. As Anna Karenina found out, she couldn't have the love of her lover all the time, and therefore, she committed suicide, on the train. But Grannie is trying to make this her god, so to speak, love, and it's all love, and so this is all she knows, and so she's become, for this reason, she's become narrow-minded. For instance, she comes over to our house. The only thing she can do is go in the garden and work, work, work.

Because this is the only way that she seems to be able to express her love.

MRS. S. (*to Mr. and Mrs. P.*): You know, maybe you haven't thought about it like this, but this has obviously been a big puzzle and a big source of heartache, because you can't be sure whether your mother-in-law loves you or whether she doesn't love you. She does loving things. She does things that look like they're unloving. And, how many years have you been married, now?

MRS. P.: Twenty-four.

MRS. S.: Twenty-four years. (*To Mr. P.*) It's still a big puzzle, and apparently you have seen the pain that this has brought to your wife and you can't figure it out either, because I think you see what Gary sees. There's a loving basis, but some of the behavior doesn't match, either.

MR. P.: Right.

MRS. S.: Now, I wonder about Gary's explanation, and I think he's given us something we can look at. And that is that your mother's attitude toward you is so completely focused on you that she hasn't thought about herself, and as such, it looks like she's smothering you all. Isn't that what you were talking about?

MRS. P.: Yes.

GARY: I, of course, I was giving you a general theory. If you want to . . .

MRS. S.: I was asking you for validation as you see it, now.

GARY: I would not say it's smothering. No. I would say an overconcern, or a—caused by her, probably from the very time she was born, trying to be all love, from some misdirection in the child (*inaudible phrase*). Yes. (*Inaudible phrase, stops, lowers voice.*) Approximately, yes.

MRS. S.: And so, what we're dealing with, then . . .

GARY: For instance, she tried, she wanted to come down and live with me this year. I mean, it's the same thing.

MRS. S.: Uh-huh. And how were you able to say no? 'Cause apparently you did what Father was never able to do.

INT.: Why would you at this point bring up the fact that Gary could do something Father couldn't do?

MRS. S.: I thought it was safe to begin to rub things a little bit. I've already put a cushion in for the father when I said that he had a way of handling his mother. Now I'm saying that Gary could do things differently from his father, but I'm trying to make it an individuation thing instead of a comment on who's better or best.

INT.: Were you trying to imply that Gary could do something different with his own mother, that is, say no to her, too?

MRS. S.: I wasn't thinking of it like that. Gary was again coming in as a peacemaker, but he was also trying to put something together for the mother. It was a gift, peace with a gift, but he couldn't present it clearly. I was hoping to objectify this whole situation a little.

INT.: Did you assume that the too loving accusations were a comment on his relationship with his own mother, on the way his mother was dealing with him by being too loving?

MRS. S.: Oh, yes, the way the mother dealt with Gary, the way the mother dealt with the father, the way the father's mother dealt with him, and the way people insist on calling this loving when they're actually killing each other. This smothering.

> GARY: I never did say no, but I went down to look at things, and I sort of lived day by day, and then I said, "Well, I'll see if I can find a place in [*dormitory*]." And one guy dropped out and it just seemed to work and I was able to get into [*dormitory*].
>
> MRS. S.: Well, now, what you're saying is you did not . . .
>
> GARY: It was just luck, let's put it, that I . . .
>
> MRS. S.: . . . you did not want, then, or feel that it would be fitting or even gratifying for your grandmother to be living with you.
>
> GARY: In some ways, perhaps I thought that I could help her, or she could help me, or both. In other things, I really want to be with my friends.
>
> MRS. S.: Well, naturally.
>
> GARY: So I really did want to go to [*dormitory*].
>
> MRS. S.: But the dilemma for you . . .
>
> GARY: At least, consciously . . .
>
> MRS. S.: . . . but the dilemma for you was how to say no to Grandmother without hurting her feelings.
>
> GARY: And as it turned out, just lucky.
>
> MRS. S.: And so the situation managed.

INT.: Why does he say he was just lucky?

MRS. S.: Because that's how it happened. It's a very interesting sequence. His grandmother asked to live with him, but it didn't turn out that way. So I interpreted for him that he was able to say no. But in this context he can't get the credit for saying no, because it doesn't fit the situation. If he puts it as a series of circumstances, as luck or an accident, it's okay.

INT.: Actually, this wasn't luck. It was luck that a room appeared, but he went down to the dorm to see if he could get a room there, and a boy happened to be leaving.

MRS. S.: The luck came in that another circumstance appeared.

INT.: You have a nice phrasing for it: "And so the situation managed." All by itself.

MRS. S.: If I push him too far in this, he'll have to be crazy again, because we haven't done enough preparation yet. I have to go carefully.

MRS. S. (*to Mrs. P.*): Now for you, you—sometimes I guess you can manage this way, but you don't want to say no either because you'll hurt her feelings.

MRS. P.: That's it.

GARY: And sometimes we're lucky and sometimes we're not.

MRS. P.: Yes, well, sometimes she comes in and she starts in. She just takes over.

GARY: That's true.

MRS. P.: Well, then, where's my place?

MRS. S.: And you've always felt you had to let this happen? That if you said no, Grandmother would be hurt.

MRS. P.: Yes. Yes.

GARY: And I have had a dilemma, which side to pick. Should I take my mother's side or my grandmother's side? And I've sort of been waiting and waiting.

MRS. S.: Is there a side? Is this a matter of sides at all?

GARY: I think it is.

MRS. P.: (*Inaudible phrase.*)

GARY: Well, I—at least I have to see things clearer than I did as a baby. At least this is something. At least I have to see, ah, see an ace as an ace, so to speak.

MRS. S.: As we near the end of the interview, he's becoming clearer about his dilemma. Whose side should he take, Father's side or Mother's side? At this point, Grandmother and Father are symbolically about the same. He's taken another step.

INT.: What are you aiming for when you talk about sides?

MRS. S.: I'm saying, "It's not a matter of sides when you consider your own interests." That's what I'm aiming for. You don't have to decide on whose side the power lies. It has to be done in terms of what fits you.

INT.: You're looking for an individual decision rather than a coalition decision?

MRS. S.: That's a good way to put it. If somebody who is involved in something that refers only to him has to make a decision as if it concerned other people, this is going to reinforce his feeling that he can't take charge of himself. He has to continue to be victimized by somebody else. Your "coalition decision" is a good word for that.

MRS. S.: Who's the mother in the household? Your household.

GARY: Of course. My mother.

MRS. S.: Yes. All right. All right. And Grandmother is Grandmother. She's not Mother.

GARY: Yes. That should be—the Bible says there's a place, you know, there's places for everything.

MRS. S.: Now, we'll come back to you. Because apparently (*to Mr. P.*) you too have been caught in this thing, that to say no to Grandmother would hurt her feelings, to your mother.

MR. P.: That's right.

MRS. S.: Well, how have you tried to handle it? We've got one idea that Gary has used sometimes. And we know that Mother hasn't been able to do this, so she lets these things happen. Now, what have you tried to do to say no?

MR. P.: Well, sometimes, just saying no, ah, ah, but ah, that is, I'll do that, in the case where it means anything as far as the family is concerned. Ah . . .

MRS. S.: Did you know anything about Grandmother wanting to live with Gary, for instance? In school?

MR. P.: Yes. Well that, ah, is, was a question of approval or nonapproval. I mean, that we really didn't, ah, didn't, ah, have too much opinion on that, as far as what was best to do. Because Gary had spent quite a bit of time in the hospital here, and, ah, and had had this, ah, breakdown, and so we thought maybe it would be helpful for him, in that case, now. (*Mrs. P. and Gary talking in background.*)

MRS. S.: Wait. I got caught in crosscurrents. Gary and Mother are talking, and this young man (*Tim is making a noise*) is being like a little mouse (*laughing*) and Dad is trying to answer. Now look, what I asked about Dad's being able to say no to Grandmother, his mother. And then we posed the question about what did he do when Grandmother wanted to live with you, and it was obvious that you didn't want her to and it wasn't fitting. And you were just commenting?

MR. P.: And, ahhh, there are times when, ah, I just sort of let time lapse to see if, ah, how it works out, so I, ah, without trying to create a situation.

MRS. S. (*interrupting Gary, who tries to speak*): Just a minute. (*To Mr. P.*) Till time, if you can let time go by, maybe things will work out, and Gary has suggested that if maybe you get a lucky break of some kind . . .

GARY: I said I was lucky.

MRS. S.: Well, all right; if you are lucky. Whatever. A lucky break or something. You couldn't fall back on these two things.

GARY: I, I get an awful feeling when Grannie comes to visit me as if there wasn't anything there. I mean, because she is all love, I guess she stifles the rest of her emotions.

MRS. S.: You know, Gary, if your mother and father could really understand, and I'm going to try to help them, because you're saying something very important, and that is that she is not the kind of strong person that she appears to be. That actually she wants so much to be loved, and this is what you feel. (*Mr. P., Mrs. P., and Gary all talk together for a few seconds.*)

INT.: What you say there isn't what Gary said at all. You could derive it from what he said.

MRS. S.: That's what I did. I derived it, so that I could make my point. Because he's been trying to make pleas. Remember when he said further back that when Grandmother comes, she works in the garden, work, work, work?

INT.: He does make her sound pretty sad.

MRS. S.: That's right, and yet she's perceived by the family as a victimizer. I'm trying to cut through this. One of the problems here is that the wife can't see herself as acceptable in the eyes of her mother-in-law. This is really saying that she doesn't see herself as acceptable at all. The mother-in-law is a vehicle by which this comes about. If everybody in the family sees the grandmother as a victimizer or as somebody who inhibits them, they will all experience low self-esteem, and they will have to form all kinds of coalitions to outwit the grandmother.

Gary is now intimating that the grandmother is pleading for some kind of acceptance herself. I'm going to use Gary's perception to try to take the situation out of the ego-assaultive framing the wife puts it in, and put it in a framing which will allow her to cope differently. It was quite interesting; after this interview the wife made some changes concerning the mother-in-law's visits, and those changes stuck. She told the mother-in-law very quietly that she would like to have her call before she came over.

INT.: When you make this shift, it is partly that it will be harder for you to get the family to stand up to the mother-in-law if you go along with the idea that she's a victimizer?

MRS. S.: If I continue to behave toward her as though she's a victimizer, I'm telling these people that they are victims and I'm not helping them much. It's like people who come in and complain what poor teachers their children have. If I say, "Yes, you're right, that teacher is a victimizer," then I am cutting off avenues for these people to grow.

INT.: Part of the shift is to define the grandmother as a victim herself.

MRS. S.: Sure. I think a lot of therapists forget that if they make a change over here, they're automatically producing a change over there.

INT.: Were you looking for an opportunity to make this shift and so decided to pick something from what Gary said, or did his speech decide you to do it?

MRS. S.: I was looking for an opportunity to do it. I knew that was the way I wanted to end the interview.

INT.: This strains a little, as if you were reaching.

MRS. S.: I was looking for it, yes. I was consciously thinking of a way I could reduce this victim-victimizer situation. I thought that this would be helpful in getting Gary off the hook.

GARY: (*Inaudible phrase*) we're getting closer to her now.

MRS. P.: You see, she was so young when her husband died.

MRS. S.: How old was she?

MRS. P.: She was only forty, ah, oh, forty-two, I guess. I think she was eight years younger, but she was, well, she has a marvelous talent for nursing. She's wonderful when anyone's sick. I mean, this is when she's the best. When I get sick, oh, then she is just marvelous. Had she gone ahead and taken up nursing and had

some life of her own, but she didn't, she didn't do a thing. So she
has no life, except ours.

MRS. S.: Let me pose something to you. Here is a woman who you
speak about in superlatives about her ability. You've been talking
about her in one way as though she were such a strong person
she could dominate everybody else, and you also have a feeling
she's so weak that if you say no, she will fall over. Are any of
these things true? Or is— (*Mr. P. interrupts.*)

INT.: When you ask, "Are any of these things true?" what are
you after?

MRS. S.: One of the things I'm after is to point up the discrepan-
cies. I'm putting the question in terms the people use, as though I'm
accepting that the mother-in-law could really be all of these contradictory things, but by saying, "*Is* she any of these things?" I pin them
down.

MR. P.: Well, not weak, she gets very angry if, ah . . .

MRS. P.: She would get angry. If we ever said no—this is the thing,
if we said no, she would be so angry she'd probably . . .

MRS. S.: And who would drop dead?

GARY: Anger is often . . .

MRS. S. (*overlapping*): Who would drop dead?

GARY: . . . from fear.

MRS. S.: Who would drop dead if Grandmother got angry? (*Pause.*)

MRS. P.: Nobody. And she would lose so much because she wouldn't
come around and she wouldn't even see the children.

INT.: Do you have a term for this "Who would drop dead" technique?

MRS. S.: I use it rather frequently to try to show that the thing
that has been labeled with survival significance is purely a delusion. So
I go back to the literal survival effect, which is dropping dead. I try to
divest the victim-victimizer situation of survival significance by pointing
out the reality, which is, "How close are you to literal death?"

INT.: You take what they imply and carry it to its logical extreme.

MRS. S.: I do this frequently. I have another question that goes
like this: "Did you ever see the cause of death on a death certificate
that you said no to somebody? I've never seen that."

MRS. S.: Ah, wait. I want to tell you something. Didn't she say, "You never darken my door again"? So what happened when you darkened it? She said, "I'll buy you a dress," maybe, hm?

MRS. P.: Yes. Yes.

MRS. S.: That doesn't sound like it fits, does it?

MRS. P.: No. No.

MRS. S.: Doesn't sound like it at all, does it?

MRS. P.: Actually, I think you have hit on something, here. Because I do think the few times that I have kind of, you know, reared up, that she would back down. I think maybe she recognizes strength. Maybe that's it.

MRS. S.: You know, after a while it won't even be that you have to be so strong to overcome somebody, or you have to go and pick them up. What's the reality? Here is a family in which you're the mother, you're the father, you're the wife, you're the husband. These four are your children. How come Grandma has something to say about the lives of other people?

INT.: You're labelling each one's function here, but the gist of what you're saying is, "How is it that some other woman has something to say about your life?" Yet you, as another woman, are saying that. It must put the family in a curious position.

MRS. S.: I'm not the grandmother, that's what saves it.

INT.: You've phrased it as, "How come Grandma has something to say about the lives of other people," not "the lives of her family." It's almost a paradox, because it implies, "You shouldn't let yourself be influenced by an outsider like me."

MRS. S.: That's no different than my telling people that each one must take charge of himself. I'll say, "Who goes to the toilet for you?" —things like that.

MRS. P.: But how, how do you make her realize that maybe three or four times a week is more than e-enough? I mean, she c- (*sighs*).

MRS. S.: Well, you can see that . . .

GARY: I haven't seen the problem because I've been at school so much. I've never really seen Mother's pain. I haven't really seen the (*inaudible phrase*). I've sort of, what I've done is shut my eyes towards it.

MRS. P.: Eight-fifteen. I mean, a lot of times I have something else planned. But there she is at eleven o'clock in the morning.

MRS. S.: Well, I can't—and as you probably recognize, we don't have any ready-made solutions—but this I can tell you. That is, that right at the outset, the two of you, certainly as far as your mother is concerned, felt in some way at a disadvantage. You wanted her to like you. You wanted her to bless this thing which was so much love between you. And it didn't happen, and I think, as Gary suggested, not because she didn't love, but because she was scared and naïve and didn't know. And so, you've felt always at a disadvantage ever since.

MRS. P.: Yes (*inaudible phrase*) guilty.

GARY: I feel, the one reason, I had some reason. I didn't know what, but I wanted her down there. I think the reason I wanted her down there is that she would be away from our family, and the family could be itself. I think if there were, there was some urge that wanted her to be down there, there was some urge that wanted her not to be down there, this was the, in my subconscious that I wanted to help the family by pulling her away.

MRS. S.: If you had Grandmother with you, then she wouldn't be bothering Mother and Dad. She'd be, you'd have the pain of it.

GARY: I didn't think of this consciously.

MRS. S.: No, it just came out today.

GARY: Yes, that's right. I think, maybe.

MRS. S.: I think you have a point. And what I want to say is that nobody has to be a victim of Grandmother, because I think Grandmother is somebody who's got a great deal, and I think outside people would be very surprised to hear Grandmother spoken of in this kind of way. So this means that all of you have somehow, without meaning to, gotten into some kind of a delusion with her, that can be taken care of very nicely when we work it all out. And you (*to Gary*) won't have to be the rescue man.

INT.: Why did you keep talking about the grandmother at this point?

MRS. S.: Because in talking in this way about the grandmother, I'm giving a message to the other people that they've got something to offer. I am saying that when they understand all they have to offer, they won't have to feel like victims.

INT.: It's going pretty far to say that all of them have a delusion about her. Is this again trying to spread the symptoms around the family, rather than pin them on the patient?

MRS. S.: Oh, yes.

INT.: Why do you say, "An outside person would be surprised to hear Grandmother spoken of like this"? Do you tend to bring in the idea of what the outside world will think?

MRS. S.: Not very often. It fitted nicely here, because I wanted to make the point that the family saw her in a way that might be different from the way others on the outside would see her, where she wouldn't be in the same system with them. Someone outside the system can have a different experience with the person. It's a matter of shifting the perspective.

MRS. P.: She gets so mad at us.

MRS. S.: That's all right.

GARY: We've got to be subtle. Now, especially.

MRS. P.: I know, but even when eating and she tries to force you to eat, you just have to say no.

MRS. S.: You know what you do then? "Thank you, Grandmother, for thinking about me." And go right on eating what you yourself want to eat. And Grandmother will feel valued, and she will not control you.

INT.: A few minutes ago you told them you had no ready-made solutions, and yet here you give them a solution. Do you think the mother-in-law is so demanding that they need practical advice at this point?

MRS. S.: Yes. I'm giving the mother an illustration of how it can be done. Sometimes I do that, sometimes I don't. It depends on how great the demands are and whether the people have something to work on. You notice I don't tell them what to do, I give them an illustration of how it could be done. In a sense, that's being a model.

INT.: Is this something you tend to do toward the end of a session?

MRS. S.: Toward the end of the session I might ask, "What has this all meant to you, what did you learn?" or I might say, "Where do we go from here?" or I might say, "During the next week it seems to me you ought to get some evidence of thus and so," or I might prescribe a symptom. There are all kinds of things I might do.

INT.: What do you mean, prescribe a symptom?

MRS. S.: You can prescribe a symptom in one of two ways. One is to ask them to do explicitly what they've been doing implicitly. Let's say the man is accusing the woman of nagging, and the woman is denying it, and the woman is accusing the man of being passive and not talking to her. I then give them directions that make them do the same things on purpose. Or I might reverse the role. One time I had a woman who was complaining about her husband spending too much money and he was complaining about her being stingy, so in this instance I asked them to reverse their procedures. She wasn't to have a single thing to do with the money and he was to take care of all of it. Sometimes I will do a little teaching. For instance, if I have people who don't listen to one another, I'll tell them there are two ways to make sure somebody hears you. One is to be sure you have his eyes in your focus, and the other is to touch him and then ask, "Are you feeling the touch?" To get them used to a new way of asking for attention. Or we might come up with a whole new aspect, vague, about one part of the mother's life, or something like that, so I ask if they have some old albums around, or obituaries, to try to get the facts together. This is of value in terms of the facts per se, but it also says you can find out, you don't have to have a cover on any of this stuff. There is no dangerous information.

> GARY: What I say is usually, "No, thank you, *please*." And then she gives me more. But I have been insistent. I have tried to be insistent 'cause I do want to be a good runner, and if you eat too much of the wrong thing, you're not a good runner.

MRS. S.: You notice this reference to being a runner. Gary spent some time in the hospital after his second breakdown, which occurred early in treatment, but when he came out he went back to college and finished the year very well. The main thing was that he wanted to be an Olympic runner. So this little, skinny boy got himself ready for the Olympic tryouts, literally made his meek little body into Olympic material. He won third place in a college cross-country track meet and got a medal for it. But it was such a terrible idea to the family that he wasn't going to go and be a professor that they put a damper on the whole thing. They said, "What do you want to be a runner for? You're going to be a teacher," implying, "My God, how can you have such low aspirations?" And of course, just before the Olympic tryouts, he had another breakdown. I had been forced to discontinue the case before therapy was completed, and I wasn't seeing the family at the time, but I heard that he carried the medal around with him in the hospital. A gold and gray medal. He brought it out in front of everybody, mother and father too. I tried to make arrangements for the family to see another therapist, but that wasn't successful and they dropped out of treatment altogether. The girls did well. Lois blossomed at school and won a scholarship to go round the world, and Gail moved out, got an apartment and a job. So there were some things I felt pleased about.

MRS. S.: Yes. Well, now we have to stop at this point, and we'll meet again next week, and I think we will make great progress.

GARY: Perhaps. (*Mr. P., Mrs. P., and Gary all talk at once.*)

MRS. S.: And I want you all to know it was a pleasure. Father. Lois. Mother.

MRS. P.: Thank you so much.

MRS. S.: Tim. I've got the wrong hand, haven't I? This is not the right hand.

GARY: (*Inaudible phrase.*) It's good enough.

MRS. S.: It's nice to see you. Gary, a pleasure. (*All talk at once.*) Goodbye. (*Noise of people leaving, tape recording ends.*)

INT.: Do you name each one to emphasize your relationship with him, or to identify each one as separate?

MRS. S.: I think names are the most direct way of giving a message of individuation.

INT.: Why do you say it was all a pleasure?

MRS. S.: Because it was. I enjoyed the treatment. I wouldn't say it if I hadn't enjoyed it. Sometimes I'll say, "It was pretty sticky today. *I* thought it was pretty sticky."

INT.: You try to end with something personal.

MRS. S.: Well, I feel that none of these families have ever had somebody else in their environment giving out clear reports about them. So I do as much of that as I can. For instance, I have a perforated eardrum, and I've been wearing a paper eardrum. Sometimes the paper eardrum slips and that sets up a disequilibrium in my head. I'll go into a treatment hour and I'll say, "You know, if you see me like this, it's because my paper eardrum slipped and this causes me certain problems in listening. If I ask you to repeat, it may be because you're not talking loud enough, we'll find that out, but it could also be because of this defect I have." That already says you can talk and be clear about anything. It also says that people's behavior need not be related to expectations about whether they are acceptable, lovable, sick, bad, stupid, or crazy. So I do that kind of thing too.

INT.: With a paper eardrum!

MRS. S.: With a paper eardrum.

3]

The Eternal Triangle

An interview with Don D. Jackson, M.D.

INT.: What did you know about the Starbucks when they came in to see you?

DR. J.: I knew they had an eighteen-year-old daughter, Sue, who had a psychotic breakdown while she was away at college. I was on an extended visit to the city where the family lived. The college psychiatrist, whom I didn't know personally, telephoned me, and said that he had learned that I was going to be in that city for a while, and asked if I would consider taking the girl on. He had her on the acute ward and she was suffering from paranoid delusions, was hallucinating, and so forth, but he felt that she was calm enough to be sent home. When she arrived, I arranged to have her put on an open ward in a hospital and went to see her. She was still acting pretty far out, rolling her eyes and telling me confidentially about a servant she thought had raped her. I spoke to her parents on the phone and set up an appointment for all three of them. This is the session we're going to talk about here.

INT.: Was Sue their only child?

DR. J.: They had three other children: Peter, seventeen; Charles, fifteen; and Laura, thirteen. I didn't see any of them at first.

INT.: What were the parents like?

DR. J.: They were wealthy, upper-class people, both in their forties. The father was a businessman. He was the one with the obvious charm, but there was something pompous and pseudo-executive

Don D. Jackson, M.D., is Director of the Mental Research Institute, Palo Alto, California. He has published many articles on family research and therapy, is the editor of *The Etiology of Schizophrenia* (1960), author of *Myths of Madness* (1964), and co-author of *Pragmatics of Communication* (1967).

about his manner. The mother was a fading beauty in cashmere and pearls. She'd been worn away by a life of psychosomatic illnesses, and you had the constant impression that she had just taken two aspirins and was tolerating you from her bed of pain.

INT.: Did the parents know that you were planning to include them in therapy?

DR. J.: No, and when I spoke to them on the phone I deliberately left it vague, because they had a reputation to uphold. I suspected that the last thing they would want in that city was to be identified with psychiatric treatment of any kind. As the tape recording begins, you'll see how cautiously I had to proceed.

Initial interview with the Starbuck family

DR. J. (*to Sue*): Ah, I think you better sit down and let me bring up the ground rules first . . .

SUE: Okay. (*Laughs.*)

DR. J.: You'll notice that I make that kind of remark to Sue throughout the interview. What I am doing initially is to say to her, "Don't make a fool of yourself, because we'll lose the ball game if you do." All the parents would need is for her to misbehave, and they'd both jump on her and we wouldn't get anywhere. So I immediately focused on her by telling her to behave. I always do this with disturbed schizophrenics because they can keep themselves so worked up in a pointless sort of way.

DR. J.: And then, ah, in the first place I'm seeing you—have a chair—deliberately, ah, in this room, because whenever I can I like to record family sessions. Now if it makes you nervous, we'll dispense with it.

SUE: Not me. (*Laughs.*)

DR. J.: The reason is that, ah, when you have three people, and a therapist, things are said that, ah, don't become clear until I hear the tape myself . . .

MR. S. (*overlapping*): Slowly.

DR. J.: . . . in the interim, and also there are sometimes questions about who said what which we can, ah, settle by actually playing it back.

INT.: Why did you make that remark about playing back the tape?

DR. J.: This is partly to tell the identified patient, "I'm not necessarily going to believe what's said against you. If your parents don't understand you and vice versa, it may not be just your fault." I'm also trying to put them all on an equal level, which is not done by saying, "You all have problems," but by saying, "It's all so very complicated that we have to have a tape and look into it again and then we can be objective."

INT.: You suggest that you're not up to understanding matters without a leisurely listening any more than anyone else.

DR. J.: Yes. It makes me equal too.

DR. J.: I think it's, it's a useful thing. It saves a lot of needless, ah, kind of bickering . . .

SUE: (*Sighs.*)

DR. J.: . . . that can go on. But the other is the more important, that I, ah, myself have to listen to it.

INT.: Was that a way to engineer a conversation that wouldn't be just bickering?

DR. J.: No. This is something I wouldn't usually say, and I'm surprised that I did say it, because I don't like to make people aware that we might trap them with their own recordings. The feel I got of the family over the phone must have given me the idea that the daughter was going to be accused of things that weren't so. That there was confusion. Ordinarily I wouldn't point out future difficulties.

MRS. S.: We're used to a tape recorder. [*family friend's*] younger brother has one.

DR. J.: Good.

SUE (*overlapping*): Gosh, I don't care, it doesn't bother me. I can say it whether it's being recorded or not.

INT.: Did that give you the idea that Sue had something she was ready to come out with?

DR. J.: Yes. I was already becoming uneasy that she was going to lay some bomb on the table. I thought that it might literally be incest, and I wasn't too far wrong. One of her delusions was that she had been raped by a servant while her mother stood by, giving him advice of a mechanical nature. There was an actual incident, when she was twelve or thirteen, when a servant did feel her up or was just kidding her, but it was nothing much. The delusion was really based on the involvement she had with her father. It came out in a later interview that he was in the habit of walking about nude with the bedroom door open. She complained, she said it was very provocative, which embarrassed him very much. Also, she used to climb into bed between her parents on weekend mornings, even when she was in junior high school. When they locked her out, she'd go round and climb in through the window. I didn't know any of this yet, but something about her manner gave me the feel of Joe McCarthy with the 202 names in his briefcase. I was afraid she was going to blow the thing open before I could get started.

> MR. S.: It would pay, I would think, to have one of us talk at a time if you expect to be able to read it back on the tape recorder, so let's not two of us try to talk at once.
>
> DR. J.: Ah, the reason I wanted to get together with you is that although Sue has a therapist of her own, ah, and although she's getting of an age where she'll be, ah, moving on in the world, there are certain, ah, family considerations that still come up, ah, for example, there's what to do with her in the next few months, for example . . .
>
> SUE: Well, I have some ideas of my own. (*Laughs.*)
>
> DR. J.: That's right, but these also involve your parents.
>
> SUE: Oh, necessarily they do, I understand that.

INT.: I was wondering why you let that statement of the father's go.

DR. J.: I'll let a lot go in the early sessions if I think it's not leading to disaster. I think that these patterns are redundant and are going to be repeated, so I'm not worried about missing anything. It's not the old analytic idea of attending to every word with "evenly hovering attention." What I am concerned about is that somebody will be so humiliated that they'll withdraw, or that there will be violence of some kind that will break up the group, or that somebody will be made such a fool of by a coalition of the other two that the sides will be drawn up and it will be impossible to break them down. That kind of thing I will interfere with, even in the first interview.

INT.: You weren't worried that the father was coming in as president of his company?

DR. J.: I couldn't care less. I'm learning something about him, you see. I don't know him well enough to say, "Oh, come on now."

INT.: Did you have a reason for Sue's having a therapist of her own, as well as coming into family therapy?

DR. J.: I've found that most youngsters this age, since they are half in the house and half out of it, like to have a private therapist who sees nothing of the family. They feel as if that's the part of them that is leaving home. Otherwise they take family therapy to mean that they are being kept as a child. This girl, later on, would complain bitterly to her therapist about certain things I did. She had the feeling that with me she was being treated like the daughter, when she was about to become a young lady.

INT.: What did you mean when you spoke of "family considerations"?

DR. J.: I assumed that Sue's breaking down while she was away at school so that she had to come back to the family had to do with unresolved family business, though I didn't want to lead her to think that this was the only thing that was important. Later, when she started to go steady with a boy and got engaged and finally married him, there was a lot of friction. It showed that the family really needed her as a scapegoat.

INT.: There's quite an edge in your voice when you're talking to Sue. I gather you're still keeping her in line.

DR. J.: Right. This is where the nonverbal factor comes in; you have to have a picture of her. She was a very cute, very attractive girl, but malicious-looking with flashing black eyes and a little grin as if she was about to say, "Ask me, kid, I've got something to tell you." So I'm saying, "You're still a daughter." But you notice how she backs right down. I think this is what gives you confidence. It's not that you've intimidated her, the point is that you've got a little cooperation game going. If she had said at that moment something like, "What's that sound?" you would get an entirely different interview.

INT.: How did you get her cooperation?

DR. J.: I just looked at her as if to say, "We're going to play this game now," and she was willing to go along with it. Why, I'll never know.

DR. J.: Ah, and there's the question if she should live at home, ah, of how people are going to, ah, interact with each other. Ah, there are certain past issues which are still very much in her mind, and, ah, so that I think that, that there's a real reason for these meetings. Now what I would suggest is that if we get through this one with any kind of, ah, progress, ah, and this is shared, that we then plan to have some other get-togethers after you get back [*from a planned trip*], ah, on a kind of *ad hoc* basis . . .

SUE: Mm-hm.

DR. J.: . . . from time to time, ah . . .

SUE: Well, that's . . .

DR. J.: . . . because I don't think all the family problems can be settled by having individual therapists. Ah, when I say family problems, I mean things like (*pause*) decisions.

INT.: I gather this is an attempt to commit them to coming in again. You say, "If we have progress," but you imply, "No matter what."

DR. J.: What I would do now is probably be more flip about that and say, "If we all leave the room alive." I'd make it as bad as possible so that they would be tempted to fight me by not having it be that bad.

INT.: That's an odd phrasing: "family problems, I mean things like decisions." A problem isn't the same as a decision. It's a little deceptive, as if you wanted to make it seem that family therapy wasn't going to uncover too many skeletons.

DR. J.: I can't explain why I put it that way. All I can say is that this may have been part of a general attempt to seduce the parents and not frighten them. I don't think that at this point they thought they had anything to do with Sue's illness, although later on they each thought that the other one had a great deal to do with it.

INT.: What is your rule for bringing the whole family in? Do you always start by seeing just the identified patient and the two parents, or do you sometimes have everybody come in?

DR. J.: I don't think there should be any rule about this and I might have done a little differently here. But with a girl who is this sick, something active has to be done. If she didn't stay in the hospital, there would have been a very serious problem about where to put her. Then there was the possibility that she might get shock treatment. I think the siblings are apt to be on the side of the parents against the patient, and I'm usually not prepared to deal with them right away, especially in a case like this. If it's more obviously a family difficulty of some kind, like a marital problem where children are involved, sure. I think it depends on the therapist. It would have slowed me down to have three more youngsters in there. I thought I had enough to do with just the mother.

INT.: Did you see the other children later?

DR. J.: Yes. In the beginning, the two boys were away at school, but I included the little sister in some of the meetings. Then Sue improved so much, started to live away from home and so forth, that it turned into marital therapy and I just saw the parents. Sue is married and doing quite well now. The younger sister got pregnant at the age of fourteen or fifteen, and I worked with her individually and she pulled out of it well. Then I took on the older boy, who was floundering around at college, no serious symptoms, but confused. I felt like a paperhanger with bad glue, running around, never organized the way I would have liked to be.

INT.: Do you think you could have avoided this if you had seen them all together from the start?

DR. J.: I don't know. It was an unusual circumstance. All these children were growing up and getting to the point of leaving home. If you see the whole family as a unit, there may be some benefits, but it gets the kids reinvolved. I think you have to play it by ear.

SUE: Yeah. Well, I'm, right here I think we have an eternal triangle.

DR. J.: Mmm.

SUE: And I think maybe we're seated wrong for it, but I think it's, very much, there.

DR. J.: Mm-hm.

SUE (to parents): I don't know whether the two of you understand what I'm talking about.

INT.: What was your private reaction when she used that phrase "eternal triangle"?

DR. J.: It made a tremendous impression on me. I've used it a number of times in talking to groups. I often am impressed with the apt remarks that schizophrenics come out with.

INT.: You say "Mmm" in such an uncertain way there.

DR. J.: I think Sue's remark delighted me, but it also made me nervous, because I thought this might be the bomb I'd been expecting. So this is a mixed reaction of, "Is it—or not?"

INT.: Do you often get an identified patient who says right out, "It's not me, it's all of us?"

DR. J.: Yes, but she doesn't mean that at all. This is a one-shot kind of ploy that has no substance. I had a patient, a schizophrenic girl, who came bouncing in and said, "Mother had to get married, so I'm here," which encapsuled a whole history I won't go into, including the obvious. But this didn't mean that she could stand up to her mother or that she really understood her problems.

INT.: Sue uses the remark to implicate her parents rather than herself.

DR. J.: That's my impression. But why she said that about the seating, I don't yet understand.

INT.: What was the seating?

DR. J.: She was between her mother and father and I was across from her. This has always puzzled me, because the way she saw the triangle, she should not have been sitting between her parents. She apparently didn't think of herself as mediating between them, the way the child with the problem usually does.

INT.: She says later to her father, "You're torn between Mother and me." Perhaps she was thinking her father should have been in the middle.

DR. J.: That must be it. In one of the later interviews, he banged the table, red in the face, and said to the women, "I'm sick and tired of the two of you dragging me into this." He was always being called into their fights as a mediator.

INT.: Then it wasn't an oedipal triangle.

DR. J.: It all depends which side you stand it on. The parents were very distant with each other, and they needed the girl as a cross monitor. In that sense she was in the middle, though she wasn't seeing it that way.

MR. S.: Is that a problem according to the ground rules that you're ready to discuss now?

DR. J.: I made my speech, ah, so now I'm, ah . . .

MRS. S.: Well, what are the ground rules?

SUE (*simultaneously*): Well, do you want me to bring up my medical considerations before we go on?

DR. J. (*to Mrs. S.*): Hmm?

MRS. S.: The ground rules just as, ah . . .

DR. J.: Oh, I wanted to point out that the ground rules are I do like to record, although I take responsibility for this, for the anonymity of the material, and that, ah, secondly, that I did want to introduce early the notion that we'd, we would meet again, because, ah . . .

MRS. S.: I'm agreeable.

SUE: Sure, so am I.

DR. J.: I do think that, that there are some things to be done, it's not simply a case of Sue having had some difficulty and then, let's get her patched up, but there's going to be . . .

SUE: Uh-huh. This *is* my difficulty, Dr. Jackson.

DR. J.: Which?

SUE: This, right here, these three.

DR. J.: Mm-hm.

MR. S.: The, the lack of conversation, or just these three people?

SUE: Conversation, yeah, but communication has been cut off for various reasons, and I don't think I'm entirely to blame for it.

DR. J.: Mm-hm.

INT.: At the beginning of this part, Sue tried to bring up her medical problems. Were you trying to bypass that?

DR. J.: My reaction here was that Sue made her parents nervous by acting as if she was about to come out with something. I thought then that it was more specific than it turned out to be. She had a propensity for making them nervous anyway, because they never knew what she was going to do or say next. Both the father and the mother are saying, "What is there in the ground rules to stop Sue from speaking out?" I'm about to let her, and then it occurs to me that for ethical, not legal, reasons, I have to tell them that I intended to record and use this material. I felt we were going to get into something they wouldn't want publicized, and I wanted to make it clear that I would take responsibility for not spreading it around the community with their names on it. I should have mentioned it earlier. But the mother and I are both reacting to the tone, the maliciousness, of the way Sue says, "Should I bring up my medical problems?"

INT.: By saying it, though, she is making herself the scapegoat and taking the focus off the family.

DR. J.: All I can say is that you don't know Sue. Her medical problems could turn out to be quite provocative. I thought she might say, "How come my hymen's perforated?"—some "medical problem" like that. It turned out that she was talking about a bona fide hospital-type question, but I couldn't know that beforehand.

INT.: This is the second time you've referred to the ground rules. Here, by putting "meeting together as a family" in the rules, you take something you're not sure the parents will agree to at all, and present it as if they had no option.

DR. J.: Yes, I'm putting pressure on them, but I had to proceed very carefully. I knew that the parents were upper-class people and they indicated on a number of occasions a fear of some kind of leak. I didn't know at that point how bad a marriage they had. Naturally, they didn't want any more strain.

INT.: There's another thing about these rules. You bring them up at the start of the session and then don't specify what you mean except to say that you're going to record and that you want them all to come in together. Are you using ground rules in an idiosyncratic way, or are you just being ambiguous?

DR. J.: I'm being ambiguous. I'm warning them that this kind of therapy is different and I'm spelling out some of the things that make it different, microphones and so on. If they have some questions about how it's different, the very way they ask and what they ask will tell me something.

INT.: Yes, but ordinarily, if someone lays down the ground rules, you might expect him to say that the first rule is that everybody can say whatever comes into his mind; the second, that certain things won't be talked about; and so forth. All you say is, "I'm recording, and we're going to meet again."

DR. J.: With a healthier family, let's say with an "underachiever" family, or with one in which it looks as if a lot could happen in a relatively short time, I might structure certain things as specifically as I could, to try to save time. With a family like this, since I don't know if the parents will come back, or if the girl won't go so crazy that she will have to be locked up and won't be able to come to the sessions, I'm not sure that ambiguity isn't a good thing.

INT.: I take it that you would prefer to be fairly unstructured with this kind of a family.

DR. J.: I think so. This family was extremely rigid; they only appear unstructured.

INT.: Could you give an example of a family with whom you would be specific about the ground rules?

DR. J.: With couples with symmetrical difficulties, where each is trying to match the other tit for tat, I'll say, "Now one of the ground rules is that we won't refer to anything in the past. We'll meet once a week and let's agree that we won't go any further back than that." I'll get that specific because they waste so much time saying, "Well, you remember in 1923 when you . . ." With this family, I have a feeling that if I said to the mother, "One of the ground rules is that the mother will have to say whatever comes to her mind," she would say to me, "Are you implying that I am dishonest? I'm just trying to help Sue." It would be misinterpreted.

INT.: When the father calls you on these ground rules and asks whether or not the daughter's remark comes under them, you don't say yes or no, you just say, "I made my speech." Why don't you answer his question?

DR. J.: Because I don't think it really is a question. He's talking to me but he's really asking whether he should answer his daughter's statement. I'm telling him, "Go ahead, deal with your daughter."

INT.: He is a proper organization man, trying to find the framework for what sort of a conversation this is supposed to be.

DR. J.: I feel that he understands the framework completely and misuses it, so I'm not going to give him any more help.

INT.: It sounds as if you are deliberately trying not to structure anything, so you will be free to block whatever the family is trying to do.

DR. J.: Free, to me, is not to give them so much direction that they know how to use it against you.

SUE: Before we get launched, can I ask you a couple of questions? Like first of all (*lowering voice*), going to the bathroom is kind of difficult. (*Laughs.*)

DR. J.: Hm? Oh!

SUE: Going to the bathroom . . .

DR. J.: Uh-huh.

SUE: . . . in that, maybe it's tension but maybe it's something else too. Also I, I don't know whether this has any connection, but I would like to try it without medication for a while.

DR. J.: Sure.

SUE: Okay, will you tell them I can then?

DR. J. (*overlapping*): Sure, uh-huh. As far as going to the bathroom, this is, ah, usual, I would say, and, ah . . .

SUE: Well, I'm either constipated or have diarrhea, or hard stools.

DR. J. (*overlapping*): I got a report from Dr. Smith that your physical was just fine.

SUE: Good.

DR. J.: So, ah, nothing to worry about there.

DR. J.: See, she said it: "Before we get *launched*." She also keeps saying, "I don't think it's all my fault," and so you pick up the idea that any missiles that get shot, she is going to shoot.

INT.: Why does she suddenly switch to this innocent medical business?

DR. J.: I really don't know, except that she may have been more daring than she could tolerate. She could say some of these devastating things, but following through was another story. She really never attacked her parents in a straightforward, durable way for two minutes at a time. She would say something, as when she accused her father of walking about naked, and then in two minutes she would disqualify it.

SUE: Well, an interne called Johnson did it on me.

DR. J.: Yeah.

SUE: Poked around quite a bit. (*Laughing.*) Who's Dr. Smith, by the way?

DR. J.: Dr. Smith is the, is the woman, ah . . .

SUE: Oh!

DR. J.: . . . in the ward . . .

SUE: Oh, yes.

DR. J.: . . . in her forties . . .

SUE: Um-hm. Light blond?

DR. J.: Um-hm.

MR. S.: Do these drugs cause constipation?

SUE: Well, I'm constipated anyway, if they do, then (*laughing*) maybe I'd better not have them—occasionally have trouble. I, ah, it's, I think there's one thing that needs taking care of but I think I still have the fissure . . .

DR. J.: Mm-hm.

SUE: . . . which let's get rid of please, one way or the other.

DR. J.: Ah, I think that, ah, if you do have a fissure, ah, that you should take it up with Dr. Brown, ah . . .

SUE: Uh-huh.

DR. J.: . . . so that he can give you, ah, one of these things that softens the stool and makes it, makes it get well fast.

SUE: Okay.

DR. J.: Ah, in other words, I think all problems relating to physical illness, ah, or physical complaints . . .

SUE (*overlapping*): Well, I don't know simply who to take what to.

DR. J.: Yes, should go to him because he knows more about it than I do. I've been away from it too long.

SUE (*overlapping*): Well, yeah, I really, you know, I don't know exactly who to take what to. (*Laughing.*) It's just one of these (*inaudible phrase*).

DR. J.: Sure.

SUE (*sighs*): Okay. Well, let's go.

MR. S.: That's a mechanical problem that many people have and there is a positive answer to it, so I'm . . .

SUE: Yes.

MR. S.: . . . sure the medical doctor can clear that up very quickly.

DR. J.: You notice that I'm on a spot there. I don't want to drop the topic because I can't without punishing her. I don't want to say, "This is no place to bring this up," because, after all, I let it happen, so I'm trying to get out of it with the least pain to everybody by saying, "I don't know much about it, so take it up with your medical doctor." The other thing that occurs to me is that about two years after this, the mother had a hemorrhoidectomy. She was a great hypochondriac, and her internist's chart was about four inches thick, without any major illness. When Sue takes this role, it's certainly in concert with her mother.

SUE: Okay, that's all I had to say on that score. Daddy, do you under—

DR. J. (*interrupting*): What about the communication?

SUE: Do you understand the eternal triangle in that, ah, what, ah, how

I see it and I, I don't know if Mother sees it the same way I do.

MR. S.: Well, ah, I suspect I know what you're talking about. I was (*Sue overlapping, inaudible section*) don't know why it has to exist.

DR. J.: This is really both data and problem. The father is saying, "I know what you're talking about," and he sounds a little bit pleased. This is what happened almost every time Sue indicated that something was going on between them.

INT.: He sounds both pompous and pleased. Or perhaps the pompousness is a protection against seeming too pleased.

DR. J.: Yes, some kind of mixture. But what do you do with it? Would you say to him, "Are you flirting with your daughter?" You could make a joke of it: "Ha, ha, ha, you're flirting with your daughter." Or you could say, "I'm sorry, old man, but you seem sort of pleased when your daughter makes up to you." This was one of the problems, how to get in the fact that she had a way of titillating him, without getting him on the defensive. It took quite a while before I could even get near this.

SUE (*to father*): Well, here's Mother, and here's me, and here's you, and you come down the center and you get pulled apart pretty decently sometimes (*laughs*) by it. I think you probably feel torn between the two of us at some times, and sometimes (*sighs*) I think this has been something that's been present from just about all of my life.

DR. J.: Just to remind you, this is a young woman on a mental ward with seventeen other patients, who has had all these wild ideas and is still entertaining this rape thing. However, you'll notice that in certain contexts, and for short periods, she sounds not only normal but very precocious.

INT.: If you hadn't known that this girl had been in a hospital for a breakdown, would you have been able to tell it from this interview?

DR. J.: I don't think so. Of course, I had seen her in the hospital before the interview, so I was already prejudiced. She was behaving pretty weirdly there, calling attention to herself and telling everybody about these fantasies, hallucinations, she had. So I am surprised at how well she handles herself.

INT.: Did this make you hopeful about helping her?

DR. J.: I feel that most acute psychotics can be helped, and if they can't, the fault is usually with the therapy. Chronic schizophrenics are another matter. There you've got all sorts of other factors to deal with. But I don't see why a breakdown in a college girl of this age shouldn't have a good prognosis.

MR. S.: Is it bothering you or bothering me?

SUE: Oh, I think it's bothering all of us, I think it has to.

MR. S.: Well, I didn't *feel* bothered by it.

MRS. S. (*overlapping*): Well (*inaudible phrase*).

DR. J.: Um-hm.

SUE (*to father*): Well (*laughing*), I'm glad you *don't,* because you're on a heck of a spot.

MRS. S.: Well, I don't know, Daddy's my husband and I think we understand each other and . . .

SUE: Oh, I know but I think I come between you sometimes, or he comes between us to mediate, because I, I think, sometimes we have our run-ins and Daddy mediates pretty well, on one side or the other.

MRS. S. (*overlapping*): Well, everybody has run-ins, once in a while . . .

SUE: I know . . .

MRS. S.: . . . you have them with Dad too, occasionally . . .

SUE: I know, but it seems that you and I (*laughs*) more often do than Dad and I. I'm sorry about it and I really want to change it, that's one reason why we're all here, it's 'cause I, I hate it, really I do. (*Pause.*)

DR. J.: Sue's therapist had not been seeing enough of her to have primed her to say this. They had only had one, maybe two, get-acquainted visits, so this can't have been put in her mind by a therapist.

INT.: She's reviewing the whole family problem.

DR. J.: That's right.

INT.: Were you thinking that at the time?

DR. J.: I was probably thinking, "How much of this can we all handle?" and looking for a way to break in with humor or something. One of the ways in which family therapy is different from individual analysis, which is how I was trained, is that in analysis you listen to everything and you try to get the patient to say more and more. But in family therapy that is not often the case; in fact, it's often *not* the case. You don't want too much or it will get in the way. You don't have this privilege of saying, "Yes, go on," while you sit and take it all in.

MR. S.: Well, I, ah, do you want me to do something about it, or do you want Mother to do something about it?

DR. J.: You can't do it, ah . . .

SUE (*sighs*): It's not that simple.

DR. J. (*overlapping*): It's not either or . . .

MRS. S. (*overlapping*): You can't do it with one person.

SUE: It's not that simple.

MR. S.: Well, do you have some request as to how you'd like to have us clear it up?

SUE: Well, I think . . .

DR. J. (*interrupting*): I don't think that's a fair question.

SUE: No. (*Laughs.*)

DR. J.: Let me interrupt, ah (*to Mr. and Mrs. S.*), let's try to understand. You're, you're getting some kind of an eloquent plea, here, and a very touching one, to be sure, and I want to know what each of you understand by it because I, I certainly don't know, I don't live in your family.

DR. J.: That was a very good aside, if I say so myself: "I don't live in your family." It's not a bad statement, it's not offensive, yet after it has been said, you suddenly realize that the person is saying, "Thank God." So, although it is a request for information, there's a piece of information being given as well. You'll notice too that there's a shift in me here. Sue has convinced me that she's not going to ruin the game by taking over.

INT.: She's very cautious.

DR. J.: Cautious and well put, so I am willing to relax and say, "O.K., now let's get at 'em."

INT.: You take the daughter's part very feelingly here.

DR. J.: Right. But I try—and this may not be therapeutic technique, it may be just a personal bias—to reward schizophrenics when they say something correctly. I make it a point to see that they get a boost.

INT.: To imply that they're not so crazy after all.

DR. J.: Yes. But there must also have been a feeling of relief in me when I realized that she had her chance to burst her bomb and didn't.

INT.: When you say, "This is an eloquent and touching plea," you're not just rewarding the girl for being clear and perceptive and well-mannered, you're also saying to the parents, "She's not as dangerous as you think."

DR. J.: But I wasn't able to say that until I found out that she really wasn't. Up until then I wasn't sure what she might do. There was an episode in the hospital, her first or second day there, when she walked up to one of the nurses and hit her because she thought the nurse was laughing at her. The element of craziness and violence was still present.

> DR. J.: What do you think of this idea that there is some block in communication?
>
> SUE: There is . . .
>
> MR. S. (*simultaneously*): You're speaking to me now?
>
> DR. J.: Mm-hm. (*Pause.*)
>
> SUE: I can tell you what the block is.
>
> DR. J.: No, you give your dad a chance now. (*Laughs.*)

INT.: Why did you ask that question of the father?

DR. J.: I always go to the father first, in almost any situation. The myth is that the father is in charge of the family, but he usually knows less about what's going on and feels more insecure about it because he is out of touch and often dominated by the wife. Also, for cultural reasons or perhaps because of the nature of therapy, the fathers are the hardest to keep involved. So I try to help them make what they have to say worthwhile.

> MR. S. (*laughing*): I don't know of any block in communication. Ah, I have always, for many years, felt that, ah, Sue was a pretty good girl and, ah, I was very liberal with her and ah . . .
>
> SUE: Mmm. Yeah.
>
> MR. S.: . . . her mother, to offset my liberalness, ah, would, ah, be extremely strict with her . . .
>
> SUE: Oh, Daddy, now wait a minute . . .
>
> MR. S.: . . . and, ah, then . . .
>
> SUE: Wait a minute . . .

MR. S.: . . . there were some times you . . .

SUE: I needed discipline . . .

DR. J. (*simultaneously, to Sue*): You do get your chance (*laughs*) to rebuttal, but, ah, we're getting what we're looking for.

MR. S.: Two at once here.

SUE (*overlapping*): Go on.

INT.: What were you looking for?

DR. J.: Evidence from the parents about the conflict between them that the daughter has started to hint about. You notice that I can say that kind of thing and Sue can get it, but the parents don't do anything with it.

INT.: You ask them about a block in communication and you get this evidence about the triangle. Is this a way to ask for one thing and get another?

DR. J.: Oh, you always assume that what they tell you will only be tangentially related to the block and for a very good reason, because who knows what the block is.

INT.: Then why do you use this "block in communication"?

DR. J.: It's just a good ploy. It's better than saying, "You have problems," because then somebody might say, "Well, I don't think I do." But it's pretty hard for them to deny that there is some block in communication. It's an irrefutable statement.

MR. S.: Ah, so I, ah, sometimes resented Mrs. Starbuck's discipline, ah, to what I thought was an unnecessary degree. I think as the years have gone on I realize a little more that, ah, probably she was right, but it used to, ah, bother me considerably . . .

DR. J.: Mm-hm.

MR. S.: . . . ah, especially inasmuch as, ah, the two girls will start recriminations, neither side will accept, and shut up, after the first disciplinary comments and, ah, therefore it gets to be an argument . . .

SUE: And there you land in the middle.

MR. S.: . . . and that's when I try to interfere, ah, and, ah, of course that creates probably this triangle which you refer to.

SUE: Well now, as far as this is concerned . . .

DR. J.: Wait a minute, now, wait a minute! (*Sue laughs. To Mrs. S.*) Ah, you were brought into this by . . .

MRS. S.: Well . . .

DR. J.: . . . by indirection. Ah, do you feel you need some help in, in making, ah, your wishes known to Sue in such a way that it'll be more expeditious?

INT.: This phrase of the father's, "the two girls start recriminations," is odd; it puts them in the same generation.

DR. J.: That's what he did all along. As I've said, although there were three other children, it was characteristic for Sue to get into bed between him and his wife on mornings when he wasn't working, and they would read the funnies together. This girl was someone he could use a lot.

INT.: Why did you stop Sue there and turn to the wife?

DR. J.: Well, the father is leaning over backward to acknowledge that this matter of discipline is not all one-sided, but he has made himself sound a little too much like the lily. He is taking the nicer position of being the more liberal, and I don't think that he can do this and not have the wife react to it. I don't want Sue to come in here because he is saying something primarily about his wife and I think it's only fair to indicate to her that she has a right to speak too.

INT.: It sounds as if you are going around the table, taking each one in turn. Would you have gone to the wife next, even if the husband hadn't brought her into it?

DR. J.: I would have gone to the wife next, unless they had raised something so interesting or heated that I lost where I was. Ideally, I would go to the wife, but especially after this kind of speech.

INT.: When you turn to the wife, your whole tone changes to a more seductive one.

DR. J.: Well, she is a martyr and if I said, "Your husband just took a swipe at you, aren't you going to do anything about it?" she might say, "Oh, I get this all the time." I'm trying to draw her out.

INT.: Do you use the phrase, "Do you need some help?" hoping that she will deny that she needs help?

DR. J.: Right. What I am doing there is to ask whether the problem is between her and the daughter or between her and the husband. The way I put it makes it a little preposterous that she will pick that first arm of the Y to go down, the one making it a problem between herself and Sue. I don't think that most women would feel that they need help in making their wishes known to their daughters.

I'm hoping that she'll say the problem is the husband's interference, which, as you'll see, she does.

> MRS. S.: Well, my feeling has been that I didn't get the backing up I should have had. When it came to matters of discipline, I was often crossed . . .
>
> SUE (*overlapping*): I'm with you there, on discipline . . .
>
> MRS. S.: . . . and the discipline was necessary, but—and unfortunately she's the only one of the four that that's applied to.

INT.: This is a very mixed remark. The mother picks on the father, but by the time she's finished the sentence, she's turned around to pick on Sue.

DR. J.: As I got to know the mother later, I felt she was consciously apprehensive that her social life, her way of living might explode. And so here, where she is being careful with the father, I think there was an element of not wanting to cause trouble.

INT.: That's a very skillful, vague comment she makes. She gets them both in one sentence without being too hard on either one of them.

DR. J.: Her tone implies: "Both of you are so difficult." It isn't complaining, exactly; it's a patient, put-upon tone.

> SUE: Well, you know, Mother, I'm really with you and I feel that this is something that you've had to do pretty much on your own and I've been, I've needed it, I've needed it so badly, and I've had to learn a lot of it on my own in the last three weeks (*starting to cry*). It's been rugged, it's been hell, and I think partly that's because you didn't get the support from Daddy that you needed.
>
> MR. S.: I would agree that it was probably . . .
>
> MRS. S. (*simultaneously*): Well, I think that's pretty hard to say . . .
>
> MR. S. (*overlapping*): I would agree to that . . .
>
> SUE (*simultaneously*): It's hard to say but it's the truth, and I think it's . . .
>
> MR. S.: Uhh . . .
>
> SUE: . . . it's no condemnation of anybody in this room.
>
> MRS. S.: The thing that was hard for me . . .
>
> MR. S.: (*overlapping*): (*Inaudible phrase*) lack of experience . . .
>
> MRS. S.: . . . and I always knew why Daddy did the things he did, it was because he loved you so much.

INT.: When the daughter says to the mother, "I'm with you on discipline, Daddy didn't support you enough," she seems to be taking her mother's part.

DR. J.: She could also mean, "This is one of the few things we are in agreement about."

INT.: She uses this discipline issue in a curious way. She accuses her parents of being hard on her by being too easy on her.

DR. J.: Well, you can take it both ways. It's bad if you discipline somebody for their own good, and it's bad if you don't discipline them because you love them so much. She's got a beautiful area to be ambiguous in.

INT.: She's also pretty ambiguous when she tells them, "You haven't helped me to discipline myself. I've had to learn it on my own."

DR. J.: "Especially since I've been crazy." She says the hospital experience has taught her this, very explicitly.

INT.: At the same time, both mother and daughter are busy taking it easy on father when they're really ticking him off: "It was because he loved you so much," and "It's no condemnation of anyone in this room."

DR. J.: They've got another area of agreement. They don't see it this way, but if you look closely at this matter of discipline, you see that each pair has an area of agreement against each third person simultaneously. There's Dad protecting Sue against Mother's attempts to control her, Mother and Sue disapproving of Dad for doing it, and both parents controlling Sue so ineffectively that she had to go to a hospital.

SUE (*sighing*): I know and I don't condemn you for it, Daddy, but I just think that you were a little bit blinded by it.

MR. S.: I agree. I said I was learning (*Sue sighs*) slowly but had progressed quite a bit more recently.

SUE (*overlapping*): Discipline's so important, Daddy, it governs everything, it, it's your whole life, make or break, really.

MR. S.: Have you seen current or recent evidence that the situation still exists?

SUE: You mean my, a lack of discipline in me?

MR. S.: No, I . . .

DR. J. (*interrupting, to Mr. S.*): Oh, I think . . .

MR. S.: . . . I mean lack of support from me?

DR. J.: I think if you . . .

SUE: No.

DR. J.: . . . pursue that line, you'll be getting yourself into . . .

SUE: Yeah . . .

DR. J.: . . . a trap you don't need to fall into and . . .

SUE: . . . and I, I don't, my answer is no, anyway.

INT.: It's a nice way of turning a man in a different direction, to say, "That's a trap you don't need to fall into."

DR. J.: The reason I said it is that I don't think the father is asking a genuine question. I don't think he expects or desires the answer that the question seems to ask. What he is saying is, "I have improved, and I can prove it by the fact that I am willing to ask, 'Have I improved?' " If I took the opposite tack, I would say, "I hope you put an honest question." But I think that would be a very untherapeutic thing to say.

INT.: Why did you stop the argument at that particular point?

DR. J.: I'm not sure, but in hearing it now, I suspect it was because Sue was getting a little carried away about the discipline, when she says it was her "whole life."

DR. J.: . . . we can assume that, that people do the best they can. I, I would not hear of it otherwise, because (*sighs*) people . . .

SUE: Well, oh . . .

DR. J.: . . . try to do the best they can so that they won't, ah, be in pain in any way.

INT.: When you say, "I wouldn't have it otherwise," you're taking an extremely arbitrary position. You certainly could have it otherwise.

DR. J.: Well, I don't have much tolerance for this business where a therapist says, "We are all going to do such and such," and then somebody says, "Why do we have to?" and he says, "Well, it has been shown that the best thing that can happen is for you to do this," and so on. I would much rather have it be idiosyncratic and imply that maybe I am peculiar. That way I take responsibility and say, "Be my guest."

INT.: Without giving your reasons.

DR. J.: Right. So I can't be hung on them. But this gets back to the ground rules. The ground rules have never been spelled out, so the ground rules are whatever the ground rules come to consist of. Here, for example: "I won't tolerate any belief other than that all of you are trying as hard as you can try." I honestly believe this, but it is a tactic too.

INT.: It's a way of exonerating people and implicating them at the same time. When you say that people do the best they can because they want to avoid pain, you bring up the question of whether what's best for them is best for anyone else.

DR. J.: Well, they do what they do for selfish reasons. But I'm trying to bypass the issue of blame. If there's anything that wastes time, I think it is recrimination, and this is what we almost get into.

INT.: It's partly an efficiency move.

DR. J.: Yes.

INT.: That's a little odd, because you do have time if you want to take it.

DR. J.: I'm not thinking in terms of how much time but in terms of how to use that time. It's like the crisis in pneumonia. You're building toward a certain peak where things can go one way or the other. A person may be months recovering from pneumonia, but if he passes the crisis, he'll make it. It's not that you don't want to waste time, it's that if you don't use your time right, it can be dangerous and harmful.

INT.: In other words, you want to control the timing.

DR. J.: *Timing.* That's the word.

SUE: I won't condemn anyone, I won't condemn anyone, I don't, I think it's normal for him to be that way.

MRS. S. (*overlapping*): I've always felt that it was especially hard for you, Sue, but when the time came when Dad did back me up all of a sudden . . .

SUE (*laughing*): Oh, yeah.

MRS. S.: . . . because it was *you.* (*Laughs.*)

SUE: Well, because it was inconsistency, it was, it was very much inconsistency.

MR. S.: A change of pace, with me.

SUE (*overlapping*): And, well, you both have been kind of inconsistent with me and that, those, that's one of the inconsistencies that's made my life a little hard.

MRS. S.: What do you mean by being inconsistent towards you?

SUE: In, sometimes in your behavior toward me. (*Pause.*)

MR. S.: Sometimes I back you up, sometimes I don't.

SUE: Yeah.

MRS. S.: Is that what you mean?

SUE: Yeah.

MRS. S.: What about me? Where have I been inconsistent? (*Starting to cry.*)

SUE (*to mother*): Not as much you, really.

MRS. S.: But I really want to know. (*Weeping.*)

INT.: When the daughter says it's inconsistency, it's unclear whether she means the mother's or the father's.

DR. J.: But she gets them again. She's already scored against her parents for not disciplining her properly. Then if they change sides about discipline, or change their minds, she gets them on that too, because they are being inconsistent.

INT.: She's an extremely clever girl. You can see how her mother would lose in debates with her. The mother is more limited, which I think is unusual in the mother of a schizophrenic.

DR. J.: Except that this mother was not. One day, quite a while afterward, the mother and Sue had an argument and the mother said, "Now you go to your room," meanwhile holding on to Sue's wrists, and Sue said, "But I can't, you're holding me." This episode made her mother's contradictory tactics, the double-bind aspects, very obvious to her. Her therapist felt she began to be less vulnerable to her mother after that. There's a lot to this woman that we miss in the tape; her martyred looks, her sighing, her whole mien.

INT.: She's perpetually hurt?

DR. J.: Yes. Here, for instance, she's weeping and asking supposedly helpful questions, like, "I want to know where I've been inconsistent," when what she really means is, "Tell me how I've hurt you, just kick me in the side now that I'm lying on the ground."

INT.: I just think that in that interchange the daughter is a pretty fair competitor.

DR. J.: It's partly because you're thinking of it verbally. This is a woman who managed to get a number of surgeons to operate on her for conditions they ordinarily would not operate for. She got them to do an exploratory laparotomy and a laminectomy for pain, and in neither case did they find any pathology.

INT.: It's an interesting definition of a controlling woman.

DR. J.: It was only in direct debate that the daughter could outwit her. For instance, she would "lose" an argument with Sue, Sue would storm off saying, "I won't do it," and then the mother would have three other children to relate this to and say, "Don't turn out like Sue, oh, I know you never will." It would make the father angry, he knew this was completely unfair, although he wouldn't do anything about it.

INT.: Then part of his behavior with Sue was protective, it wasn't altogether seductiveness.

DR. J.: Yes. It's fairly evident that he was trying to compensate. There was a grandmother in the picture too, the mother's mother. During the period when Sue was still quite crazy, the grandmother called her up and berated her severely. She said, "You're no good, you're killing your mother." After that, Sue made a suicide attempt, or threatened to; it was quite an emergency. The grandmother lived nearby, so she was in the picture too.

INT.: Do you ever bring in the third generation?

DR. J.: I have, but I didn't here. If I had it to do over again, I still don't think I would have brought in the grandmother. There were a lot of relatives in the area; she was reputedly quite a matriarch. I don't know whether I could have done any good with her or not.

> SUE (*tearfully, to mother*): Well, you haven't as much. There, there is one area, Mother, where you have, and that is, we have discussed this before and I, it's an open wound and I don't know if I should go into it or not, because . . .
>
> DR. J. (*interrupting*): I want to raise something else first, ah, and that is, ah, you've been in tears, and your mother is, and, ah, it's obvious that you're both upset, although . . .
>
> SUE: I'm not . . .
>
> DR. J.: . . . well not . . .
>
> SUE: . . . as much as she is, that's one thing.

INT.: I take it both the mother and the daughter are weeping. Was there any particular reason for interrupting them at this point? Have you anything against letting people weep and show emotion?

DR. J.: No, but I usually will comment on it if nobody else does. The mother is crying all through this, but she doesn't say, "You upset me," or give any idea why, and nobody else says anything, and yet they're all affected by it.

INT.: It's interesting that you bring up the weeping not in terms of those who are weeping, but in terms of the audience for it. I gather you wouldn't say to them, "Can we get an understanding of why you're weeping?" or something like that.

DR. J.: If I ask that kind of question, it's usually because I'm at a loss for anything better. If I say to somebody, "Why are you doing such and such?" I don't really expect him to have any idea at all.

> DR. J. (*to Mr. S.*): Yeah, yes, and I wonder, you know, what's this doing to you? (*Pause.*)
>
> SUE: Hurt. (*Sighs.*)
>
> MR. S.: (*Pause.*) Well, I (*laughs*), I guess I've gotten kind of immune to it over the years, um, ah, the . . .
>
> SUE: (*Laughing, inaudible words.*)
>
> MR. S.: . . . the tears are rather easy, in this family . . .
>
> DR. J.: Hm.
>
> MR. S.: . . . to come by . . .
>
> SUE: (*Laughs.*)
>
> MR. S.: . . . and, um, while I . . .
>
> SUE: (*Loud giggle.*)
>
> MR. S.: . . . I'm disturbed. (*Breaks out in laughter.*)
>
> MRS. S.: (*Laughs.*)
>
> SUE: (*Laughs.*) You too?
>
> MR. S.: (*Laughs. All three continue laughing.*) I can do it too.
>
> DR. J.: Mmm.

INT.: Your question must have hit the father hard, from the amount of time it took him to answer. He's starting to cry too, isn't he?

DR. J.: Yes. As he says, "I can do it too." It's funny, it's hard now to think of him as having wept.

INT.: I suspect you touched it off by your inquiry. The father is so accustomed to their being upset and to his being the one who upsets them that it threw him when you made that switch.

DR. J.: Yes. When one of the women would start to weep, the other would too, and it really left the father out in the cold. I'm bringing him back in.

> MR. S.: Ah . . .
>
> SUE: I've seen it . . .

MR. S. (*laughing*): So I've practically become immune to tears, they don't bother me at all. I, I certainly am (*sighs*) sorry to see, ah, Mrs. Starbuck hurt by, ah, things that Sue was saying . . .

SUE: Oh, I don't mean to hurt her . . .

MR. S.: . . . and ah . . .

SUE: . . . that's not the point.

DR. J. (*interrupting*): I wonder that she was crying necessarily because she was hurt. Has that been established?

MRS. S.: Me, you mean?

DR. J.: Yeah. I, this would be an easy assumption but I don't know that it's so. Was this the only reason?

MRS. S.: A good deal of the time it has been.

SUE: Is it now?

DR. J. (*overlapping*): Well, I mean right now. Were you crying now because you were hurt, do you think?

MRS. S.: I don't know what you mean. (*Pause.*) Because I was (*word lost in crying*).

DR. J.: Yeah, because you, you responded to, ah, your daughter with I think a rather touching closeness, I don't think it was just a hurt.

INT.: This is one of those instances in which it would be very easy just to go along with the premise they're establishing, which is that the daughter hurt her mother and they're weeping. Did the mother do something to make you feel it wasn't so?

DR. J.: No, I do this often. This is simply taking the motivation that has been labeled in a negative way and labeling it in a positive way, whatever you want to call this technique.

INT.: It really gets their attention.

DR. J.: That's not surprising. If they have been defining what they are doing in one way for many, many years, and if I can suddenly define it another way, it shocks them a little out of believing that they're always right.

INT.: Why do you pick "hurt" as the word you relabel?

DR. J.: It may have to do with the enigma that the mother presents to me as well as to the other two. I am saying, "Let's not be so quick about applying the usual labels to Mother, she's a little bit more enigmatic than that."

INT.: You made the same kind of shift when you interpreted the daughter's aggressive manner as "touching." There you were saying that the daughter was not as threatening as she seemed, and here you're saying that the mother is not as vulnerable as she seems.

Dr. J.: Yes.

Int.: But why did you choose this method? You could conceivably have gone along with the mother by saying, "Well, about your being hurt, in what instances?" or "How did it happen?" or whatever.

Dr. J.: I could have, except it would be totally pointless. I see relabeling as the only hope. Another possibility would be the *reductio ad absurdum,* where I would commiserate with her, talk about the cross she bears and the scientific fact that anyone else would have been completely crushed by it, so that she finally has to say, "You know, I didn't say it was *that* bad."

Int.: Are you trying to shift the emphasis from the idea that the mother is a victim to a realization of closeness?

Dr. J.: I don't care about closeness, really. All I am saying is that if A does X to get B to do Y, and establishes a pattern of A–X, B–Y, then once the pattern has been established, A doesn't know whether it is A–X, B–Y, or whether it's really punctuated B–Y, A–X. Like the joke about the mouse in the experiment who says, "I get that guy to feed me every time I push the lever." I am only interested in breaking up the way they tend to label a particular pattern. Now a nice way to do it is to put it into a "good" framework, a warm, happy framework.

Int.:   Are you also trying to point out the system that's operating?

Dr. J.: You don't really point it out, you disturb it first. Otherwise they'll never see it, because A will always say, "Well, I think it's A–X, B–Y," and B will always say, "No, it's B–Y, A–X." You can upset the system by saying, "Well, I think it's C–Q," so that both of them are confounded. But I think that you should stress positive motivations where you can, because they are the most acceptable. If I say to you, "I think you are not telling me the whole answer because you don't think I'll understand," it's a lot better than saying, "I think you are too stupid to tell it to me straight."

Int.: You give the mother an alternative which is better than being hurt. You are forcing her out of her position of being the martyr, but in a face-saving way.

Dr. J.: Yes. Within the framework of saying, "Maybe the way you have been looking at it is wrong." Supposing I say, "You've got the idea that Alaska is a terrible place because it is always cold," and so on, "but you've never tasted whale meat." Then if they say, "No, I haven't tasted whale meat," this reinforces a new way of looking at everything, because if they are wrong on one detail, they might also have misjudged Alaska.

INT.: This has repercussions on everyone else too. The daughter is going to be a little less sure that she is hurting the mother when the mother weeps, because you have questioned that labeling. You did the same thing when the women were weeping, by talking about the impact of the weeping on the father. I'm sure the women had never thought of it in this way before.

DR. J.: Yes. The sequence of funny lines and the delighted way the two women laugh together indicate that they must have been struck by a new point of view. But that time I don't think I did it deliberately.

SUE: Well, I supported her and I think this is upsetting her.

MRS. S.: Oh no, that doesn't upset me. You see, something you've never understood is the relationship between Dad and me.

SUE: Yes, I understand it, better than you think.

MRS. S.: I don't think it's possible at your age to understand it . . .

SUE (*overlapping*): Oh, eh, now what's my age? I have an awful lot of insight and I've been told by other people that I have a great deal more insight than most people my age.

DR. J.: But you haven't been married for a long time.

SUE: (*Laughs.*)

MRS. S.: That's just a basic fact.

DR. J. (*overlapping*): This, this makes a difficulty . . .

MR. S. (*overlapping*): But I never understand . . .

SUE (*overlapping*): But I've seen, I've seen you two more objectively than you think I do.

DR. J.: I would buy that, but I think you still have something to learn here.

SUE: Oh, sure.

INT.: Why do you say to Sue, "You haven't been married a long time, you still have something to learn?"

DR. J.: Because the mother has said something that is just as true in the way it's said as in its opposite. "You don't understand about your father and me," can mean, "You don't understand the love we have, but you also don't understand the hate we have." And I think this was true. Sue hadn't been married a long time, so she couldn't have quite an accurate picture. This is quite pretentious of Sue.

INT.: It's a nice way to tell her to keep out of it. Your remark doesn't point to something she can interpret as a defect in herself, it's just her age.

DR. J.: If she stays in it, the mother is going to say something like, "Oh, your father and I got along beautifully until you came along." I'm trying to tell her, "Look, don't destroy this. When your mother is able to say this kind of thing, sit back and listen because there is information there." This is an accurate thing the mother says: "You have never *understood* about your father and me." Sue thought they were much closer than they were. Well, she did and she didn't. Overtly, she thought they were much closer.

INT.: It would be possible to interpret what you are doing as either supporting the mother or helping the mother draw a generation line.

DR. J.: I'm doing that too. But Sue can find out something if she'll only stop and listen. I can't say to her, "Now look, take my word for it, your mother has just said something important," without shutting up the mother, so I don't know what else to do except to look at Sue and shake my head.

INT.: There must be a set of ways to quiet someone graciously. This one wouldn't fit everyone. But I would never have guessed your reasons for doing it.

MRS. S.: I think you've always underestimated the, the feeling that Daddy and I have for each other and it's only . . .

SUE: No. No. I think you two are the happiest married people I think I've ever seen and I think you have a . . .

MR. S. (*low voice*): Thank you.

SUE: . . . deep, deep and unusual love that not very many people find, and I, I wouldn't ruin it for the world and I wouldn't want to hurt either of you and I don't mean to hurt either of you by saying anything I say in here.

MRS. S. (*starting to cry again*): We don't take it that way, darling.

SUE: All right.

DR. J.: But you see, we're off on this hurt kick now, and I don't think this is what, what was important. I think your mother was responding to you out of passion, not out of, ah, being hurt . . .

MR. S. (*interrupting*): *Com*passion?

DR. J.: Hm?

MR. S.: *Com*passion?

DR. J.: Yeah, and because there is something touching about what you've been through recently as only you, as you know only too well, but I wonder if, ah . . .

MRS. S.: I think you've put your finger right on a very important thing, Dr. Jackson, because that is (*wavering voice*) exactly my feeling.

INT.: "Passion" was a peculiar word to choose, somehow.

DR. J.: It was entirely spur of the moment. I might have said "compassion," but I didn't think of it, the father did.

INT.: This wasn't an attempt to try to get several things into one word?

DR. J.: No, no. I'm sure it wasn't. I was just trying to build up the positive aspects and "compassion" would have been much the better word.

INT.: "Passion" is interesting because it's not just positive. It implies something more, some kind of intensity.

DR. J.: This is probably what the father was correcting. He was trying to help me by saying, "You're talking about the positive elements, so you must mean compassion." They had plenty of passion together. They fought each other, they hit each other.

INT.: Then you were coming too close to the truth.

DR. J.: Yes. The father's very helpful, as you notice, in several places.

SUE: Well, that dis-discipline issue is why (*wavering voice*) I went through it in a big way . . .

DR. J.: Mm-hm.

SUE (*starting to cry*): . . . and I had to learn it the hard way. I had to learn to sleep, when people around me were screaming . . .

MRS. S.: We all do that, too.

SUE (*crying*): Not this way, Mom, not screaming like that. (*Pause, Sue sobbing.*)

MR. S.: Why were people screaming, even in the dormitory?

MRS. S.: No, I think she means her hospital brush.

DR. J. (*simultaneously*): She's talking about the experience of a mental hospital, which can be . . .

MR. S.: Oh.

SUE (*still sobbing*): . . . with everything locked, and no one trusting you, and people really crazy around you, really bad cases, permanent cases.

MRS. S.: That's a terrible experience for anybody to go through.

SUE (*sobbing*): It was hell, you just don't know, you've no idea (*sobs*), when the only thing that was wrong with me was emotional . . .

DR. J. (*to Sue, loudly*): All of a sudden, you get on the band wagon and bail your mother out. Your mother starts crying, then you start. Now I, I think, this is one of the . . .

SUE (*interrupting*): (*Inaudible phrase*) told me to release a lot of emotion over that . . .

DR. J.: You, you have some chance to release some emotion, ah, and I . . .

SUE: No, I haven't . . .

DR. J.: I think you have, I, I think you should, I don't mean that you don't have a lot still in you about this, you'll never forget this experience, but I think it's important for you to realize that just when we were, when I was talking to your mother, you stepped in with your problem . . .

SUE: All right.

DR. J.: . . . and this is, this may be part of the eternal triangle that we're talking about, ah, that it's got three sides and . . .

SUE (*overlapping*): Well, how is it part of that?

DR. J.: . . . each person in his own way keeps boosting it along.

SUE: How is part of, how is this part of that? You mean I interfere when . . .

DR. J.: Well, I think I understood your mother a little better and just at that moment is when you started on the, the business about the horrors of the mental hospital. I agree with you with them but . . .

MRS. S.: We all do. (*Laughs.*)

INT.: Your voice is very sharp when you interrupt Sue. I get the impression that you've got your finger on something, that you've pinned down some invisible adversary.

DR. J.: I think that's true. I consider this a typical rescue, one that I've experienced in many other sessions.

INT.: What gave you the clue to this? Was it the hysterical exaggeration in Sue's voice?

DR. J.: Yes. I'm not saying that she didn't have a tough time in the hospital, although it was not quite a state hospital she was in, but I think she is trying to use tonality to involve you. The way she says, "You have *no idea*," it doesn't ring quite right.

INT.: By pointing out that whenever the mother starts crying, the daughter interrupts in this way, you are also isolating a rule.

DR. J.: That's right. I don't say it, but the implication is that the mother lets it happen. If I rescue you, you are letting yourself be rescued.

INT.: This brings up an interesting comparison with individual therapy. In individual therapy, you would naturally focus on the one person. In family therapy, you would have to take into account the effect of whatever you said on the others. If you had never done any individual therapy, your first thought might be how to reach the other people by directing a remark to one.

DR. J.: Even in family therapy I don't think you can focus on more than one person at a time. I have a stock phrase which usually gets a couple laughing: "It seems to me the two of you deserve each other." But I don't say this to the two of them together; it is said in connection with some particularly horrendous accusation that one has made about the other. You might say jointly to a couple who are trying to destroy each other in some symmetrical way, "You're really ruining each other," and it may be a correct thing to say, but it does very little good because the wife will reply, "No, he's ruining me," and the husband will say "No, she's ruining me."

INT.: Well, a therapist might say to a husband when the wife is being particularly difficult, "Your wife is a very difficult woman to resist." It's a way of saying to him, "I understand the trouble you are having with this woman," but it's also for her.

DR. J.: Yes. She is overhearing it. I think this is what brings a different element into family therapy, rather than the idea that you can aim your remarks collectively.

DR. J.: But I, I think also that we've got to understand that there are an interplay of forces here, that . . .

SUE: I don't see how the forces work, here.

DR. J.: That's right, and I don't see too clearly either, except when I see shifts like this, it, it alerts me to them. I can't tell you what you were doing, but I think— (*Sue interrupts.*)

INT.: What do you mean when you say, "When I see shifts like this, it alerts me to the forces that are at work"?

DR. J.: I was working on the mother and she was responding with a certain amount of feeling, and at this point Sue cut in. Now there was no need to protect the mother, nobody was being unpleasant to her, I was in charge, so why did Sue cut in?

INT.: It was something unexpected.

DR. J.: I mean a shift in that sense, yes.

INT.: Which alerts you to the fact that there is something meaningful here.

DR. J.: Right.

INT.: Do you look to these moments to tell you what's really going on in the family?

DR. J.: Very much so. At this point in the interview I wasn't thinking about the family "rules," but I think that in general I do watch for clues to family homeostasis. I don't pay so much attention to the content as to the kind of a shift that doesn't seem to fit. During one of our structured interviews, the parents were discussing a proverb, and the father was very polite to the mother while they were alone, but the minute the boy came in, the father took over and said, "Now this says that rolling stones don't gather no moss—now you understand what moss is?" He just sounded different. You got the feeling that there was some kind of shift in him, he became all at once so positive and pedantic. That alerts me, not knowing what the motivation is.

INT.: You wait for the inconsistencies, and that gives you a clue?

DR. J.: Right. Much more than the content, or slips of the tongue.

INT.: And you are sharing with the family the idea that these shifts are important and that you don't know what this one was about?

DR. J.: I show that I do know what it is by calling it a rescue operation, but this still doesn't label the content of it, its specific meaning in this context.

INT.: Some therapists wouldn't feel they should share with the family in this way. You are telling them what your operational methods are, what you are looking for.

DR. J.: I'm not doing it deliberately at this moment, but I do try to do it when I think of it. I try to make each member of the family a monitor of the other's behavior, in terms of shifts, so that later on the father can say to the mother, "Why do you jump on me, you were just talking with Sue and all of a sudden . . ."

INT.: Are you trying to give them an example of how to do this?

DR. J.: I'm trying to act as a model, yes.

INT.: There's a fine distinction between "helping them understand the shift" and giving them a model of how to handle each other tactically.

DR. J.: In this case, I'm both telling them how to recognize this kind of shift and being the model for the way to intervene when it happens.

> SUE: Well, maybe it's just attracting attention to myself.
>
> DR. J.: No, I don't think it's that simple. Ah, I think you have somehow become a spokesman for the family, and it's a very burdensome role to be in.

INT.: For someone who was assuming, ten or fifteen minutes ago, that these parents had no awareness of any connection between them and their child's problems, or at least no willingness to concede it, this is going pretty far, isn't it?

DR. J.: Not if you think of what the parents have been able to do. They have been able to come forward, and now the problem is to get Sue out of the way so that she doesn't become an obstacle. The mother is weeping, the father is in tears, there is something happening, where before I wasn't sure what they would accept.

INT.: But you are going so far as to say that the family has problems for which Sue is the spokesman. Do you feel safe enough to deal with that this soon?

DR. J.: All I can say is that I must have been impressed by the mother's tears, the father's tears, the extent of the movement. Compare this with initial interviews in which the two parents sit solidly united on one side of the room and the patient sits isolated on the other. In this interview you get a feeling of divisiveness, implications on the mother's part of other problems, and so forth.

> SUE: Well, I can tell you one thing I understand right now, not exactly a spokesman but I'm bearing most of the burden of my own emotional independence, and I'm not getting much help from my mother, and I'm sorry, I mean there are a lot of factors that are

innocent and not exactly realized but (*sighs*) are a result of this. It makes, it makes it necessary for me to do most of it.

DR. J.: Mm-hm.

SUE: My own emotional independence is necessary at this point.

DR. J. (*overlapping*): Well, if this is true, your mother is losing something too, so that I think it's still . . .

SUE: Oh, I know . . .

DR. J.: . . . in that sense it's a family problem.

SUE (*to mother*): I can, I can appreciate and sympathize with your position very much, but I am—me, and sometimes I get (*crying*) a little bit confused about who me is. (*Pause.*)

MRS. S.: Darling, that's part of growing up.

SUE (*crying*): No, it, will you please let me? (*Sobs.*)

MRS. S. (*simultaneously, crying*): I want you to . . .

SUE (*crying*): Oh, you say that but you don't *feel* it. I've said this to you before.

MRS. S. (*overlapping, crying*): If you could see inside me, you'd know how I feel.

SUE: I'm not the only one who's said this, Mother, why do you think I—you don't think I'd cook that up on my own, do you? (*Sighs. Pause.*)

MR. S.: I don't know what more we can do to let you grow up, Sue. We sent . . .

SUE: Let me . . .

MR. S.: . . . you away to school at the early age of, first year of high school . . .

SUE: Well. (*Sighs.*)

MR. S.: We talked you out of staying away for the last two years, that's true, and brought you back home . . .

SUE (*low voice*): I didn't want to . . .

MR. S.: . . . because you, ah, were getting very rough, tough, tomboyish, and you were going into a third and fourth year of high where in a marooned state like that existed in Arizona, you had no companions older than yourself . . .

SUE: All right. Skip the reasons, I realize that.

MR. S.: . . . so we did bring you back home. I'm saying the one time we imposed upon you we brought you back home for two years.

INT.: I noticed that while you were listening to the tape, you were shaking your head.

DR. J.: I was thinking, "How can the father have said this?"

What he is talking about is a breakdown Sue had when she was fourteen. The way he puts it is almost unbelievable. He says that this was part of their helping her to grow up, when it was really a horrible breakdown.

INT.: Why do you keep silent during this interchange?

DR. J.: I had no idea about all this, you see. I didn't know anything about the family history.

INT.: You don't usually inquire into the family history to acquaint yourself with these past events?

DR. J.: Not initially, no. I think taking a history is a matter of debate. I feel I do better if I don't know the family background and get a feel of the situation first. If I know that she has done this, I am apt to ask about it and get off onto all sorts of things.

INT.: In the beginning you say to these people that one reason for them to meet together with you is that certain past issues are very much in Sue's mind. What strikes me is how few past issues you work with. You take the present conflict, even let it run on, then make your assumptions and work with that.

DR. J.: I'm not sure how much my knowing every single thing would contribute. I have no objection to taking a history if it can be used dynamically, right at that moment. I recommend it to some of the people I supervise, not so much to collect facts but because it is a way of getting into another area where things are not so disturbing.

SUE: Well, I . . .

DR. J. (*interrupting loudly*): Now here we have . . .

SUE: . . . understand this . . .

MR. S.: . . . then we sent you away again . . .

SUE: Oh!

DR. J. (*overlapping*): Here we have the two sides of the family.

SUE: I didn't say this . . .

DR. J.: We have the tears on the one side and on the other side we've got the president of [*father's company*] talking.

MR. S.: Um-hm.

DR. J.: This is the way you would read a balance sheet . . .

SUE: This is a businesslike attitude toward something you don't be businesslike . . .

DR. J. (*to Mr. S.*): . . . and you know it doesn't fool me, because I, I know that you're affected by both of the tears and that this resorting to the balance-sheet approach and adding and subtracting, "This is what happened," ah . . .

SUE: You don't do that with life.

DR. J.: . . . is, is something that must leave you disturbed somewhere inside, it just doesn't, you don't even *sound* very convincing, and yet you're an extremely successful person, so the business side of you must be convincing, but this side of you isn't, and I think this is something we want to try to get back to and that is what, what, what do you do for crying, you know? I, I gather you cry too some but (*female sighs in background*), from what was said, but, ah, I mean there is a kind of tragedy here and in the last few minutes you've been sort of staying out of it.

INT.: To the mother you've said, "You're not as hurt as you think." Now you say to the father, "You're more upset than you show." Do you often do this when people act as though they weren't worried or upset?

DR. J.: Yes. It's partly punishing them for saying that no message is the message. I tell them, "If you think that you can just sit there and let other people make fools of themselves, it's not going to work."

INT.: But he hasn't been sitting there. He sat through the exchange between the mother and daughter, but then he stepped in with this story about the daughter in high school.

DR. J.: But that is still being out of it. He refused to take any part in the emotion. Here were the two women, pleading with each other and hating each other and so on, and he's sitting over there reciting facts. I'm saying to him, "You are not going to escape."

INT.: Your manner is extremely provocative. Was this tactical, or were you really annoyed?

DR. J.: I do use this tone tactically but in this case I was probably pushed into it because I was so repelled by his going on about schools in the face of all that was happening.

INT.: You're giving him the "You're denying your true feelings" line.

DR. J.: But I think he gets the message, "Look, you're going to be involved with us whether you like it or not, so you might as well get into it." For example, I rarely say to somebody, "You've been very quiet lately." Instead I say, "Boy, we sure are getting volumes from Aunt Mary!" Then she'll look puzzled because she hasn't said anything, and I hope she gets the idea that not being involved is an involvement and it's going to be labeled as such.

INT.: It's somewhat facetious to say that the customer is always wrong, but in this interview the daughter acts aggressive, and you indicate that she ought to go in the other direction; the mother gets upset, and you indicate that she ought to go in the other direction; the father acts businesslike, and you indicate that he ought to go in the other direction.

DR. J.: I really think that's the whole story, because what they ordinarily do is like the "Anniversary Waltz." I would say, yes, everybody is wrong, not because they are wrong in the ordinary sense, but because they are doing what they are doing at home and it hasn't worked. The thing is to convince them that they are wrong for the right reason. Then they are American and God-fearing and all, but they are just misguided.

INT.: You use a humiliating tone in talking to the father, but it's humiliating in a very special way. You're criticizing him for not doing what is in his best interest. He can't say, "You're humiliating me," because you're on his side.

DR. J.: If you tell somebody that he can do better than he is doing because you really think he can, rather than simply to cut him down, you may be humiliating him in one sense, but you are also elevating him.

INT.: I suspect that right there you have the essence of therapeutic technique; this mixture of forcing people to behave differently but phrasing it in such a way that they can't resist it because you are on their side.

DR. J. (*to Mr. S.*): I don't think you do really stay out of it. What happens?

SUE: Is it fair to?

DR. J.: It isn't a question of being fair. I don't think he *can*. I think, ah . . .

SUE: Well, if he is managing succex-, successfully to stay out of it, I don't think it's right. (*Laughs.*)

DR. J.: Well, I don't think (*laughing*) he does stay out of it, he feels it somewhere.

MRS. S.: 'Course he feels it, he feels it deeply.

SUE: Well, I appreciate that. I didn't think he was a vegetable. (*Pause.*)

DR. J.: That was a compliment.

SUE (*laughing*): Oh, it was. I know you . . .

MRS. S.: All right now, this is . . .

SUE: . . . feel things pretty deeply, Dad.

MR. S. (*low voice*): Thank you.

MRS. S.: This is something right here. That was a compliment, I know, but the delivery of the compliment was a little rude and sassy.

DR. J.: She smiled when she said it, very warmly.

MRS. S.: I didn't see the smile but I heard the tone.

INT.: Why did you say, "That was a compliment"?

DR. J.: Because I assumed that as soon as the mother starts labeling things, particularly in this sentimental "He feels it deeply" way, she has them so far away from what is happening that somebody has to point out the relevance of other things as they occur. I am sure that she is a focal point at that moment, and that a siren could go off next door and they wouldn't notice.

INT.: Were you also trying to soften the daughter's comment?

DR. J.: I think I was showing the father that I wasn't sure that he could hear his daughter, particularly in this context, with his wife acting the way she was. I was insulting him, I suppose, by saying, "I have to explain her comment to you." On the other hand I was saying, "It's my business to interpret you to each other."

INT.: You seem to have been a little clairvoyant there. The mother comes in and begins to attack the daughter for what sounds on the surface like a rather sweet remark.

DR. J.: I don't think it was clairvoyance, I think the mother probably was competing with me. Instead of saying, "Oh, I didn't realize it was a compliment," she immediately takes the opposite point of view: "You don't know my daughter better than I do." Which I think is understandable. However, this little exchange raises a technical problem. If I can, I'd rather ask another member of the family about the meaning of what was just said, to keep it intra-family. The trouble is that if I say, "What did you think of that?" the mother can say, "Well, obviously it was a facetious remark." Then I have to top her by saying, "I didn't hear it that way at all." I don't like to get into that position. You don't want to ask somebody to come forward and then chop him off. I don't know what the answer is, but I think it's usually best to ask a member of the family to interpret what went on.

INT.: You're saying that what you say is very different depending on whether it follows or precedes what the family member says. Here you set them up to attack what you said, if they so wished.

DR. J.: I think as long as the therapist is feeling up to it, that's the better way to do it.

> SUE: Every time I try to be adult, I get squished, just like that. I'm being . . .
>
> MRS. S. (*overlapping*): Sue, I'm speaking . . .
>
> SUE: . . . sassy or I'm being impudent!

INT.: All through this interview, the daughter complains that she's being treated like a child.

DR. J.: Yes, but she introduces that note as much as her mother does, by going back many years: "Now you're telling me what to do."

INT.: By demanding that she be treated as an adult, she ensures that she will be treated as a child.

DR. J.: Yes. And what she is objecting to here is that the mother reinterprets her remarks, decides what they're supposed to mean. But they can only really mean that if the daughter sees the mother as being more powerful and brighter and so on than herself. I don't put up with it from her, because I think that she and her mother are nearly peers.

INT.: The mother and daughter are both playing some kind of powerlessness game. The daughter says, "You treat me like a child," meanwhile acting like one, and the mother answers by weeping and being hurt.

DR. J.: It's an odd interweaving of levels. The mother says the daughter is immature and irresponsible and hysterical. At the same time she says, "Look how you hurt me," as if the daughter should be able to contain any kind of behavior the mother doesn't approve of.

INT.: And the daughter is always complaining to the mother, "You give me no help in becoming emotionally independent," which sounds like a contradiction, but is probably the only accurate way to describe the way the mother deals with her.

> MRS. S.: No, this is—Sue, I'm speaking to Dr. Jackson and trying to explain that that would have been my reaction to it. Now let me . . .
>
> SUE: Your reaction . . .

MRS. S.: . . . finish . . .

DR. J. (*simultaneously*): Yeah, let, look . . .

MRS. S.: Let me finish, Sue, because I'm trying hard to help get . . .

SUE: Go on.

MRS. S.: . . . to the root of this . . .

SUE: Go on.

MRS. S.: . . . and perhaps I'm supercritical of it. I don't question the fact that I am . . .

SUE: Mm-hm.

MRS. S.: . . . but I think there should be an effort made to correct what can be causing the mistaken impression . . .

DR. J.: Mm-hm.

MRS. S.: . . . because I know the, the mistaken impression is not only *my* mistaken impression. I mean, I don't like to see Sue putting herself in a position where people could *unjustly* criticize her.

INT.: The mother translates Sue's remark not as something she would criticize but as something that would offend others. She pushes off her own dislike of what Sue does onto these "others."

DR. J.: This is a very common parental technique; it's certainly not confined to sick families. "I know the real world better than you do, so when I'm speaking I'm a representative of other people you're going to run into and they'll feel exactly the same way." There's a certain amount of reality to this, which makes it very hard to deal with.

INT.: Did you see it as something this particular mother did a little more than other people?

DR. J.: Yes. She set herself up as someone with very proper standards and saw the daughter and father both as people with improper standards, thereby forcing them into a coalition which she then was repelled by. Even though the father was successful and so on, she saw him as boyish and rude and thoughtless, too much influenced by his work and his office. But there's something else here that I think is perhaps more important. Notice how quickly, when the mother said, "I may be wrong, I'm only trying," the daughter forgave her. I think the instantaneous way these two could get together as soon as a coalition was proffered is a sign that something could be done with it in therapy. A good prognostic sign.

INT.: I never would have seen that.

DR. J.: It happened so quickly. The daughter's tone softens, as if to say, "I know, Mother, I know." It shows that they can respond, if only on an instant-to-instant basis. To me, this is a kind of plus the therapist has to work with.

INT.: How do you mean, plus?

DR. J.: Their ability to influence each other momentarily means that you may be able to help them to stay on longer time segments together. If they can do it at all, you might be able to help them to extend it so they can get along for a whole luncheon together. You wouldn't hope for a whole week, but—two hours.

> SUE: I realize that, Mom, but you, I've also learned to be a lot, a great deal more kind in my man-, my speech and manner, since I entered [*hospital*], necess-, necessity demanded this, because you just don't be mean to people who are in trouble and have problems . . .
>
> MRS. S.: No, you don't . . .
>
> SUE: . . . and I had to learn to be kind, in everything I said and did, otherwise it would have repercussions.
>
> DR. J.: This, this is a, a (*sighs*) family to work with all right, ah . . . (*Sue laughs.*)

DR. J.: Sue is referring to the experience she had on the closed psychiatric ward where she was first hospitalized.

INT.: She's saying, "Mother, you shouldn't be mean to people who have just been in hospitals and have trouble."

DR. J.: A beautiful statement. It means that, and it also means, "I learned my manners after I left home. After your treatment of me sent me to a nut house."

INT.: Why did you come in then with such a personal reaction?

DR. J.: It's hard to recall the visual cues. I suspect I've gotten three messages that conflict within the last minute: the way the father's looking, the way the mother's talking, and the way the daughter answers her. And just as I thought the mother and daughter were beginning to get together, the daughter says, "I learned to behave away from home, in a nut house." It's exasperation of some kind.

INT.: It seems to be a way of putting some distance between the family and their problems.

DR. J.: Well, it makes them all equal. "I'm equally disgusted with the lot of you."

INT.: Yes, but some therapists would never come out with a

statement that showed them watching their own techniques, let alone using this as a technique. It's as though you were asking the family to go around behind the one-way screen and watch you work with them. It certainly calls them back to what they're there for, rather than this in-fighting they're engaged in.

DR. J.: It's probably true that whenever people in a family get into an unpleasant situation with each other, they tend to think very individualistically. "You're being mean to *me,* and he is not helping *me,* but he is on *your* side." If the therapist says, for example, "You're *all* this difficult," he relabels the situation as a family affair.

INT.: By presenting yourself as slightly confused, you also put yourself in the one-down position.

DR. J.: Yes. Part of the treatment of this family involved my try-ing to get the father more and more to participate, which he began to do with varying success. I think it was helpful to take the one-down with him, so that he didn't feel that I was doing something he couldn't do for his own family. I was caught up in this on several occasions when I became a little too active, I felt, and usurped his role.

INT.: As mediator between the two women?

DR. J.: Yes. And you might say, why not get the mother to be more active? I agree with Milton Erickson's statement that you use whatever the patient brings you. The girl and the mother got along much less well than the girl and the father, so he was in a better posi-tion to act as the stabilizer.

DR. J. (*to Sue*): We were just talking about what your dad might be feeling because I don't buy this, ah, (*to Mr. S.*) you know, we did everything we could for you, in quotes, as if you weren't feeling something right this minute. (*To Sue*) And now we're off on your manners, you see, um . . .

SUE: Mm-hm.

DR. J.: . . . you, you were the one who started it again by saying what you did to your dad. Your mother helped you by pointing it out, and then you help her by arguing with her over this relatively minor issue compared to the severity of the other troubles.

SUE (*overlapping*): Well, I know we had a major issue there for a while but, ah, got interrupted . . .

DR. J. (*overlapping*): But Dad's been left out again . . . see?

SUE: Uh-huh, I see. (*Pause.*)

INT.: When you do a little review like that, do you assume that bringing to their attention what's been happening will help them to change it?

DR. J.: No, I don't. It's a way of justifying your remarks. If suddenly I say to you, "You're behaving miserably," this has no effect except to irritate you, unless I can say, "because of the following." I don't think they get much insight out of it, no.

INT.: Again, you get the emphasis on the family system. You're pointing out a redundancy, a pattern.

DR. J.: But more to imply that I have some authority and can see something they can't see, rather than to make them see things my way. That would be too much to hope for.

MR. S.: That is exactly what I referred to a little while ago when I said the two of them get recriminating back and forth and they carry on until finally I step in and say, will you please shut up or stop it or . . .

SUE: Yeah.

MR. S.: . . . don't bicker so much, and, ah . . .

SUE: Well . . .

MR. S.: . . . try to—well, I don't try to separate 'em, I get, I get so annoyed that I blow up . . .

DR. J.: Mm-hm.

SUE: Yeah, and that's what I was just s-s-saying . . .

MR. S.: Uh-huh.

SUE: . . . you usually do it rather explosively . . .

MR. S.: Yes.

SUE: . . . and then it upsets us all the more, then boy, we've really got a situation on our hands.

DR. J.: The important thing here is that they missed the fact that when he comes in explosively, he does break them up. Even if it's poorly done or unpleasantly done, it breaks them up.

INT.: You made the point just now that you were trying to help the family by getting the father to mediate more effectively between the mother and the daughter.

DR. J.: Yes. He used to blow up at them, and shout at them, sometimes at one, sometimes at the other, and sometimes at both. Now, to the extent that he makes a fool of himself, he doesn't sound like a leader. Also, if he makes them both very uncomfortable, it only reinforces the conviction of each that the other one got her into trouble with Dad again. He perpetuates their dyadic quarrel this way.

MR. S.: (*Pause.*) I, um, I guess if I suffer I suffer inside, I don't show it much on the outside. I get, stomach tied up in a knot and I . . .

DR. J.: Mm-hm.

MR. S. (*sighs*): I grit my teeth and clench my fists and finally blow up, ah— (*Sue interrupts.*)

INT.: That was quite a long pause, before the father came in. Were you looking at him expectantly, waiting for him to continue?

DR. J.: I would suppose so, because he is responsive to the idea of intervening. He does enter in when he explains why he feels the way he does, and I'm encouraging him to go on.

SUE: I wish you could let it out.

MR. S.: What's that?

SUE: I wish you could let it out. It'd be so much better for you.

MR. S.: Well, over many years of discipline I guess you kind of . . .

SUE: Yeah, but you can overdiscipline yourself.

MR. S.: Well, maybe I have, I don't know. I try to conceal all my . . .

DR. J. (*interrupting*): Let's not make the mistake, Sue, of thinking that, that people can do differently easily, you know from your own experience they can't, so it's one thing to say, "I wish you'd let it out," and another thing to be able to do it.

SUE (*laughing*): Yeah.

DR. J.: Yeah.

DR. J.: One thing is fairly consistent in this interview; every time Sue brings her illness in, I won't tolerate it. She's really saying, "I've been a patient and I know; the psychiatrists have told *me* to let it out." She seemed to have decided that she would be my co-therapist because both she and I knew what mental illness was. I didn't altogether care for this. I'm always uneasy in early interviews with psychotics because they try to put the focus on their illness and things can very quickly get out of hand.

INT.: Are you also responding to a feeling that a daughter

shouldn't have this amount of freedom to comment on what her father does? Were you trying to separate the generations by implying that the girl shouldn't be supervising the parents?

DR. J.: That wasn't my reaction here. I think one generation can comment on another and the line of separation can still remain if the comment is put in the context of the speaker's generation. Like: "It's all very well for you young fellows to say you want to make a million dollars; I can sympathize with your wish, though I know it's not easy to do." I would only jump on such a remark if I thought it was intended to stir up trouble. Illness and deliberate provocation are two things I will not tolerate. Here it was the illness. I don't think Sue was trying to be provoking.

INT.: You fend off Sue and defend the father by saying, "People can't be different." It's an excusing kind of thing, as when you said, "People do the best they can."

DR. J.: Yes, but it goes both ways. I can apply it equally to the daughter: "As you learned from your own experience."

INT.: It's such a complicated statement in the context of the father's saying that it's his own self-discipline that makes him blow up.

DR. J.: Whatever they're saying, I'm not even hearing it as discipline. My remark says that whatever they're doing, it's what they have to do. I'm putting them on an equal level.

MRS. S.: Dad and I are two completely, totally different people, you know that . . .

SUE: Sure.

MRS. S.: In, in every way, but we've managed to live together unusually happily, in your own words.

SUE: I know.

DR. J.: The mother was in a peculiar bind at this time. She hated her husband, intensively and actively; he did a lot of things that humiliated her, including bringing women he was going around with into the house. Yet she was maintaining the fiction that they had a happy marriage. She would naturally resent her daughter for claiming to be more of an expert on her husband than she, the mother, who had known him many years longer. On the other hand, if she was really to be an expert on him, she would have to admit the truth about him, which would refute this good relationship she claimed they had.

INT.: This may be why she uses the word "unusual." It can be taken any way you like. The surface idea here is that the marriage is fine, but the implication is that it's unusual that they could stay together because they don't get along. You wouldn't raise any question about the "unusual" happiness of the marriage?

DR. J.: No, especially not in the first interview. I'm trying to get them to keep coming, so I'm in no position to indicate that they're going to be under scrutiny.

MRS. S. (*starting to cry*): How do you suppose it happened?

SUE: Well, you were in *love*.

MRS. S.: That's not enough . . .

SUE (*overlapping*): It took a give and take process, it took a lot of working out ups and downs, a lot of discussion, and I think you've even seen argument.

MR. S.: That's normal.

MRS. S.: That's right.

SUE: I know a lot more about marriage than you give me credit for.

MRS. S.: But you know what I think has made it possible for us? Is learning to accept each other as we (*voice wavering*) are.

SUE: Well, sure, you'd have to, otherwise you never would have even got to the altar. (*Long pause.*)

DR. J.: To me this is so terribly pathological that I feel I've got to do something and yet I can't tell the mother to shut up. I don't know what to do. But this is a bad point, I can feel it.

INT.: Sue says, "I think you've even seen argument." Had the parents had arguments in front of the daughter, or was she just guessing?

DR. J.: I think they had arguments fairly often, but I don't think the daughter knew with certainty how bad the situation was. The mother gave me a letter which she had written the father but never sent, the daughter was six months old at the time. It was really a fascinating document and foreshadowed a lot of things which came to pass. They had only been married a little over a year, and the mother was already saying that she didn't know if she could go on in the relationship, that the father was too much involved with the daughter, was ignoring her and so on. Yet the father at that time had given evidence of being involved in his first extra-marital activity. So even then, at the age of six months, the daughter got the blame. I was cued into this by a statement the mother made during a later interview when she said to Sue, "For the past twenty years you've interfered between your father and me." The girl at that time was nineteen! It's nearly twenty years later, and nothing has changed. The baby is now a college woman, and the same thing is going on.

INT.: Did you appreciate the switch the daughter made? The mother says, "What has made our marriage possible is learning to accept each other as we are," and the daughter says, "Well, you'd have to, otherwise you'd never have even got to the altar." Then there's a big silence.

DR. J.: From altar to altercation!

INT.: She refutes everything she's been saying.

DR. J.: Yes, there's a little bit of sanity in that she goes overboard and then retracts it. "What you're saying, Mother, is obvious—that Daddy and you can't stand each other."

INT.: I take it that this sort of "togetherness" would make you feel you had to come in.

DR. J.: It would make me very uncomfortable to see this going on. To me it is highly pathogenic. I think it's the therapist's duty to catch some of these things, so that the participants can learn to recognize the general configuration of this kind of brainwashing.

INT.: Why do you call it brainwashing?

DR. J.: Well, that's just a way of putting it. It sounds as if the mother's brainwashing the daughter, but it takes two to tango, so that's oversimplifying it. The mother is saying, "Okay, you said the Emperor had his clothes on. I'll go along with you, but if you now deny that you said it, you'll open up a schism between your father and me that you can drive a truck through." So the daughter quickly says, "I don't want to do that. Yes, of course you're in love!" But she has to pretend she's crazy in order to accept this.

MRS. S.: We got there awfully fast. (*Laughs.*)

MR. S. (*laughing*): I don't think we analyzed it very thoroughly at that time.

MRS. S.: (*Laughs.*)

MR. S. (*laughing*): Oh, I did quite a bit . . .

MRS. S.: Oh, you were a cold-blooded man, at least as I look back on it (*laughs*) now.

MR. S. (*overlapping*): Well, I was older than you were and I had spent more time thinking about marriage than you had, although . . .

MRS. S. (*overlapping*): Hm. Remember, we start earlier than you do.

MR. S. (*overlapping*): So I had, I had, we—all right, maybe, all right, I'll take that back, I didn't, thought about it longer but (*sighs*) I had thought about it long enough to get it spelled out in my own mind pretty much what I expected and didn't expect and, um . . .

SUE (*interrupting*): Anyway, we're off the issue (*sighs*), which I think is why you're squirming, Dr. Jackson (*laughing*). This, this is not really the issue.

INT.: What was this squirming Sue refers to?

DR. J.: I think Sue's remark probably referred to something I was doing that I was not aware of. I imagine I was figuring out what to do about this critical exchange between Sue and her mother, and feeling impatient because I hadn't done anything about it yet.

INT.: Sue diverts everyone from the issue that caused this flurry by saying, "We're off the issue." You had gotten to why Mother and Father got married, and whether they even thought about it at the time. But the daughter says that's not the issue.

DR. J.: Well, the father said something classic, not in this interview, but shortly after. He wanted to indicate how much his wife and he were in love, so he said that they got on a cross-country train together and by the time they got off, they were engaged. The mother found this a rather licentious statement; she didn't like it at all. But they were engaged and got married rather quickly, despite some family questions.

INT.: When the mother says, "You were cold-blooded," does she mean "You maneuvered me into this?"

DR. J.: The implication is that he pushed her into it, yes. The other implication is the rather obvious one, that she was pregnant. It's better to have it that he pushed her than that they had to get married.

INT.: The daughter would be even more a cause of resentment if she had been what forced them into marriage.

DR. J.: That's right.

INT.: One more question about this remark of Sue's. Do patients often comment that freely about you?

DR. J.: No. but I had a rapport with Sue from the minute we met.

I don't know entirely what it was based on. But I did not find her remark surprising.

> DR. J.: No, I was squirming because I, I don't, ah, I'm trying to think which is the most useful aspect . . .
>
> SUE: Well . . .
>
> DR. J.: . . . of this to break into and, ah . . .
>
> SUE: The most useful as far as my health is concerned now is the issue about my independence.
>
> DR. J.: Ah, but that, that will take some getting together, so that that to me is the groundwork. Ah, I'm trying to deal with your mother's statement, ah, I suppose more than any. Um, you see, you see, Mrs. Starbuck, from what you've said, you've put Sue in a rather impossible position, because she will have to assume that she either is an illegitimate child (*Sue laughs*) or adopted or, ah, that mental illness is completely a matter of biochemistry, for which there is no good scientific evidence.

DR. J.: That's a rather brave thing to say, isn't it?

INT.: It's especially brave in view of the fact that you take these ideas of heredity which generally you attack—and attack later in this interview as the parents come up with them—and use them against the parents. You're saying to them, "If you treat Sue as though she couldn't come from your marriage, you're acting as though there were no heredity involved."

DR. J.: Yes. It's a tricky use of heredity. It's saying, "You're not treating Sue as if she were really your daughter," which is more of a pangenetic concept. Actually, I'm on safe ground, because I can assume that they will think I'm talking about the ways she is like them, which are good. What is bad about her is the way she is *not* like them.

> SUE: I don't think it's mental illness . . .
>
> DR. J.: Ahh . . .
>
> SUE: . . . I think it's emotional.
>
> MRS. S. (*overlapping*): I don't understand what that means, Dr. Jackson.
>
> DR. J.: Well, if you say that, that you and your husband have gotten along, you know, so well, and how have we managed to do this, ah, then obviously this means that she is the moldy fig, she is the troublemaker, the, the, you know, I, I mean (*Mrs. S. overlapping,*

inaudible phrase) it cuts her out from the family in a way that I don't think you mean to.

INT.: That's pretty direct.

DR. J.: I think it was partly desperation. Time was going by, and I didn't know quite how to break into this. I'm almost focusing the blame on the mother. I don't think it's very adroit, because it invites Sue to come in and say, "Yes, I am a poor orphan."

INT.: You don't consider it productive to support her like that?

DR. J.: No. She does this all the time. I don't think anything she does routinely is very useful. She can always be dramatic about "You don't appreciate me," and I assume this is standard with her. What I should have done is to say to the mother, "You know, I think you and Sue have a lot in common."

INT.: You mean, instead of putting it in a negative way, "You people are cutting Sue out," you should have said, "You, Sue, and you, Mother, have a deep harmony."

DR. J.: As a matter of fact, they do; they just don't see it that way. I did try later to get the mother to agree that her daughter looked like her, but as you'll see, it didn't work.

INT.: That's such a different orientation from the old days. It was thought then that the way to treat the schizophrenic in the presence of his parents was to show how the parents are cutting him out of the family, that is, to be supportive. I'm interested to know why you wouldn't consider this helpful.

DR. J.: It might be helpful if the patient is taking everything on himself. We had to do a structured interview recently with a boy who had been labeled a mental defective. The boy would say, "I'm just a dope," or, "I should go out and get a job." He would never realize how the parents were cutting him out. When they could actually be confronted with this in not too maladroit a way, it was useful. But it's a limited tactic because you can't go any place with it. Also, showing how the patient is being left out doesn't exactly bolster his self-esteem. But at least he learns to recognize what's going on.

MRS. S. (*to Dr. J.*): No, my object was to point out that, um, we must learn to accept each other as we are . . .

SUE: Well, you don't!

MRS. S.: . . . and that Dad—(*To Sue*) Dad and *I* do.

SUE: You don't! You *two*, yeah, where do *I* stand in this? I don't get accepted for a person, for an individual, for an adult. I'm a child, and I'm very painfully reminded of it every time you get a chance to, every time. The minute I say something like this . . .

DR. J. (*interrupting*): What I was going to suggest is that, this, um, this is my hypothesis, I don't have good evidence for it, ah, except from experience and from what little you've already said, um, I think we could at least entertain the hypothesis that one reason you and your husband have accepted each other so well is partly because you could see in Sue that part which you were not accepting in the other person but were completely unconscious of.

SUE: Oh, boy!

DR. J.: This goes as far back as the Bible, you know, when you, this business of when Jews don't eat pig.

SUE (*overlapping*): In other words, the things that they can't accept in each other are in me . . .

DR. J.: Mm-hm.

SUE: . . . and I've just sort of gotten them from them both.

MR. S.: Could you repeat that again? (*Laughing.*)

INT.: You're saying that Sue represents the unconscious side of them. Why do you bring in the unconscious here?

DR. J.: I think using the unconscious as a ploy is a perfectly legitimate way to get people to consider a different point of view. I don't think it accomplishes anything to say, "You may not agree with me but I *know*." On the other hand, I would use it to get people to look at things a new way.

INT.: That's interesting. A lot of therapists would avoid making such a theoretical statement about what they think the trouble really is, knowing the other people aren't seeing it that way at all. It's almost as if you were explaining the case to a colleague.

DR. J.: No, all I'm doing is trying to give the parents a different way of viewing what they're doing to their daughter, one that will cause them to be less judgmental.

INT.: What is surprising is that in general your therapy seems more a "behavior" therapy than an "insight" therapy. Yet you seem to be giving them insight here.

DR. J.: I think it's behavior therapy. When you use the insight ploy in this way, you're not really referring to some kind of unconscious that they don't know about and you do; you're using it to stop them and say, "Listen to me, because I have knowledge that you don't have—pay attention." Then if they say, "You're wrong," you can say, "You can't prove I'm wrong. If it's unconscious, how can you know?"

INT.: You see it as a tactical thing, rather than as "helping them understand."

DR. J.: Yes.

INT.: Because an outsider might think you were trying to give these people insight.

DR. J.: You can tell the quality of the insight when the father says, "Would you repeat that?"

INT.: Naturally, they're not thinking that they're making the child a scapegoat, and that's what you're implying.

DR. J.: No, I'm saying that they're doing it unconsciously. They don't have to say they're guilty, they can just say, "We didn't realize it."

INT.: There's a fine distinction here between a tactical maneuver and an insight maneuver. If you were going to try to give them insight into this, would you go about it differently? Suppose you thought it was very important for the parents to discover that they're doing this?

DR. J.: I would tell them to treat the daughter the way they are already treating her, and let *them* discover how they're treating her. In other words, try to produce a "runaway" in the system. That would produce more "insight" than just telling them what I think they're doing. I would say, "The thing to do is be very firm with Sue, and the two of you must stand together and treat her like the child she is." Prescribing the symptom is more likely to produce insight than telling people how the mind works.

INT.: Would you use this tactic with a chronic schizophrenic's family in which the parents are saying, "We're very happy," and seem totally unaware that their child's problems have anything to do with them?

DR. J.: About a week ago, I saw a family with a boy who was supposed to be mentally defective, and of course wasn't. I urged the mother to keep the father from being so benevolent to the son, because he was ruining his own life. As soon as I touched on this, the differences between the parents started to come out. If I had tried to give them insight into what they were doing, they would have said, "Oh, Bill is so helpless, so sick, we've got to help him," or "Dr. So-and-so says we should do such-and-such."

INT.: At the end of this interchange, you brought the Bible in. Was that for some particular reason?

DR. J.: I knew the mother came from a very religious family. I was saying to her, "Don't start arguing with the Bible."

INT.: You have quite a bit of ammunition, with both psychiatry and the Bible thrown in.

DR. J.: Well, I keep a lot of little clichés and examples in my mind, from a variety of sources. If this were an Oriental family, I might have brought in something from Zen or Taoism.

> MR. S. (*cont.*): I don't, I think I follow you.
> DR. J.: I may not . . .
> MRS. S. (*overlapping*): I'm sure it's true. (*Laughs.*)
> SUE: I got it. (*Laughs.*)
> DR. J.: I may not be too clear but I'll try. What I'm trying to say is, ah, that maybe one of the first things we could again examine as a hypothesis, and look for data for, is that some of the things that Sue does that are difficult and cause trouble are exactly the things that you (*to parents*) do not complain about in each other, you two . . .
> MR. S.: Um-hm.
> DR. J.: . . . but they have been put into her, where they are then dealt with.

INT.: The way you say, "One of the first things we could examine as a hypothesis, and look for data for," seems to set this up as a scientific enterprise.

DR. J.: Oh, well, everybody believes in science. I'm saying, "This is not just personal opinion, it's something we're going to work on."

INT.: There's a funny quality here of "Let's you and I examine what terrible things you're doing." Do you often say this sort of thing?

DR. J.: I think I say it very often: "I don't really know; I have a few ideas, but I need your help." Anybody who says he won't help is pretty bad.

> MRS. S.: That's exactly right. I can give you . . .
> SUE: Boy!
> MRS. S.: . . . specific instances of it.

DR. J.: See how quickly the mother agrees with me? If you call something to people's attention by saying: "You may not have been aware of it, but this could have been going on," they tend to seize on the idea that it was unconscious. The avidity with which they seize it gives you an indication of how "unconscious" they really are. These parents were at each other's throats, they just hadn't publicly admitted it.

> SUE: It's so true. I mean things . . .
>
> DR. J. (*to Mrs. S.*): Thank you!
>
> SUE: . . . things that you don't (*laughs*) like.
>
> MRS. S.: Well, I have recognized that and I've even talked about it (*inaudible phrase*).
>
> SUE (*overlapping*): Well, the things you don't like in each other are here in me, and I'm sorry, that's just the way I am.
>
> MRS. S.: Darling, nobody minds the way you are.
>
> SUE (*overlapping*): Well, all right . . .
>
> DR. J. (*interrupting*): Here you go lousing things up again! Your mother says something to be helpful again and you start off on one of your speeches.
>
> SUE: O.K.

DR. J.: You see, I'm trying to get my point across to the parents; the mother says she's gotten it, though I don't believe she has, and the daughter says, "It's all my fault," to take the focus completely off what I'm trying to do.

INT.: One might assume that this has touched some family chord or the daughter wouldn't come in so quickly. Again, you seem to feel pretty free to quiet Sue down.

DR. J.: I wonder why I feel more free with her than with the parents.

INT.: I don't think you'd say, "Here you go lousing things up again," to the mother. You make it sound very affectionate.

DR. J.: It's mainly that I have a way, not entirely intentional, of establishing a signal system with the identified patient, of indicating: "You're crazy, but you and I know that's not all of you." And it gives me greater leeway.

INT.: You seem to be suggesting you're more comfortable with the schizophrenic.

DR. J.: I can do this with a married couple, with whoever is the identified patient, in the sense that they've agreed that he drinks, or she steals. You can say to somebody, "You really are a mess," and have it sound hopeful. Here the mother hasn't admitted to anything, so if I criticize her, it's all negative.

INT.: When you say to Sue, "Here you go lousing things up again," you introduce the assumption that she can stop. Is that what you mean by "hopeful"?

DR. J.: Yes.

INT.: Perhaps you're not so sure the mother could stop.

DR. J.: If the mother said something was wrong with her, then I could give her credit for being wrong in a way that meant she could do better. If the mother were saying, "I haven't been doing well with my daughter," or "It's all my fault that my daughter is this way," then I could say, "I'm sure you're not wrong all the time."

INT.: It's an interesting point, that with someone who's taking the blame you've got something to work with. I wonder if it's also that you feel parental toward the girl. Some therapists feel parental toward the whole group, and they treat the parents like children, as if they haven't matured enough to be adults. But you treat the parents like adults, and the girl like a child.

DR. J.: When the child is there, it's easy to be against the parental coalition. If only the parents are there, then there isn't a coalition. You can make one by treating both as younger and pitting them against you. In some marital situations, the couple achieves its strongest rapport in being against you.

INT.: Do you use this consciously as a tool to get them together?

DR. J.: Yes. But it's not as hard to do with a symmetrical couple as it is with people like this who have a third person to focus on. Even if they were to get together, they would only get together over that person.

INT.: If the parents sense that you're aligned with the child, does this make a problem for you in handling them?

DR. J.: Sometimes. I try to keep it even, but every so often I get caught. I saw a very beautiful girl a few months ago who got married and then had a psychotic breakdown. She was supposed to be crazy, unable to get a job, and so on. We established a rapport very quickly, and then I invited the mother in. The mother started saying to me, "What are we going to do about her?" and "She shouldn't see her ex-husband," and "She doesn't know what she's doing." The girl and I were talking past the mother to establish certain rules which sounded very sensible, such as what she'd do with her attorney, where she'd look for work, and so on. After the session, the mother went back to the psychiatrist who had referred them to me and said that I must have seen the ex-husband before they came in and made an agreement of some sort with his family. I thought I was being nice to the mother, but I was obviously mistaken. The patient left a good deal taller, and the mother resented it. So I do get caught. But to get back to Sue, did you hear her say "O.K."? It was a perfectly straightforward, evenly modulated "O.K."

INT.: Nothing crazy about it. I think that's also because you're treating her as though she were sane. You react to her as a young girl who's intruding or interrupting her mother. There's no quality of handling somebody who is disturbed.

DR. J.: No. And her tone implies, "I get the point, let's go on to something else," which is a good sign. She could have gotten angry.

INT.: I think if you had been the least bit patronizing, she would have. But it's a sane "O.K."

DR. J. (*to Mrs. S.*): Can you think of an example?
MRS. S.: Yes I can, a very specific one.
DR. J.: Good.

INT.: Here, when the mother does agree with you, even though it's doubtful whether she really does, you're so nice about asking her for an example. Is this to test her out, or is it to go along with her?

DR. J.: This is to say, "We're in as much need of examples from you as we are of examples from the patient. It's again a way of equalizing them.

MRS. S.: My husband is chronically, and I congratulated him today, he is chronically late, unaware of the passage of time, which was an extreme irritant to me because I was a prompt person when we were first married, and I adjusted along the line to him. I'm a little late now, and he's a lot better about getting to places earlier. But Sue had the same lack of sense of time, completely (*Sue talking in background*) and I was determined that she was going to learn (*laughing*)—I'm being honest about this . . .
DR. J.: I hope so.

Dr. J.: Here I'm struck by the cleverness of the tactic. The mother says, "I'm being honest." It's as if I excused myself for putting the finger on you by saying, "I am being honest, for which I deserve praise." That's why I don't go along with the people who believe in thinking disorders.

Int.: It could be argued that thinking-disorder tactics are extremely skillful. This is a beautiful one. I also noticed that the mother, after agreeing so nicely about their doing these things unconsciously, gives it a twist that gets her out from under. She says, "I was aware of my husband's influence, and I fought it." It's the father's influence that is unconscious.

Dr. J.: You're right. She puts me in my place by saying *she* wasn't unconscious. But at the price of admitting to some marital conflict. One thing about saying that something is unconscious is that they can't refute you. The only way they can refute you is to say, "No, it was conscious," which puts them on the way to admitting what they are doing.

SUE: I have learned, a lot.

MRS. S. (*overlapping*): I was determined that she was going to learn so that she wouldn't impose on other people by forgetting time.

MR. S.: So she wouldn't be like her father. (*Laughing.*)

MRS. S.: No, that isn't what I mean, because, so that she . . .

DR. J. (*overlapping*): All right . . .

MR. S. (*overlapping, laughing*): That's a fact.

DR. J. (*overlapping, laughing*): That sounded like what you meant. That's fair enough.

SUE (*overlapping*): Yeah, I think you've done a fairly good job.

Int.: Why did you come in then?

Dr. J.: Everybody's taking his hair down. Father says *mea culpa;* mother says, "I didn't mean it." They're having a moment of togetherness. I'm always willing to underline this if I possibly can, because I think these moments are all too infrequent.

Int.: It's a mixed moment of togetherness. Father has just interpreted Mother correctly by saying, "You mean you don't want her to be late *like me*."

Dr. J.: Yes, but that's an admission. Mother says, "Let's all be honest," and everybody is being honest. Father said that about his lateness right after his wife said, *"I'm* able to be honest."

INT.: He forced her to take it back. She then slid into a bit of dishonesty by saying, "That isn't what I said."

DR. J.: But girlishly. And Sue isn't taking her usual role as the moldy fig. She is being honest enough to say, "I think you've done a good job." Everybody's just charming—but oh, for so short a time!

> MRS. S. (*to Sue*): I think you've been wonderful about it. You, you bucked for a while but you finally saw the reasons why it was necessary to be on time, because it often imposes on other people, it imposes on . . .
>
> DR. J. (*interrupting*): Ah, but you said something else that supports my thesis, I'm happy to say, you said she bucked for a while. In other words, if you think of a child as being pretty malleable, ah, why wouldn't she have learned to be right on time from the beginning? So . . .
>
> MRS. S.: I don't think of a child as being malleable. Sue has never been in her whole life, from the time she was born.
>
> DR. J.: Oh.

DR. J.: This is my fault. I set this up. I got a little competitive with the mother and said, "Aha! You've proved my point," but it was a weak tactic because then she could say, "That doesn't prove anything at all; it was inherited." I pushed her into this position.

INT.: You pushed her to contradict herself. She's been saying it's the father's influence, not heredity.

DR. J.: Yes, but I could have handled that better by not meeting the mother head-on.

INT.: When you said, "You proved my thesis," did you mean that Sue wouldn't have resisted unless there were some conflict between the parents?

DR. J.: I'm saying that she's getting reinforced by the father, yes.

> MR. S.: Malleable? (*Sue laughs.*) Is that what you said? Never been malleable?
>
> SUE: Um-hm.
>
> MRS. S.: There's never been one, this is my trouble, there's never been one thing which I considered as normal teaching or training on the part of a mother, and a mother's responsibility to her children, which hasn't been a struggle with Sue.
>
> SUE: Ohh, I don't think that's a fair comment. I think that's highly unfair and it blames me for something . . .

DR. J.: But . . .

SUE: . . . that isn't totally true.

DR. J.: Now wait a minute . . .

MRS. S. (*overlapping*): Darling, no.

INT.: The mother goes pretty far there. "Sue has never been normal" is what she is saying.

DR. J.: It's irrefutable, this kind of talk: "She's been that way ever since she was born."

INT.: Yet five minutes ago she was agreeing completely with you. When you said, "Sue's troubles are not inborn, they come from you," I think she must have heard it as a criticism of the way she brought Sue up, not as a reference to the father's reinforcing the daughter.

DR. J.: That's the trouble with her technique. She cuts me off, as I'm sure she does other people, and ends up in a worse position than she would if she could wait a moment.

INT.: That may be the main weakness of mothers of schizophrenics. They come in too soon every time, then they struggle to get their feet out of what they got into.

DR. J. (*to Sue*): Ah, how can it be fair or unfair?

SUE: Well, I haven't bucked her on *everything*. I couldn't possibly have . . .

DR. J. (*overlapping*): It isn't—well, who is *you*, when you were a little baby? Your mother is talking about back to the crib.

MRS. S.: (*Overlapping, inaudible phrase.*)

SUE: Well, I know, but I couldn't possibly have re-rebelled on everything or I'd be faster in a mental hospital than I was.

DR. J. (*overlapping*): So don't buy the statement.

SUE: (*Sighs.*)

DR. J.: Don't buy it!

SUE (*starting to cry*): I don't, I'm not buying it.

DR. J. (*overlapping*): Your mother's expressing her feelings about this. It isn't a fair or unfair statement because it's . . .

SUE: Hm.

DR. J.: . . . simply a reflection of what she's feeling.

MR. S.: That's her training, all right, and you can . . .

MRS. S. (*overlapping*): Well, I (*Mrs. S. and Sue talk at once, words unclear*) completely frustrated because simple, basic things, no matter how hard I tried, I could never seem to get the results. I mean, how you hold your fork at the table . . .

DR. J.: Um-hm.

MRS. S.: . . . table manners, just habits that are instilled in children by their mothers, that *must* be.

INT.: You come in so persistently there, as if you feel it's very necessary.

DR. J.: I would have to see a movie of it to know, but I would suspect from the tone of the voices that this is one of the recurrent vulnerabilities. To me, this is high-class brainwashing. The mother saying, "I know, darling, I'm only telling you this for your own good," and Sue saying, "You're being unfair," meanwhile starting to go downhill, showing some moisture in the eyes and so on. I consider this whole argument of the mother's, about Sue never being malleable, as pretty psychotogenic, a devastating thing to say. I'm almost pleading with the girl, "Don't *buy* this!"

INT.: You seem to have a strong aversion to what you call brainwashing. Is that partly why you turned on the parents before and said, "The problem isn't Sue, it's what's going on between the two of you"?

DR. J.: If the brainwashing bothered me, it was more from the standpoint of Sue's being so confused that she would accept her parents' distorted view of things. I wasn't really blaming them. I think I went into it more as a reaction to her prostituting herself in order to be their daughter. So I think it would be more a question of attacking the psychosis, as John Rosen says. You're not fighting the patient, you're fighting that crazy aspect of her. In the same way, you're not fighting the parents, you're fighting their contribution to her craziness.

INT.: You take the daughter's side very feelingly here and completely dismiss the mother. It does sound as if the mother had provoked you.

DR. J.: Only because her tactics are so good. She has to deny what she's doing by saying, "I'm putting the finger on you, Sue, but only for your own good, and I wouldn't do it unless I were a mother. It's a mother's duty to suffer." She's gotten it all in there. I am provoked, not by the mother's chicanery, but by the very mechanics of what she did. I don't think there's the least bit of motivation there, it's almost instinctual for her to do that. It's as if you were asking what an animal experiences when it gets a scent. Does it know it's a coyote out hunting, or does it just react?

INT.: You seem to be saying that you can't blame someone who acts like this any more than you can blame a hunting dog who chews up the neighbor's rabbit. It's a curious reason for not blaming someone. In other words, you're provoked by the psychosis again.

DR. J.: Yes.

INT.: In dealing with this, you don't say to the mother, "This is not the way to handle your daughter." You say to the daughter, "You don't have to buy this."

DR. J.: I must admit I'm a little proud of this. I said, "Your mother couldn't help it." That makes the mother equally irresponsible in her behavior. If I turned to the mother and said, "That's not the way to treat your daughter," it makes her saner than the daughter. This way it's: "Your mother couldn't help what she said, so don't take it personally."

INT.: You're bypassing the issue of blame again.

DR. J.: Yes. If the daughter hears herself being treated this way by the mother, unless she realizes that the mother does it because she "can't help it," she's going to blame her.

INT.: It must have an effect on the mother when you don't call her on this directly but tell the person she's talking to not to accept what she says. It cuts her out.

DR. J.: Yes. She doesn't like that. But it's content-less, so she can't do much about it. Whereas if I attacked her directly, she'd say, "I'm as good a mother as anyone else."

INT.: To say to the daughter, "You don't have to buy it" is also asking for a major change in how they talk in that room. If she doesn't have to buy it, she doesn't have to argue about it, which sets up a new precedent in the family. It implies that no matter what anybody says, the others don't necessarily have to take it as the ultimate truth; they don't even have to react.

DR. J.: If you classify the kinds of remarks a therapist makes, one category would refer to what is said and the other would refer to the rules of communication. What you're talking about would fall into the second category.

INT.: The phrasing you use here falls into that category. All through this family interview, you come in with bargaining or game-playing terms. When people start getting caught up in their own feelings, you cut them off, using some phrase like, "Don't buy it," "It's a trap you don't have to fall into," "You won't win this argument." When you do this, you bring in the idea that feelings are tactics, that they take place within an interactional framework.

DR. J.: Yes, but you have to remember that feelings are also pre-tactical. It's not easy to remind yourself that your response, however emotional and purely nontactical, will be seen as tactics because that's the kind of environment we live in. You've got to help people to interpret their own reactions.

INT.: But using tactical phrasings yourself is a little different from directly interpreting reactions as tactics.

DR. J.: Well, I don't see how you can come out directly and interpret somebody else's feelings in a group, or even in a dyadic situation, as tactics. If somebody comes in and says, "I've got news for you, I'm dying of cancer," it doesn't matter that he's simply reporting on what his internist has told him and his depression about not wanting to expire; it's a tactical situation once he's said it. Then if he adds, "Oh, don't let me upset you," you think, "Now he's really pulling my leg." I think this is what the psychotic is up against. Because of his training, he doesn't recognize the effect of that kind of a statement on a group. But it's no use saying to the man with cancer or whatever, "Your misery is having all kinds of effects on other people," because then he'd say, "Oh, I didn't mean that at all," and you'd feel doubly bad because he was dying and here you'd made him feel terrible. If you could say, "Well, if you've got enough time left, perhaps you could help Christ do some of his unfinished work," that would be a way to get it into an interactional framework.

> DR. J. (to Mrs. S.): But where was the, where was the other side coming from, you see?
>
> MRS. S.: Um-hm.
>
> DR. J.: I mean kids are little. If they don't do what you say, do what you tell 'em to, you can beat 'em, or you can scare 'em to death, or you can brainwash 'em, you can whisper to 'em while they're asleep, ah . . .
>
> MRS. S. (laughing): Well, I never heard that one, I should have heard that one!
>
> SUE: It works!

DR. J.: You notice here that I went just a little bit too far. I used one, two, three phrases, and then a fourth, which was one too many.

She picked it up and said, "I should have heard that one." Just as an experiment, I would like to sit down with a family like this and deliberately behave in a way to get myself annihilated. I think I could predict beforehand that if I used certain too explicit, or too extravagant, or whatever, expressions, the mother would invariably cut me down. You have to know when to stop. I could hear this coming: first, second, third, fourth, and then she wipes me out by changing the subject.

DR. J.: What, where was the other side coming from?

MRS. S.: The other side of . . .

DR. J.: The negative side. If she . . .

MRS. S.: . . . of Sue?

DR. J.: Yeah. If she was late, for example, until she finally got over it, that there had to be some reason why she was late, why she didn't do what you said right from the beginning. This is (*inaudible phrase*).

MRS. S. (*overlapping*): Well, I believe, I believe firmly, as far as this time thing is concerned, that some people are just born without an acute sense of time, and others are born with a better sense of time. (*Sue laughs.*)

MR. S.: You think that's an inherited characteristic?

SUE: No, it's something adopted.

MRS. S.: I'm not at all sure it isn't inherited. If you look, if you look back through the families on both sides, you can find plenty of evidence. (*Laughs.*)

DR. J.: As an aside, the letter I told you about was written at seven or eight o'clock in the evening, when the father had not shown up for dinner. This was early in the marriage. She talks about sense of time *now*, twenty years later. And in that letter she talked about time: "You don't show up for dinner; you don't even tell me you're not coming." It's marvelous how this genetic idea will spare her twenty years of suffering as she looks back. She doesn't even have to think about all the examples the father set for the little girl.

INT.: What is curious is the way the mother blames the child for things that she claims were born into her. If she was born that way, how can she deserve to be blamed?

DR. J.: Well, the mother's tone is complaining, yet she speaks in a kind of forgiving way too. But the fact that she's forgiving them all the more reifies the fact that they're terrible. It's a tough one to deal with.

> DR. J.: But that's— (*Mrs. S. laughing.*) You know, there, there actually is no scientific evidence to date for any particular personality trait being inherited, let alone something as specific as time.
>
> SUE: (*Inaudible phrase*) must be adopted.
>
> MRS. S.: Is it then a form of imitation?
>
> SUE: Um-hm.
>
> DR. J.: Well, at least until there's evidence to the contrary, I think we would have to assume that this is a good bet. And why wouldn't a daughter want to imitate her father?
>
> MRS. S.: Well, I think she would.
>
> SUE: Pretty thin thing to go by. (*Laughs.*)

INT.: Are you assuming a metaphorical conversation here about mental illness and inheritance?

DR. J.: Yes, sure. But I did do something rather good there, when I got back to the father. We got off onto genes, but just saying it's not genetic doesn't do a bit of good. I shifted to the father, a true live participant. "Why wouldn't the daughter want to take after her father?" That was a pretty good move, I think.

INT.: You make it sound so acceptable for a daughter to imitate her father.

DR. J.: Yes. Judging from what I know of the mother, when she says something bad is inherited she's not going to blame her own side of the family. It's a way she can reproach her husband without coming right out and doing it. I'm countering that.

INT.: Listening to that conversation about which side of the family the trait came from, I took it more as: "It was independent of anything we did. It was in the genes."

DR. J.: In my experience, with these families, when something about the two sides of the family comes up, it's usually the other side that's stupid. Your side is stupid because your people moved around a lot or had a bad time during the depression.

INT.: When you're speaking to the mother, you don't say, "Do you suppose Sue imitated her father?" and wait for the mother to say, "Yes," and then say, "Why shouldn't she imitate her father?" You're a step ahead. You're slipping in a premise that's accepted before it's really agreed to. The mother replies as if this had been assumed all along, saying, "Yes, why shouldn't a daughter imitate her father?" when it's never even been discussed.

DR. J.: You're right, but it's also a matter of making use of the natural coalition formations. In families in which the mother is threatened and needs this particular kind of power, she will, in order to show that she is as competent as the therapist, almost invariably not refuse certain kinds of bait. It happened over and over again with this family. Here the mother denies her genetic theories and goes back to blaming her husband. The reason for it is that she cannot keep from trying to top me at my own game. If I can say something she has to agree with if she is going to be co-therapist, she will suddenly find herself taking a position she hadn't meant to take.

INT.: There seems to be a process of therapy of constantly using what people *have* to do in relation to you. It's very evident in the way this woman goes with you.

> MRS. S.: I think I did with mine. I think it's a perfectly normal thing to do, but I think it can be exaggerated too. And in our particular case I think it was, and I think it was not only Sue, I think the same situation existed in reverse with her next younger brother. And that's why there are two other members of the family. (*Pause.*)
>
> SUE: I don't get that.
>
> DR. J.: That's why there are two other members of the family?
>
> SUE: I don't understand that.
>
> MRS. S.: Because when there was just you and just Pete, and Daddy and me, and you'd been Daddy's girl from the word go . . .
>
> SUE (*overlapping*): And Pete was yours.
>
> MRS. S.: . . . very openly about it, and Pete came along and was an easy-going, peaceful, humorous, relaxed little guy, who relaxed *me,* when you two have always been so high-tension that you exhaust me, to tell you the truth, a good many times, and Pete had the opposite effect. And it was only too obvious that if we just stayed that way we were going to have a family split right smack down the middle with a, Daddy and you on one side and Pete and me on the other, which is not a healthy situation in my book. You remember, Bill, when I said to you, "There's only one thing to do and that's to have at least one more child quickly, and get us out of this." And your grandmother was horrified when Laura was

coming, and doubly horrified when I said, "Yes, and I'm going to have another one as fast as I can." (*Laughing, everybody laughs.*) And although there was another girl and another boy it didn't happen that way.

DR. J.: Um-hm.

MRS. S. (*Sue talking simultaneously, words unclear*): . . . that way, and I fought for years to try, I could lean so easily on Pete now that I could make him into just a leaning post, but I won't do it to him. It nearly killed me to have him gone four years too (*starting to cry*) but I won't do it to him. (*Pause.*)

INT.: That's the first time I've ever heard that motivation for having a child. The coalitions are so tight that you need another child to break them up.

DR. J.: I don't know what you can do with that speech, she said so much. She lashed out at her husband, her husband's family, her daughter, all under the guise of explaining why she had to have another child.

INT.: Do you think this was calculated?

DR. J.: I don't know. But something set her off.

INT.: It's possible that this speech is an indication of some kind of turning point. Looking back over the interview, the daughter seems to have fallen into line with you very quickly, and the father did too, after you called him on not showing his feelings. The only one you haven't been able to involve is the mother. Daughter and husband are to blame, but not her. So you say to the parents, "You may have unconsciously put some of your problems into Sue." The mother won't agree with you, because that would be an admission of guilt, but she can't deny your statement because the behavior was "unconscious." Her tactics are to agree at first and then slide into a different position. So she says, "You're right, my husband's problems are in Sue, and I have tried to get them out of her." The husband says, "So she wouldn't be like me," and you agree. To avoid exposing the rift between them and to refute you, she starts to suggest an alternative, that Sue was impossible from the beginning. You push her on it a little and she makes the remark about the baby who was born resisting her. She's been blaming Sue throughout, by weeping and being hurt, but this is the first time she's blamed her openly. When you then turn to the daughter and say, "Don't buy your mother's statement," you cut her out without directly attacking her. Her reaction is to come over to your side and be co-therapist. So it seems that you have now succeeded in reaching or touching each person. Since the mother is the hardest to pin down, this scene could be significant in establishing you with the family. Would you agree that something like that is operating here?

Dr. J.: I think that's right, yes. It's the kind of thing you have to do over and over, but especially in the first interview.

DR. J.: I lost that—to have him gone four years?

MR. and MRS. S. (*simultaneously*): He was away at school for four years.

DR. J.: Oh, I'm sorry!

MR. S.: We, ah . . .

DR. J.: I get you.

MR. S.: . . . much rather, Mrs. Starbuck'd much rather have him around home, but in order to give him his independence, and build it up, and tear him away from the apron strings, we . . .

MRS. S. (*overlapping*): And not let myself lean on him . . .

MR. S.: . . . deliberately encouraged him to go away to school, which he liked . . .

DR. J.: I see.

MR. S.: . . . which he liked to do . . .

SUE: (*Overlapping, inaudible phrase.*)

DR. J. (*overlapping*): He's in prep school?

MR. S.: He's in prep school in [*city*].

DR. J.: Um-hm.

MR. S.: He's coming home this June and, ah, I think, going to [*university*].

DR. J.: Um-hm.

SUE: Now I really admire you for it.

MRS. S. (*overlapping*): Which has been his own decision, there hasn't been any pressure from either of us on that.

MR. S.: Um, well, um, coaxing, but nothing, no insistence.

SUE: Well, anyway I, I think it's a fine thing.

DR. J.: Who is Sue supposed to look like?

MRS. S.: I think she's a cross. I always have. (*Laughs.*)

SUE (*to mother*): People tell me I look like you.

MRS. S.: Well, they say you look like Daddy, too.

SUE: More, more like you than more like, than like Daddy.

MRS. S.: You analyze it yourself sometime.

SUE: Well, my high-school graduation pictures were . . .

DR. J. (*to Mr. S.*): What do you say?

SUE: . . . dead ringers for yours.

MR. S.: I think she favors me more than her mother but she, ah, ah, definitely is a mix.

DR. J.: Um-hm.

MR. S.: She's got my eyes and my thin face, whereas her mother has a wider face and, ah . . .

MRS. S.: (*Laughing, inaudible phrase.*)

MR. S.: I think her physical long muscles are a little more closely resembling mine.

MRS. S.: I disagree with you there.

SUE: Uh-huh, I (*inaudible phrase*).

MR. S. (*overlapping*): I don't know, I never analyzed it distinctly, you asked . . .

MRS. S.: To look at Laura, physically Laura is, is . . .

MR. S.: Much closer.

MRS. S.: Laura is you completely, physically.

MR. S. (*simultaneously*): Much closer, much closer.

DR. J.: Um-hm.

MR. S.: This question was, which do I think she resembles the most? (*Sue talking in background.*)

DR. J.: Well, yeah, and some families will have, ah, you know, grandparents on each side and the child will be known more as a Jones than a Smith, but . . .

MR. and MRS. S. (*simultaneously*): Um-hm.

DR. J.: . . . is it, is this obvious in your families? In your relatives?

MRS. S.: Uh-uh. No.

DR. J.: Ah . . .

MR. S.: Well, it's, ah, very obvious in our other two children, I think, or other three children, ah . . .

MRS. S.: Oh, I don't.

MR. S.: . . . that she f-, they favor one side or the other? (*Pause.*)

MRS. S.: No. I think Laura, of the four of them, is the one you can pick out the most and say, she is so and so.

MR. S.: Starbuck, yes.

MRS. S.: Laura is, yes, there isn't any question at all. But she's the only one I feel you can say that about.

SUE: Charles is a, is a true [*mother's family name*].

INT.: Why did you make that remark about which of her parents Sue was supposed to look like?

DR. J.: Because it was my own personal opinion that Sue was very much like her mother and I felt that it was about time to get the two women together. They'd been talking about heredity, family, and so on, and I was trying to say to the mother, "Well, as an outsider, it appears to me that Sue looks very much like you, because she's also beautiful." If she had looked like her father, I never would have done it.

INT.: The effect was to bring about another little rift between the parents, because the mother then disagrees with the father.

DR. J.: I was surprised. I didn't think that anybody would think other than what I thought, which was that Sue looked like her mother. And the mother tells Sue, who is very attractive, "You don't look anything like me." I thought this was heartless.

INT.: The mother says she's a cross. Cross to bear, if anything. You do ask whether father's pushing daughter to give mother the business—a subject you were on earlier.

DR. J.: When I introduced this other idea, I really expected they would agree with me. The assumption is that if you look like somebody, then you've inherited some of their other genes. It doesn't necessarily follow, but it makes a good premise.

INT.: You're adopting their genetic theories in order to go along with them again.

DR. J.: Yes. I tried to beat the mother at her own game, but she stopped me.

> DR. J. (*to Mrs. S.*): May I see your hand? (*Mrs. S. talking simultaneously, inaudible phrase.*)
> MRS. S.: It's an X-ray burn, Dr. Jackson.
> DR. J.: Oh.
> MRS. S.: (*Laughs.*)
> DR. J.: From what?
> MRS. S.: Uhh . . .
> MR. S.: X-ray. (*Mr. and Mrs. S. laugh.*)
> DR. J.: Treatment for what?
> MRS. S.: Treatment for, ah, a malignant, ah, ah . . .
> DR. J.: Bone?
> MRS. S.: . . . can't think of it—yes, when I was five years old.
> DR. J.: Mm.
> MRS. S.: As a matter of fact, I saw [*radiologist*] yesterday, he had

some beautiful, ah, color photographs and X-rays that he took of it which he uses constantly (*laughing*) as demonstration.

SUE (*laughing*): Ooooh.

MRS. S.: I'm lucky I have it, that hand.

MR. S.: Lucky you still have what's left.

MRS. S.: Yeah.

DR. J.: I'm, the reason I asked was I, ah, wondered if, if either of you had any, ah . . .

MR. S.: Hereditary defects?

DR. J.: No, no.

MRS. S.: (*Laughs.*)

DR. J.: No, ah, psychosomatic difficulties. Are there any headaches or ulcers or, you know. I haven't, ah . . .

MRS. S.: I have no . . .

MR. S. (*simultaneously*): I haven't had any . . .

DR. J. (*overlapping*): I don't know who your physicians are . . .

MR. S.: Mrs. Starbuck (*tape recording skips*) severe arthritis.

DR. J.: Hm?

MR. S.: Severe arthritis which, ah, is aggravated by tensions.

DR. J.: Whereabouts?

MRS. S.: My spine, when I fell . . .

MR. S. (*simultaneously*): Neck.

MRS. S.: . . . and I have three disks in my spine and five damaged vertebrae on my . . .

DR. J.: Mm-hm.

MRS. S.: . . . lower spine . . .

SUE: Is it psychosomatic?

MRS. S.: . . . from a fall and—but arthritis, ah, developed about three years after the fall.

SUE: Is arthritis psychosomatic?

DR. J.: Some forms . . .

MRS. S.: It can get tangled up in it, yes.

DR. J.: . . . but if you have an injury, you can certainly make it more painful when your muscles tighten up.

SUE: Hm.

DR. J. (*to Mr. S.*): Are you in reasonably . . .

MR. S.: Very good health. I have no physical problems that I know of.

SUE: Well, I'm glad someone doesn't. (*Laughs.*)

MRS. S.: Well, I think we're an extremely healthy family. I think that our, our overall record for all six of us for all the years is . . .

SUE: You make up for some of us.

MRS. S.: . . . remarkably good.

DR. J.: Mm. Well, ah . . .

SUE: Well, Mom, your health has never been too sharp.

MRS. S.: Honey, you have worried about it . . .

SUE: Well, you know why?

MRS. S.: ! . . much too much.

SUE: You know why? Because it's always been thrown up to me.

MRS. S.: I doubt that.

SUE: No, Mom, I think that . . .

DR. J. (*to Sue*): You aren't going to win this particular agreement, and . . .

SUE: I know.

DR. J.: . . . we're running out of time and so I want to, ah . . .

MR. S.: Why, I—may I just clarify this one thing that I think she's refer- (*tape skips*). Mrs. Starbuck did have TB as a child . . .

SUE: Yeah.

MR. S.: . . . and we have constantly warned Sue, "Now don't run yourself down."

SUE: Yes, and when I wouldn't stay in bed when I was sick it was thrown up to me that I might get TB, and it was the only means of disciplining me.

MR. S.: I have done that, I have done . . .

MRS. S. (*simultaneously*): I haven't . . .

SUE (*to mother*): You haven't. It's been mostly you, Daddy.

MRS. S.: I don't even know this existed.

SUE (*overlapping*): Whenever I didn't behave and when I wouldn't be disciplined one way, you would throw my health up to me to discipline me and scare me into it by using my health. And this is maybe part of my problem.

MRS. S. (*overlapping*): I never have heard it. I've never heard that before.

SUE: Well, I've heard it. I can give you a couple of specific instances.

DR. J.: You won't win this argument.

SUE: I know I won't. But I'm just saying it, so that they both . . .

MR. S.: Well, I have said it, in that I, ah . . .

DR. J.: Yeah.

MR. S.: . . . you caution your children, "For heaven's sake don't ruin your health." I mean it's one of the normal things . . .

SUE: Yeah, but it was brought in when it didn't need to be a couple of times.

MR. S. (*sighs*): All right. All right.

INT.: Do you usually ask about psychosomatic difficulties?

DR. J.: No, I don't. I think the mother must have winced or conducted herself in some way to reveal this neck problem she had. She had some kind of tension reaction. She used to take hold of her neck, twist her head, do something to indicate pain.

INT.: Did you know she had a medical file about four inches thick at this time?

DR. J.: No, I didn't. I think I was trying to switch the topic from that last area of disagreement, and her neck movement and the scar on her hand from the bone tumor must have given me a cue.

INT.: The mother got herself into quite a corner there. Although she says they're all so healthy, she herself isn't.

DR. J.: She was really very healthy except for a bad knee cartilage. She's telling the truth about being healthy; she just had that thick file. And the daughter correctly picks it up, saying, "Is it psychosomatic? Is it? Is it?"

DR. J.: Ah, I wanted to, ah, get onto the business of the next few weeks, ah, this is, ah, switching abruptly, but as I say, we are running out of time. Ah, as I understand it, you, you all are going on a vacation, or a quick business trip or something.

MRS. S.: (*Inaudible phrase.*)

MR. S.: Half and half.

DR. J.: Half and half. And you will be gone, roughly?

MR. S.: Nine days.

MRS. S.: When will we be home? Saturday? A week from Saturday?

MR. S.: Yes. Nine days.

DR. J. (*to Sue*): Now, ah, in the interim, ah, will you, whether you like it or not particularly, but will you, ah, be willing to stay at [*hospital*]? (*Pause.*)

SUE (*sighs*): No.

DR. J.: No? You don't think you need it?

SUE: No. (*Pause.*)

DR. J.: But where would you have in mind staying?

SUE: Well now, I have, this is something I intended to bring up today. I have talked to a friend of mine, not Betsy Albright because I saw your point, I talked to Debbie Carter this afternoon and her family have sold their house. She was desperately looking for a roommate to share an apartment with, and I'd *love* it. I asked her, she didn't ask me, I asked her, and I think this is just what I need, not as a geographical excuse, or escape, but . . .

DR. J.: Where is this?

SUE: I'd like it to be in the area, somewhere.

MRS. S.: You mean she doesn't have an apartment yet?

SUE: She doesn't, she wants someone to room with. And I think it would be fun, and I think it would be a good idea, considering the situation as it is now, not to escape, as I say, but to be independent. (*Pause.*)

MR. S.: Have her parents approved of her renting an apartment?

SUE: Well, she's done it before . . .

MR. S.: She has?

SUE: She just ran out of a roommate because her roommate was getting married.

MR. S.: She's been living alone already or indepen-, independently?

SUE (*overlapping*): No, well they haven't moved out of her house yet, but they're going to.

MR. S. (*overlapping*): But she's living in an apartment, you say?

SUE: She has, yes.

MRS. S: Yes, I know that.

SUE: And I think, you've always told me, well, if I could support it all right I'll get a job. If Daddy can, if he feels like . . .

DR. J.: Well . . .

SUE: . . . he can help me, fine. If not, I'll get it on my own.

DR. J.: I think it is obvious, Sue, from this conversation today, that there are currents, ah, here that are pretty strong, and that you have the, the unfortunate tendency to try and buck them, ah, to your own . . .

SUE: I don't see that.

DR. J.: Well, ah, I, think you, I can appreciate the spot you're in but I think you're . . .

SUE (*overlapping*): It's the worst spot (*inaudible phrase*).

DR. J.: . . . trying to use a bulldozer instead of a, a scalpel, ah, in getting, ah, cutting through some of these, ah, currents.

SUE (*overlapping*): Well, yeah, the things, the spot I'm in is, these are the ties that bind and . . .

DR. J.: That's right.

SUE: . . . they're binding a little too tight now, and this is my trouble. This is the whole thing. This is what is wrong with me.

DR. J. (*overlapping*): But I wonder if you won't really put us, ah, and this will include you, ah, on the spot if you insist on doing something in the next nine or ten days.

SUE: Why? How could I do that?

DR. J.: Because we haven't really gotten, ah, any feeling from your folks about how they feel about your independence, ah, this, the problem that you have had this upset . . .

SUE: I know how they feel.

DR. J.: . . . and, yeah . . .

SUE (*overlapping*): Well, this upset is the result of this situation right here, and I know how Mom feels, she doesn't like it.

DR. J.: But since you have another forty or fifty or sixty years to live, ah, I wonder if you can't make the sacrifice of postponing this for the next couple of weeks, or nine days, or whatever it is, and working . . .

SUE (*overlapping*): Well, I know, but I think these . . .

DR. J.: . . . on your problems . . .

SUE: Yeah.

DR. J.: . . . until we can go into this at a . . .

SUE: I know, I don't, I'm not saying, get this apartment right away, because I don't think Debbie . . .

DR. J.: Good.

SUE: . . . is ready to and I'm not either. But I'm just saying this is what's going to hap-, what I'd like to have happen.

DR. J.: Well, that's fair enough. But I think your folks would rest easier if they knew the general course of things for you while they were gone. (*To Mrs. S.*) Wouldn't you?

INT.: What are you after here?

DR. J.: Well, the parents are going on a vacation, at least the father is, because it's partly business. I don't want them to get out of family therapy by having Sue get into some kind of scrape while they're gone. If she had another psychotic blowup, they might withdraw from therapy, put her back in a hospital, and turn her into a chronic patient. I hadn't anticipated Sue's reaction. I thought she was relatively happy at this hospital.

INT.: So when you started this discussion you were just clarifying the fact that she'd be on the ward while they were on vacation.

DR. J.: Yes. Then the three of us would get together when they got back. Actually, Sue is very reasonable about this; she backs right down.

INT.: You keep hitting one point, which is getting her to go back to the hospital. I gather that you're trying to arrange a protective situation for her and a peaceful one for them while they're away.

DR. J.: I felt that if she could make it, she would have made some headway by the time they got back. If they had to come back on an emergency basis, she'd end up in an insane asylum.

MRS. S.: Oh, yes, I couldn't go.

SUE: Well, well, I understand that.

DR. J. (*to Sue*): And I don't think you can afford for your mother not to go.

SUE: She has to go, she needs the vacation.

MRS. S.: (*Overlapping, inaudible phrase*) couldn't.

MR. S.: Whether you need it or not, you wouldn't leave.

MRS. S.: No, I certainly couldn't.

SUE: Well . . .

MR. S. (*to Mrs. S.*): You certainly need it, you've been through an awful siege here for the last, ah, two months.

SUE: I think it's my fault, I'm sorry.

MRS. S.: No, Sue, a lot of it is something which I tried to explain to you before, is my problem which I must live with, and nobody can take it away . . .

SUE: I know, I know.

MRS. S.: . . . and you mustn't try to because it's mine . . .

SUE: I'm not.

MRS. S.: But you are if you can say that, though. There is now a hope that we will be able to work this thing out mechanically and I will be out from under a great deal of the pain (*starting to cry*), which is wonderful, and I am quite encouraged at that, but it isn't going to be an immediate thing, and it's something I have to live with and you mustn't take it on yourself.

INT.: What problem are they talking about?

DR. J.: Mother's burden.

INT.: You mean the daughter?

DR. J.: Yes, but she also has the neck problem. There's the pain in her neck and the pain in her neck sitting beside her. Father's saying that what with one pain and another, Mother needs the vacation. He's pressing Sue to behave herself so that her mother can get away, and the mother is saying, "I couldn't go if I didn't know where Sue was."

INT.: Not all parents would take a vacation when their child was on a psychotic ward.

DR. J.: Well, if they had nothing to do with her breakdown, why shouldn't they go? I felt it would put too much burden on the therapy if they cancelled the trip, or if the mother stayed home. It would mean that she would have to deny all the more that she had anything to do with Sue's illness.

INT.: Why would you assume that she'd have to deny it all the more?

DR. J.: Because it would be making her that important to Sue. I think if she becomes that important, she becomes that guilty too, or that responsible. It can never be a positive thing.

INT.: You mean the more she extends herself to Sue in this crisis, the more she's conceding blame for Sue's being in the crisis, and the more she will not want to concede it?

DR. J.: Yes. The more vital I am to you, the more responsible I am for what happened to you, and the more there is to deny. I think if the mother had stayed home, we would have heard her emphasize what kind of care Sue was getting, what kind of medication she was on; she would have taken charge in a nonpersonal way. What she did do was to leave an aunt in charge, and it worked out very well. Sue got along with the aunt; she came home from the ward on a couple of occasions and spent the night with her.

> SUE: I won't, Mom, but listen (*wavering voice*), this isn't surgery, is it?
> MRS. S.: Yes, it's a new kind of surgery, and you mustn't—well, why, why act that way? Dad and I are very . . .
> SUE: Well, it doesn't . . .
> MRS. S.: . . . encouraged.
> SUE (*crying*): . . . it upsets me to see you go in the hospital all the time, Mom, it naturally does.
> MRS. S.: I don't go in all the time, I haven't . . .
> SUE (*crying*): Well, you've been in plenty, you've been in and out, a lot.
> MRS. S.: But isn't that my problem?
> SUE: I know, but it affects me, of course.
> MRS. S.: It affects all of you. I know that.

INT.: Sue doesn't object to her mother taking a vacation, instead she objects to her mother leaving her to go into the hospital. Perhaps it's a way she does object to the vacation.

DR. J.: Yes. You notice that the conversation is quickly shifted from the question of whether Sue is going back to the hospital to whether Mother's going in or not. Sue says, "You're in the hospital all the time." Then the mother has to say, "No, I don't go in very often." Then Sue says, "Oh, yes you do." It's a reversal of roles, it's again this switch of generations. In a fraction of a second, the mother is in Sue's position. At the same time, she's denying it: "Worry about me, only don't make it obvious."

(*Tape recording distorted here, words unclear.*)

DR. J.: . . . some sort of steps, because I, I'm not about to, ah, (*tape recording skips*) sitting tight so that your folks can go off into the sunset together, and, ah, have the peace of mind in knowing you'll be looked after.

SUE: Well, if I can come home sometimes, perhaps even spend the night there sometimes, and be with my brothers and sisters . . .

MRS. S.: They aren't going to be there.

SUE: Where are they going to be?

MRS. S.: On again, off again, well, Charles is on a school camping thing and Laura . . .

SUE (*overlapping*): How long is that going to last?

MRS. S.: (*Inaudible phrase*) and you know you don't want to be with Aunt Louise, 'cause she's there.

SUE: I don't mind her that much.

MR. S.: (*Female sighs in background.*) But you fight with her.

MRS. S.: And you said you didn't want her.

SUE: Well, I don't mind her that much.

MR. S.: We have to have Aunt Louise there to take care of the house while we're away, and take care of . . .

SUE (*overlapping*): Well, fine, swell, then we'll go up to [*lakeside resort*] as a result of her accepting all our hospitality, huh? I'm willing to buy that.

DR. J.: Will you make this sacrifice for now? I mean I think you . . .

SUE (*overlapping*): Well, as long as I don't have to stay there pretty, a lot, and I can come home, maybe spend the day or so at home and, and, so long as I don't have to make it as permanent as, as it is now, I mean as frequent as it is now.

MRS. S.: But (*inaudible phrase*).

DR. J.: Yeah, I think that, that the idea of going home, you see, involves all kinds of imponderables. I mean, I don't know what Aunt Louise is like, and how the two of you get along, and so on.

Y-you do have a fair amount of freedom on the ward, and . . .

SUE: Well, could I have a car while, while you're gone? (*Pause.*) Why not?

MRS. S.: Well, that's, I tried to explain to you the other day, that's a practical thing too, you see, honey, the use of the car, the . . .

SUE: Well, we do have two cars.

MRS. S.: One's being turned in.

SUE: Do you have to do it now? Because now that you're going, I don't have any way to get out, and I'm going to need it.

DR. J.: We're talking about a matter of nine or ten days.

SUE: I know, but nine or ten days locked up in the hospital is just . . .

DR. J.: You're not locked up. You'll be, you've got . . .

SUE: I'm not locked up . . .

DR. J. (*simultaneously*): I hope you're . . .

SUE: . . . but I can't get very far on foot.

DR. J. (*sighs, laughs*): You can go into town to movies and, and so on, and also, I think you're going to be pretty preoccupied with getting a couple of these things straightened out, these, these very personal . . .

SUE (*simultaneously*): Well, this is the one that needs to be straightened out and these meetings are what's going to straighten it.

DR. J.: No, I mean this is one thing, but there are some personal things that, that you mentioned . . .

SUE: Yeah, well . . .

DR. J.: . . . that you also need to do some thinking about.

SUE: I don't know if you've talked to the, to Dr. Brown or anyone else, but there was one that was partly imagined.

MR. S.: Imaginative, did you say?

SUE: Imagined. Things weren't quite as serious with that pervert as they, they were made out to be.

DR. J.: Sue's talking about the delusion she had that she was raped.

INT.: And she now is able to say that it was imaginary?

DR. J.: No, she says more accurately that it was partly imaginary. After all, there was a real incident with the servant.

INT.: She trails the word "imagined" off and the father fills it in.

DR. J.: What's interesting is that the father responded right away to this, and with good reason, because the delusion was a kind of symbolic statement of what was going on between them. She's very clever. I'm not sure but what she isn't baiting him a little: "Do you know whether I'm going to say it or not?"

DR. J.: Yeah, but this is, is also something to work on, how come, you see, you got so upset?

SUE: Yeah, well, I know there are a lot of personal problems, but . . .

DR. J.: I, I know that this is putting you on the spot, but the mechanics of it is, are such that I think, ah, you would be doing yourself a favor to be the hero right now. You, you'll have your innings.

SUE: Oh, yeah, as long as I don't have to be there the whole time, I'll do it. (*Crying.*) But you can understand how I've seen enough.

DR. J.: Yeah, yeah.

MRS. S.: We all do.

DR. J.: Except that this is a very different ward.

SUE: I know, but there's still the same, a lot of them the same basic elements. (*Pause.*)

DR. J.: Yeah, and these are some people you can, you can also learn a great deal about life from.

SUE: Oh, I know, you can learn a lot, in some, in some ways, you can learn a lot more about life . . .

DR. J.: That's right.

SUE: . . . from them.

DR. J.: This won't be wasted.

SUE: No, I know it won't. But I'm just saying I'd like to get a chance to get out too. And I'd like a chance to . . .

DR. J.: I heard you.

SUE: . . . be on my own for a day or a night.

DR. J.: Loud and clear!

SUE: (*Laughs.*)

INT.: Just now, you said to Sue, "Will you make this sacrifice?" Here you say, "You would be doing yourself a favor to be the hero." She's already the sacrificial victim, or scapegoat, but you're turning it and making it positive.

DR. J.: Making it voluntary, yes. Also, she had a particularly upsetting experience on the closed ward in the first hospital she stayed in. I'm trying to sell her on the idea that it would be best for all concerned if she would stay where she was, which was an open ward. I was afraid that another break might put her in a closed one, and she might have a very bad reaction which would set her back a lot.

INT.: Was it deliberate on your part to refer to it as a sacrifice?

DR. J.: Yes. After all, they are going off on a vacation, so she really is making a sacrifice. If they were at home, whatever she did would be negotiable from day to day, but they're taking off for ten days, so she's stuck. It is a sacrifice.

INT.: You're also playing on her repeated statement that she wants to be independent. She's said before that she has been given her "independence" by being sent away to a hospital, but you say to her, "This could be something for your real independence."

DR. J.: I don't know how much I knew about her background then, but she did have a long record of acting the spoiled child, so that there was something for her to gain in accepting someone else's advice and sticking to it, even if it wasn't good advice.

DR. J. (*laughing*): Then can we arrange to get together, ah, when you get back, because, ah, if Sue keeps progressing the way that she has been, then there will be this question of where should she go. Home . . .

MR. S.: Yes.

DR. J.: . . . or to elsewhere, and then it, it's going to involve the very same problems that we were talking about today in emotional terms, it's not just a practical matter, because, ah . . .

SUE: Well . . .

DR. J.: . . . there's bound to be feelings about it.

MRS. S.: Yes, I'm sure there are. I just hope that— (*Sue interrupts.*)

INT.: You're not trying to sell these parents on becoming patients in family therapy, as some people might; you're selling them on a return home to deal with a situation. From what you said before, I take it that you had the feeling that they wouldn't accept the idea of family therapy.

DR. J.: I did from the beginning, and I think I was not mistaken. The mother was a very proud woman, very active socially, and it was clear that she felt all of this as an affront. It wasn't until some months later, when we got into the marital therapy, that she ever acted as if she had something to be there for.

INT.: Did you feel that you could get them back more easily by putting the emphasis on practical matters?

DR. J.: I had a feeling that we'd slide into family therapy without announcing when one thing became another. Remember, when the girl was fourteen, she was expelled from a school in Arizona and had some psychiatric help at the time. She had already been labeled as a patient and the troublemaker in the family, so it didn't surprise me that the parents took that attitude.

INT.: This goes back to the very beginning of the session when you turned "problems" into "decisions." Here again you imply that they are people who are facing difficult decisions, not people with problems.

DR. J.: Yes, the situation is complicated and decisions have to be made; anybody can accept that without admitting he's neurotic.

INT.: Particularly nervous people.

DR. J.: Well, I felt that the parents were going to be more difficult than they were. I think that they turned out to be less difficult because they were against each other and neither one would let the other withdraw. But we had a problem finding a time when everybody could make it to an interview.

SUE: Well, emotional independence is important to me and I think it's a very real issue.

MRS. S.: Darling, nobody in the world knows more that emotional independence is important. And you don't know this any more than I do.

SUE (*overlapping*): I know. But it's a very real issue, and it's one that I've had to do most of, mostly on my own, right now.

MRS. S.: Everyone has to do it himself.

SUE (*overlapping*): Yes, but you have made it a little hard.

DR. J. (*interrupting*): There you go with that bulldozer again. Mm!

SUE: I don't (*sighs, inaudible phrase*) now.

DR. J.: You just plowed right into this, you know, as if you could beat your mother down after twenty years . . .

SUE: I don't want to beat her down.

DR. J.: . . . of fighting with her.

SUE: I don't want to beat her down. I'm just saying that 'cause of the kind of person she is I'm doing most of it. I don't mean to plow her down.

DR. J.: But that's something to feel proud about, it's, ah . . .

SUE: Yeah, well, it's not making it any easier, it's just confusing me as to who I am.

DR. J.: We'll get you straightened out as to who you are.

INT.: All through this, you handle the girl in relation to her mother without ever commenting to the mother directly.

DR. J.: The girl knows, just from my expression and tone, that I'm saying, "You can do better than your mother." In that sense, I'm using her rivalry with her mother. It sounds as if I'm picking on her, if you don't hear it right, but I'm not. I'm saying, "You can handle her yourself if you want to." There was an element here of Sue's being "not as good as" the mother. The mother obviously felt she was a better person than the girl, more moral, more mature, more whatever. So I think the girl was spoiling for a fight over it.

INT.: The girl must feel somewhat a helpless victim with the mother, but the image you use in connection with her is a bulldozer. It's almost a *reductio ad absurdum* to carry it that far, when all she's doing is making a noisy protest and not winning.

DR. J. (*to Mrs. S.*): But I lost the point that you were going to make about . . . (*Pause.*)

MRS. S.: I'm afraid I kind of did too.

DR. J.: You started to say about the practical issues, that there would be emotional, ah . . . (*Long pause, unclear what's happening.*)

SUE: Told you she didn't like it.

MRS. S. (*crying*): I want you to do it, Sue, I . . .

SUE: I know you do.

MRS. S.: I've wanted you to for a long time, but I want it to be done the right way. I want it to be done so that it's going to be a good thing for you.

SUE: Right. Well, I know what's good for me.

MRS. S. (*overlapping*): I think sometimes you don't know all the things that are good.

SUE: Well, yeah, but I'm me and I know me pretty well, in some ways.

MR. S.: You've not quite lived twenty years yet . . .

SUE: It's all right. I've had to live with myself . . .

MRS. S. (*overlapping*): (*Inaudible phrase*) a long time . . .

MR. S.: And, and, you're setting out to go on your own as though you were . . .

SUE: Out? I'm not saying I'm doing . . .

MR. S.: . . . a thoroughly adult, of-age person. I didn't object to living at home until I was twenty-four, and I am sure I was dictated
to and dominated and many things that I didn't like, but, ah, I felt
my place was to be at home until I was out earning my own living
and, ah, fully of age.

SUE: Necessarily I'll be around. I couldn't help but being around, I
want to be around, that's one reason I want to be . . .

MR. S. (*overlapping*): Honey, your room is in the far part of the
house, you have a private entrance, you can come and go as you
please, nobody stops you.

DR. J.: We are already getting into the issue that I was hoping we
wouldn't get into (*laughs*) because I think it is a little . . .

MRS. S. (*overlapping*): I, I don't think we are ready to get into that
one.

DR. J.: Now, I want to . . .

MRS. S.: Let's just get through the next nine days.

INT.: Why did you open up a discussion of emotional problems
which you now try to shut off?

DR. J.: What I was trying to do before was to get the mother to
come out with anything else she had to say about the problem of Sue. I
wasn't looking for emotional problems. I suspect I was trying to see if
she had anything else that she would bring up after they left and spoil
the thing. I must have said "emotional" to jog her memory, so that she
would get out whatever she had in mind. And of course now they're
talking about dependence and independence again.

INT.: The girl says something interesting. She says, "My wanting
to be independent doesn't mean that I want to leave you."

DR. J.: She even says, "I *have* to be with you."

INT.: It's when she went away that she had a breakdown, both
times, so that's really quite a realistic statement.

DR. J.: It also poses the question whether she really can leave.
They don't know whether she's staying out of love or out of weakness.

DR. J.: Yeah. I want to make one, one comment, though, about this.
Ah, you know, the way the two of you treat Sue, you would think
that she was a lot older and a lot tougher than she really is. You
know, she, she raises her voice, you weep, you take this, ah,
"Well, now, you got to understand," sort of approach, and here's
a kid who, who has just gotten off the, ah, mental hospital ward,

all shook up, confused and, ah (*to Sue*) you called me today to find out the results of a physical examination, to show that, that there, you know, that you still are feeling quite anxious about things, ah . . .

SUE: I'm not so confused, though, I'm getting squared away, I'm confused in some things . . .

DR. J.: No, no, no, what I am trying to say to your parents is this, this, in a way this is a very peculiar situation. (*To Mr. and Mrs. S.*) You tell her she's a little girl, but the way the two of you treat her, you would think that she was a great big tough—something.

MRS. S. (*overlapping*): I don't tell her she's a little girl.

DR. J.: Well, she is.

SUE (*simultaneously*): Well, you treat me like one.

DR. J.: Well, in many ways you are.

SUE (*simultaneously*): Well, you treat me like one.

DR. J.: That's understandable.

SUE (*simultaneously*): Well, all right, I expect in many ways I am, but they treat me more like a child than I am.

DR. J.: But they also treat you more grown up.

SUE: There's another inconsistency, that they treat me, and this confuses me and it messes me up. (*Starting to cry.*)

DR. J.: Well, I think this is worth thinking about. (*To. Mr. and Mrs. S.*) The, the fact that she can hurt you the way she does makes her seem a lot more tough than she is. She just isn't that sure of herself.

INT.: Do you have any comments on that?

DR. J.: Yes. The issue, you see, is apparently dependence and independence. Is Sue ready to pull away, is she ready to go out, and so on. She's pushing independence, though she disqualifies herself too. But the way she puts it sounds as if she's being unloving and so she gets blamed. I'm trying to turn it and say, "Look, she's just a little girl, and if she says untoward things, it's partly because of her age and naïveté." I'm trying to reestablish the generations: "You're up there and she's down here, and what's this bickering about?" Also, if you notice, I'm distributing the blame. Sue has agreed to accept the blame and be the patient, and I'm trying to spread it a little, so we end up even. So I say to the parents, "You're not perfect either." Sue was able to handle this, though she almost spoiled it by coming over to my side and saying, "There's another inconsistency."

INT.: What's curious is that you've just said to Sue, "There you go with that bulldozer," as if you yourself were reacting to her the way the parents do.

DR. J.: Yes. If I were really distributing the blame, I would have said, "She gets me that way too," so that we really had it spread around.

INT.: You mean you might ordinarily have included yourself in the picture?

DR. J.: This is pretty early, but I think it's a reasonable thing to do, to make the parents feel that their reactions are not so unusual, that anybody could have them.

INT.: It sounds as if you are attempting a completion of some sort with this interpretation. When you talk about the daughter hurting the parents, this refers back to several places in the interview when you questioned whether the mother was really hurt or the daughter so harmful. Is this an attempt at some kind of overall unity? Are you tying things up with what went before?

DR. J.: I'm not sure that I did it deliberately here. I'm not very good at what one would do in writing a speech, putting in a beginning, a middle, and an end.

INT.: This interpretation is really a statement about the "eternal triangle" the interview began with. Do you often summarize in this way, so that people have something to take home with them?

DR. J.: I do try to give some kind of punctuation: The End. I'll give a little speech, as I did here, or I'll say, "I think we all have a lot to learn; maybe by the next time we can give thought to this or that."

INT.: Sometimes you end an interview by giving out a piece of homework which you call an "intervention." Can you think of an example of an intervention you gave this family?

DR. J.: In a later session, I tried to get the mother to be actively critical of the father and to get him to accept it on the grounds that it would be good training for him. He saw himself as being terribly patient with her, but although she was always nagging at him, she didn't see herself as being critical. My suggestion did seem to have the effect that in the next few weeks they had some open quarrels, more straightforward quarrels, which upset her more than it did him. But it took the pressure off Sue a little.

INT.: How did you phrase it to the mother, to get her to be more critical?

DR. J.: I said that I didn't think she knew how to argue, and I thought she needed practice in arguing. She nagged, she whined, she moaned, but she never came right out and said anything. In another interview, it turned out that the husband gave his secretary the family books to keep. The wife was very upset about this because it made her feel left out, so I said, "All right, you take over the books." She didn't want to do it, she preferred to be hurt about it, but in the end she agreed to take them over.

INT.: Why did you ask her to do that?

DR. J.: I think she had good reason to feel left out. On the other hand, she didn't know how to get herself in, so all she did was stand on the sidelines and complain. It was a way of taking a small thing that could be handled practically and focusing on it.

> SUE: And I'm, one reason why is because another thing is the inde-pendence, emotional independence. If I were, I know we're not islands, we all need de-, dependence emotionally on somebody, but there's someone else now that I'd rather be emotionally inde-pendent [sic] on than my family, and I mean it with all my heart.
>
> MRS. S.: But that's good, that's exactly what we think would be a fine thing. We weren't finding any objections.
>
> SUE (overlapping): But the kind of people you are, it's going to be kind of hard (Mrs. S. laughs) because you're both very dynamic.
>
> DR. J.: Well, let's see. We, we haven't established that yet. But can we get together then when you get back?
>
> MR. S.: Any time . . .
>
> MRS. S. (simultaneously): Oh, yes.
>
> MR. S.: Gladly.
>
> MRS. S.: Absolutely.
>
> DR. J. (simultaneously): Fine.
>
> MR. S. (overlapping): I'd like to solve this out. I think these conversa-tions have been very helpful and . . .
>
> DR. J. (interrupting): Well, I think you'll find them a little upsetting for a while, and I don't, ah, you know, ah, underestimate this. I'm not asking you here without realizing what I'm asking of you. Be-cause it isn't easy. But on the other hand, ah, you've got some-thing worth saving over there. (Pause.)

INT.: Why wouldn't you go along with that remark of the fa-ther's?

DR. J.: Because I don't want to enter into any obvious coalitions.

The father was making a bid to get together with me, but here's the mother and the patient being left out. If I can say, "You don't quite have the picture," it makes us all equal, because none of us knows what it's going to be like.

INT.: What's interesting is that you do make coalitions with people; you just won't let them make coalitions with you.

DR. J.: That's right. Although I can't avoid it with the mother of a schizophrenic. I've never found a way to get around giving the impression that she's helping me.

> MR. S.: We certainly do. Anything and everything that would give her just the perfect life, that wouldn't (*inaudible words*) . . .
>
> SUE (*overlapping*): Nothing's perfect, Daddy.
>
> MR. S.: . . . as good as we can give her.
>
> DR. J. (*to Mrs. S.*): I'm expecting you to get something out of it too. Um, I'll call you then and, ah, I'll be gone, also, Easter and next week, but I'll call you when I get back. You should be just about back then, and see if we . . . (*Unclear exchange between Dr. J. and Mrs. S.*)
>
> MR. S.: The first part of the second week would be better. I'll be in [city] the last part, the eleventh, eleventh of May, ah, around the sixth, seventh . . .
>
> DR. J. (*overlapping*): Well, I get back on the eleventh, unfortunately.
>
> MR. S.: Oh.
>
> DR. J.: I leave on the fourth and get back on the eleventh. Ah, how long are you . . .
>
> MRS. S. (*overlapping, to Mr. S.*): Are you going to [city] on the eleventh, you say? You aren't going to be gone long, are you?
>
> MR. S.: No, I'll be gone that weekend.
>
> DR. J.: (*Unclear remark to Mrs. S., who laughs.*) Oh, that's all right.
>
> MR. S.: That means I'll be gone till Friday night. I'll be back in just two days.
>
> DR. J.: Nice meeting you. See you in a few weeks then.
>
> MRS. S.: Goodbye. (*Family leaves.*)
>
> MR. S. (*coming back in*): Can you and I have a little, ah, discussion or instruction? Should I have some instruction on these conferences? I came in here totally blind and unprepared for what we were going to do and why, and I . . .
>
> DR. J.: That's right.
>
> MR. S.: . . . deliberately stayed quiet as much as possible because I didn't know what tack you wanted to follow.

DR. J.: These are not, ah, these are deliberately arranged to have everybody present, and I, I think that, that although you are doing this on faith now, maybe you will see why. That this is not, that if I thought it was useful to see you and your wife and say, "Treat Sue so and so," you know, and take this attitude, I would do it, but I think it is just a waste of time. I think it is only by our understanding how the three of you get along, and I mean the three of you . . .

MR. S.: Um.

DR. J.: . . . that we can get anywhere with this, really.

MR. S.: But do, do you want me to speak up and . . .

DR. J.: I wish you would.

MR. S.: . . . and spout out whatever comes to my mind, and . . .

DR. J.: Yeah.

MR. S.: . . . or stand by and let you maneuver the thing until . . .

DR. J.: No.

MR. S.: . . . I'm asked a question?

DR. J.: I wish you would say anything, including objecting to what I say.

MR. S.: Well, I deliberately stayed as much . . .

DR. J.: Yeah.

MR. S.: . . . out of it as much as possible today because I, I thought that it was your operation and you were maneuvering it the way you wanted to.

DR. J.: No, I hope in the future you will say anything. I mean that.

MR. S.: All right.

DR. J.: Good. Oh, here, this is the way out.

MR. S.: Thank you.

DR. J.: Right. (*Tape recording ends.*)

DR. J.: What's too bad here is that the father was obviously feeling a little in the one-down position. I don't know how you could get around that, because he was such an important executive that he'd be bound to feel one-down for a while.

INT.: I should think that if you built him up and sent him out too pleased, you would have a coalition with him which would be noticeable when he got downstairs and joined his wife and daughter.

DR. J.: Yes, it's something they would pick up immediately. That he was cheered up.

INT.: But I gather that you didn't mind seeing him alone for a few minutes.

DR. J.: No. If he repeated this maneuver, I would block it by indicating somehow that it was not acceptable. But I don't see any reason for affronting him now, because he didn't know any better.

INT.: I take it this is not the way you would prefer to end an interview.

DR. J.: No. I might have prevented the father's coming back in if I had asked him if he had anything more to say, as I did the mother. This may have been partly why he came back. People often call up or indicate in various ways that the interview wasn't finished, that one person ended up and the other ended down. If I can, I even everybody up before we close.

INT.: All through this conversation, you've put an emphasis on making people equal, putting them on the same plane.

DR. J.: It's particularly important to do this at the end. If we end on your last statement, this either puts you in charge or makes you the moldy fig. That's why I want to be the one who terminates.

INT.: One general comment before we end. You talk about your therapy in a strategic way, with the emphasis on manipulation. Yet with this family, you lean over backward not to appear manipulative. You seem to like to show the family when you are baffled or perplexed, or if you have a private opinion or a personal reaction, you often share it with them. I should think that this would tend to make you seem less manipulative and to invite trust.

DR. J.: The only objection I have to the idea of being less manipulative is that I don't know what you could do to achieve that. I'm not trying to act as if I weren't influencing people, because influencing people is what I'm there for.

INT.: Just the same, I think that you, more than most therapists, would say, "You got me on the spot there," or "You confuse me." You take a straightforward position of someone who is in a situation rather than of someone who is managing a situation.

DR. J.: You notice that this tends to come up when *I* am saying, "I am confused." If *they* say, "You are confused," then I will rephrase it in some way, unless there's something I can make out of the statement.

INT.: You prefer to determine who has the right to say what.

DR. J.: Yes. I'm fairly autocratic, but in such a way that they can't easily object to it.

4]

The Growing Edge

An interview with Carl A. Whitaker, M.D.

INT.: What contact did you have with the Fairchilds before this interview?

DR. W.: I had seen them once previously.

INT.: Then this interview isn't the first one?

DR. W.: No, but it was a continuation of the first one in the sense that I was still working out the terms of therapy with the family. This is a preliminary stage that I don't even think of as therapy yet.

INT.: Did you see the whole family at that time?

DR. W.: Just the mother and father and seventeen-year-old son. A psychiatrist in south Georgia wanted me to see them because the boy was threatening to beat up the old man. He'd already hit him a couple of times, and it had gotten around the community. The parents were very upset, especially since the father is a respected professional man, a lawyer. So they went to get the boy psychiatric help. But they didn't realize, when they were referred to me, that it would mean treatment as a family.

INT.: How did you handle that?

DR. W.: When they first came in, the son said he was there because Mother and Dad needed help. The parents said they were there because the son needed help. I agreed with both sides and said that I wouldn't see any of them unless they were all three present. I told them that if we had another meeting and anybody was missing, there wouldn't be any meeting but that I'd charge them anyway.

Carl A. Whitaker, M.D., is Professor of Psychiatry at the University of Wisconsin, Madison, Wisconsin. He has published a number of articles, is the author with Thomas Malone of *The Roots of Psychotherapy* (1953) and editor of *Psychotherapy of Chronic Schizophrenia* (1958).

INT.: Is this standard procedure for you?

DR. W.: Yes. Therapy has to begin with a fight. If they capitulate before they telephone, there's no problem, the fight can go almost unnoticed. But ordinarily there's a structural fight.

INT.: What do you mean by that?

DR. W.: A fight over who controls the context of therapy.

INT.: How can they capitulate before they telephone?

DR. W.: It depends on whether the referring doctor has made them understand that they'll be seen as a family. If they haven't accepted this, I have to make it clear that I won't see them any other way. I want it to be understood that I'm in charge of what happens when they get here. The only thing they're in charge of is whether they come or not.

INT.: I take it that you use "coming in as a family" more as a testing ground for this issue of control than as a stand you take about therapy. It's not that you believe in seeing only families.

DR. W.: You're right. I don't see only families. The fight will sometimes be about some other issue. But with these people it was about coming in as a family.

INT.: How did you deal with them?

DR. W.: Well, when I said I wanted to see them all together, the son said, "I'm not coming back. I'm going to New York tomorrow." Father said, "How?" Son said, "By plane." Father said, "Who's going to supply you with money?" Son said, "You are." Father said, "I'm not going to give you money to go to New York." Son said, with Mother nodding agreement, "There you go, always refusing me things!" It was a ludicrous scene; here was this boy with his dark glasses and his dandyish manner and his green cravat, Father who looked foggy and not with it at all, and Mother who was fluttering about like an old hen. The son was being so utterly disdainful of these people. Well, the meeting broke up without any decision having been reached and we made no further appointment. But I'm always available after the first interview to anybody I've seen, unless I've already decided that we can't work together. So three days later, Father gave me a call. The boy had blown up again, everything was a mess, it was worse than ever. I said, "Do you want me to save a time for you?" He said, "What are we going to do?" I said, "You're living with him, I'm not living with him, don't bother me with it." "Well, you're a psychiatrist." I said, "I'll be glad to see all three of you if you want to come in." He said, "Well, the boy won't come in." "Then what did you call me for?" "I just want some advice." I said, "Look, I don't know anything about your life, I have troubles enough living my own." He said, "Well, I can't control him." I said, "Why don't you call the police?" He said, "I can't call the police. Can't you suggest anything else?" So I said, "Well, I'll tell you. I'll be glad to see you and your wife and your son *and* your four other kids too." He said, "You mean expose those little children to this horrible mess?" I said, "Look, they've been living in it for years." So we made an appointment for the whole family. A half hour later, I got a call from Mother. "Did you suggest to my husband that we should bring those four little chldren into your office?" I said, "No, I didn't." "Well, he said you did." "I just suggested that as a substitute if he wasn't willing to call the police." She said, "I think it would be just criminal, to bring those little children in." I said I wasn't interested in whether she approved of it or not, I would only be willing to see the three of them plus the four kids and did she want me to cancel the appointment Daddy had made. She said she'd talk it over with him and hung up. To my surprise, they showed up in the clinic, which was quite a thing for a man of his status and wife and kids to do.

INT.: What you do is to give them one set of terms, and then if they turn those down, you give them another set which is twice as bad. If the three won't come in, the seven have to.

DR. W.: That's right.

INT.: Isn't that taking a chance that they may not come in?

DR. W.: I don't care if they come in or not.

INT.: You want them to care, though.

DR. W.: If they're coming, I certainly do want them to care. I want all the affect they have, and that may not be enough. If it isn't, I'll have to supply the rest.

INT.: You certainly put roadblocks in the way of this man.

DR. W.: That's right. He can come in on his hands and knees. I see this as the administrative battle I have to win. I'll give you another example. A boy showed up after he'd been in therapy for four years, a typical, schizy sort of boy. It turned out that he had a father, a mother, and an identical twin brother who was the success of the family, belligerently counter-schiz, and probably part of the pathology. I said, "I don't know if I'll see you without your twin." He didn't think that would be possible. So then he asked, "Will you see me twice a week? My father will pay for it." I said, "I don't even know if I'm going to see you at all yet." We ended without deciding anything. But he came back again and we had a continuation of this. He said he didn't like my attitude, so I said he was free to leave, and finally he did. A short time later, the mother called and made another appointment for him. This time, I had another therapist in with me. He said, "I don't want him in here too, my father can't pay for two psychiatrists." I said, "This is the same as two meetings a week, only we have them at the same hour." He said, "Why do you need somebody else?" I said, "Because you scare me." The next time he came in I had the other doctor in again and the fight went on. I wouldn't agree to give the other doctor up, unless I felt I could do without him, and I wouldn't agree to cut my fee. He asked if there wasn't some other way, so I said he could go back to his first therapist, who was in another city. He said, "I can't do that, I'd have to change colleges." So then I said, "By the way, if you decide to go on with me, and you talk to your father about it, I want you to make it clear to him that I wouldn't have another interview with you without your brother *and* your father and mother. Because it looks to me as if they're in here whether we want them or not. And I'm not going to have them in as ghosts."

INT.: I take it that until you win this round, you don't feel it's really therapy.

DR. W.: It may have a therapeutic effect, but I'm not playing at being therapeutic. I'm trying to get the field sterile so that I can work. Otherwise there's no sense starting.

INT.: It's a double framework. You want to control the therapy but you don't want to control their lives. As you said to this father, his life is his own business.

DR. W.: Sure. It's up to him to control his child. But what he wants is for me to control his child. So I say, "The people who do the controlling for the people who can't control are the police. Not psychiatrists. But if you want to come in, I'll try to help you figure out how to control him yourself."

INT.: If he accepts coming into therapy under the conditions you present, he has to get his son in. But if he gets his son in, that means he can control his son. So if you win this particular administrative battle, you have already produced a change. It's already therapy.

DR. W.: It is as soon as that happens. But chiefly I want it very straight that when he comes in here I'm in charge. I'm not going to be with him the way he is with his son.

INT.: You give him a model for being an appropriate authority.

DR. W.: That's right. If he won't accept this, I say, "Then don't bother me," which is another kind of model. He can behave the same way with me that his son is behaving with him, only I don't have to be hurt by it.

INT.: Does it sometimes happen that when you say, "Don't bother me," they take you up on it?

DR. W.: Sure they do, and this may have been what happened with this family. After the second interview, they never came back.

INT.: When you demand that all the children come in, I get the idea that you're redefining the son as one of several children.

DR. W.: I don't think I did it consciously for that reason, but I was very much aware that the son and the mother were the parents in this family and the father was the child.

INT.: Do you think the mother understood what you were talking about when you said that bringing in the children was a substitute for calling the police?

DR. W.: Good Lord, that was so clear compared to the usual confusion this family was in.

INT.: What do you think decided them to come back a second time?

DR. W.: I suspect they pushed each other in. The parents were pressing for the boy to get help, and the boy was pressing for the parents to get help. But I had my doubts. I wasn't at all sure that the boy was going to let me come in a second time with the kind of power he saw operating when I took charge of the threesome. Because he suspected that I was going to break up his entente with Mother. At the same time, he wanted to get free, to get out of that crazy house. So that may have helped.

INT.: You said that in the first interview you agreed with the boy that his parents were sick and with the parents that the boy was sick. Is this a way to avoid siding with anybody?

DR. W.: I think it has to do with my moving up to another level of abstraction. The son is dealing with the parents and the parents are dealing with the son. I deal with the threesome, with the bigger unit, as though I weren't concerned with its components. This is the unit that they use to make war with. When there's trouble, they split and play one off against the other. I was trouble, and they would try to use me against each other too. But I refuse to get drawn in on this level. They have a common enemy, rather than a person they can use to side with. It becomes a battle between them and me, rather than between themselves.

INT.: It's a way you get them together.

DR. W.: That's right.

INT.: Who was present at this second interview?

DR. W.: There were the two parents, who were in their forties; Eric, the seventeen-year-old boy; Kathryn, who was ten; Eliza, eight; Dirk, six; and Margaret, four.

INT.: Do you remember the seating arrangements?

DR. W.: I was sitting at my desk and the mother was on one end of a semicircle facing me which went: Margaret, next to her, then Eliza, then Dirk, then Eric, who sat near the door, then Kathryn, then Father. Eric and the mother were sitting across from each other; they had a corresponding radius.

INT.: Had you previously explained to the family about the tape recording?

DR. W.: No, I decide about these matters as I would the kind of anesthetic. It's not a social issue. But there's one other thing you ought to know about this interview. Just five minutes before they came in, I had been talking to a medical student who had a fellowship to work with me, and I said, "Look, why don't you come in to this interview and run the tape recorder?" So he just sat over in the corner with the earphones.

INT.: Did you need him to run the tape recorder, or do you just like to have someone else in the room?

DR. W.: This illustrates an important aspect of the way I work. I didn't need him to run the tape recorder. But introducing a stranger into the interview set the whole framework up differently. For one thing, the presence of an outsider made it the whole world. It's also possible that having an audience brings out the ham in me. I feel I work better with someone else there. But mainly this is a way I add an extra quantum, a random element, which can give the whole process a twist. Whatever comes of it will be unforeseen and unexpected. This is what I look for in my therapy all the time. Events that occur out of nowhere, which I haven't pre-planned, which I've never had happen before. When I push what a colleague of mine in Georgia, John Warkentin, used to call "the growing edge."

INT.: In other words, by asking this boy to come in, you plan a situation in which something you didn't plan for can take place.

DR. W.: Yes. But I have the feeling that if I had arranged for this guy to come in weeks beforehand, and told the family about it, that would have killed the possibility.

INT.: It's a mixture of planning and not planning. Like the Zen saying, "You can't do it by trying, but you've got to try."

DR. W.: That's right. I'm very deliberate in the beginning of therapy, but my hope is that if I set things up right, these events will take place which go past my "point."

INT.: Which make you know when your "point" is there.

DR. W.: Yes. I have to get it started, but after that point is reached, the book writes itself. This is what I'm always aiming for.

Initial interview with the Fairchild family

DR. W. (*referring to a "butch" haircut on Father*): You got the kind of brush I've been trying to find.

MR. FAIRCHILD: (*Inaudible phrase.*)

ERIC (*apparently referring to his tie*): I love pink. It does something for me.

DR. W.: It does something for you? It gives you a sort of feminine tone?

ERIC: Right. I've got it.

DR. W.: Well, you may need more than a feminine tone. But at least we got here. I thought last time maybe we weren't ever going to get together again.

MRS. F.: Well, I guess fate . . .

ERIC (*overlapping*): I'm not sure.

MRS. F. (*laughing*): . . . plays a role.

ERIC: This will be the last time though.

DR. W.: Again?

ERIC: Again. Definitely this time though.

DR. W.: Well, why, why did you come if this is the last time? That doesn't make much sense, to, ah . . .

ERIC: Well, you see I really don't have much choice. I really (*inaudible phrase*).

DR. W.: Well, (*Eric continuing, inaudible*) if you don't have much choice, why don't you leave it open, maybe we can get together once a week for the next two years.

INT.: I notice you come in talking to the father but immediately turn to the son. Is it usual for you to go right to the patient?

DR. W.: Yes. With a psychotic like this boy, I try to get immediately involved. The reason the psychotic is talking crazy is because he's trying to find someone who will listen past the level of social games. So I don't postpone my participation till some other time. For instance, in one first interview with a family with a schizophrenic girl, I turned to the girl after I'd been talking fairly emptily with the parents and asked, "What are you here for?" She said, "Contact is very good for colds." I said, "How long have your parents been cold?" And she said, "Twenty years." We went on talking schizophrenese like this without any hesitation.

INT.: It's not quite clear what this exchange between you and the boy is about. Why does he say, "I love pink"?

DR. W.: I think I was looking at his tie. It was one of these flowing scarves in an extremely loud color. This was his façade, his way of saying he didn't belong in this picture, like his statement that he was going to New York. I move in here because I think the whole process of therapy is breaking the mask. Otherwise it becomes supportive therapy, and to me that's useless. Supportive therapy merely means that you're going to postpone the administrative fight indefinitely.

INT.: So you join issue with him right away. His feminine tone isn't going to be enough to get him out of there.

DR. W.: Yes. That's why I follow up with the remark about their having come. This is to all of them, but I'm also telling the boy that his presence is a contradiction of his pretense of being out of it.

INT.: You're approving of his goals at the same time that you're criticizing the way he's trying to reach them. The statement "You may need more than a feminine tone" sounds rather ironic but it also implies that he is embarked on an enterprise of some moment.

DR. W.: Yes. I'm saying that I know he's up to something. We're part of a big plan.

INT.: He reacts to that by saying, "This will be definitely the last time."

DR. W.: And I suggest again that this is a contradiction. If he doesn't want to come, why is he here?

INT.: He answers, "I was forced to come." Now your answer to that is very strange: "If you don't have much choice, why don't you leave it open, maybe we can get together once a week for the next two years." If he doesn't have a choice, he can't leave it open. Only somebody with a choice could leave it open.

DR. W.: I'm again answering the contradiction. He has admitted he has a choice about coming when he says he's not going to. He also says he was forced to come. I pick up the two sides of the coin. First, since he's admitted he has a choice, then why doesn't he choose to come? Second, since he doesn't have a choice, why doesn't he let me make it for him?

INT.: It's a double-level response, it catches him either way. I think part of its effectiveness is in your tone, which implies "Why don't you swing along with me?"

DR. W.: Sure. Since he's such a willing victim, why doesn't he decide to be my victim?

INT.: What do you make of that statement of the mother's, "Fate plays a role"?

DR. W.: Well, this is what I mean by the battle. She's saying the same thing as the son, that it isn't their choice if they're there. I'm telling them that as long as we avoid the decision that we're all going to be responsibly in this, there's no sense having these meetings. I'm pressing for a settlement.

INT.: It seems absolutely crucial to you right now that they concede that they're going to keep on coming. If they don't do that, nothing happens.

DR. W.: It's not them, it's myself I'm concerned about. I don't want to commit myself if the therapy is not going to come to anything. They're saying, "I'll sleep with you tonight but I won't marry you." I'm not interested in that. These torn-away fragments of patients hurt me. For example, there was this woman I was recently working with, a very exciting gal who had a brain injury and couldn't talk. I got more and more involved with her and all of a sudden they whisked her away to an institution. That hurt me for a long time. I'm trying to avoid that.

INT.: It's a curious emphasis on what happens to you, not to them. You say you want them to commit themselves not because it will be bad for them if they don't, or lessen what they could get out of therapy, but because it will be bad for you.

DR. W.: That's right. It's a self-protective device.

INT.: It would make a difference in the way patients would react to you, I should think, if you insist on being able to make a commitment to them.

DR. W.: Sure. This gives me the right to raise hell with them if they back down on their commitment to me. Because it's a bilateral commitment.

> ERIC: (*Inaudible phrase*) but I won't be here. I'm definitely going. I just cannot stand this existence any more. Not this business, *existence*. Absolutely. I'm living as if, ah, I was a hermit or something, I don't know. I don't care . . .
>
> DR. W. (*overlapping*): Well, you're hiding in that cave behind those black glasses. I can't even see the cave you're in.
>
> ERIC: (*Laughs.*) No, I wear them all the time, though. I, I rarely go out, now. I just sit around the house (*inaudible phrase*).
>
> DR. W. (*overlapping*): The windows of your soul are covered over, huh?
>
> ERIC: Pardon?
>
> DR. W.: The windows of your soul are covered over?
>
> ERIC: You might say that. I'd just rather not go—I don't care how I look any more, I don't move in the right circles any more, I don't —nothing bothers me now, that's why I'm leaving. I can't have a calm and peaceful point of view toward him, it's completely ruining my life. And that's the way I am when I'm at home. Always, I always have been, and I always will be. That's why I've got to get out, as soon as possible.

INT.: What does the boy mean when he says, "I don't move in the right circles any more"?

DR. W.: I assume he means he's trying to get out of the homosexual circles he's been in. The right circles for him would still be the high-school squares. He's apologizing for the affectation.

INT.: When he says he can't stand this existence, is he alluding to his fights with his father?

DR. W.: Yes. He's telling me that he's nothing, that he rarely goes out, that he has no life of his own. He's presenting himself at the level of being a patient, or a mechanism that the family uses. So I'm talking to him past that level, as a human being with a soul.

INT.: You're thinking of this as a scapegoat situation.

DR. W.: I assume the identified patient is the Christ, that he's agreed to sacrifice himself, to be a nobody. I'm saying that he doesn't have to be.

INT.: You start talking in a poetic, symbolic way here when you speak about the cave he's in, and the windows of his soul. Do you often use this kind of language in therapy?

DR. W.: I use many different kinds of language, the Bible, jokes, vulgarity, free associations, fantasies that happen to flit past. It's usually not deliberate. I'm convinced that my therapy is mostly operated by my unconscious. It's as though I were on a bank fishing, not really trying to catch anything, but every once in a while something gets hooked on my line and I haul it up. This is what I look to for evidence of what's happening in the therapy, what we're up to.

INT.: What are you up to here?

DR. W.: Well, in the beginning, with that business about the feminine tone, we were talking about the front the son puts on. Now he's drifting toward agreeing with me that we're here for something significant. He's starting to talk about what's behind the front. He starts to use a subjective, introspective language. He doesn't just say, "I never go out," he calls himself a hermit. So I go on with this language and talk about the cave he's in, the cave behind the dark glasses, then I move on to the windows of the soul. I assume we're moving further and further into psychotic-type material. When a patient does this, I'll go even further and get a step ahead. If he doesn't go with me, I'll back off.

INT.: And you want to go in the direction of this material?

DR. W.: Yes. As I said before, I want to get behind the façade. Another way I'll often do this is to pick up words that seem to have special meanings for people. Many times you get a word that stands out because of the way it's said. I'll even stop and go to the dictionary. I have three of them right here.

INT.: You mean you look up the meanings and the derivations and discuss them with people?

DR. W.: Yes. I feel that I'm sharing part of my ignorance with them. I don't know what the word really means for them, and often they don't either. So I look it up in a slang dictionary and often it has a meaning which they didn't know about but which fits in exactly with what they are talking about.

INT.: To get back to your symbolic remarks here, they sound almost as if they were in quotes. You say that in these instances your unconscious is operating, but here it seems to be a very controlled unconscious.

DR. W.: It's true that I'm less apt to be personal in the beginning. It's almost straight tactics, we haven't got any real intimacy yet. I hadn't thought about this before, but I'm always anxious and a little irritated with a new patient. I remember saying to my secretary, "If you ever get me two new patients in the same day, so help me I'll shoot you." Because I have to reset my sights from the personal involvement I have with the patients I'm currently seeing to all of a sudden putting on the act of being a psychiatrist.

INT.: Do you see "acting like a psychiatrist" as a way of getting into therapy?

DR. W.: Yes. I can give you a good example of this process. I saw a nurse who had just left a young doctor she'd been married to. She was three-quarters drunk when she came in and was debating psychotherapy versus suicide versus going to Europe and living with some man who wanted her to join him. I said, "I'm not interested in seeing you when you're still trying to make up your mind. Why don't you decide what you want to do first and then if you want to make an appointment, call me." A week later she was back, but she still didn't know what she wanted to do. I got increasingly aggravated. I said at the end of the interview, "Look, we haven't got anywhere today, you just wasted twenty-five dollars." She said, "I'd like to come back." I said, "Okay, but it doesn't look as if we're up to anything." She came back and we still didn't make any headway, so she said, "Shall I make another appointment?" I said, "Well, it looks as though we're locked, whether we like it or not. I don't like it, and I still don't know what it is you want, but there isn't much either of us can do about it now."

INT.: That's an odd way of winning this administrative fight you've been talking about. First you make it more and more difficult for people to come into therapy with you. Then all of a sudden you reverse and tell them they haven't any choice about it because "it's already happened."

Dr. W.: Well, I think of myself as having to be captured by the countertransference, if you want to use that term. Until that time, I don't think of us as being in therapy. We've been considering therapy, testing each other out, but there comes this point when we move into a process that carries its own direction and is self-moving. Now, the girl I'm talking about was a messy person to get mixed up with, the kind that goes out into the community and gets herself pregnant and then comes in and debates whether she should get an abortion or not. I really didn't want to take her on, I knew she'd be too painful. But I knew at the same time that there would be a point, if she kept pushing, where I'd be captured.

Int.: So part of it is that they have to keep pushing. Is there anything else a patient could do to capture you?

Dr. W.: Another part of it is just time. If they stay with it long enough, they're apt to get me. But it has to be in the therapeutic setting. I can associate with colleagues, or residents, and never turn it on or never let it get turned on.

Int.: The "it" being?

Dr. W.: My perception of myself in them, or my attachment to them. Where I see more and more of myself in the other person. This ties me.

Int.: You see it as an experience for yourself.

Dr. W.: Yes. Because I'm trying to expand myself. That's what I'm here for. I'm looking for an experience that will excite me and open me and cause me to grow. I went down to a seminar in group psychotherapy in New Orleans two or three years ago and somebody asked, "What is your purpose in doing therapy?" And I said, "Well, I want to experience some more of myself." They spent the next two or three days trying to figure that out. Why was I doing therapy for my own sake, not for the sake of my patients? I think that's just a little more honest way to express the facts.

Int.: At any rate, if you get that experience, you know it's therapy.

Dr. W.: That's right. If I'm tied, I know they're tied too.

Int.: It's possible that when you and a patient "just happen" to get tied together, it's no accident. It's a natural outcome of the idea that they've got to provide something for you, not vice versa. You don't say to the girl, "You can't come into therapy with me." You suggest that if she won't commit herself, she's not worth bothering with. But if she does commit herself, she's worth your while. A lot of people couldn't resist that. It's a negative come-on.

DR. W.: I'm not at all averse to thinking of it in this way. I started this strategy way back, when I got sick and tired of simply assuming that people were going to go on with psychotherapy. Every time anybody said anything negative about the process, I would take it seriously and carry it to its logical extreme. If they said, "I may not want to stay," I'd say, "Why don't you give the whole thing up? If you want to come back, you can. I won't disappear. But maybe I'm not the person you want to work with, or maybe it's not therapy you want." And I never got anywhere. I didn't get a single person to stop.

INT.: It's a technique that could have its disadvantages. Do you ever find yourself getting stuck with someone by telling them to go away when you really do want them to go away?

DR. W.: It does happen. I had a horrible battle with a girl recently who showed up in the waiting room and just felt she needed some therapy. I was very busy and I thought the situation wasn't that critical, so I told her to go see someone else. But I found that I was discouraging her from coming to see me as if I were already involved with her. I didn't take her on, but that sort of thing can be extremely disconcerting.

INT.: Would you ever deal with a patient by trying to persuade him directly that therapy would be a good thing for him?

DR. W.: Oh yes, I would do that with anybody who is really interested, who says, seriously and honestly, "I want to grow." I had one patient, a very decent man, whose wife had been in therapy and had urged him to come and see me. He was one of these people who lead tight, mechanical, adequate lives, but there was nothing he could point to as a problem. So we discussed what he could get out of therapy. I said to him, "I think that essentially you're living a good, well-compensated, well-operating life. But if I were you, I'd want to go into therapy. I should think that you would come out of it with a kind of full-throated living process which you really don't have now. You do a lot of things, you have a lot of fun, but they seem to have a kind of child-like play quality rather than the profound satisfactions which I think are possible for you or for anybody else."

INT.: In other words, you don't see therapy as merely a matter of helping people who have broken down and have to be put together. You do what one could call "expansion therapy" too.

DR. W.: I see all therapy as expansion therapy, as leading fundamentally toward growth. The patient is up to the same thing I'm up to.

> DR. W.: Maybe the best way to get out is for you and I to help you restructure the home. (*Pause.*)
>
> ERIC: Actually, I think this thing—because of the behavior patterns (*inaudible words*) I don't think that can be done. Possibly it can be—improved slightly, but I don't think it can be done, actually.

INT.: The basic issue between you and the boy still seems to be whether he's going to come in or not. He says it's pointless, because nothing can be done about the family.

DR. W.: Well, he's backing off slightly. He says it might be possible to improve it a little. In a tiny way he's accepting my orientation to change things.

INT.: What do you think enabled him to make that shift?

DR. W.: I would guess it was the fact that I was taking him seriously. I showed this in my warm feelings and my response to him. This is the ultimate patient. His attitude is: "All my efforts are directed toward going home and curing my mama." To some degree this is affectation, this being the diagnostician, the superior authority, but to some degree he's right. He's up to the ultimate therapeutic challenge, and I tell him I'm going to help him with it.

INT.: By changing the home. The implication is that if the home was nicer, if he didn't have to mediate between his parents, he could leave.

DR. W.: Yes, he can't leave until his parents get together. He's dedicating himself to making his parents happier. So I'm telling him I'll be his assistant in this.

INT.: It's part of family theory that children can only leave a happy home.

DR. W.: It's true. The only way you can pay your parents back for having given you your life is to make sure they're happy parents.

INT.: You give such an appearance of siding with this boy. You could have said "we," meaning the whole group, "are going to restructure the home." Instead you say, "You and I." I take it you don't object to siding with the patient vis-à-vis the parents.

DR. W.: This may be my training in individual therapy, but I side with individuals all the time. I start out by relating first to one, then to another. Then I move on to the twosomes in terms of their reciprocal, interlocking qualities. Then I move from these dyads to the whole. Simultaneously, of course, I insist on keeping the whole always in view. But, as I see it, the way I establish the whole is by this movement from one to the other.

INT.: You do this here, too. Within the context of siding with the boy, you say, "I'll help you restructure the home." This makes it a matter of the entire unit. You step to a higher level than the battle between the individual parties.

DR. W.: One aspect of family work is that you have to move in and out of so many combinations. You have to better the relationship between the father and mother, which I feel is the essence of freeing the child. You have to relate to the child in his effort to separate from his parents. At the same time you have to identify the operation of the threesome: "Look, Mommy and Daddy are trying to get together and all of a sudden you sneak in between."

INT.: It's a kind of balancing act. How would you describe your relationship to these sets and subsets?

DR. W.: I don't really know. I would guess that I become the third side of the triangle which is the parents, the child, and me. Maybe I'm the mediator in the angle between the generations.

INT.: That's a nice way to put it. At any rate, it seems here that you're not really siding with anybody.

DR. W.: Well, I guess that's what we would like to decide this morning. Because if the three of you don't have any hope of doing anything about it, there really is no point in our being here.

ERIC: Well, personally, I don't care.

DR. W.: I like the fact that all three of you are desperate about it. I had a telephone call from Dad, which obviously expressed his desperation about the family and what was going on. And a telephone call from Mother, and she was obviously expressing her desperation. And now you express yours and I like that.

ERIC: Do you?

DR. W.: I think a family that has that much—concern, has so much more chance to do something about it.

DR. W.: Here, you see, I'm ignoring the son's statement that he doesn't care and jumping back to where he was saying the family is hopeless. What I was doing was sticking them with the identification between the three of them. This is one of my gambits in the initial phase when I'm still being the psychiatrist. For instance, in one family I saw several years ago, the schizophrenic daughter said she was carrying her mother on her shoulders. And not more than three minutes later, Mother came along and used the same kind of phrase in regard to the daughter. My co-therapist asked them how in the world two people could be on each other's shoulders. Or Mother will say, "I feel sucked dry," and daughter will say, "I can't get out from under." I'll say, "You two don't see how much you've been helping each other. Mother, if you didn't have your daughter around, you'd be dripping milk. And daughter, if your mother weren't here to feed you, you'd be starving." This is the kind of overlapping I try to bring out, this togetherness which from their individual points of view they can't see.

INT.: When the son says "I don't care," what was your reaction to that?

DR. W.: I just don't believe such a statement. There is no such thing as ultimate biological hopelessness. This is what I see as the value of the biological model, the one you get out of medical school. I don't believe it is possible for a person to want himself dead. The organism is headed toward its own growth, within the limits of the nutrition and the possibilities from the outside, and it will push for that, regardless. When you see people under what looks like utterly impossible pressure push through it, you get an almost religious feeling about this fantastic operating power toward growth, toward extension, toward oneness. This is the model I operate from. When I hear talk like this boy's talk, I brush it aside.

INT.: With this remarkable statement that a family that is as desperate as this one shows great hope. You manage to define desperation as a positive thing.

DR. W.: I think it is. You've got a wound and it's scabbed over and festering within. The scab comes off and it looks terrible. But now at least you can get at it and start to treat it.

INT.: You're telling this family that it's exactly their desperation that makes them such a hopeful prospect for therapy. From their point of view, this doesn't exactly follow.

DR. W.: It does for me. Anxiety is the motor that makes therapy move. I frequently say, "You're not desperate enough. You're not disturbed enough to really have a go at this thing."

INT.: You're really cheering them on. "You have all three of you managed to be desperate and *I like that*." I don't see how anybody could handle that statement.

DR. W.: It sounds perfectly reasonable to me. Desperation is the proof that you've got someone who is really up to something—like craziness.

INT.: The worse they are, the better off they are.

DR. W.: Absolutely. This isn't a gimmick, I honestly believe it. If a schizophrenic youngster comes in here and tells me what a horrible thing his mother and father did to him, I say, "Look, you've got to give them credit. They made you crazy and you get something out of life. You're not out there dead like most of these characters carrying a brief-case." I differentiate crazy from insane. The insane are what Christ called the "whited sepulchers." The ones who go to jobs every morning in gray flannel suits.

INT.: A lot of people who work intensively with schizophrenics seem to get more of an appreciation of craziness and less of an appreciation of ordinary life.

DR. W.: It's true. I'm envious of people who have had an overt craziness. I've had my moments and shades and shadows, but never the full-blown creativity that some of these people have available to them. They may never get around to using it, but they've got it right there. I think this is why the psychiatrist frequently gets into craziness with his mind. He's hoping to find it in himself. You can divide people into two groups: those who have been crazy and are trying to get over it, and those who haven't been crazy and are trying to get there. And I'll say to a crazy person, "You're stuck with two lives. I want you to stay crazy, but I also want you to live out there with those insane people, because that's the world you have to live in and you can get something out of that too."

INT.: Do you prefer to work with schizophrenics rather than people with less interesting problems?

DR. W.: I don't necessarily prefer schizophrenics, but I like my cases to be as bad as possible. That's partly why I took up family work. An old psychiatrist I knew in Georgia once told me, "The reason you took up couples therapy is because you got bored with individuals." When I take on a family with a schizophrenic and an arthritic and an ulcer, I've really got something to work with. It's more of a challenge, more vivid.

INT.: And, as you said just now, it shows more hope.

DR. W.: That's right.

INT.: Well, if redefining things as positive is therapeutic, your framework, being positive to begin with, is really helpful.

DR. W.: At the level you're talking about, the level of strategy, it is helpful, and it makes good sense. But at another level, it's my declaration of faith in the human order.

> ERIC: Well, I really don't care whether we get along or not.
>
> DR. W.: Well, I'm not talking about getting along. I'm talking about getting less desperate, or getting more out of life. I assume you'll be leaving the family, one of these days.
>
> ERIC: Do you . . .
>
> DR. W. (overlapping): I would like to see you—well, of course, you're growing up, you can't stay in the family all your life.
>
> ERIC: Oh, yes. Well, I am leaving, as soon as I graduate from high school.

INT.: The son again says he doesn't care whether they get along or not. It's possible that when you say, "A family that has so much concern has a much better chance to do something about it," he takes it to mean, "has a better chance to learn how to get along together."

DR. W.: You may be right. He thought I meant that I was going to help make them happier with each other and a natural consequence of that was that he wasn't going to get out. So I say clearly that I'm not interested in making them happier.

INT.: You're saying that the problem is how to get them separated from each other, at least as far as the boy is concerned. Is this the approach you usually take when the patient is a child this age?

DR. W.: Yes. I'll say right out that he's going to be leaving and I'll help him to do it.

INT.: That's a remarkable switch he makes after you say that. He's been saying he's going to New York tomorrow. You then put it on a reality level about his leaving and he picks it up on the same level and says, "I'll be leaving after I finish high school."

DR. W.: He's really been saying, "I don't want any part of a therapy that binds me further to these people." Now he's testing me, cornering me, to see if that's what I'm going to do. So I put it to him straight that what I want to do is reconstruct the family so that Mother and Father will be together where they belong and he won't be in the bed between them. So that he can really go off and never come back. I think that's why he makes that switch.

INT.: There's a kind of meta-conversation going on here with the parents. You're putting in the premise that therapy is going to involve getting the boy out of the home, which is probably not what the parents are thinking it's going to do at all.

DR. W.: Sure. They're the biggest problem. They need him at home. If they're going to sit around hating each other, he's going to have to stay to keep them from killing each other. So the message may really have been for them. I frequently talk to one person through somebody else.

INT.: Family therapists often seem to talk repercussively. Do you consciously choose out A to say something to in order to get a message across to B or C?

DR. W.: No, because my framework is one of reacting directly to what comes along. I was trying to look at it from a more strategic framework when I said what I did.

INT.: Why wouldn't you say right out to the parents, "You've got to let your son go"?

DR. W.: Because I assume that at any particular point the dynamics are so thoroughly fed back and forth that there's no one person who is doing anything to the other. It's a joint arrangement. So I just set it up that he'll be leaving.

INT.: What stands out here is that you've been focusing almost exclusively on the patient. I realize that you want to get immediately to the psychotic, and that in any case what you say to him is also for the parents. But a lot of therapists wouldn't do this at first, for fear of reinforcing the family's conviction that it's the patient who is the problem.

DR. W.: I've already dealt with the problem of who is the patient in the first interview by agreeing that each of them is. But my basic assumption is that whatever I do with any one of them includes the whole family. If one of them wants to involve me, I'm involved. If the boy wants to talk with me for the whole of every interview while the parents just sit, that's all right with me.

INT.: Many family therapists would say that isn't family therapy, it's treatment of the individual in the presence of his family. Would you really talk with just one member for the whole interview?

DR. W.: Sure, so long as I felt involved. If I was getting bored, or if he was tricking me, or seemed unreal or unrelated, then I might object.

INT.: Another therapist might say, "I'll stop him if I feel that his behavior is interfering with the therapy." But you say, "I'll stop him if I get bored."

DR. W.: I don't look at the cause and effect between me and the family. I just assume that if it feels right inside me it must be right with the therapy.

INT.: It seems to be so here. Within the first few minutes of this interview, the boy has come back from his far-out position and is talking sense.

> DR. W. (*overlapping*): I would like to see you, ah, get some of these tensions you have about—it, and about yourself, straightened out before you leave, but that's your business.

INT.: There's something I'd like to get at here. Throughout this interview you have a particular way of using "it." For instance: "I'd like to see you get some of these tensions you have about *it* and about yourself straightened out." Are you being deliberately ambiguous, or are you putting a lot into this one word, or what?

DR. W.: I wouldn't know. But the association I just got to your question was Groddeck's *Book of the It*. The original term in German for *Id* was *Es*. Freud translated it *Id* and Groddeck refused this and called it the It. He said, "We don't live life; It lives us."

INT.: It's that passive tense which therapists and disturbed families seem to use equally. "It" is always "this thing that just happens to me," not "this thing that I do to myself."

DR. W.: I suspect it's a loaded word of mine. "It" can mean, as I think of it, "this whole mess you're in," "the thing that brought you here," "leaving home," "the relationship between you and your father," or even "the collective unconscious."

INT.: By not naming it, you avoid being specific about anything that could be queried at that point.

DR. W.: That may be why I use it, I don't know. But this next thing is very clear to me. I say to the boy that getting his tensions straightened out is his business. What I'm saying, and I do this very deliberately, is that the boy can leave home without solving his problems, that he has a perfect right to do this, just as he has a perfect right to kill himself. But I would rather he solved them before he leaves, because that would mean he was leaving to go to something, rather than running away from something.

INT.: You're recommending what he ought to do, but telling him that it's his business whether he does it or not.

DR. W.: Yes. At that point I'm accepting him as an independently activated person who came today because he wanted to come, not because he was forced to. He can go to New York too, but if he doesn't go and comes back for therapy, I consider this to mean that he chooses to be here.

INT.: It's part of the process of defining the contract.

DR. W.: Yes. I do this very carefully and in great detail. This is again what we've been talking about; I'm protecting myself. I don't want to set out on a long journey unless we've got enough money to get all the way through, or at least a good part of the way.

INT.: This initial capital is that he has to choose it for himself.

DR. W.: That's right.

INT.: To go back to the business of "life lives us," the big problem in therapy seems to be not to let the patient deal with therapy in the same passive manner as he deals with the rest of the world. So you offer him two alternatives which amount to the same thing. Whether he accepts or refuses the terms of your contract, you define this as his choice.

DR. W.: Yes. I don't accept the passive tense.

ERIC (*overlapping*): But I have no tensions to worry about, at least with some people.

DR. W.: I'm sure.

ERIC: They don't faze me at all. When I get away, I obviously don't think of them. They don't bother me at all. That's why I have to leave. Because when I am home I just can't do anything. My father won't give me a penny.

MRS. F. (*overlapping*): Why do you send birthday presents to the children then if you don't worry about them? Why do you remember their birthdays then?

ERIC: Why shouldn't I?

MRS. F.: Well, okay, you say you forget about us, you remember them (*inaudible words*).

ERIC (*overlapping*): Well, I might not give a damn about you or your husband . . .

MRS. F.: Oh . . .

ERIC: . . . but the children, you know, they still have a life to live. They may be following in your husband's footsteps . . .

MRS. F. (*overlapping*): Well, at least that shows you have a little feeling, that you've . . .

ERIC (*overlapping*): I have a little faith—in the children, yes. (*Pause.*) I plan to . . .

MRS. F. (*overlapping*): Well, we don't expect you to be on our level. After all, we're much older than you are, of course. We wouldn't, we couldn't get, um, we don't live in your generation, we wouldn't expect you, of course you would be, you're in their generation . . .

ERIC: I wish . . .

MRS. F.: . . . is the understanding. But it shows you have a little feeling, you remember them.

ERIC: Well of course I have feeling, I'm definitely not a cold person. I'm very warmhearted. I'm passionate by nature. But it's just—I cannot get along with you and your husband, and I never will be able to. I can get along with you to a degree, but *never* him—*never*—he's not on my level at all. He's an antisocial.

MRS. F.: Now listen, girls and their fathers get along and boys and their mothers get along.

ERIC: Yes.

MRS. F.: You've read all this . . .

ERIC: Of course I have, and I have, I have expressed this before, but not to the, the degree we don't get along. Not to that degree. There's a bit of friction, yes, but not absolute anarchy.

MRS. F.: Well, that's a pretty big question, isn't it?

ERIC: I'm not lying. (*Long pause.*)

(*Dr. W. turns and starts speaking to the youngest child.*)

INT.: That's a beautiful statement: "I have no tensions to worry about, at least with some people." It covers all the possibilities.

DR. W.: If he can only get away from home, he won't have any problems. This is typical. It's like the woman who says, "I don't know why I can't get along with my husband, I get along fine with everybody else."

INT.: And Mother comes in and says, "Why do you send birthday presents then to the children, if you don't worry about them?" I think that's an extraordinarily insidious move.

DR. W.: She takes his remark and expands it to imply that he's turning on the children. "The poor little children who are starving to death because they don't get enough affection from you." It's standard with the mother-father game.

INT.: You see the father in there too?

DR. W.: Sure. My prototype for this sort of thing is the schizophrenic girl who had a dream in which she was in a state hospital hall and her mother had her up against the wall and had both hands around her throat. She was going to kill her. The girl looked down at the other end of the hall where her father was rocking in his chair, paying no attention to anything. Then she saw Father nod his head and knew that this was it. Mother was just the executive secretary.

INT.: Except for a few mutterings, this is the first time the mother has come in. How would you describe what she is doing?

DR. W.: There are several things she's doing. One is to reattach the boy to herself as "father" to the children. It was very clear in the interview that the father was a piece of cardboard and the son was the gigolo and the mother was just sexy for the son. They were sitting directly across from each other. And she's saying, "Don't leave me, think of our poor children."

INT.: It's the way some wives will say, "You must have some feeling, you're kind to the children."

DR. W.: Yes. The quality of her voice is completely seductive. You can almost feel her stroking with it. And when the boy says, "I'm not a cold person," he's making it a straight-out sexual question. Except that it really isn't sexual, because with her seductiveness she's making him into a baby.

INT.: Or into her husband and her baby at the same time.

DR. W.: Yes. She puts him into her generation while telling him that after all he isn't in her generation.

INT.: The boy then answers her by saying that it's not her he can't stand, it's his father, and instead of replying that it's normal for boys and their fathers to have some difficulty, she says that boys and their mothers *get along*. So that you have to step-think to keep up with her.

DR. W.: Well, the boy is saying that his father is an antisocial so-and-so. Inference: Goad me once more and I'll clobber him. She says, "Let's not, we're in public. Let's just talk about the combinations that work well, the dyads that are nice."

INT.: The boy answers the other implication that it's normal for them to be the way they are. He says, "A bit of friction is normal but not absolute anarchy." He's quick, but you'd have to be to keep your feet in that. This woman is so fast, on so many levels, that I'm surprised he isn't crazy.

DR. W.: If he isn't, it may be because the mother has allowed him to direct his anger at her against the father. And also to transmit her anger at the father against the father.

INT.: You mean if he wasn't able to beat up his father, he'd be crazy?

DR. W.: It's possible.

INT.: Do you feel that beating up your father is a healthier thing than being crazy?

DR. W.: It's more interpersonal, at least. Being crazy is settling for masturbation, for a hermit life. Any interpersonal living is more healthy in that it's more open to change over the course of time.

INT.: At this point, you turn to the youngest child. Just before you make this shift, the mother has been doing a number of things to the boy. She's been taking cracks at him while seeming to compliment him, and she has redefined him in two or three different ways. Now when she does this, you don't intervene. You wait and then turn to somebody else. Is it typical for you not to break up an exchange like that?

DR. W.: Yes. I would assume that this is a self-contained, self-locking system, one that I wouldn't open at this stage because it's too delicate. This homeostatic, stabilizing force which binds them together, and which also brought them in, may well be put on the table here to test whether I'm going to destroy it. So I let them have their tête-à-tête. I wouldn't be apt to challenge it till we're further along. Just as I wouldn't challenge Mother's craziness for a long time.

INT.: You mean mothers in general or this mother?

DR. W.: Mothers in general. I think of that as the *pièce de résistance*. And, as I often say, I don't like to start the operation till I'm sure of the anesthetic.

INT.: What do you mean by the anesthetic?

DR. W.: The anesthetic is our relationship. I'm not going to start cutting anybody up until we're very secure in that.

INT.: That's very different from the idea of the therapeutic relationship as a warm human encounter.

DR. W.: To me therapy is like a surgical operation. I know

there's going to be pain. The relationship is what makes the pain bearable. And I'm very careful not to go any faster than I think they can tolerate.

INT.: Are there cases where you feel you can move in right away?

DR. W.: Oh, yes. I've had one-interview treatment many times. I think the difference is whether they accept the structure, whether they take their part of the responsibility for what is happening, so that I can feel free to accept my part without having to take theirs too. Several years ago, a man showed up suddenly in the outer office and said he had to see me immediately. I asked him to come in and he sat down directly opposite me so that we were face to face. He said, "I'm a homosexual. Can you do me any good?" I said, "It depends on whether I'm a better partner than any partner you've had before." He said, "I don't understand." So we talked on, clarifying this, and all the time he was swinging his leg back and forth. After a while I said, "Look, if you want to kick me, kick me." So wham, he did, and wham, I kicked him back. Then we both blushed. I said, "Man, wasn't that fun?" And he said, "You mean you enjoyed it?" I said, "I think it was wonderful." He said, "Well, I'll be damned, that's all I wanted to know," and he got up and left. I never saw him again.

INT.: What did you make of that?

DR. W.: Well, he was carrying the responsibility for what he was and asking me a direct professional question. I was offering what was available in me. But I haven't the vaguest idea what really happened. Perhaps he took it to mean that it was all right to be a homosexual, or that everyone was a homosexual in some sense, so he didn't have to worry. I don't know.

INT.: You took his leaving so decisively as something positive?

DR. W.: No, it was his not coming back. I've had several things like that happen. There was another man who came in and said, "I'm a good husband, a successful businessman, a good father, my life is going beautifully, but I'm not enjoying it. What's wrong?" And I said, "I don't know, but what about the guy who trained all those people you're talking about?" He said, "You know, I never thought about that," and he turned and walked out. I never saw him again either. I assume that he must have gotten something out of this or he would have come back, to find out what I was doing, or why I didn't do more, or whatever. But to get back to this first point, I think that the question of why you can move in at some points and not at others has to do with whether the patient accepts his separateness within the togetherness of the therapy process.

INT.: I gather, then, that one reason you don't go in and break up the entente between the mother and the son is that they haven't accepted this structure of yours. The contract isn't settled yet.

DR. W.: That's absolutely right. The fact that the two of them are having a kitchen fight, or a bedroom fight, is something I don't feel I have any right yet to do anything about, or even to look at. It's their own private world.

INT.: You wait quite a while before you turn to the child. Are you waiting to see if they're going to go on?

DR. W.: I don't know. I would assume that I had decided not to get involved with those two and that I'm accepting the father's nobody-ishness.

INT.: Are you accepting it or pointing it out?

DR. W.: It may be the same thing, but it's a direct denial of him.

INT.: So you let them finish and then turn to the youngest child. Why did you choose her?

DR. W.: As I remember, she was looking at me, so I started to speak to her.

INT.: Aside from the fact that she was looking at you, is it also that you prefer to work involved with people? So if the mother and son are shutting you out, or if it's not anything you care to join, you'll turn to someone else to get involved?

DR. W.: That's right.

INT.: Some therapists will instruct people to talk to each other while they're in the room. I take it you never do anything like that.

DR. W.: I never did it that I can remember. I guess the reason is that I feel that when they do this they have a bilateral role-playing arrangement. With couples, one is usually being the patient and one is being the therapist and every once in a while they'll flip and go the other way. I'll tell them, "This worked out fine during the first period of your marriage, but now you've gotten to an impasse, you're locked, just the way a therapist and his patient often get. And I'm taking over. You're just a couple of amateurs and you've failed. If you face this fact, maybe we can go on from there."

INT.: Here, instead of stopping the mother and son, you turn to the child. This is a message, too, to ignore them like that.

DR. W.: I'm certainly pushing the family out in front as though to turn my back on the twosome. The inference is that I wasn't getting anything very straight from them, so I'll go to the one who's most apt to be honest, the littlest one. But what I'm really trying to show, I think, is that I'm interested in everybody's idea of what we're up to.

INT.: Are you trying to get some clues from the child as to what's going on?

DR. W.: No, I'm not so much interested in the information as in the contact. The little child values me. And I love talking to kids.

INT.: Some therapists will do this to make it very clear that they see the problem as a family problem, since they're bringing even the youngest child in.

DR. W.: That's part of it. I'll often make this kind of switch with couples. I'll ask the husband, "Now tell me what's wrong with your wife?" in cases when she's supposed to be the patient. Then instead of asking the wife to tell me what she thinks is wrong with her, I'll say, "Okay, what's wrong with your husband? He's just finished raking you over the coals, now it's your turn." Then I may never get back to the question of what's wrong with the patient. I'll say, "Why don't the two of you tell me what's wrong with the third patient, the marriage?"

INT.: Instead of turning to the youngest child, would you sometimes turn to the father and bring him in? If it's a silent father like this one?

DR. W.: I don't know. I think here I was just going along with the father's passivity, but I usually try to get the father to have his say before too long. I think of the father as being at a distance. The mother and the child are biologically unified, but he's a social accident, an outsider. Therefore, if he has anything to say, it's usually apt to be hidden as soon as the people close to the problem, like the mother and patient, start defining what's going on. It's that way in a staff conference; you usually start with the youngest or most inexperienced member there, because if you wait until he's listened to all the others, his own ideas will become influenced or inhibited. So I will often go to the father first, or to the youngest child, who is the other person who is distant.

INT.: Would you go to the father first if it was a family in which somebody besides a child was the problem?

DR. W.: If it was a case where it was the father's sister who was sick, and she was living in the home, I might go to the mother. I try to move from the outside in.

INT.: You might have started here with one of the other younger children.

DR. W.: I prefer the youngest one I can get hold of. Children past five or six get very self-conscious, and in this kind of setting I assume that I wouldn't get any contact with the oldest girl at all. Too shy, too afraid of exposing herself. But the little ones are more available.

INT.: Perhaps you're also turning to this little one for some relief after that mother-son scene.

DR. W.: Sure. I'm tired of these dreadful characters neutralizing each other. With the little kids, I can forget about them and have a ball.

DR. W. (*to Margaret, age four*): What do you think about the family? (*Pause.*) You don't know? Or are you just holding out and won't tell us? Whose side are you on? Dad's or Mother's or your brother's?

MARGARET: Mommy's.

DR. W.: You're on your mother's side. (*To Dirk, age six*) How about you? Whose side are you on? (*Pause.*) That's a heck of a question, isn't it? Truly an unfair question. (*To Eliza, age eight*) You got a side?

ELIZA: Yes.

DR. W.: Oh, good, what side are you on?

ELIZA: My brother's and my mother's and my dad's.

DR. W.: Oh-ho, you one-upped me all right. Your brother's and your mother's and your dad's. Well, I think that's nice. (*To Kathryn, age ten*) How about you? You got a side? Would you be on my side?

KATHRYN: Mm-mm.

DR. W.: You wouldn't be on my side? Oh dear. Whose side are you on?

KATHRYN: My dad's and my, my brother's side.

INT.: When you ask one kid after another whose side he's on, I assume you're starting with the youngest and going up the scale.

DR. W.: Yes. I start at the bottom and work up, because, as I said, there's greater spontaneity in the younger ones. I take the little girl first and then the rest of the children can smile and be with her and then move with me.

INT.: You get a response from each of the children, but you don't stop and deal with that response. You go on to the next. Is that deliberate?

DR. W.: Yes. I'm just getting them related to me. Bringing them out of their isolation, making them feel that they belong here, that I need them.

INT.: Why do you do this by asking them whose side they are on?

DR. W.: I always assume there are sides, especially in a family like this one. The struggle between Father and Mother is the basis of this whole chaotic thing. And Brother is drawn in by them on one side or the other.

INT.: But you say there are three sides. There's Daddy's side and Mommy's side and Brother's side.

DR. W.: Yes. Brother has a side because he's fighting to get free from being used by the two of them. The mother and son combination exists to save the mother from being honestly involved with the father. It's a way of avoiding the real battle.

INT.: You not only define these three sides, you assume that each person must be on one of them.

DR. W.: Sure. I don't think that anybody can be on more than one.

INT.: The little girl says she's on Mommy's side. Then you go to the younger boy, but you don't get any answer from him.

DR. W.: No, and I didn't want to press him. His shyness and withholding made me back away.

INT.: The next oldest girl doesn't take a side either.

DR. W.: Yes, she fixes me. Here I'm trying to expose her and she answers in a beautiful way to solve the whole problem. She's on everybody's side. But I felt that this was just a social gimmick. She didn't want any trouble.

INT.: When you move on to the oldest girl, you take a different tack. You say, "Would you be on my side?"

DR. W.: I was being directly seductive. The mother and son had a combine, maybe we could have a combine.

INT.: You didn't get one. Her "Mm-mm" is pretty noncommittal.

DR. W.: I didn't get it overt. I might have gotten it.

INT.: Were you being seductive because you felt like it or because you wanted to balance the mother and son?

DR. W.: I think I had detected something in the oldest girl that gave me the idea that I could get her out of this peculiar repetitious business they were all involved in. And that I could establish a relationship with her that was more adult than the toy kind of relationship I was having with the others.

INT.: The conversation about sides comes directly after Mother has been trying to stress the harmoniousness of the family. You're contradicting her by assuming that fighting is going on in the family and it's just a question of whose side they take.

DR. W.: Oh yes. I'm agreeing with the son that she's misrepresenting things.

INT.: But in a very indirect way. On the surface, you're just making friends with the little children.

DR. W.: That's right. I wouldn't tackle the mother directly for some time. I would want her to understand that whatever I do, I do in their best interests. That I'm not just humiliating her or attacking her or proving her wrong.

INT.: A lot of therapists would say they won't tackle someone directly because they don't want to get into a power struggle, or that therapy wouldn't get anywhere if they did. You put it more in terms of the value of the personal relationship.

DR. W.: I don't ordinarily think of therapy as something manipulative. I think more in terms of, "They're up to something and I'm trying to help." Now this doesn't mean that I don't ever work on a purely technical level. I do, in the beginning of therapy especially. I think it's possible to do therapy of a less disturbed person on a fairly straight, technical level. But when I'm working with people who are very upset, the quality of the relationship becomes crucial. I had one patient who had a fantasy that he'd been working on for fifteen years. It had to do with a family of thirteen adopted children, each of them about nine or ten when he adopted them. The patient was a kind of older brother to these imaginary children and kept them properly disciplined and out of trouble with the law. When he started to describe the fantasy to me, I said, "How about my taping that? We can listen to it again and maybe even get it transcribed." We did, and I almost lost a patient.

INT.: Why was that?

DR. W.: Because I wasn't taping it for purposes related to him but for an ulterior motive on my part. I was only interested in it for my research. He sensed that and became genuinely cynical about me as a person. Therapy started to go wrong, so I said to him, "Look, I guess the reason we lost our verve with each other is that I double-crossed you when I taped this. I should have told you that I was doing it because I felt it might be worth using in teaching my residents. It was dirty of me and I hope we get past it." Of course it's different if I include the taping in the original contract, but if a patient has something that I suddenly want to tape, that's using him.

INT.: You're talking here about "manipulating" someone in the sense of exploiting him, doing something that isn't for his sake but for your own. How different is this from using therapy with patients to expand yourself or increase your own growth?

DR. W.: There's a real difference. If I do therapy to expand myself, both the patient and I get something out of it or it doesn't happen to either of us. Making the tape for the residents didn't give the patient anything, it was using him.

INT.: There seem to be two extreme positions therapists can take with regard to manipulation. There are the therapists who set out deliberately to manipulate a person so that he will change his way of life. Then there are the therapists who claim they aren't manipulating the patient at all or even trying to influence him. You seem to take a middle course.

DR. W.: I'd rather put it that I'm on both sides. It's obvious you can't change people without manipulating them, but on the other hand you aren't going to be of any use to them if you set yourself up as a person who only tells them what to do. I'm not trying to control people, I'm trying to help them to inherit themselves, or help them emerge, or however you want to put it.

INT.: The problem is how to be manipulative and how not to be at the same time.

DR. W.: It's a hard thing to get around. When people come to me, that automatically makes me a significant person. The only way I can counter that is to make it clear that I'm not interested in being a significant person to them, I want to be a significant person to myself. I hope that will give them the courage to become significant to themselves too.

DR. W.: Your dad's and your brother's. Well, we've got almost all the variations, haven't we? I didn't even know Dad and Brother had a common side. (*Pause.*) You mean there's Dad and Brother against Mommy, huh? (*Pause.*)

MRS. F.: She's a girl (*laughs, and Dr. W. laughs*), favors the boys, and the boy favors the mother. (*Laughing.*)

DR. W.: Well, I don't know . . .

MRS. F.: This is it, not favor, but (*laughing*) I guess it's just the normal . . .

DR. W.: A regular family structure. (*Mrs. F. laughs.*)

INT.: Now you say, "I didn't even know Dad and Brother had a common side." This is probably a completely new idea in this family.

DR. W.: One of the things I assume is that in any mixed group there are not only all the combinations of male and female but there are all the males against all the females. I discovered this in group work, where after the third or fourth session you find all the men on one side and all the women on the other. I'm just acknowledging that this is another one of the dynamics that are operating.

INT.: It's not exactly just one of the dynamics in this family. It's a loaded combination that has to be kept out of sight, because it also includes the idea that the men are against Mommy. In a family with a schizophrenic, if somebody suggested that Dad and Brother were against Mommy, you'd expect Mommy to come in like a shot, and I notice that Mommy does here.

DR. W.: It may be that I was responding somewhere inside me to Mother's previous statement that girls like the father and boys like the mother. I may have been setting out to sink the first gaff in her by pointing out that the boys like the men.

INT.: You aren't just saying that boys like men but that they get together with another man against Mother. You shift from who likes whom to who's against whom.

DR. W.: Well, she puts it right back again. The boy likes the mother.

INT.: Then you both laugh. That's a strange laugh of hers.

DR. W.: Yes. It's a psychotic laugh. But this is the laugh that covers the hostility. She and I are clear that we're after each other, but we're still doing it with the greatest delicacy and social comfort.

INT.: She doesn't reply to your suggestion that Dad and Brother have a side, she replies to your previous statement that the girl is on

Dad and Brother's side. You're offering her two propositions and she chooses to go after the first.

DR. W.: This is a technical maneuver that I use many times. I'll drop in a statement while we're talking about something else, and they can't really challenge it because we're on the other subject.

INT.: You say X, Y, and Z, and Y gets in there some way.

DR. W.: That's right. And I'll command them to talk about Z so that they can't get at Y unless they really insist. And so Y sits and they can't get away from it.

INT.: When you put in "The men are against Mommy" within the framework of whose side the girl is on, the mother can't suddenly come out and say, "What do you mean, against Mommy?" without making an issue of it.

DR. W.: That's right.

INT.: But she still answers that point, when she says the boy naturally favors the mother. So how can he be with Dad against Mommy? It sounds like a non sequitur, but in that context it's not.

DR. W.: Yes, she's countering me. She's also going after the girls. Everybody would really favor Mother; the only reason they don't is that they are mean, damn females. It's only because they're of the wrong sex that they're against their good old mother.

INT.: It's just an accident of birth. She doesn't have to appear to be attacking anyone.

DR. W.: That's right. And I say, "Well, I don't know." I'm not going to fight it but I don't quite agree.

INT.: You drop in that "I don't know" in such an offhand way.

DR. W.: This is a standard procedure of mine. I call it "seeding."

INT.: You seed an idea and drift away and leave it.

DR. W.: The most frequent pattern I use is never to repeat something I've said. If I'm talking with the parents and I say something that's loaded for the mother and she says, "I didn't hear you," I say, "Well, Dad heard me and I'm not going to tell you because it's put in now, but you don't have to worry, everything that goes into the computer stays there." Two minutes later I say something to him and he says, "Would you say that again?" and I say, "You see, Mother, this is exactly what happened a minute ago. I'm not going to repeat it for him either." I never come back to those things.

INT.: Is this partly because you feel it's a stronger way to get a point across, a kind of subliminal flash?

DR. W.: No, it's more the other way round. They're trying to get me to say it again so that they can cut it off. When I say it again, my affect is gone. It's like a wife asking for the second time, "Do you really love me?" Then she detects the coldness in her husband's voice and says, "I don't believe it." This fixes him, because the first time he meant it.

INT.: The next thing you say is very curious. Mother is again saying that it's normal for children to favor the opposite parent, and you say, "A regular family structure." You seem to be agreeing with her, but your tone is very flat, almost ironic.

DR. W.: You could say that I'm agreeing with her, except that when she says that her family is normal, she means the opposite. She means that it's an unfortunate trick of fate that she has all these females to contend with. I'm breaking up her suggestion that this is an unusual family.

INT.: That's pretty subtle. I wouldn't have gotten that meaning from her remark.

DR. W.: I introduce the idea that anything that happens in a family is normal whenever I think they're trying to say, "Look how strange we are," meaning that other people in the family ought to be different. It's a standard response of mine to any ploy that has to do with how abnormal the family is.

INT.: What gets complicated here is that you're getting at the mother's real meaning, which is the opposite of her stated meaning. And you do it by agreeing with her ironically. It's a curious double-level way of dealing with two incompatible positions.

DR. W.: I'm just hanging her on her own remark.

DR. W. (*to Dirk*): That's some red shirt. You know, I've got a red shirt just like that, and I'm very fond of it.

MR. F. (*to Dirk*): Don't be so modest.

DR. W.: No, it's got a stripe.

MR. F. (*overlapping*): He's got one, he's got one like this home too. I like that one myself (*inaudible phrase*). (*Pause.*)

DR. W.: I'm talking here to Dirk, the boy who bypassed me before. I couldn't get to him, so I came back to pick him up.

INT.: Your tone changes when you turn from the mother to the boy. It gets warmer.

DR. W.: I said this about the shirt with a lot of feeling, because I have a red shirt which my fourth daughter made for me last Christmas and which I like very much.

INT.: What do you think brought the father in just then?

DR. W.: I would imagine he was about to feel isolated. There's nobody left for him.

INT.: Did you isolate him on purpose?

DR. W.: Maybe. I may have been angry at him for being so indifferent, so aloof from it all.

INT.: You pick out something that you and the young boy have in common and he comes right in. He seems to want to share in this shirt affair.

DR. W.: Perhaps it was because we were talking specifically about things, instead of these loaded problems about the family.

INT.: Also, he may have been reasonably sure by now that you could handle the mother without disaster.

DR. W.: It could be.

DR. W.: Well, what are we going to do? I think of us as kind of being here this morning to see if we can make up our minds whether psychotherapy is worth getting into, and whether the three of you can make up your minds to, ah, spend that much time, and effort, and money, trying to work at it (*pause*) and I guess I need to get fairly clear where I stand with it, and then tell you the rough, rough outline of how I feel about this kind of work, I mean I don't think of it as being anything particularly exceptional, I think of it as being the kind of thing that's worth time and effort. I would, as I said last time, be willing to work with the three of you. I would not be willing to work with any part of the three of you, either one or two, or any combination, because I think this would be denying the situation as it seems clear it exists. I'm glad to have the kiddies in, I think they belong in, I don't think they have to be in every time, but I think they have to know, and I'm glad to tell them, that the family is upset, and they've known it for a long time. I think they know probably as much about the upset as any one of the three of you do, because I trust children's intuition and their understanding to be very deep in these very early years. I don't think they need to be in every time, but I'll be glad to have any of them who want to come, or any of them you want to bring, or all of them, if you feel you'd like to bring them. I think each time they come they contribute, and I think each time they come they get something from it. They get something from it because they have a sense of their family trying to do something about itself. And I think this keeps them from being panicked, ah, in their bed at night by themselves, or being panicked, ah, at what they overhear, or what they think they overhear, or what they're afraid is going on, and, ah, I think the real facts are never as dangerous or as frightening as the fantasies and dreams that children can have about this, particularly when it involves their mommy and their daddy.

INT.: Right after the exchange about the shirt, you launch into a long speech about therapy. It's almost as if you had completed something, wrapped it up.

DR. W.: I think of this as a point where I've made contact with the entire family, kind of shaking hands all round. Now we're moving back to talk about what we are here for. Are we ready to structure this thing?

INT.: You start with that at the beginning of the interview, and you don't get it resolved, so you go into a diversion. Now you get back to the issue again.

DR. W.: I'm not sure I'd call it a diversion. What I did during this time was to set up the issue differently.

INT.: That's true. You've brought in everyone in the family and made it clear that there's a war on and everybody's taking sides. It would be very hard for them to say, "Why should we come in as a family?" because you've redefined the problem as one in which they all have a share.

DR. W.: Exactly.

INT.: I notice that you go back to saying you'll just see the three of them. The other children are welcome but they don't have to come. Why is that?

DR. W.: Before, when I wanted to see the three of them and they wouldn't come in, I said, "Okay, then bring the seven in." But the seven are to bring the three in.

INT.: You mean that they'll be glad to get back to three now that they've had the ordeal of seven?

DR. W.: That's right. Because when I get the seven of them in, it turns out that five of them are on my side. From the mother's point of view it's even worse, because it's clear that the females are against her, which makes three, and she knows the father automatically is against her.

INT.: And you've lined up big brother with Daddy and gotten together with Daddy and little Dirk.

DR. W.: So we've really got Mother isolated, haven't we? She's got nobody on her side.

INT.: This operation of yours with the children has isolated both parents. This may be the first time they've only had each other in years.

DR. W.: If they won't come together on purpose, I have to get them together by default.

INT.: In this speech, you seem to be trying to persuade the family that therapy will be worth their while. Why, then, do you say that you don't think of it as anything exceptional?

DR. W.: I meant that the family is nothing exceptional. I said "it," meaning the kind of problem we'd be working on.

INT.: It's that "it" again. It runs through this whole speech. And there are some other puzzling things. For instance, you say that the little children have to know about the upset, so they won't imagine that things are worse than they are. On the other hand, because they're children and have a deep intuition, they've known about it for a long time.

DR. W.: This is again talking to the parents through the children. The parents have maintained the fiction that the children don't know and that to know would upset them. So I take the responsibility for "upsetting" them by letting them in on the fact that the family is upset. Then I laugh at the parents for making believe that the children don't know by saying that of course they've always known.

INT.: You seem to be talking here about a kind of double-level knowing.

DR. W.: Yes. At the same time that I'm talking about what they openly know, I'm also talking about the Biblical, the carnal "know." This is a real part of my conviction. These kids have known about sex, they've known about Mommy and Daddy for a long time. They also know about the family upset, even though they pretend not to.

INT.: You don't say it openly, but there is a suggestion in this speech that the family upset is the same kind of open secret as what goes on in the parents' bedroom.

DR. W.: Yes. I use the framework of sex to talk about it, but what these people are really afraid of is that they're killing each other. The violence is usually thought of as a disguise for sex, but I suspect it's the other way round.

INT.: What stands out is that you speak to the parents as if both you and they know what this family upset consists of, but you never make it explicit what that is. Do you mean the boy's violence at home?

DR. W.: No, his symptom doesn't concern me at all. Anyway, I assume that's no secret. I felt that what the parents didn't want the children to know was the level of the affect of their disturbance, not anyone's misbehavior as such.

INT.: By family upset, then, you mean the struggle between the parents.

DR. W.: The struggle between the three, really. Because it's a three-person upset. If Father and Mother were willing to accept their own war, they wouldn't need the boy to conduct it for them. This is David fighting Goliath for Mother.

INT.: We've got what you mean by the upset, but there's still a question whether the parents are taking it that way. There's been no concession on their part so far that there is a war, let alone that the boy is fighting it for them.

DR. W.: I assume that on some level they know perfectly well what I'm talking about and that the children do too. This is also part of what I'm telling them.

INT.: Without clearly telling them anything. What I'm really trying to get at is the ambiguity of this speech. You're letting the parents know that you know what's going on without ever saying what that "it" is. You're speaking as ambiguously as these people themselves could ever do.

DR. W.: You're exactly right when you say that I'm talking the way they do. The only way I can treat very disturbed people is to get involved with them. And the only way I can do that is to get involved the way the mother got involved. So I double-bind the patient and he double-binds me, just like mother and son do. I really believe that the only person who gets to be a psychotherapist for schizophrenics, or maybe for their families, since that's possibly the same thing, is someone who is schizophrenogenic.

INT.: Therapists who work with families of schizophrenics often seem to talk like the people in those families. It's not unusual. What's hard to get at is the difference between what the therapist is doing when he talks this way and what the family is doing.

DR. W.: I've wondered about that myself. An ex-patient of mine who was in treatment with our group in Georgia once said to me, "Every one of you was just like my mother. You were doing the same things to me that she did. But I found the difference. When I tried to break out of this with my mother, she would twist it. Push it tighter. When I tried to break out of it with you, you loved it." It occurred to me later that part of it is that the patient is not my child and therefore I don't have to keep him. Now there's always the question of whether, if he were my last patient, I'd ever let him go. I suspect I'm like a mother I once had in a mothers' group. She had ten children and one of the other mothers said to her, "Why did you have so many?" and she said, "That's the only way I can keep from spoiling the youngest."

> DR. W. (*cont.*): I would (*pause*), I would not be willing to go on catch as catch can. I think if we go on we need to decide, and we don't need to decide it today, but we need to decide before we go much further, whether you're willing to undertake this as a long-range project, all three of you. Ah, I would not like it, unless all three of you made your own individual decision about this. I would accept it and assume it to be my responsibility as a physician to work with it, if just Mother and Daddy made the decision and insisted (*to parents*) that your son come along. I would much rather he came because he wanted something out of it for himself, (*to son*) but I would accept their decision, ah, if they, ah, decide that's the way it has to be.

DR. W.: When I say, "You don't need to decide today," I'm trying to keep them from making a pseudo-decision. This is a standard administrative demand of mine. "Go home and sleep on it, and if tomorrow morning you still want to come, call me and we'll make an appointment. Or call me six weeks or ten years from now. I don't care when you decide, but when you do, I want to be able to count on you."

INT.: Is it enough of a commitment if they make a plain, direct statement that they agree to come in?

DR. W.: It is if I feel they're being genuine. But essentially it's the state of the relationship that tells me. It has to be based on an understanding that we are jointly up to something long-range. That's when I think the formal process of psychotherapy begins.

INT.: In trying for a commitment, you have a way of going up to these people and backing off, going up and backing off. First you pressure them to come in, then you say, "You don't have to decide today."

DR. W.: I think there's always this alternation of withdrawal and approach. It's like a courtship dance. And the question is not, "Do you love me?" but "Are you going to marry me?" I'll back up to see whether they'll come toward me, then I'll come forward because I'm interested.

INT.: You'd have to move back so that they can come forward. Otherwise it wouldn't really be their decision.

DR. W.: I'd say it was in order to make it a reciprocal decision. I back up to see whether they will take their share of the responsibility and then I move forward to tell them that I'm willing to take mine.

INT.: In this next exchange, you say, "I would not like it unless you all three of you made your own individual decision about this." Do you really think it's possible for them to make individual decisions to come in together?

DR. W.: They make them covertly, even though they don't admit it. They may go home and sit for six months and then somebody will say, "Oh, this mess, maybe we ought to go back and see Whitaker." Somebody else will say, "All right, if you want to," and the other one will say, "I'll go along if the two of you are going."

INT.: What's "individual" in this becomes very peculiar. Suppose the father doesn't make an individual decision to come in and the son hauls off and hits him and the father decides to come in. You can't really say this is the father's individual decision.

DR. W.: Well, I assume that in all these families there's a constant confusion about boundaries. I remember one time when the father of a very psychotic boy brought up the fact that they were going to buy a car. The next week I said, "How about it, Dad, did you buy your new car?" And he said, "No, we haven't made up my mind yet."

INT.: You start mixing the pronouns yourself in this speech. "I would work with it if just Mother and Daddy made the decision and insisted that *your* son come along. I would much rather *he* came because *he* wanted something out of it for *himself,* but I would accept *their* decision if *they* decide that's the way it has to be."

DR. W.: You have to remember that I'm looking first at one, then at the other. It wouldn't be so confusing if you had been sitting there.

INT.: It's just that you go into such a fast alternation. In talking about B's decision you address yourself to A, and in talking about A's decision you address yourself to B, and you keep rocking it back and forth. It's almost as if you were countering this tendency you've described, which is that whenever these people are faced with a commitment, they slide in and out of each other.

DR. W.: It could be. It's certainly a strange speech.

INT.: The other strange thing is that just after you've said that you want individual decisions, you say that it's all right if the parents bring the son in.

DR. W.: I don't care who brings who in. I'll take each one's presence in the office next time as evidence of his choosing to be there, no matter who makes the overt decision. I didn't say it here, but it would be equally acceptable to me if the son brought the parents in.

INT.: You again set it up so that whether it's an independent choice, or whether somebody else does the choosing, it's still each one's choice.

DR. W.: Yes. The only thing I wouldn't accept is if any two came in. All three have to be there. This is what I keep pushing.

INT.: You wouldn't see the parents alone? Some therapists will bring the child in at first but then drop him and concentrate on the parents' relationship. Since he's only the surface symptom.

DR. W.: I wouldn't do it with this couple. They'd say, "We love each other. There's nothing wrong with us. It's just that boy."

INT.: Are there situations in which you would do this?

DR. W.: For me it depends on how old the child is. With a younger child, from four up to perhaps nine, I might be tempted to offer this alternative. Or if the child had already made a move to break away from home. I once saw a couple with a schizophrenic daughter of seventeen, she was out on a pass from the hospital. After the first interview, she ran away. She was found and brought back to the hospital, but the parents came to the next interview alone and I said to them, "By running away, your daughter has said she doesn't want to be part of the family. I take that seriously, I take it as a *fait accompli*. I'll work with you as a couple but I won't work with you and your daughter." And this is what we did.

INT.: What was different about that case? This boy wants to run away, he just hasn't done it.

DR. W.: That's the difference. I feel he can be helped to do it a better way. That's why it has to be the three. The way he's trying to leave is just going to get him tied tighter into the family.

> DR. W. (*cont.*): The other thing that I think is important for me to say is that I do not feel that I am competent to do this alone. I, ah, as I sometimes say to patients, I'd be glad to take out an appendix with a good operating-room nurse, but I wouldn't even touch a gall bladder or a, whatever else, hysterectomy, without a good surgeon right there beside me or on the other side of the table, and I feel the same way with this kind of thing. I do not think it's possible, by myself, ah, I don't think I'm strong enough. So if we decide to go on, either today or sometime in the very near future, I would want a second psychiatrist in with me, at each interview, ah, as I want to be strong enough, or want your therapist, the two of us, to be strong enough so that you can depend upon us, and I don't think I can do that alone. I might make it, but I don't want to take any chances, I'd rather play it safe. (*Pause.*)

INT.: If you don't mind, I'd like to stop here for a moment and go into your reasons for having a co-therapist. First of all, how did you start doing this?

DR. W.: In 1945, when John Warkentin and I were working together in Oak Ridge, one of us would come out of an interview all excited and try to tell the other what a wonderful experience this had been. But the other wouldn't be interested. So one day one of us said, "Look, why don't we see patients together and then we can both talk about the same interview." After we tried it, we saw so many advantages in it that we never gave it up. This was even truer after we started seeing chronic schizophrenics, couples and finally families.

INT.: Why was that?

DR. W.: I doubt that it's possible to handle any family with just one therapist. I don't think one therapist alone possesses the amount of power necessary to get in and change the family and get back out again, without getting stuck in the people salad. Even when I think it might be possible, I'm usually not willing to take the chance. I'd rather get a good double team and be sure.

INT.: The other member of that team is another therapist, I gather, not a social worker or a student or something like that.

DR. W.: Yes. Another professional therapist. Although I think of the team itself as being the therapist. For instance, my resident and I are treating an older woman with a menopausal depression. She misidentifies and calls him "Whitaker," as though she were trying to make it clear that we're a team, even though most of what's been going on has been with me.

INT.: You still see it as team therapy even though the other therapist doesn't take an equal part?

DR. W.: That's right. Even if he is relatively inactive.

INT.: When you talk of wanting extra power to handle a family, is part of it that you don't want to be too outnumbered?

DR. W.: No, I think of it as adding power to myself. The other person gives me security, a feeling that I'm not isolated, that I'm not going to be ham-strung by my attachment to one or my antagonism to another. I'm able to keep clear of entanglements.

INT.: The presence of the other person gives you a platform outside the family structure. It's not that you want another therapist for the different skills he might bring, but because he becomes part of your own apparatus in dealing with the family.

DR. W.: In effect, yes. Although his skills and knowledge are very important. If in the middle of the operation I'm suddenly not quite clear whether this is the bile duct or the aorta, I'll say, "Bill, what do you think?" But this is a secondary gain. I've learned that you can go on holding a family together and staying with it without changing it. I'm not willing to do that any more. I want to get in with enough power so that I'm going to be able to get out. I don't want to stay the rest of my life with my finger stuck in the dike.

INT.: Is the team always two people or do you sometimes work with more?

DR. W.: We tried all sorts of combinations, but two was the basic concept. We'd occasionally split it up; one therapist would see the patient for one interview, the other for the next, and then we'd meet together. Or one would take one spouse, if it was a couple, and the other would take the other, and the next time we'd have a four-way meeting. We found it worked best if we alternated the individual patients rather than if each therapist saw the same patient. But we'd make sure that there were always four people there in spirit. The structure was always there.

INT.: Do you find that having two therapists makes therapy shorter?

DR. W.: There's less chance of its being interminable or never getting off the ground, but I can't prove it's shorter. It's just that the therapist is more adequate. In a serious situation like this one, where the father and mother are grossly disturbed, I would never go on without a second therapist.

INT.: You felt that the father and mother were that upset?

DR. W.: I think that anybody with any experience would have taken a look at them and decided that they were both crazy in the direct insane sense. What I had already been told about the family confirmed this, too: how crazy the situation was in the community, how utterly out in left field the father was, and how disorganized the home was, wild, chaotic, with no reality controls at all.

INT.: Are there families you would see by yourself?

DR. W.: Yes, if it's a concerned family, with everybody interested in doing something about the problem.

INT.: Do you usually bring in another therapist when you're working with individuals?

DR. W.: Always, with a VIP, or a millionaire, or a reputable psychiatrist, or a patient who has had two or three previous therapists whom I think of as good ones. And I'll do this with families in which there is a strong possibility of violence. In one family I saw before I left the South, the husband had tried to hire someone to kill his wife and the FBI picked it up. Since they said they were ready to try to go on living together, they were sent to me.

INT.: Is part of it a responsibility problem, that you don't want to be the only one on the spot in case there is violence?

DR. W.: Well, that's helpful, but again it's not the main reason. I think it's mostly that the twosome is greater than the sum of its parts. The twosome becomes the administrator. When I'm alone, I have to be both the person who has fun with the little girl and the reality person who has to figure out what we're going to do.

INT.: It gives you the freedom to be personal, to do what you feel like.

DR. W.: Yes. I can take the next hour and just play with the little four-year-old. This might be a tremendously powerful experience. Mother might see the fun she could have by being loving with her daughter. This is one of my standard moves in therapy with the family.

INT.: So far we've been talking about the advantage for yourself of having another therapist in. Does it free the other therapist too?

DR. W.: Yes. Because one can be the administrator while the other plays. Or one of us can move in on one person while the other stays with the other one. Who does which can change from moment to moment.

INT.: I take it that you tend to keep in balance with each other. If one of you stops playing and becomes the administrator, the other will fill the place you just left.

DR. W.: Yes. It's usually complementary.

INT.: You don't pre-set things, such as deciding before an interview that one will be the supportive one and the other will be the reality one?

DR. W.: No, it happens dynamically. Let me give you an example of this freedom I'm talking about. I was asked in on a case with a very schizy, overt homosexual. It was one of the last interviews, and he started telling us that he didn't want to talk about his real life situation because he didn't think it pertinent. He hedged all around this, and finally I said, "It sounds to me as if you're talking about your being a homosexual, and you don't have to tell me about it, but I'd like to explain to you how I feel about homosexuality. I often have a feeling of envy toward somebody who has been overtly homosexual because that's a life experience I've never had. When you talk about this, I have the feeling that you're somehow denying the fact that you've always had a sense of lovingness with men that I'm not sure I'll ever have, having missed that experience." This startled him and he became flustered. During the next interview, which was the last one, he talked about how much my statement had meant to him. Now I think that if I had been his therapist I probably would not have been free to say this, either because he might take it out to the community or because it might precipitate both of us into some kind of panicky feeling about each other. With the other therapist there, I didn't have to worry about this.

INT.: The fact that you're two therapists suggests the idea that you're like two parents. Do you think of yourselves as creating a therapeutic family for the patient? Does one become more the mother and the other more the father?

DR. W.: No, I think of us as both the parents. We take both parts interchangeably, like hermaphrodites. It is like a family in that we tend to represent the older generation and treat the patient like our child. Or, if I'm alone, I'll think of myself as a kind of prime parent, not sexually identifying.

INT.: Whether you take the parts of mother and father or not, you're still a pair. If, as is often noticed, the schizophrenic patient is adept at splitting the parental pair, I should think that he would also try to split the therapist pair.

DR. W.: He does, and this is what we deal with all the time. I remember one instance in which Malone said to a patient, "Look, you can make love to Whitaker but he and I have been sleeping together for years and years and years. We had a particularly good night last night, and I don't think you have the slightest chance of getting anywhere, but why don't you go ahead and try?" We would handle it in this kind of crazy, symbolic language, but we wouldn't evade it, we'd meet it directly.

INT.: You assume that it's therapeutic if they attempt to split you and don't succeed.

DR. W.: I think of that as crucial. If they split the therapists, there's no way around it. You're up the creek with a hole in the canoe.

INT.: You could see that having two therapists there would almost invariably tempt the patient to try to split you. Did anyone ever succeed in doing that?

DR. W.: There was one schizophrenic patient who blasted Warkentin and me apart. At first, therapy went so well that we started to take turns with him. Then things became so difficult between us that we decided to drop the case. But I think that's why most therapists will take on one schizophrenic and then never take on another. Because the patient will split him into his masculine and feminine parts and he's not sure he can get them back together again.

INT.: I should think that working in a team would be useful because it would allow you to handle this splitting in an easier way. With two bodies, it becomes a more obvious operation.

DR. W.: I think so. It also allows us to demonstrate what a confident, direct relationship can be like. Co-therapy with us was a recurrent process of arguing, even fighting. I'd say to the patient, "Look, that s.o.b. is twenty minutes late today; you just sit there while Mother and Daddy get this straightened out." And we'd fight throughout the whole interview. We would both be mad.

Int.: How mad?

Dr. W.: Really mad.

Int.: You mean you would only enact a scene to show the patient how to get angry if you really were angry?

Dr. W.: This would not be an enacted scene!

Int.: In other words, you would just happen to get angry while the patient was around.

Dr. W.: Well, it could be that he was part of it. The other therapist may have been late because the last time he thought I was stealing the patient and this time he was going to keep me alone in there for twenty minutes so that he could be mad at me for having an interview without him. But we would have it out right in front of the patient.

Int.: This becomes another example of how you refuse to let the patient split you.

Dr. W.: That's right. The great advantage of it is that you're able to show the patient how to be challenged and how to handle this verbally.

Int.: We've talked about the advantages of co-therapy; what about the demerits?

Dr. W.: Over a long period, you may find yourselves locked in like a husband and wife, so that the two of you can't talk openly. You build up tensions and you have to adapt to them somehow and so you get into a pattern of stalemating and stultifying each other. For example, what began to happen with Malone and myself was that he was so incisive in his interpretations that I would tend not to interfere, whether I agreed with him or not. Or he would know that I would be tempted to move in fairly early in the relationship, so he would sit back and let me go ahead.

Int.: You could also see this as a division of functions along the lines of what each of you could do best.

Dr. W.: Yes, but at times this tended to keep the other on the outside.

Int.: You've said that you want to work out a contract with a family in which you're in charge of the situation and can make it go where you want it to go. I should think that when somebody else, a peer, is in there, you would also have to work out a reasonably clear arrangement with him.

Dr. W.: Yes. In the beginning it may sometimes be difficult. Since I've come to Wisconsin, I've been working in collaboration with six or seven psychiatrists, seeing couples, and at first I felt a little skittish about this. I didn't know what was going to happen. But so far it's worked out very nicely, no problem.

INT.: Do you think this is partly because you come in as the authority in this situation?

DR. W.: I'm not sure. I'm certainly still wearing some kind of halo that has to do with being from far away, or perhaps it's because I'm the only one in town who does anything except individual therapy.

INT.: But when you were working with therapists of equivalent experience, did you ever find you had trouble?

DR. W.: Occasionally, as in the case I mentioned of the patient who broke up Warkentin and me. We finally had to take it to the whole staff, and they recommended we drop the case.

INT.: You had a super-authority to go to.

DR. W.: Yes. But we very seldom had to use it.

INT.: You say that you feel it frees you to have another therapist in with you. Many people might find it restricting to have that to deal with as well as the family.

DR. W.: I think that's because they've never done it. After I came here I suggested to two of the residents that they see a patient together. They had one interview and they bent my ear for two solid hours telling me what a wonderful experience this was. One of them said, "I had more ideas in that hour than I had in a whole year of seeing patients alone. It was all of a sudden as if I was free." We used to define the requirements in terms of whether we could be either therapist or patient to the other person. If you have enough respect for him, you can do it.

INT.: In your talk to this family, when you say you want another therapist, you put it in terms of not being strong enough to handle them alone. This sets up a peculiar situation. You're stepping one down when you say that you're not strong enough. This makes it impossible for them to hang you on omnipotence, because you're conceding your weakness to begin with. At the same time, this is going to make them want to build you up. With two people there, it's going to cost them twice as much, and I should think that their natural reaction would be to try to make you stronger, so that you can do without the other person.

DR. W.: People often ask me if we couldn't drop the second therapist. But once I've decided to have him in, the therapist has been structured as a twosome. And no matter how well things progress, I wouldn't feel that we could go back to one.

INT.: Once you start with a team, you've got to be not strong enough right through to the end.

DR. W.: Yes. The only way we would modify it would be to cut down on the frequency of the visits. Or to alternate, making sure that the two therapists are always there in spirit. When we get going, it becomes a question not of strength but of who is the therapist. It's not me, or him, it's us, and if you change that, it's like starting with a new therapist.

INT.: The twosome becomes a new person.

DR. W.: Yes. And a proof of this is that when I'm seeing a couple in co-therapy, I can go to a cocktail party and meet the couple and be perfectly comfortable, and so can the other therapist. There isn't the uneasiness that is usually present when an individual therapist meets the patient socially.

INT.: I wonder what the difference is between the relationship of the co-therapists in the room and the relationship when they get outside. You say that you'll sometimes insult each other or fight. If you're outside having coffee, would you be so likely to take the same tone with each other?

DR. W.: No. Outside it's a relationship between professionals or just an ordinary friendship. Inside it's psychodrama, if you will.

INT.: The courtesy rules are different in the room than they are outside.

DR. W.: The courtesy is what takes place outside. Inside we call each other names. I can tell you one thing; I'm a lot more mature in the office than I am outside. My thought about it is that the professional fragment is a pie section that goes deeper in but isn't the whole circumference. When a patient attacks me, he may go way in, but he doesn't attack the rest of me, just that particular area.

INT.: You can't take it personally, because he isn't attacking you, he's attacking the new therapist you've created. That may be part of the freedom you describe.

DR. W.: That may very well be the way it works.

DR. W. (*cont.*): I would think of a minimum of once a week as being a, a usable kind of relationship. I would feel it necessary to charge you a twenty-five-dollar fee for each of the therapists for the regular process interviews as we went along, which will amount to a couple hundred dollars a month. (*Pause.*)

MRS. F.: What do you think, John?

MR. F.: Well, I don't know.

MRS. F.: Ah, I think it's just that, ah, we must get this, ah, element of violence out of our family, it's getting worse and worse and we certainly, we all get upset, but I mean it gets to a point where you're breaking things and, ah, completely going off beam and, ah, which is rather a contagious thing when you have so many people in the same family, it just goes on and everybody does it after a while. It's something that's got to be defeated.

INT.: Is this the first time you've brought up the subject of the fee?

DR. W.: I think so, yes.

INT.: The mother turns to the father and asks, "What do you think?" As usual, he's almost inaudible.

DR. W.: He really is. Two hundred dollars a month and he's speechless.

INT.: The mother's next speech implies that there's a little more violence in the family than has been revealed. She seems to be saying that other people are being hit besides the father. "Everybody does it after a while. It's contagious."

DR. W.: I thought she meant that she might catch it. "I might go mad."

INT.: When there's a mysterious statement like that, do you ever try to get at the facts behind it?

DR. W.: No. I remember one poor man who spent an hour telling me about himself, and he finally said, "You don't seem to be listening." I said, "Well, I'm not interested in facts." I thought he was almost going to fall out of his chair. It never occurred to him that there was anything in life besides the facts.

INT.: Do you feel the same way about taking a history?

DR. W.: When I was first practicing and teaching, I used to take exhaustive histories, but I've stopped doing that now. I take a few notes for myself during the first interview, but that's about all.

INT.: You don't feel you need information about what led up to the boy's hitting his father?

DR. W.: No, I don't want that part of their life, they can have it. I've got two couples: one whose daughter is in a sanatorium and one whose daughter is away at college. And with both of these couples, the absent child is thrust at me with a horrible drive and insistence. I say, "Look, I'm not interested, I don't care what happens to her, quit telling me, leave me alone." And they say, "Well, what are you interested in? Shall I tell you about me?" "I'm not interested in the facts about you either." "Well, what are you interested in?" "I'm interested in *you*."

INT.: What do you mean by "you" as opposed to what they mean?

DR. W.: I'm interested in the person. They say, "Well, that's what I am, my children, my husband, my home, my past." That doesn't make sense to me.

INT.: How do you define this person you're interested in?

DR. W.: The person who is sitting here with me. The person who keeps me from feeling lonely during that hour.

INT.: You block off everything that isn't their action in connection with you.

DR. W.: Sure. "If you're not interested in me, I don't want to listen to it. Don't bother me with what happened to you last night or yesterday."

INT.: There's something strange here. This discussion with you about this family isn't going to have a past, because, as you say, "they can have it." And it's not going to have a future, because so far they haven't come back. That doesn't seem to matter to you either. For you, therapy seems to be a matter of the instant moment, as when you kick a guy and he kicks you back.

DR. W.: That's right. I believe the transference is in the here and now.

    ERIC: Well, I'm definitely leaving. However, I'd be willing to fly back to come to the sessions. I'm getting out of here, I can't stand these people, and I'm not going to be near them. But I certainly would want to come back and straighten out their problem. I say *their* problem because I think it's more theirs than mine, I think.

    DR. W.: Certainly they were here first.

    ERIC: I have been caught up in it, it certainly wasn't *my* fault I was born, and I was, ah, became a part of this triangle which once was only two points.

DR. W.: Mm-hm, I sure agree with that. I think the other question, and the question that I addressed myself to a few minutes ago when I said I would like a separate decision from each of you, is that in the process of your being caught up in the family structure that you're caught up in, it has done things to you which I think you can gain from by *really* getting yourself out, rather than physically walking out. I think physically walking out does not get rid of your parents. This is, ah, a sort of a scientific fact that we, ah, are stuck with. That they will always be your parents, and that you will always be like Daddy, and like Mother, inside of yourself, and that one of the big things I think of this working toward is helping you to get free inside of yourself, to be a separate person in a, ah, less guilty, ah, less defensive, less, ah, reaction against them. (*Pause.*) And, ah, I think this would be advantageous to you.

DR. W.: Just now we had the mother agreeing to come in, or at least conceding that something has to be done. So the boy says he's willing to come in too. He's willing to fly back from New York.

INT.: That's a concession. But he makes it clear that he'll only do this to help his parents, because the problem is "more theirs."

DR. W.: I point out to him that if the problem is "more theirs" it's because they were born first.

INT.: It's a phrasing that takes the blame away. The boy can accept being part of the problem too, because he was born into it.

DR. W.: Yes. As he says, "into a triangle that once had only two points." It's a nice way to put it. As if the "set" were already there for him to walk into.

INT.: In your next speech, when you say to the boy that he's caught up in the family structure, you again use a phrasing that blames nobody. You could have said, "caught up in the struggle between your parents," and it would have put them on the spot. Do you deliberately choose a neutral phrasing?

DR. W.: It's not deliberate. Here it may have been because I tend to think of the family as a set of vectors, rather than people.

INT.: This subject keeps coming up, but it's rare in talking to you that you describe something you do as an action that has a purpose in relation to somebody else. You prefer to describe it as an expression of you in some way. Now it could be that both ways of describing the thing are equally valid. You wouldn't express yourself differently, and yet it can be seen manipulatively, too, because it's appropriate to get someone to do something.

DR. W.: This is a strange business, and I don't know how to answer that. I don't have any problem with your seeing my use of the term "family structure" as an attempt to manipulate. But if you mean that I use the term so that the family can't wriggle out of my definition of the problem by saying I'm attacking them as people, this wouldn't seem accurate to me.

INT.: There's always a question of deliberateness versus calculatedness. You take a master tennis player. His opponent is on one side of the court, so he puts the ball into the opposite corner. If you ask him why, he may well say, "That's just the way my arm swung." It's what he's programmed to do. But if you try to describe what he's doing, you are likely to say that he put the ball there so that his opponent couldn't reach it.

DR. W.: I wouldn't argue with what you're saying. The way I look at it is that there are three levels of operation in therapy: the tactical, the strategic, and possibly a level beyond this which I don't have a name for. In the first category, I would put the immature hypnotist who tries to, and maybe does, get rid of a hysterical paralyzed arm. Now this may be valuable, it may be dangerous, and it may be the best be can do. The person who manipulates on a purely strategic level may be just a technically good therapist. I do that myself and I don't have any ethical scruples about it. The third level, which is what I think we're struggling with, gets to an area where you can't be deliberate any more. I'll give you an example. I had been seeing this older woman with a post-menopausal depression; she had already been to another therapist when she came to me. I saw her about fifteen or twenty times, and at about this point began to act meaner and meaner with her. This was strategic, or partly strategic, and she began to get angry with me, but she wouldn't come out with it. One day she came in wearing red shoes, and I commented on how pretty they were. The next week she came in wearing black shoes. The next time she came in, she was wearing hospital slippers, those canvas scuffs. She seemed about to express her hatred of me, and was talking about going back to her previous therapist. I found myself concentrating on her slippers and all of a sudden I leaned forward, seized her foot, and began to draw my initials on her shoe. I went through three or four pens before I found one that would do it.

She tried to pull her foot away before I was finished, and I got angry, but she apparently saw my anger as something different from the taunting, derisive meanness I had been showing her before, because she gave in and was with me. She realized it was very important to me whether she belonged to me or to the other therapist. This was a very significant moment for both of us. But I didn't plan it, and I still don't know what meaning it had in the therapy.

INT.: Suppose you were an outsider trying to make sense out of this for other people who wanted to know how you work or to understand the process of therapy. Can you conceive of any way to present what you were doing in terms that were not strategic?

DR. W.: I don't know how you would describe it. To me, this is beyond the dance. It's not interpersonal. All of a sudden I'm not interested in the woman, I'm not interested in myself, I'm interested in the shoe. This is a creative moment. I had no sense of its being a creative moment when it was taking place, but fifteen minutes later it suddenly occurred to me that I hadn't completed the action and I went back and put her initials on the other shoe. So that there was a His and Hers, like the towels. That second gesture may have been strategic.

INT.: You're saying that the first action is something that can't be duplicated.

DR. W.: That's right. It's something that just occurs. I keep telling the residents, "You know, I've never done this before in my life." The satisfaction I get out of it isn't just based on the relationship, it's the satisfaction that comes from the breakthrough of a new set of thought connections. For many years I used to struggle with never saying the same thing the same way. If I can't think of anything different to say, better not to say anything. I still pretty much go by that. Not in this initial structuring, but as we go on. I don't ordinarily say anything unless something occurs to me that has some pertinence.

INT.: It's how to describe what you do that becomes the problem. You could say it's like a child building up a pile of blocks. Sometimes he's doing it to impress his parents, and sometimes it's just for his own pleasure. But if the parents are there while he does it, an observer would describe it in relation to his parents no matter what the intent.

DR. W.: It can be very hard for an outsider to tell the difference. This may be related to the reactions people have to my going to sleep in therapy. I'll go to sleep for a short while and have a dream and then wake up and tell the patient about it. I don't know whether this is fantasy, or a pseudo-hypnotic experience, or an ordinary dream. And I'm never aware of being sleepy, the first thing I'm aware of is coming out of the dream. But many patients will say to me, "You're not really sleeping, you're just closing your eyes, it's just a fake."

INT.: Do you ever drop off to sleep like this in an ordinary situation?

DR. W.: No, it only happens in therapy. I've even done it in front of a movie camera. It's been going on for fifteen years. There was another period when I would get into fights with patients. This wouldn't be deliberate, it would be a bilaterally activated process. I'd get madder and madder and the patient would get madder and madder, and we'd end up in a wrestling match.

INT.: Is the sleeping bilaterally activated too? If you're in a trance, somebody must be putting you in a trance.

DR. W.: I never thought of it that way. I suppose you're right.

INT.: Would you say the same of these spontaneous moments of yours?

DR. W.: Oh yes. I'm sure they arise in response to the situation as it's developing.

INT.: In one sense, then, they don't "just occur." You yourself don't make them happen, but something in the relationship makes them happen.

DR. W.: That's true. Just before one of these moments, I'll be aware of a quality of resonance, a physiological resonance, between the other person and me. Even though I'm almost unaware of him while the particular action is going on.

INT.: To get back to the question of how to describe what you're doing, you're being spontaneous here, but at the same time there's the underlying suggestion that it's exactly these moments that make therapy go well. It's like Zen; the best way to live is to be spontaneous but at the same time you have to plan.

DR. W.: Let's put it this way. I'm not spontaneous in the beginning, I'm aiming toward the point of being spontaneous. When you've reached that point, you don't have to do any more, it just happens. It's like pole vaulting, when you're finally over the bar and gravity does the rest. I'll give you one other example of this. I was seeing a man who had had three or four previous therapists, a weird, schizoid man who came in with a fabulous double-binding arrangement of impotence and omnipotence and all sorts of off-edge moves. I played the same game back to him, so that I was one step ahead of him all the time. This was all deliberate and he didn't know what to do about it. But one day I was playing a tape recording of bird calls to one of the residents and the patient walked in and it turned out that he was an expert ornithologist. We had a tremendously exciting half hour, even though the next day we went back to the same game playing.

INT.: Is it moments like these that you see as producing change in therapy?

DR. W.: I don't know. All I can say is that the more of these moments I can get into therapy the more useful I think I am. But you're right that there's a basic contradiction there, because it's like saying, "The only completely successful strategy to use with another person is to get to the place where neither of you is concerned with strategy at all."

DR. W. (*cont.*): I'll agree with you that the problem did not originate with you. I would even go so far as to say that it didn't originate with them either, that Dad is what he is because of his mother and father, and Mother is what she is because of her mother and father, and that what they could do about it they have done, for reasons which are not pertinent, but that whatever it is, you're stuck with what it has done to you, or what life has done to you, and the effort to get beyond that pain, to get bigger, to have, ah, more adequacy in constructing a life of your own that's worth something to you, I think is worth your spending time and effort and (*laughing*) Dad's money. But I'm prejudiced, it's my racket. It meant a lot to me, when I had my psychotherapy, and that's I guess the real, the only real evidence you have.

INT.: Any comment on this?

DR. W.: I guess it's just my preaching impulses coming out.

INT.: It seems that you're again absolving everybody of blame. It's not the boy's fault and it's not the parents' fault and it's not their parents' fault. And they have done what they could have done for reasons which are not pertinent. What do you mean by that statement?

DR. W.: That I'm not going to go into all the reasons why they couldn't do any better than they did. I'm making them responsible for where they are and where do they go from here.

INT.: The implication is that since they did what could be done then, they'll do whatever can be done now. By complimenting them on having done their best in the past, you catch them on current responsibility.

DR. W.: Yes. This is strategic. I face them with the fact of their decisions. They decided in the past to do what they did and they're now in the process of deciding what to do next.

INT.: That "it" comes back again. In talking to the boy about his disturbance, you say, "what *it* has done to you," and then shift to "what *life* has done to you." Now "it" could conceivably refer to what the parents have done.

DR. W.: No, I think of it as their pathology and their parents' pathology.

INT.: But you don't get more specific. You make it more distant —life in general. It sounds as though you were being ambiguous again.

DR. W.: I don't think so. It obviously isn't just the parents. At this point, they're stuck with the effort the boy's making to get beyond the pain, too.

INT.: This speech almost implies that they're stuck with having to go into therapy.

DR. W.: Well, this is the way I read this boy's behavior. He's the one who, by attacking his father, drove his parents to a psychiatrist. I'll frequently say to a teenager, or sometimes even to a younger child, "Do you think it's possible that you did all this stuff for the past three, four, five years just to get yourself in here?" Or I'll say to a wife, "If your mother had been all that bad, you'd never have come in here, you'd have just stayed dead in your marriage. But your mother somehow gave you something else. She kept goading you so that you wouldn't just fold up and be your husband's housekeeper. You ought to congratulate her for that, even though you can blame her for the rest."

INT.: That's really turning blame into credit. Everybody is to be congratulated.

DR. W.: Sure. I always pick up the deliberate aspect. "If you hadn't been this disturbed, you might never have amounted to anything. Now you're about to catch fire and do something."

INT.: Do you usually try to sell people on psychotherapy as directly as this?

DR. W.: No, it's just that in this second effort to get the contract settled, I'm apt to push a little harder. Particularly since they have proved a second time that this is necessary.

INT.: Do you take it as a discouraging sign when you don't get the contract settled quickly?

DR. W.: Not necessarily. We're still in what I call the referral stage. We're still trying to work out an arrangement for referring them to psychotherapy. This can go on for a couple of years.

INT.: It's a bit complicated, because you're referring them to yourself. It's a little different from referring them to psychotherapy.

DR. W.: That's why I tell them I'm prejudiced. I'm saying that I know they might not trust my opinion, because this is the way I earn my living.

MRS. F.: Well, I can show you that's true in my own case. I'm sure that I was much too dependent all my life. It was only when I'd lost my, all my family and just had my mother, who's very old now and has had a stroke and, ah, she was always the, all my—I couldn't move without her, she was the, the great outstanding one, I mean I'm sure that I had to ask her to do every little thing all my life. And now I realize I'm a free person and now I realize that all these years I was so dependent, terrifically dependent, and as you say even when I was, no matter how far away from her I was, you still have this feeling, unless you break the ties. And . . .

ERIC (*overlapping*): Well, I can see that with the children. Eliza and Dirk are more attached to you than Dad or any, Dad or the rest of the family. (*Inaudible phrase.*)

MRS. F.: Well, I have to work on that. (*Pause.*) I think . . .

DR. W. (*overlapping*): This may be worth saying something about, because I think the two of you are saying something that maybe you haven't put together yet, and maybe I can help you put it together. What Mother is saying is that she knows she was sick, she feels she is better, than she was, whatever. And I think she's acknowledging something that you (*to Eric*) have been saying, that in her sickness you suffered. And I think the problem that we're up to is how to help you with getting past what she brought to her motherhood of you. That she, the mother that you are stuck with, is not this person here, but the woman you lived with fifteen years ago, or twelve years ago. And she is saying to you, "That woman was a very dependent, mother-dominated person, and therefore she was inadequate as your mother." And I think this takes a lot of guts on her part, I want to congratulate her on it. Many mothers never admit it.

DR. W.: You'll notice that this speech of the mother's about her own past is in response to my saying it's not pertinent.

INT.: Do you think she means she's had therapy herself? She draws such a close parallel between herself and you.

DR. W.: She's saying, "I'm a case, just like you were." But I don't think she had ever had any therapy. I think she was trying to keep her son from thinking about what I had just said. So she leads off in another direction.

INT.: She's also going along with you by saying that just leaving home doesn't help. You have to break the ties.

DR. W.: This is standard with this kind of mother. To define what it is they're doing by saying they're not doing it.

INT.: What do you mean?

DR. W.: She says, or implies, "You must break the ties with me," which is straight upsidedown. You see, she ends on an alternative: "It's no good unless you break the ties." That's where the boy comes in saying he can see that the children are more attached to her, and she answers, "I have to work on that." She sounds as if she means she's going to help them break the ties. But it's like the hypnotist saying, "You see, I'm not going to hypnotize you, don't you, don't you, don't you?"

INT.: The tearful tone of her voice suggests, "How can I bear my life without my mother, and how could I bear my life without you?"

DR. W.: Or: "How could you bear your life without me? If I can't get along without my mother, you obviously can't get along without me. But you certainly should."

INT.: It's interesting that she brought up her mother. It seems true of nearly every disturbed family that at least one of the mother's or father's parents is involved.

DR. W.: I keep a watch on how many minutes after the beginning of an interview one of the adults says, "Mother."

INT.: When the mother talks about how important her mother was to her, would this give you the idea that you ought to bring her mother in?

DR. W.: No. I don't ordinarily take on the extended family, unless there's some specific reason for it. There was one case in which I decided to bring in the brother of a psychotic girl and his wife because the mother was crazy too and had too little reality sense to get herself and her daughter to an interview. So I got the brother and his wife to come in with the girl, and I kept them together in therapy.

INT.: If the mother's mother here were living in the house, would you bring her in?

DR. W.: I probably would ask her to come in if it seemed clear that she was involved. That is, if they kept talking about her.

INT.: When you turn to the boy, you make a pretty free translation of what his mother just said. She has said she was too dependent on her mother, but she doesn't define herself as a patient or as someone who used to be sick, by any means.

DR. W.: I would say that anybody is sick who at her age still thinks of her mother as "the great outstanding one."

INT.: But it's doubtful that her statement would be construed as an admission of illness, either by her or by most people.

DR. W.: I do this sort of translating all the time. I could just as well have said, "Mother is telling you about her craziness," and pushed it a lot further.

INT.: You make another free translation when you say, "She's acknowledging something that you have been saying, that in her sickness you suffered." She isn't acknowledging this at all.

DR. W.: I assumed that her statement about her ties to her mother also referred to the boy's ties with her.

INT.: Well, you've got her admitting that she was sick, admitting that in her sickness she drove her child crazy, admitting that she's been an inadequate mother, even though she's better now. Then you congratulate her on having the guts to admit all this, when she hasn't admitted any of it.

DR. W.: It really leaves her stuck. If she says now that she's never been sick, she's showing that she hasn't any guts. And if she says I'm wrong, she's saying she still is as bad off as she was fifteen years ago.

INT.: Talk about a benevolent double-bind! You do this so casually that I gather it's somewhat routine for you. To take what little they do concede and go with it like a rocket.

DR. W.: I wasn't aware of doing that at all.

INT.: It's a complex speech. But there's another aspect to it. You say to the son that the mother he's stuck with now is not the problem. It's the mother he was living with fifteen years ago.

DR. W.: It's the introject he's struggling with, yes.

INT.: You're assuming that a person can have a trauma which affects his behavior years later. If the boy is sick, it's not because he's responding to the way his mother is dealing with him now, but because he's responding to his idea of how she's dealing with him, based on the way she dealt with him fifteen years ago.

DR. W.: Actually, I think both are true. She is describing the quality of her sickness, which set him up to be super-sensitive to what sickness there is left. What maturing she has done since then has not made it possible for him to get past the hypnotic spell she started in the beginning. Like the neurotic sheep business. Experiment with them, then put them back in the original fold, and the neurosis is all gone, but one tenth of one percent of the initial stimulus precipitates the whole thing again.

INT.: There's no evidence that the mother is any better now than she was before, except for her statement. But she's saying that things are better, and that she's healthier, and that she's doing her best, and you're accepting this positive statement of hers.

DR. W.: I'm catching her with it, yes.

INT.: What I'm trying to get at is the difference between the way a concept can be used as part of therapy and the way it can be used to explain therapy. For a long time, it seemed that the only possible explanation for the way these people behave was the presence of introjects. Now if you start to look at the situation they're in, you feel that you don't need the introject explanation. The situation itself is enough to account for it. If you put aside the introject as an explanation and look at it as a tactic in therapy, this concept is very useful. The mother has offered you a way to make it easier for her by saying that she used to be sick but now she's better. By saying to the boy that the mother he's living with now isn't the same one that set him up to be so badly off, you can provide a graceful exit for her. At the same time you're redefining his perception of her by making her seem stronger.

DR. W.: Yes. I may be encouraging him not to be so concerned about the present situation because she's better now and he can go ahead and fight her. This is a standard tactic of mine, now that I think about it. I'll say to a child, "Look, I think your parents can stand a great deal more than you think they can. I'll help them if they get disturbed by what you're up to." Or for the same reason, I'll be mean to them myself. Here's a case in point. I was seeing a bitter, sanctimonious man together with his wife, and six or seven interviews along I climbed all over her, blasted her to bits. She was crying, and the husband said he had never before heard anybody say to her the same dreadful things he used to say to her. In a strange kind of way this made him more loving to her, even to the point of suggesting that they come at 12:00 so that they could have lunch together at 1:00. And they'd been living in a state of armed warfare for fifteen years. But this was in one sense a pure trick. When I attacked the woman, I did it with a lot of lovingness for her and probably ended the interview with my arm around her shoulder as she went out.

INT.: Reading this speech of yours to the mother, one would think you were putting it on slightly. But the tone of your voice is quite genuine.

DR. W.: It occurs to me that I was quite tender in this, comforting both the mother and the son.

> MRS. F.: Probably because the younger ones (*laughing*) fight it more. I think this is it.
>
> DR. W. (*overlapping*): Well, sure, I think it's, it's a lot of . . .
>
> MRS. F. (*overlapping, laughing*): They're more independent. I suppose maybe I had—you see that was my problem. Eric was the only one for so long. Of course, ah, it was a very bad thing to do, but I, I just, ah, mothered him too much, but, ah, it's a little difficult when you have these varying—see one's here, one's there, which is a good thing, I know.
>
> DR. W.: You've got a, you've got a group therapy against you now.
>
> MRS. F.: A group . . .
>
> DR. W. (*overlapping*): First it was just one to one, just you and Eric . . .
>
> MRS. F.: Yes (*laughing*), fight to the finish now.
>
> DR. W.: Now you're in, you're in the big time.
>
> MRS. F.: Mm-hm. (*Long pause.*)

INT.: The mother is laughing her strange laugh again.

DR. W.: I think she may have been a little embarrassed by all the congratulations.

INT.: She sounds pleased, too. I'm sure she came in expecting you to tell her what a bad mother she is, so she goes into this business about, "I used to be bad but now I'm better." You tell her not only that she's better but that she's great, which probably allows her to admit to more than she otherwise would.

DR. W.: I set that up. I admitted that I used to be bad myself. Psychotherapy has helped us both, even if she hasn't had any.

INT.: What does she mean, "The younger ones fight it more"? That the younger mothers fight their mothers more than she did?

DR. W.: It's hard to tell. It sounds to me as if she's being modest about my compliment. If she's a better mother now, the younger children should get the credit. Because they fight her domination more.

INT.: You then tell her that she has a group therapy against her.

DR. W.: I meant that Eric was her sole therapist in those days. Now she has a whole group. I think I'm supporting her implication that it was a good thing the other children came along to stop her overmothering.

INT.: She comes back with "It's a fight to the finish," and you agree by saying, "You're in the big time." It's curious that you define therapy as a fight not only to people you might be talking to about therapy but to your patients as well. It's a rather explicit statement of what therapy with you is going to be like.

DR. W.: That's true. It's already been a fight. I've been lining them up.

INT.: When you say, "You're in the big time," you put in another element. You frame up the whole sordid battle she's in as something heroic and grand.

DR. W.: That's right. She's in Madison Square Garden now with the pros.

INT.: You have a way of emphasizing the positive all through this, but just offhand, just with the back of your hand.

DR. W.: I may have got this from Dr. Richard Felder, who joined our group fifteen years ago. He had no background in psychiatry, his background was in internal medicine and he had no training in defensive dynamic thinking. So he saw everything as possible. It didn't make any difference what it was, he never saw it as a defensive move "against," it was always a positive move "for." The first time I ran into that, it really rocked me.

INT.: It's such a contrast to the type of therapy that shows how unsavory people are, that takes the line of, "Let me help you understand how you are exploiting your child," and assumes that once the parents understand this, it will help them to change.

DR. W.: That's the sorriest business I ever heard of, this business of "If you figure it out, that will solve it." I believe that insight is a by-product of change. You have to go past it to see what it is.

DR. W. (*to Margaret*): Are you wishing for a little sister or a little brother?

MRS. F.: We've been wondering about this, we haven't said anything but I think we're going to have it around December.

MARGARET: What's that? (*Apparently pointing to mother's stomach.*)

MRS. F.: Hm?

MARGARET: That?

MRS. F.: You've been telling me I was getting awfully fat, haven't you, since the middle of the year? (*Pause.*)

DR. W.: I didn't realize I was, ah . . .

MRS. F.: Well . . . (*Laughs.*)

DR. W.: Excuse me.

MRS. F.: (*Laughs.*) That's all right.

DR. W.: Precipitating a family secret here.

MRS. F.: (*Laughs.*)

DR. W.: Anyway, I would like to make a guess that everybody knew, even though they may not have said anything.

MRS. F. (*laughing*): No, I'm sure they knew. Kathryn and Eliza have had so many teachers drop out in the middle of the year.

DR. W.: They know what happens then?

MRS. F. (*laughing*): Oh, they certainly do.

DR. W. (*to the children*): Did you know that birds and bees were just like people? They have babies too? (*Pause.*)

MR. F.: Those things are unimportant to the boys.

DR. W.: Hm?

MR. F.: Those things seem to be rather unimportant to the boys. The girls are much more . . .

MRS. F.: I don't know.

DR. W.: Gosh, not this little boy. (*Alluding to himself.*)

MR. F.: No?

DR. W.: I don't know about that one (*indicating Dirk*) but this one. Gosh darn, when I had a little sister, it changed my whole life.

And a little brother. (*To Dirk*) Would you rather have a little brother or a little sister?

MR. F. (*to Dirk*): Now don't look at the other end of the room. You know.

MRS. F.: How about you, Eliza?

ELIZA: I'd like a brother.

DR. W.: You need a brother? You sure do. (*To Dirk*) You're sort of outnumbered, aren't you? (*Mrs. F. laughs.*) You and Eric ought to get together, maybe the two of you could sort of equal up this struggle.

MRS. F.: Well . . . (*Laughing.*)

DR. W.: Do you and Eric ever get together and fight Mommy?

DIRK: No.

DR. W.: You don't? Good gracious, it sounds like a natural combination. Because the two of you might have a chance to, ah, win.

ERIC: That's a rather—you know, he takes more after my father.

MRS. F. (*laughing*): You did at that age too.

DR. W. (*overlapping*): Well, ah, Dad's stronger, he's gonna link up with strong—maybe the three of you could get together. (*Mrs. F. laughs.*) You know, the men against the women.

MRS. F.: Mmm. I think you did it fairly much too, Eric.

ERIC: I hope not. (*Long pause.*)

INT.: This is the second time the mother-son thing has come up and there's been a silence and you've turned to a child. Why do you again do this rather than bring in the father?

DR. W.: I don't know why I didn't bring the father in. I'm sure I was aware of his suffering; he was obviously the most isolated one in the whole setting.

INT.: You did get together with him at one point, when you were talking about the little boy's shirt.

DR. W.: There may also have been points where I was communicating with him nonverbally, which wouldn't show up in the recording. He was sitting close to me physically, so that he and I could have had a kind of unspoken entente, a resonance.

INT.: When the mother goes on about her past and the difficulty she's had with the boy, many therapists would say to the father, "Weren't you around?" or something like that. Would you ordinarily have done this? That is, was it unusual for you to leave him out at this point?

DR. W.: I'm surprised at it, so I think it was unusual. I may have been waiting for him to sense that I could handle Mother, so that he could feel safe enough to get in verbally. Or I may have been emphasizing the family imbalance by focusing on the mother and the children, who were the overt force in the family, and ignoring the father, in hopes that he would react by trying to get back in.

INT.: This silence again follows a scene between the mother and son at the end of which the mother says that things are pretty good. I was wondering about the reasons for this. Were you again thinking that something had come to completion?

DR. W.: I remember I did think that the first time. But ordinarily if I'm silent, it's because I don't have anything I want to say. I wait for something to erupt in me, or to erupt in them. I'm not usually thinking about what we're going to do next, or what we've just completed.

INT.: You just sit and see what goes.

DR. W.: If I'm quiet long enough, they'll often ask me what I'm doing. I'll say, "I'm waiting for something to happen."

INT.: If enough doesn't happen, something will.

DR. W.: That's right.

INT.: What happens here is that you spring a pregnancy on the family. Did you already know the mother was going to have a baby?

DR. W.: They hadn't told me, but it was noticeable.

INT.: You get back to this point about the carnal "know." The children really know about the baby. Why do you then ask them if they know about the facts of life?

DR. W.: I'm again opening up a subject that's a secret in this family. I'm showing the parents that it's okay for them to talk with their children about sex, because they know about it anyway.

INT.: I notice the father comes in then, something so unusual for him, and contradicts you, or contradicts the mother, at least. He says the boys aren't interested in that sort of thing.

DR. W.: He's talking like Mother about what's normal. It's normal for boys not to be interested in sex. In other words, "Be like me and don't notice these things." So I try to give Dirk a way to admit that he certainly is interested.

INT.: You still don't get a confirmation from the boy. Father has to tell him to speak up.

DR. W.: Yes. "Don't be inhibited, speak up." Which of course inhibits him.

INT.: Here I notice that you bring the subject back to the question of sides. Which sex this baby is going to be is obviously a loaded subject in this family.

DR. W.: Father has already made it a matter of sides, the boys versus the girls, so I'm just going on with that. I say the little boy certainly does need a brother.

INT.: Not only that, you ask why he and Eric don't get together and fight Mommy.

DR. W.: This is realigning the family in a different way. Before, I put Eric and his father against Mother, now I'm putting the two boys together. I'm again changing the coalitions.

INT.: You're not only changing them, you're putting your weight behind this one. You say that the two boys might have a chance to win, that it's a natural combination. And everybody starts talking.

DR. W.: Yes. That upsets them. You notice that Eric comes in and says of Dirk, "He takes more after my father." The implication is that Eric goes with the mother.

INT.: When you say, "He's going to link up with the strong," do you mean that Dirk will want to side with his strong father?

DR. W.: I'm not sure. I could have meant the father would want to side with Dirk. My immediate association was that Dirk was the healthiest of the males. He was the only person with any strength in the family. But essentially I'm trying to set up a male combination.

DR. W. (*to Dirk*): Did you know Mommy was gonna have a baby?

DIRK: Mm-mm.

DR. W.: You didn't? I think you're kidding me. (*To Eric*) Didn't you tell him Mother was going to have a baby?

ERIC: No. (*Pause.*)

DR. W.: Did you figure out any names?

MRS. F.: That's something to work on, isn't it?

MARGARET: I already made up something.

DR. W.: Oh, you already thought of some names? What names did you think of?

MARGARET: Susie, Wendy, and, um, Jane.

DR. W.: You sound very prejudiced. (*Mrs. F. laughs.*) What if it turns out to be a boy, will you name him "Jane"?

MARGARET: No, I'll name him Bill or Tom or, ah . . .

DR. W.: Bill or Tom, that sounds good.

MARGARET: . . . or Joe or, um . . .

DR. W.: How about Bradley? Or Carl, you can name him after me, how about that? (*Mrs. F. laughs.*)

MARGARET: Nah.

DR. W.: You don't like that name, it's kind of a stiff name.

MARGARET: I could name him Eric, maybe.

DR. W.: Name him Eric?

MARGARET: Yeah.

DR. W.: You love Eric, I guess, huh?

MARGARET: Maybe Bill . . .

DR. W. (*overlapping*): You're buddies, aren't you?

MARGARET: . . . maybe Dick, maybe, ah (*inaudible phrase*).

DR. W.: Gosh, you're really a name catcher-upper. (*To Kathryn*) Did you have a name for the baby? Hm? What would you name the baby?

MRS. F.: Well, can you think of a name, hm? Hm? (*Pause.*)

INT.: You ask the older boy why he didn't let his brother in on this secret. Is this another way to get them together?

DR. W.: I suppose so. To make them men in a man's world.

INT.: How far along was the mother in her pregnancy?

DR. W.: As I remember, it must have been four or five months.

INT.: Did you find it strange that she hadn't told the younger children?

DR. W.: No. In many families nothing is said about it until it's so obvious that it's impossible to avoid. Then when the children finally do bring it up, it can be passed off as a fact of nature. Not "We're going to have a baby," but "There's a baby in the tummy."

INT.: I take it you're talking about disturbed families.

DR. W.: Yes. You notice the schizophrenic quality of making it something that just happened, rather than something they did. As if this were an immaculate conception.

INT.: Do you have any special reason for asking about names for the baby?

DR. W.: Looking back, I assume that I was trying to unify the family. We've set up a whole series of subgroups and discussed splits, and now we arrive at a unified project. We did this before, if you recall, when we went from the discussion of sides to the question of coming into therapy.

INT.: You're also taking this particular "it" and giving it a name. You even suggest to the little girl that they name it after you.

DR. W.: I would guess that I'm being seductive again.

INT.: You could have said, "Would you name him after Daddy?"

DR. W.: That's true. Apparently I'm determined to keep Dad in the background. I'm not only refusing to talk to him, I'm not going to let him in on what's going on.

INT.: There's a quality here of treating playfully what could turn into a serious obligation. If the children really did decide to name the baby after you, the parents might feel they had to go through with it.

DR. W.: Yes. A good example of what Mother called "the fight to the finish." I play with serious issues all the time. Later in this tape, we go on to play about marriage and incest. But the fact that I'm playing has nothing to do with the seriousness of what we're up to.

INT.: This remark about naming the baby after you certainly precipitates you into the middle of the family.

DR. W.: This is consistently my pattern. I precipitate myself into the situation very quickly, any way I can, and then struggle to get the position valid and usable and significant.

INT.: You leap and then you look.

DR. W.: Well, I'm sometimes very cautious, as in all the structuring I do. But in a relationship with children, or where I'm less concerned with the long-range objectives, I may plunge in.

INT.: Throughout this session, you seem to alternate between the structuring, which is mainly directed at the threesome, and jumping in with the kids.

DR. W.: I get intimate with youngsters very quickly, and it seems to me that this has developed over the years. It was true when I was doing child-guidance work and work with delinquents, and it's even truer now, although I don't see children alone any more. When I work with a family, I'll frequently do a lot through the children rather than working directly with the parents.

INT.: That's certainly true of this interview. Most of the time you're talking with the children, and even when you do address the parents, it's usually as representatives of the family rather than as individuals. You hardly ever have a direct personal exchange with either of them.

DR. W.: That's because I don't get involved with people unless they're willing to get involved.

INT.: While we're on the subject of the children, could you explain in a little more detail how you handle them, what your policy is if they get too disruptive, and so forth?

Dr. W.: I'll give you an example. I was seeing a family with two little boys, and during the first interview one of the children got onto the subject of money, so I said, "You want some money? I'll give you five bucks. Come on over here and turn over my knee." So he did, and I gave him five paddles with my hand, and he got back up and I said, "You want some more money?" He said, "Sure," so I gave him five more. In about three minutes he was sort of clowning around, so I said, "You want some more? How much do you want?" and he said, "Forty-five," and we went on. I was whamming away, using both hands, and the father was standing there with his eyes bugging out. Here was this aggressive five-year-old and I was paddling the dickens out of him, just for fun. In the second interview the question of limitations came up. I started playing with the boy, and I didn't mind his hitting me and tearing the pipe out of my mouth and that sort of thing. Every time I'd light my lighter, he'd spit on it, until I had a handful of spit, and Mother was sitting over there in her compulsive way just having fits. I had told her, as I usually do, that this was my office and I'd set the rules, and she was to stay out of it. So she couldn't stop it, but she couldn't stop her horror either. Then I began to set the limitations. The boy came over to my desk and I said, "That's my desk, you can't play with it." But I let him operate in complete freedom in regard to me as a body.

Int.: It sounds as if you were splitting yourself into two aspects, the personal and the professional. He can spit on your hand but not on your desk.

Dr. W.: That's right. "You can't fool with my grown-up self, my grown-up world, but you and I can be kids together."

Int.: What do you do when the playing gets too rough?

Dr. W.: I deflect it, so that I don't get harmed. This boy's drive to hurt me was fantastic. He turned a standing ashtray over so that the edge of it was on my toe and jumped up and down on it. So I suggested we scratch each other, because I loved scratching people, and he didn't go for that but instead he started biting. I said, "Okay, if I can bite you in return." Then I just kept biting harder and harder till he gave up.

Int.: You handle these children by refusing their invitation to fight back.

Dr. W.: I have a book on Aikido, the Japanese art of defending yourself without harming the other person. You don't throw your opponent; if he strikes at you, at the end of his strike you back off, turn slightly, then take his hand and give it a little pull, so that he goes on past you, using his own energy. You just continue his movement which was directed at you and which ordinarily you would resist. If he's harmed, it's his own energy that's harming him. I think this is what I do.

INT.: So much work with psychotics depends on deflecting what they try to do to you without harming them in return.

DR. W.: I learned much of this technique working with small children.

INT.: When you set the limitations, is it usually in this benevolent game framework?

DR. W.: No, it's direct restraint. I'll say, "Now look, Bill, not the tape recorder." If he keeps at it, I'll move him physically. And if I have any feeling that he's going to push it, I'll be absurd. I'll take something absolutely insignificant and forbid it, such as, "You can take my left shoe off but not my right one."

INT.: The more insignificant it is, the clearer it is that you're the one establishing the rules.

DR. W.: Yes. But then I'll go back to playing again; there's always this alternation. With this boy, for instance, in the first interview I was expanding the initial positive relationship, the lovingness, the fun. Then in the second I went on to set up a fairly hard-boiled limitation pattern.

INT.: In that order.

DR. W.: In the beginning, yes.

INT.: How do you handle it if the children start teasing each other or create diversionary quarrels while you're trying to talk to the parents?

DR. W.: If they're young, I may handle it physically by seduction. I'll get them over to me where I can hold them on my lap or muss their hair, while I go on talking to Mother and Dad.

INT.: Would you ask them to leave the room? Arrange for them to get a glass of water to get them out of the way?

DR. W.: No, I would never do that. It would give me the shivers. If they were older, I'd shut them up the way I do with adult patients when the two therapists are talking. "Mama and Papa are fighting now, just keep quiet and listen."

INT.: If things are getting hot between the parents and the boy starts to act up, would you make an interpretation such as, "I notice that when you two start to quarrel, your son does such and such"?

DR. W.: No, I'm pretty sparse with that sort of thing. I guess it's because I don't believe in understanding.

INT.: In regard to the parents, I take it that your rule is that you take charge of the children in your office. You don't require the parents to discipline their own children while they are there.

DR. W.: I forbid them. I say, "This is my house," and I use this term all the time. This is again to make it clear that I'm in charge of the process.

INT.: You use your policy with the children to set up limitations for the parents.

DR. W.: Well, they're guests, and they have some right to discipline their children if they want to. But they mustn't push me around or challenge my super-status.

INT.: In what way do they have some rights?

DR. W.: In the beginning, if they come in and the child starts pulling the cushion off this old sofa, say, where it's nothing I care about, and if I haven't yet established any relationship with him, I'll let the parents stop him if they want.

INT.: I take it that you don't step in on family quarrels. If the boy tries to hit his father, you don't intervene.

DR. W.: Oh, no. That's their business.

INT.: How do you deal with a horrified mother watching you collect a handful of spit?

DR. W.: I just laugh at her. This is for her too. I want her to realize what she's depriving herself of. I'm making the child respect my authority but at the same time I'm giving him the exotic experience of enjoying the physical contact. The little boy I was telling you about took off my shoes, and I took off his shoes, and he got into mine. Then I put his shoes into mine and the little fellow made believe he couldn't find them when it was time to go home. But this is really training in intimacy, both for the mother and for the child.

INT.: On having the children in, is it general policy with you to say as you did here that they're welcome if the parents want to bring them, but it's not essential that they be there?

DR. W.: Yes. Except when the child is the symptom, and then I insist that he be there because this means that he's part of the parents.

It's a three-person bed rather than a two-person bed, so I have it in.

INT.: Do you worry about an absent member or an absent sibling who may be contributing to the problem in a way you don't know about?

DR. W.: If things aren't moving, I'll often push to have somebody else come in. In some long-term problems I've had, it has sometimes occurred to me that therapy was a failure because I didn't insist on a brother's being there. Or sometimes, if the parents repeatedly mention a child, I'll say, "If this child is going to be here in spirit, ghost-fashion, then I'd rather have him here in person. Bring him." There's also the situation I had here, where the parents are opposed to bringing the children in. That automatically becomes a challenge, and we get in a fight over who controls the therapy. At that point I can do nothing except defeat them or acknowledge my impotence.

DR. W. (*to Kathryn*): How about telling me the little kiddies' names now, so I can get to know them a little bit. What . . .

ELIZA: Jenny.

DR. W.: What? What's yours?

MRS. F. (*laughing*): You thought of, she thought of the other name, Jenny.

DR. W.: Huh?

MRS. F. (*overlapping children's voices explaining that Jenny is their old kitty*): We can't name the baby after the cat.

DR. W.: Only wanted to know who you're calling, whether you're calling the baby or the cat.

ELIZA: Our old, our old kitty's named, ah—no, Muffy . . . (*Overlapping voices.*)

DR. W.: Oh.

ELIZA: Muffy, 'cause, um, we used to have a cat but she ran away, so we got another one and we still have it (*inaudible phrase*).

DR. W.: Mm. (*Mr. F. and others talking in background.*) (*To Margaret*) What's your name? Hey, sweetie-pie, what's your name?

MARGARET: Margaret.

MRS. F.: (*Inaudible phrase.*) It's Margaret, isn't it?

DR. W.: They call you Margie?

MARGARET: No.

MRS. F.: We call you Meggie, don't we?

DR. W.: Meggie?

MARGARET: Mm-hm.

MRS. F.: And this is Eliza.

ELIZA: I guess so.

MRS. F.: (*Inaudible phrase.*)

ELIZA: Eliza.

DR. W.: Do they call you Lizzie?

ELIZA: Yeah. (*Laughter.*)

DR. W.: I think that's a nice name. Do you like it? Or do you like "Eliza" better?

ELIZA: Lizzie.

DR. W.: You like Lizzie better, okay. We'll cross Eliza out. You can just use that when you write your name. (*To Dirk*) What's your name?

DIRK: Dirk.

DR. W.: Dick? (*Laughter.*)

MR. F.: With an "r."

DR. W.: Spell it for me, will you?

DIRK: D-i-r-k.

DR. W.: D-i-r-k. Oh, that's a nice name. And what's your name, big guy?

KATHRYN: Kathryn.

DR. W.: What do they call you?

KATHRYN: Kathy.

DR. W.: Kathy. Is it spelled "k" or "c"?

MR. F.: No . . .

KATHRYN: No (*spelling*), K-a-t-h-y.

MR. F.: But Kathryn is the name.

DR. W.: K-a-t-h-r-y-n or e-r-i-n-e?

KATHRYN: r-y-n.

DR. W.: Gee whiz. How old are you, Meggie?

MRS. F.: (*Inaudible phrase.*)

MARGARET: Four.

DR. W.: Two? Four?

MRS. F.: Four.

DR. W.: Gee, you're big. How old are you, Lizzie?

ELIZA: Eight.

DR. W.: Eight. Dirk, how old are you?

DIRK: Um . . . (*Doing it with fingers.*)

DR. W.: Six, hm? My golly. And how old are you, Kathy?

KATHRYN: Ten.

DR. W.: Ten. (*Long pause.*) What do you think about this family fight, Kathy?

KATHRYN: I don't know.

DR. W.: Does it scare you?

KATHRYN: Mm-mm.

DR. W.: You think it's just like families are, huh?

KATHRYN: Yes.

DR. W.: I think you're right. How about you, Lizzie, do you get frightened at the family fights?

ELIZA: No.

DR. W.: You're not really afraid of what's going to happen? That's the nice thing about kiddies, they seem to know more about how families get along than older people do.

INT.: What's this about calling the baby after the cat?

DR. W.: The little girl may have thought I said, "Tell me the little *kitty's* name.

INT.: But you were asking her to tell you the names of the other children.

DR. W.: I wasn't asking her, I was asking this of the oldest girl. The little one may have jumped in because I had turned away from her and she felt jealous.

INT.: Did you have a reason for putting this question to the oldest girl?

DR. W.: She was sitting next to the father, sharing his withdrawal, so I was bringing her in by asking her to be the mother and name the children.

INT.: When you go to each one and ask the name, is this to get to know them?

DR. W.: To know them and to line them up. I pull them all together around me. Then I apparently use this group-therapy structuring to assault the threesome.

INT.: How do you do that?

DR. W.: By asking the oldest girl again to take charge and tell me what's going on with the family. She's the mother. First child is always the mother.

INT.: As a law of life?

DR. W.: Yes. She was there first, you know. She's the one who had to take over the baby while Mommy got the dinner. And she gradually takes over the family while the parents struggle, and frequently grows up to be a pseudo-mother, or what I call a "psychiatric attendant."

INT.: What are you up to when you ask her if she's scared of the fights and then ask, "You think it's just like families are"?

DR. W.: This is really to the parents. The children are frequently not as scared as the parents think they are. Mother will all but kill the boy in a battle and she'll be shaking for hours and he'll go on to something else. He's precipitated the fight, he's aware of how far he can push Mother, so he gets her involved and proves he's that powerful and that important to her. She's afraid she's going to kill him but he knows she can't do it. It's not in the interaction that the children are afraid, it's in the withdrawal.

INT.: You offer the idea that this is just how families are. Do you really believe this?

DR. W.: Absolutely. The family is the place where you're dealing with life and death voltages.

INT.: But the kind of violence that's going on in this family isn't going on in all families. Not all sons are beating up their fathers.

DR. W.: I think they are. It may not be expressed physically, it may be expressed in a game framework, or oedipally. The son may hit the father by reassuring Mommy as soon as the father goes to work that he loves her. But this is still a pretty primitive battle.

INT.: It sounded in this exchange as if you might be reassuring the little girl by telling her that her family isn't as far out as she thinks.

DR. W.: No, I'm saying this because the parents in their panic think that this is the end of the world. They are really playing a game that I deny them. It's like saying to a crazy patient, "So you're crazy. Well, if you want to compete, I can do better at it any time than you can." In the same way I'm telling this girl, and through her the parents, "Every family has its life and death quality, and I don't care what you fight about, Oedipus, or money, or sister's a horror, it's still a normal family fight."

INT.: It sounds reassuring, but you're not contradicting the idea that the fights are dangerous.

DR. W.: Not directly, but the inference is that if they were, I'd be frightened too. I'll frequently say to patients, "So you had hallucinations, so? It doesn't concern me. I somehow don't feel upset about it." Or: "If you were really suicidal, I wouldn't sit here and be comfortable. You think you're suicidal, but I don't believe it."

INT.: There's a quality in this of undercutting their panic while not undercutting the reality of the thing they're frightened of.

DR. W.: This is what I would think of as reassurance. I'm telling them that I know they can control the situation, that they don't have to be overwhelmed by it.

INT.: And now you make a very curious speech. You say that naturally the little girl isn't afraid of the fights because children know more about how families *get along*. Here you're talking about these terrible fights and suddenly they're a way the family gets along.

DR. W.: I don't find this strange. I remember one of my students coming to me one day in horror because it turned out that his patient was all black and blue. Her husband had beaten her up over the weekend, and he had asked, "Well, why don't you divorce him?" She said, "Oh, I couldn't do that." So he said to me, "Come on in and help." So I came in and he told the story to me again in front of her. I said, "How long has he been beating you up?" She said, "Well, we've been married for twenty years." I said, "The doctor's worried because you don't get a divorce." And she said, "But, Doctor, he's so nice to me during the week." To me, this is just another way of making love. You know, the bear says it with a slap.

INT.: What strikes me is that the mother has previously said something very similar to what you're saying. She has been suggesting that the family is normal, that the little bit of dissension they have is normal, and it's really a happy, loving home. What do you see as the difference between her saying the family is normal and your saying it?

DR. W.: The difference is that the mother means that these fights aren't bad fights because it's normal for families to have them. I say that they are bad fights and that it's normal for families to have them. She's denying the fights so that she can continue to use the family as a blood transfusion for herself. I'm saying, "Every child has to worry about his mother being a bloodsucker, not just you."

INT.: It's the difference between "normal" in the statistical sense and "normal" to justify the way things are. But you come out in the same place as the mother, in a funny way, by adding another layer. The mother has said, "We don't fight, we're harmonious." You say, "You do fight, and this is what keeps you together."

DR. W.: I believe that there's a more profound and significant level below the level of the social and psychological battles. On this deeper level, the family is biologically unified and the loyalty and identification and need for each other are automatic. That's the level where they can be making love by beating each other up.

MARGARET: (*Inaudible phrase*) and got some mice.

DR. W.: You've got some mice?

MARGARET: Yeah.

ELIZA: No, we got some rats.

DR. W.: Some rats. I wasn't talking about the family, I was talking about your pets. (*Everybody laughs.*)

ELIZA: We have two rats, and . . .

DR. W.: Do they have names too?

ELIZA: Yes.

MARGARET: One is a boy and one is a girl.

DR. W.: Why didn't you bring them to the party? (*Laughter.*) You mean they can't go with you on visits?

MARGARET: Mmm.

DR. W.: That seems unfair. You didn't bring the cat either.

ELIZA: Eric was, Eric was gonna bring the rats.

DR. W.: Really?

MRS. F.: We thought the cat might (*inaudible phrase*).

DR. W.: How about a dog, got a dog?

ELIZA: No.

DR. W.: Is that all you have is just three pets?

ELIZA: Mm-hm.

MARGARET: (*Inaudible phrase*) we had a snapping turtle.

ELIZA: Someone stole it.

MRS. F.: We put it out.

DR. W.: Someone what?

MARGARET: Took my snapping turtle.

DR. W.: Took your snapping turtle?

MARGARET: (*Inaudible phrase.*)

DR. W.: Oh, good gravy. Maybe he ran away.

MRS. F.: I'm sure it did.

DR. W.: He was trying to find his way to the lake. You know I heard a secret the other day about turtles. If you ever get another turtle, you know what they like most of all to eat? I bet you'd never guess.

ELIZA: What?

DR. W.: Bananas.

MRS. F.: (*Inaudible phrase.*)

DR. W. (*overlapping*): They just love bananas. Isn't that strange?

MRS. F.: The young ones like bananas, so, ah, I'm sure we have our share of those.

MARGARET: Monkeys eat bananas.

ELIZA: We used to have . . .

DR. W. (*overlapping*): So do I. That's why I look like a monkey, because I eat so many bananas.

MARGARET: Monkeys eat bananas, and people eat bananas.

DR. W.: Do you think monkeys eat the peelings too?

MARGARET: (*Laughs.*)

DR. W.: Be kind of silly, wouldn't it? They don't really taste good.

MARGARET: (*Laughs.*)

MRS. F.: No, they don't.

MARGARET: I guess they (*inaudible phrase*) elephants eat bananas.

DR. W.: Maybe they just throw them at the people who are watching them, huh?

MARGARET: (*Laughs.*) Yeah. You can eat them. You can eat the peelings.

MRS. F.: (*Inaudible phrase*) I don't know.

DR. W. (*overlapping*): You do? You eat banana peelings?

MARGARET: (*Laughs.*)

DR. W.: People will say you're crazy if you eat banana peelings.

ELIZA: One time I slipped on a banana peel and my neck felt so swollen.

DR. W.: It's really a slippery business, isn't it? (*Margaret laughs.*) Slipping on a banana peel is just like talking to a psychiatrist, you never know what's going to happen. (*Mrs. F. laughs.*)

INT.: Any comments on this?

DR. W.: This is something I often do. I'll talk with the children, kind of free-associate with them, but use the double meanings to communicate with the adults.

INT.: For example?

DR. W.: Oh, that joke I made, when the littlest girl tells about their two rats and I say, "I wasn't talking about the family, I was talking about your pets." I'm saying that Mother and Father are rats, they ratted on Eric by calling in a psychiatrist.

INT.: Throughout this last section there seems to be a continual identification of pets with people.

DR. W.: I assume that any conversation about pets can easily become a metaphoric conversation about human beings.

INT.: Do you think the parents are understanding it metaphorically?

DR. W.: I'm sure they do in some way. You notice that the mother makes the identification herself, when she shifts from turtles liking bananas to children liking bananas. She doesn't even call them "children," she says "the young ones," so that you would almost think she was talking about animal young.

INT.: The difference is that when you slip from rats to people, you name what you are doing by making it a joke.

DR. W.: Yes. The mother does it without any facetiousness, you can't be sure which category she's talking about. That's a real quality of craziness there.

INT.: I notice that the conversation gradually leads to the subject of craziness. First you start talking in a joking, nonsensical way, then you bring up craziness. I would have suspected that you were doing this because it's a crazy family, to show that you don't mind if people are crazy, but this family hasn't been defined that way.

DR. W.: I would call it a crazy family.

INT.: I mean that the boy isn't an identified psychotic.

DR. W.: I think of his behavior as crazy in the accepted sense of the term. I didn't here, but I'll often bring up craziness and move on to the mother's and father's craziness. I was seeing a family with a schizophrenic girl and I said to her, "Look, I'm just not going to tolerate this business of you being crazy. You can turn it off and keep it turned off, and let's you and me get straight what's going on with the family." She said, "Well, I don't know anything about them." So I said, "That's fair. Mother, when were you crazy? Let's get at your craziness." So Mother gradually gets at her craziness and then we work on Dad, and each time it's, "How's your homework going, have you found out any more about your craziness?"

INT.: When you think of it, by changing the meaning of the word "crazy," you're altering the relationships between a number of people. She's no longer crazy while they're well.

DR. W.: Well, it takes three or four weeks for them to feel comfortable with my use of the word and then we use it all the time. We use it to cover anything which is non-rational, reasonable, and boring.

INT.: Did you know that you were leading up to craziness when you started talking about bananas? Was this planned?

DR. W.: Heavens, no!

INT.: What you do next is to make an association between banana peels and psychiatrists. They're both slippery.

DR. W.: I assume that they know I'm slippery and that one of the ways to make therapy less frightening is to agree that psychiatrists are weird people.

INT.: You're also setting up a precedent for your behavior. When you say, "With a psychiatrist, you never know what's going to happen," you're telling them that you're going to do the unexpected.

DR. W.: That's the way I prefer to work.

INT.: Would you also accept the interpretation that if you behave unpredictably, this makes it harder for them to handle you?

DR. W.: No question of that. It's what I was saying before about the rules. I want to have the right to lay down the rules and the right to change them too.

INT.: One of the ways to look at this interview is that you're working to define a situation in which you have maximum freedom, and you can get this freedom by saying, "There are no rules about me, I can do anything I choose."

DR. W.: I say this right out to many patients. "The rules in my house are my rules, and I'll make them any way I want to and I'll change them any time I want to, any way I want to, and that's the way it is." I met a family out in the hall last week and moved them into the playroom. I said, "I didn't tell you why I changed the hour this week and I didn't tell you why I brought you into this room, but now that you're here, I want you to know that there are several residents on the other side of the picture window and this microphone is so that they can listen." They have the right then to walk out.

INT.: Do they know they have that right?

DR. W.: If they're angry about it, I tell them. This is the one right they have left. But to go back to this other point, being able to shift your ground whenever you want gives you an immense advantage. I do it informally, too. With the two little boys I was telling you about, the kids were trying to yank the pipe out of my mouth and they finally made it, working one from each side. Then I congratulated them on having made it after I had fought them.

INT.: If they challenge you, you shift your rules to include the challenge.

DR. W.: I get over them at the next level.

MARGARET: Cats eat bananas (*long inaudible phrase*).

DR. W.: Do you think your white rat would eat bananas?

MARGARET: (*Inaudible phrase.*)

MRS. F.: (*Inaudible phrase.*)

MARGARET: He don't eat the peelings though.

DR. W.: Who belongs to the rats, are those yours, Eric?

ERIC: Yes, sir.

DR. W.: Really?

ERIC: I got them from a friend of mine who works in the endocrine lab.

DR. W.: Good for you. How long have you had them?

ERIC: I just got them yesterday.

DR. W.: Oh.

ERIC: I always . . .

DR. W. (*overlapping*): Going to breed them?

ERIC: Yes.

DR. W.: Good for you.

ERIC: In order to get small ones. I wanted to see whether I could, ah, teach a cat to get along with rats. I think in some cases you can get a cat to mother things like guinea pigs . . .

DR. W.: Mm-hm.

ERIC: This happens to be a male [*talking about the rat*] but I thought maybe I could bring out the maternal instinct [*talking about the cat*].

DR. W.: I think it's very possible. It's hard except if the animals are tiny, I suspect.

ERIC: Yeah. She doesn't seem to like them jumping all over her, though.

DR. W.: Oh, you put them together already?

ERIC: Yes, we put them together.

DR. W.: Hm.

ERIC: And after a while, it took about a half hour, she started to get rather nervous.

DR. W.: Well, there's—gosh, the first acquaintanceship like that you usually have to take it slow. Did you put the rats free with the cat, or put the cat in the cage with the rats? How did you do it?

ERIC: No, ah, the cat was on the chair, and I put both the rats under the chair. They went climbing around, touched noses (*inaudible phrase*).

DR. W.: Good. Sounds wonderful.

DR. W.: This whole conversation about the cat and the rats is straight mother-son. I must have intuited this before, when I made the joke about the rats in the family. Here the boy's the rat, and that's why I went into the breeding, because it was very clear that we were talking about an oedipal situation.

INT.: You're not listening to this as a conversation about cats and rats, you're listening to it as a metaphor about the family.

DR. W.: Yes. And I'm speaking to the boy in terms of his teaching Mother and Father how to breed.

INT.: As any child should.

DR. W.: Somebody has to. Then, you see, he describes his effort to bring out the cat's maternal instinct, but it isn't working very well. Mama's going to get him.

INT.: She doesn't like the rats climbing all over her. I'm thinking that there are two ways you could handle this. One is to do what you did, talk about the cat and the rats with the son while thinking in your own mind in terms of his situation at home. The other is to share this understanding of yours and point out to the boy that he's really talking about himself and his mother. Would you ever do that instead of going on with the metaphor?

DR. W.: I think I'd more often go on with the metaphor. Sometimes, if I'm aware of the metaphoric similarity and it's vivid to me, I'll shift and make a facetious extension of it, as I did before with the joke about the rats. But I wouldn't make an interpretation here unless I felt the meaning was pretty close to the surface with the boy, or unless I wanted to get through to Mama and Papa, who probably think of this conversation as a waste of time. To me metaphors are like dreams, and I frequently think it's more valuable not to interpret them. I'm interested in feeding the computer, not the cortex.

INT.: What do you mean when you say that metaphors are like dreams?

DR. W.: I think of dreams and metaphors and any other fantasy material as an effort to communicate something secret. The patient is trying to talk about what's wrong with him, but he has to say it in a foreign language. I'm glad to try to help him figure out what it is he's trying to say, but I don't like to work on dreams too much. Many times it's a delicate dream, and if you work on it, you're apt to reduce it to a code and then you don't get any more dreams.

INT.: I should think that if you work on dreams with people, they would tend to dream more within your theory.

DR. W.: I think so. Anyway, I believe that when people tell a dream, that's the whole communication. They don't want to hear any psychiatric nonsense about it. If I talk about a dream, it's usually to offer some crazy association that pops into my head.

INT.: That's very different from psychiatrists who interpret dreams according to a fixed system.

DR. W.: I don't have one. But in working with groups I've noticed that sometimes two-thirds of an interview will be a recital of dreams. We'll go right round the room and then we'll drop the dreams and start talking about other things. You get the idea that this is what they want out of the dream. They want to tell their secrets but in a veiled fashion, so that it comes in at another entrance.

INT.: You're very respectful of dreams.

DR. W.: I feel that to talk too much about a dream or a fantasy is somehow sacrilegious. Such a sacrifice of inner life is involved. I told you about the patient who had the fantasy of the adopted children. In the process of telling me the story of all these people, he was very sad. It was a public acknowledgment of the death of his secret world. You see, people don't know until afterwards that it's possible to increase their satisfactions by giving the dream up.

INT.: It's as though you were setting it up so that you and the patient could pay your respects to this dream he's deciding to give up. It's not really supporting the dream.

DR. W.: No, it's not. I had a patient who once said to me, "You know, I've been to four psychiatrists and the difference between you and them is that they don't stay for breakfast." You must not only be willing to be intimate, but you must be willing to accept the person-to-person level afterwards. What you're trying to do is get people out of their dreams. Dreams are not a substitute for life.

MRS. F. (*laughing*): Sometimes you just wonder how long they're going to be friends, you know, whether it's gonna—it's a basic, ah, you think something'll happen to the rat.

DR. W.: Really?

MRS. F.: It's a gentle cat, but I don't know.

DR. W.: Time will tell, I suppose. Maybe it has to do with whether the cat gets hungry or not. Keep the cat well fed, that may make it a little easier.

MRS. F.: We have n> problem, everyone feeds her, you know (*laughing*) she goes to one and then the other, so this is it.

DR. W.: Smart cat, huh?

MRS. F.: Oh, she's a very smart cat, yes. Everyone says she's hungry. The first one up in the morning feeds her, and then successively everybody gives her a little food, so (*Dr. W. laughing*) then she also goes to the neighbors, so she has no problem.

DR. W.: She gets well supplied, huh?

MRS. F.: She's smart. (*Pause.*)

INT.: The mother comes in here so quickly. That metaphor touched her.

DR. W.: Yes. She's worried about how long the rat will last, too. You hear that "it's a basic—"? That probably was going to be one of those statements about what's normal. "It's a basic law of nature for cats to kill rats."

INT.: So you say that perhaps that won't happen if the cat is well fed. Are you speaking metaphorically again?

DR. W.: I'm talking on a second level of perception to the mother and father. Father should keep Mother fed. In other words, "If you'd love Mother the way you're supposed to, you wouldn't have to worry about the little rat getting eaten up."

INT.: The mother assures you that there's no problem about food. The cat goes around to everybody and they all feed her.

DR. W.: Everybody but Daddy. But she's anxious to tell me that there's no problem.

INT.: The mother is supposedly taking this literally about the cat. Do you think she has any idea that she's talking about herself?

DR. W.: She's not aware of it, no.

INT.: And you don't feel that it would do her any good to know?

DR. W.: Not particularly. But it would do her a lot of good to know that I was with her on this. That it wasn't a private, psychotic-type, isolate thing.

INT.: If she doesn't know about it, and you're not telling her, how are you communicating the idea that you're in on it?

DR. W.: When I say, "She's a smart cat," there's something in my tone of voice that tells her I'm seeing right through what she's talking about.

INT.: It's more a sharing than a discovery. It's not the understanding that she's the cat that's going to help her, it's the knowledge that she's sharing this with you.

DR. W.: Or that she's been discovered. Whether or not she discovers it in the conscious sense is less important than the fact that someone was sharing it. It's not any more a fantasy that she can enjoy keeping up, because it's not secret any more. It's not a closed circuit within her that she can feed from. It was the same with the man with the imaginary adopted kids. Once he had shared his fantasy with me, the whole thing lost its purpose for him. Because I was in on it.

INT.: Before we go on, it impresses me how straightforward and normal the son sounds in this part compared to the mother.

DR. W.: Yes. It's the mother who is crazy. Her laugh identifies that.

MRS. F.: We have to get a dog too when we can, ah, everybody can train it, it's just that—we had a dog when Eric was small until it was eight years old, it died of old age, but, um . . .

MR. F.: I was offered a dog last night.

MARGARET (*overlapping*): We have a cat (*inaudible phrase*).

MRS. F. (*overlapping, to Mr. F.*): What type?

MARGARET: . . . eight years old.

MR. F.: (*Inaudible phrase.*)

MARGARET: But our cat . . .

DR. W. (*overlapping*): Gosh, I should think you have a . . .

MARGARET: We have a . . .

DR. W.: . . . houseful already.

MARGARET: We have a cat (*inaudible phrase*).

MRS. F.: (*Inaudible phrase to child.*) I think dogs are fun, but they're certainly just one more thing to train, you know. (*Laughs.*)

DR. W.: Oh, boy.

MR. F.: Dirk would like a dog (*inaudible phrase*).

DIRK: I would.

MARGARET: I would.

DR. W.: What kind of a dog would you like, Dirk?

DIRK: Umm . . .

MARGARET: I would like a Lassie dog.

DIRK: I would like a police dog.

DR. W.: A police dog, huh? I'll bet you would.

MARGARET: I would . . .

DR. W. (*overlapping*): They scare me, don't they scare you?

ELIZA: I would like a poodle.

DR. W.: Gosh, I'm always afraid they're going to turn into wolves.

MARGARET (*overlapping*): I would like a Lassie dog.

DR. W.: You'd like a Lassie dog? I don't blame you.

ELIZA: I would like a little dog.

DR. W.: What would you like, a spitz? You know, a spitz, the little white fuzzy ones? (*Pause.*) Or a beagle, how about a beagle?

MRS. F.: Oh, they, they say they're good, very good, with children.

DR. W.: Yeah, beagles are lots of fun, and they're good, you can take them hunting. (*To Dirk*) When are you gonna get a gun? How old do you have to be before you get a gun?

DIRK: A hundred.

DR. W.: A hundred! (*Mrs. F. laughs.*) Good gracious, that sounds like a long time to wait. The dog will get tired waiting that long.

MRS. F.: Why don't you get a ball and bat?

DR. W. (*overlapping*): You know dogs are funny. Do you know how dogs—they get old seven times as fast as people do, do you know that? When a dog is one year old, he's as old as a little boy is when he's seven. When he's two years old, he's as old as a boy is when he's fourteen. When he's three years old, he's as old as a boy is when he's twenty-one. So by the time he gets to be, you know, ten years old, he's seventy years old. Like people, and he's old and very tired and all worn out. About ready to die.

INT.: Now we get onto dogs. What's going on here?

DR. W.: In her psychotic quality, the mother is talking about the dog, the boy, Eric. He's hard to train.

INT.: Are you also talking about the boy when you say that you're afraid of police dogs because you think they'll turn into wolves?

DR. W.: Well, he's the one who brought the parents before the bar of justice. At the same time he's the acter-outer, the violent one. He could be dangerous.

INT.: As a point of information, did someone call the police about the disturbance in the family?

DR. W.: No, there wasn't anything like that.

INT.: What's this long speech of yours about the age of dogs as compared to people?

DR. W.: I'm again making the identification between humans and animals. It occurs to me, too, that when I talk about the fact that a dog ten years old is the equivalent of a man seventy years old, this identifies the son as the father of his parents.

INT.: The son is the old man.

DR. W.: Yes. Facing death. My other association is that I'm talking about death in terms of the father. Father looks dead.

INT.: There's a quickening of the pace of the associations here, and they don't follow as logically as they did before. It sounds as though you were building up to something.

DR. W.: As I said before, my therapy is often controlled by my unconscious. You're right that I'm building up to something. I'm sure I wasn't aware of it at the time, but we now move into the whole question of incest and marriage.

DR. W. (*to Dirk*): How old are you gonna be before you die?

DIRK: I don't know.

DR. W.: Haven't decided yet, huh?

MARGARET: Probably I'll be about . . .

DIRK: (*Inaudible phrase.*)

MARGARET: No, um, a million.

DR. W.: A million, huh? (*Whistles.*) Boy, how many boyfriends can you have in a million years?

ELIZA: I already have some.

DR. W.: You already have some. You're starting on your list, huh? Are you keeping a list of them in a special black book?

ELIZA: Yeah.

DR. W.: That's the old spirit.

ELIZA: I have Ricky, and, ah, the boy next door, and, ah . . .

MRS. F.: Eliza is the family tomboy, she (*laughing*) does very well.

DR. W.: Aren't you gonna leave any for the other sisters?

ELIZA: No.

DR. W.: Gosh, you mean if Kathy wants to get a boyfriend, she's gonna have to go some place else, huh?

ELIZA: Mm-hm.

DR. W.: No chance of getting them in your neighborhood.

ELIZA: And I have, um (*inaudible phrase*) I don't think I could marry him but I think I could marry . . .

DR. W.: Well, it's a little early yet. I think you have another year or two before you need to worry about that.

ELIZA (*overlapping*): I hope I can marry, ah, Dad . . .

DR. W.: I think that would be fine.

ELIZA: . . . and Eric . . .

DR. W.: Do you think he'd be a good husband?

ELIZA: Yeah (*inaudible phrase*).

DR. W.: The only trouble is with being a dad who's a lawyer like that,

he's, he's hard to be a husband because he's always going away
so much. You know, he gets called away (*Margaret talking in
background*), clients are always bothering him. (*To Margaret*) How about you marrying me? If Lizzie's gonna marry
Daddy?

MARGARET: I'm gonna marry Dirk. (*Mrs. F. laughs.*)

DR. W.: You're going to marry Dirk?

MARGARET: And Eric.

DR. W.: Well, that would be nice.

ELIZA: And I'll marry Eric.

DR. W.: You're gonna marry Eric too?

MRS. F.: He's pretty (*inaudible phrase*).

DR. W. (*overlapping*): Well, that's fine, you'll have two husbands.
That's against the law, you know. You have to divorce one before
you can marry the next one.

MARGARET: I'm gonna marry Eric.

ELIZA: Well, I'll have one husband, and if I don't like it I'll change to
the other one.

DR. W.: That's a good idea. Or maybe you could have one on Mondays and Tuesdays and another one on Wednesdays and Thurs-
days. Sort of change around. How about that?

ELIZA: Mm-hm. Then I'd have to get married almost every single day.

DR. W.: Well, you could sort of get a, you know, a sort of a revolving
marriage certificate or something. (*Pause.*) What would you do
if, ah, Kathy insisted on having Daddy or Eric for her husband?
Then what would you do?

ELIZA: I would call the police.

DR. W.: Call the police, huh? (*Laughs.*) Wow! You're playing big
stakes right off. Why would you call the police?

ELIZA: Because I'm (*inaudible phrase*).

DR. W.: Yeah. You think the police would back you up?

ELIZA: Yeah.

DR. W.: Well, that's nice. You know the right kind of policeman to
call then, huh? What's his name?

ELIZA: Um, Joe.

DR. W.: He's one of your boyfriends too?

ELIZA: Yeah.

DR. W.: Well, that's a good way of doing it.

ELIZA: (*Long inaudible phrase*.)

DR. W.: Well, Kathy, it looks like you've been out-maneuvered.
(*Laughs.*) She's not only going to take both the men in the

family, she's going to get the police to back her up. You'll have to go some place else.

ELIZA: No, I'll take all the people in the world.

DR. W.: One after the other or all at once?

ELIZA: All at once.

DR. W.: All at once. Looks like quite a party.

MARGARET: First I take Eric, then I take Dad.

DR. W.: You take Eric first, and then Dad, huh?

MARGARET: And then Dirk.

DR. W.: And then Dirk.

MRS. F. (*laughing*): Poor Dirk. (*Pause.*)

DR. W.: How about it, would that be all right with you, Lizzie? If Meggie takes Dirk? You want Dirk too?

ELIZA: Yeah.

DR. W.: The competition around here is getting pretty rough.

MRS. F. (*laughing*): It's always been very rough. (*Mr. F. inaudible in background.*)

DR. W.: It looks like the men have sort of got it made. (*Mrs. F. laughing in background.*) Do you think they're going to have anything to say about who they marry?

ELIZA: What?

DR. W.: Suppose Dad doesn't want to marry you, or Dirk doesn't want to marry you, or Eric doesn't want to marry you? Then what are you gonna do?

ELIZA: I'll still marry them.

DR. W.: Marry them anyway, huh? Whether they like it or not.

MARGARET: (*Inaudible phrase.*) Then they wouldn't go with you. (*Laughs.*)

DR. W.: They wouldn't go with me at all, hm?

ELIZA: I would put 'em on my shoulders and carry them to the wedding. (*Mrs. F. laughs.*)

DR. W.: Boy, that would be (*inaudible phrase*).

MARGARET: Dad'd kill you and then woof!

DR. W.: You'd have to get a big strong wedding gown so they wouldn't tear it.

ELIZA: If they teared it, I would kill them.

DR. W.: Tear 'em apart, hm? Piece by piece. (*Inaudible talking in background. Long pause.*)

DR. W.: This is still a double conversation. I'm kidding around with the children and at the same time raising issues for the parents.

INT.: Do you bring up the subject of boyfriends to lead the conversation to the family love match?

DR. W.: I'm not being that deliberate. It's more likely that I started to talk about it because the child was responding to me boyfriend fashion.

INT.: I take it that you prefer to lose yourself in the interaction at a moment like this, so that this is all there is, there's no other communication.

DR. W.: Yes. On several occasions a patient has come in and said, "Why don't you do the talking today? Last time you didn't say a thing." But when I would play the tape of the other interview, it would turn out that I had talked half the time. It finally dawned on me that what I said was such a continuation of what they were up to that they had completely forgotten that I had said anything. This is my concept of a perfect interview: "He didn't say a word."

INT.: So now Eliza tells you she wants to marry Daddy and you say that's fine, except you wonder if he'll make a good husband.

DR. W.: Because he's always gone. He's been gone the whole interview, too. He's only said three words.

INT.: You wouldn't make a comment to her about the fact that Mother already has him?

DR. W.: No, this is fantasy, this is play. It's a standard thing with children: "I'm going to marry my daddy." But so often the parents don't recognize that this is like playing with dolls, that it's the kitten learning to fight with its mother. And it suddenly becomes a problem when Papa gets an erection or when Mama gets a sexual feeling that makes her feel guilty. They put it on an adult level, when the child is just playing. So I keep it on the level of play. And I show the parents how this can be done.

INT.: I notice that your objection to the little girl's marrying her father is not on a reality basis of "You can't, he's your father." You object to it because he's away so much. The implication is that otherwise it would be fine.

DR. W.: I've often said that the basic contribution I make to a lot of my patients is my belief in incest.

INT.: When you talk about the difficulties of marrying men who are always away from home, I assume this is also to the mother.

DR. W.: Yes. There's no question that I'm alerting both Father and Mother to my perception of their struggle.

INT.: Again you precipitate yourself into the middle of the situation by asking the littlest girl if she'll marry you.

DR. W.: This also validates the incestual process between father and daughter, mother and son. I'm saying, "It's all right for you to marry me, I'm your father. I'm an older-generation person and the symbolic father in this household. And it's also all right for Father and Kathy and Mother and Eric to sex it up. As long as it's a game."

INT.: And as long as Father is a good husband to Mother. But you know, it's strange of you to say, "You shouldn't marry your father because he's a professional man and not around much." You're a professional man and not around much too.

DR. W.: I wouldn't have thought of that. But essentially I'm taking the standard picture the patient has of the therapist as an ideal mate and turning it by saying, "Mama really has a lousy husband, what she needs is me."

INT.: I should think the father would begin to feel quite competitive with you after hearing that.

DR. W.: I do this quite routinely. I say to the husband, "You just keep your cotton-picking hands off, I'm making love to your wife."

INT.: Do you put yourself in between them so that he will then move toward her?

DR. W.: Yes. It's to get them together.

INT.: All through this, you have a way of resolving something by putting in obstacles. In this case your own person.

DR. W.: I guess you're right. I certainly do make it personal. For instance, I'll say to Mother and Father, "Now, look, one of the problems we're going to have is that I'm going to steal your daughter and she'll never come back." I tell them that they'll worry and fret and mourn but that I think they've got what it takes to stand it.

INT.: Are you toying with the edge of a question in their minds about whether you really mean to take their daughter?

DR. W.: Yes, the symbolic act is preparation for the real loss in the future.

INT.: When you flirt with a wife so that the husband isn't certain whether you mean it or not, is it this uncertainty that you're trying to stir up?

DR. W.: I don't know. By warning the husband beforehand, I get his tacit agreement. This brings us together, too, in the sense that two men who sleep with the same woman sleep with each other.

INT.: Does a husband ever object to your flirting?

DR. W.: No, but I use facetious language, so that he has no way of doing anything about it. If he takes it seriously, I say he's a square. Anyway, he knows no psychiatrist is going to get himself into trouble like that.

INT.: That may not be so clear. You've already told this family that psychiatrists do crazy things.

DR. W.: Touché.

INT.: Now when you said, "You have to divorce one before you can marry the next one," were you consciously thinking of that as a metaphoric statement about the mother and her husband and son?

DR. W.: Perhaps not at the time. But I was aware that we were talking about incest and we were going right at it and I was going to keep at it.

INT.: Why would you want to keep at it?

DR. W.: Because this is a beautiful way to talk to the three of them about their situation. And to tell them that it's fine with me, that I don't mind their sleeping together.

INT.: You bring up some of the disadvantages of incest too. It could get them into fights.

DR. W.: That's right. I talk about the rough competition and how Eliza had better get a big strong wedding gown.

INT.: That's a strange sentence to end on, "Tear them apart, piece by piece." What are you referring to by "them"?

DR. W.: The wedding gowns for all the men she plans to marry. This is standard child therapy talk or schizophrenese. I use it all the time with families.

INT.: You've suggested that the incest process contains both sex and violence. In this last exchange, you seem to be showing the family how to play at violence as well as sex.

DR. W.: They're aspects of the same game.

DR. W. (*after long pause*): Good gracious, we're overtime already. Well, why don't you think about it, talk about it together. (*Pause.*) If you decide you want to do it, Eric, how about you giving me a ring? Since I've already had a call from both Mother and Dad. If you decide you want to do it, how about you calling me? If you can't get me here at the hospital, which is sometimes kind of difficult, call me at home in the evening. You can speak to me there. Except I'll be away—well, I leave tomorrow morning, I'll be away until Monday or the day after. I'll be back then. Okay? (*To the children*) Well, will you come back and see us? I'd love to have you come back. Bye-bye.

MRS. F.: Goodbye, Dr. Whitaker.

DR. W.: See you again. (*To Eliza*) Bye-bye. Goodbye, Eric.

MRS. F. (*referring to Dirk*): I think he wants to shake hands.

DR. W. (*to Dirk*): You want to shake hands with me? Good for you. Bye-bye.

(*Inaudible conversation under the noise of leaving. Tape recording ends.*)

INT.: Why do you say that the son should telephone you? Is it really because you've already had calls from Mother and Dad?

DR. W.: I'm trying to give all three the same credit, the same status. Although I'll frequently take the one who's least interested or more antagonistic or more dubious and give that person the responsibility for getting in touch with me.

INT.: Why is that?

DR. W.: To get him involved.

INT.: This is also setting up another obstacle; the one who least wants to come has to make the appointment.

DR. W.: Yes, and I'll be very clear about it. A wife will call up and say, "I'm very upset." I'll say, "Well, get your husband and come on in." She'll say, "My husband doesn't want to come." I'll say, "Well, don't call me till you get that straightened out. If your husband gets ready to come, then have him call me." "Well, he hates psychiatrists." "I need him if I'm going to work with you, and if he doesn't want to come, then I don't want to see you. If he has any question to ask, have him call."

INT.: Would you accept it if she straightened it out and then called you?

DR. W.: Sure. She knows I see the setup as jointly sponsored, so she'll go home and they'll make another plan.

INT.: You picked the most difficult family member to make the appointment here, too.

DR. W.: Yes, and he didn't make it.

INT.: Did you get any subsequent information on this family?

DR. W.: When I did a follow-up on the case, about a year later, the disturbances in the home seemed to have quieted down. I spoke to the father, who was quite friendly and told me that the boy had been living at home that past year and was now a freshman in the local university. There had been ups and downs, as before, but the boy was behaving more like a natural teenager.

INT.: Before we end, there's one thing I'd like to bring up. There seems to be a major theme throughout this interview, and that is a quality of playfulness. You seem to be teaching the family how to play: with names, with words, with issues, with each other. You use your relationship with the children as a way of instructing the family in how to enjoy themselves.

DR. W.: That's right. This is part of what I can do with a co-therapist. We'll say to the patient, "Don't bother us with your nonsense, we're having fun." We'll talk about what interests us, not about the patient. If something comes up that bores me in an interview, I'll frequently start reading a book, or put on some music, or make a phone call.

INT.: Is this to get people to be more lively?

DR. W.: Well, I'll say to a patient, "I've been involved with you for some time and you keep turning me down. I can't maintain my erection forever. If I lose my interest in you, you're going to have to drag me back in, and it's going to be harder every time. You'd better be aware of that, because if you lose me, it's as bad as my losing you. I can't turn myself on on purpose."

INT.: Like so much in your therapy, it has to just happen. But there's another thing about this playing. It's done in a context in which people are in absolute misery and paying money to get out of it. Yet within that context, you play.

DR. W.: That's true, and it's one of the things people can misunderstand. Sometimes someone will say to me, "You don't seem to be taking this seriously," or "Were you kidding when you said that?" I tell them, "This is a life and death job. There's nothing I do here that's for fun. I'm dead serious from the time you get here to the time you leave."

5]

Cleaning House

An interview with Frank Pittman III, M.D.,
  Kalman Flomenhaft, M.S.W., and Carol DeYoung, R.N.

INT.: Before we start the tape of the session with the family, would you describe the project you're working on?

DR. P.: The project was conceived by Dr. Donald Langsley and Dr. David Kaplan of the University of Colorado Medical Center in Denver. It is an experiment to try to keep people in acute crisis out of the hospital by using a brief family therapy approach. The project is being supported by the National Institute of Mental Health and was started in July 1964. The therapy team consists of myself, Kal Flomenhaft, who is a social worker, and Carol DeYoung, who is a psychiatric public health nurse. We plan to treat a group of 150 to 200 cases over a five-year period and contrast them with another group hospitalized through the usual channels. This first year is more of a pilot study, while we work out our techniques. We will take about one case a week for four years. The last year we won't take any more but will continue fol-

This group is at the University of Colorado Medical Center, Denver, Colorado. Donald G. Langsley, M.D., is Director of the Family Treatment Unit and Associate Professor of Psychiatry, University of Colorado School of Medicine. David M. Kaplan, Ph.D., is Co-Director of the Family Treatment Unit and Associate Professor of Psychiatry, University of Colorado School of Medicine. Frank S. Pittman III, M.D., is the psychiatrist for the Family Treatment Unit and Assistant Professor of Psychiatry, University of Colorado School of Medicine. Kalman Flomenhaft, M.S.W., A.C.S.W., is a psychiatric social worker with the Family Treatment Unit. Carol DeYoung, R.N., M.S., is a psychiatric nurse with the Family Treatment Unit. The project is supported by NIMH Grant #MH 1577.

In this interview, the conversation with the therapists has been simplified by having most of the statements of the group presented by Dr. Pittman, even though Mr. Flomenhaft and Miss DeYoung participated regularly in the conversation, and Drs. Langsley and Kaplan took part from time to time.

low-up studies and evaluate our results. We won't know who the control families are until the patients are discharged, at which point we will start the same follow-up procedures on them that we do on the families we are treating. Our hope is to show that a brief, family-oriented approach is a suitable alternative for hospitalization. We're against unnecessary hospitalization, and with alternatives such as we offer, we think most hospitalizations are unnecessary. No matter how good the hospital or how strong the indications for putting someone there, the process of removing someone from his home and declaring him a hospitalized mental patient is both regressive and stigmatizing. It has enormous adverse effects on his relationship with himself, his family, and society. It implies that he is dangerous or incompetent. Not only does it prevent his functioning, but it isolates him as the problem in the family and consolidates the family's extrusion of him, making his return more difficult. There is also the danger of hospital addiction. The family and the patient can easily get the idea that when there's a person with a problem, the only thing to do is to declare him sick, kick him out of the family, and give the responsibility to the state.

INT.: Often it isn't even a matter of extruding a person, it's having the state restrain him while he's still involved at home.

DR. P.: Sure. What makes our approach different is not whether our patients go into the hospital or not, it's the different emphasis upon who is responsible for solving the problem. We're declaring the family responsible, instead of agreeing that society is responsible. Even when we hospitalize someone, we make it clear that this will be temporary, that the person may be back any minute, and that we'll be seeing the family while he's there.

INT.: So you might use the hospital briefly.

DR. P.: Yes, although we'd prefer not to. It's hard to use most hospitals for brief hospitalization. Ours is a good hospital, a very good one, but it's set up for an average stay of twenty-five days and the wheels turn slowly by our standards. We're trying to get people back to work, which is harder to do once they get integrated into the hospital program. We do sometimes hospitalize a patient overnight, if he is really uncontrollable and the family is exhausted. We can use the emergency room of the general hospital for this and there is no stigma and no question of the person staying longer than overnight. The next morning, when the family is rested and the patient is calmed by drugs, we can proceed on a much better basis. When there's no home and no effective family, or when we're dealing with an adolescent who is appropriately leaving home, or even an adult who doesn't know whether to go home or not, we've boarded the patient at a guest home rather than the hospital. It seems more appropriate to figure out just what the patient does need and give him only that, rather than take everything he does have away and replace it with the entire hospital setting.

INT.: How long do you usually treat a family?

DR. P.: From a week to two or three months. We average five sessions over a two-week period, then maybe a few phone calls. We limit ourselves to dealing with the immediate crisis; after that we try to refer people to appropriate community services, vocational rehabilitation agencies, visiting-nurse services, and so forth. But we make it clear that we are immediately available to the family if they meet another crisis.

INT.: What are your criteria for taking cases?

DR. P.: We take, by a random selection, about one out of every four cases that would ordinarily be admitted to the hospital as acute. The admitting resident must decide that the patient needs admission. Most patients who are seen in the emergency room are handled without admission, so the patients that come to us are pretty sick. Also, the patient must live under the same roof as some other relative over the age of sixteen and must live within fifty miles of the hospital. And he must come in voluntarily.

INT.: What if the police bring someone in?

DR. P.: If there's no judge that says he has to go into the hospital, we'll still take him. We've had quite a few instances in which people were refusing to be hospitalized and we stepped in before the family got the person legally committed and prevented it. Whenever possible, we try to keep the matter of whether or not the patient is to be put in the hospital from being discussed with the family beforehand, though we can't always control this. In the family we're going to talk about, there were several people who had already told the family that the patient had to go into the hospital.

INT.: What follow-up procedures are you using?

DR. P.: We plan to see each family routinely at six months, then each year for five years.

INT.: Are you going to bring them in to the hospital, or see them in the home, or what?

DR. P.: We are training social workers as independent raters who will go out and evaluate the cases in the home. They will see not only our cases but the controls as well. As of now, we are doing the evaluations ourselves.

INT.: What sort of information are you after?

DR. P.: The same information we get during an initial interview: what everyone is doing, who is living at home, who is getting help and what sort, are there any problems or symptoms. We also have people repeat some tests we give them in the beginning of treatment.

INT.: What standards are you using for the success of a case?

DR. P.: Very simple ones, because we're setting very simple goals. We feel we've done well if we just get a family back to the pre-crisis status quo. So far we've hospitalized less than 5 percent acutely, but whether they've gotten through the crisis with fewer scars than the hospital would have left, we don't know yet. We won't know until we can compare our group with the hospital group. We are finding that only another 10 percent or so of our cases go on to be hospitalized within the year, which is a much lower figure than the hospital group's 30 percent. So we must be teaching our families to use other solutions than the hospital to handle problems. We hope our families will be able to resolve their own future crises a bit better. If not, we hope they'll seek help on an outpatient basis, preferably as a family. In many cases, I don't think we do much more than this, but there are some, such as the family we'll be talking about, in which we do set something new in motion, different ways of relating, different roles and rules for the family that allow its members to operate at their best possible level. We rely on long-term referrals for more characterological change. However, our project focus is on functioning and functional change and when we do follow-ups we ask about functional things. We ask whether whoever should be working is working, whether the children are in school, whether the wife is keeping up the house, whether anybody has been in jail or in the hospital. We also ask what subsequent problems the family has faced and how well it has handled them.

INT.: Are you using this project for research, too?

DR. P.: Yes. Besides comparing the cases we've treated with those treated by the usual hospital methods, we're trying to work out a new method of treatment. We're also hoping to learn something about crises in the family. We plan to build up a body of observations about how a crisis is handled within different types of family structure, what part the extended family plays in a crisis, what part the patient plays, and so forth. We're also trying to learn something about hospitals, what they do to people, and why families send people there. We have a psychologist, Dr. Pavel Machotka, working with us now.

INT.: When did the family we're going to talk about come in?

DR. P.: About two months after the project was started. It was our ninth family. Mrs. Willy was in her late fifties, but she looked much older. She was brought in by her twenty-four-year-old son, Paul, and her older sister, Mrs. Clapp.

INT.: When the tape begins, you're alone with them. Is this routine?

DR. P.: No, it's just that I was the only one of the team in the office at the time. Kal Flomenhaft and Carol DeYoung were at a meeting. They showed up midway through the session, and I asked them to come in.

INT.: Do all three of you usually work together with a family?

DR. P.: No, we work two together in loose rotation, with the third member behind the screen. Don Langsley and Dave Kaplan, the originators and directors of the project, and Pavel Machotka, the project psychologist, also spend a fair amount of time behind the screen. We all six talk a great deal together about what we see and do, so the ideas and even the techniques we use have come from all of us.

INT.: What usually happens to a family between the time they come to the hospital and the time they arrive at your office?

DR. P.: They are first seen by the psychiatrist on duty in the emergency room, who is one of the residents. If the psychiatrist decides that by the usual standards this is somebody who has to go in the hospital right now, and can't wait till tomorrow or next week, and if our number, about one out of four, is up, he calls us and we go upstairs to the emergency room and bring the family to our offices.

INT.: Is the family briefed on what they are to expect from you?

DR. P.: With this family, the resident did say something such as, "Mrs. Willy needs to go in the hospital, but Dr. Pittman and his group are going to try to keep her out." But we try to prevent the resident from transmitting his opinion that this is a case that ought to be admitted acutely. If he tells them this, it makes it a lot harder for us to convince the family to take the patient home.

INT.: At any rate, this family knew it wasn't going to be a straight-into-the-hospital deal.

DR. P.: Well, they knew that they were going to have to discuss it with me first.

INT.: Do you generally get any information from the resident about the family?

DR. P.: Usually we get a bit of verbal information from the resident in the process of taking the patient out of his hands, but nothing written. We do get his write-up later, but that's usually after we've seen the family ourselves. We have the old chart, if there is one, and the social worker's report, if she's seen the family. But all we usually know is that this is somebody the resident feels should be in the hospital. When I walked in to get this family, I didn't even know who the identified patient was. I found out rather quickly. As we went down to my office, Mrs. Willy was shrieking about the floods in Holland, the dikes breaking, and mud all over the streets.

INT.: What information do you take from the family yourselves?

DR. P.: Our secretary makes out a fact-sheet for base-line information such as names, addresses, and so forth.

INT.: Is there a presenting problem on that?

DR. P.: No, just factual information. With the Willys, I was able to get a bit of firsthand information by standing behind the observation screen and watching the family while the secretary had them make out the forms.

INT.: Is that what you usually do?

DR. P.: If we can. We feel we're better prepared if we're able to see who's who and what's what before we go in. That tells us a lot more than a history and diagnosis of the individual who is the patient.

INT.: What impression did you get of this family?

DR. P.: The mother's sister, Mrs. Clapp, was an overdressed, middle-aged, middle-class lady, the sort of woman who runs wedding rehearsals. The son was also quite well dressed. He had a sarcastic smile on his face and seemed terribly bitter toward his mother. The mother was sitting between the two of them, wailing and carrying on, her hair all wild, her clothes disheveled. She didn't look as if she belonged to them at all, and they looked on her as if she were a thing they had brought to the hospital to get rid of.

INT.: Did you talk much with the family before the tape begins?

DR. P.: I think I walked in and introduced myself, explained that Miss DeYoung and Mr. Flomenhaft were at a meeting, and told them something about how we operate by explaining to them about the one-way screen and the microphone. If anybody is behind the screen, I tell them who it is, but I don't think anybody was there that day.

INT.: Did you give the family any tests?

DR. P.: We were still juggling tests around at this time and didn't give any to this family. We've now started giving the tests after the first interview, because we had a number of pretty disturbed people who weren't able to fill out the forms right off, and we want it as standard as possible.

Initial interview with Mrs. Willy, her son Paul, and her sister, Mrs. Clapp

PAUL: Well, myself, mother, and my little sister who is now with an uncle in [*nearby state*].

DR. P.: How long has she been in [*nearby state*]?

MRS. W.: She just went yesterday.

PAUL: Just sent her down there.

MRS. C.: For school.

MRS. W.: I think they'll send her back. He couldn't get that transcript of grades now.

MRS. C.: He wanted to take her, for school. Thought maybe she'd be better there than . . .

MRS. W. (*overlapping*): He couldn't get that, you know, because they, ah, well (*inaudible phrase*).

MRS. C. (*overlapping*): This was so upsetting to her, and she couldn't study (*Mrs. W. talking in background*) and it was better for her down there with other members of the family. They have several girls and it would be better for her.

MRS. W.: I don't think they're going to keep her.

DR. P. (*overlapping, to Paul*): How old are you?

PAUL: Twenty-three, twenty-four now.

MRS. C.: Tomorrow.

DR. P.: You'll be twenty-four tomorrow.

PAUL: Um-hm.

DR. P.: You live at home?

PAUL: Um-hm.

INT.: From the way the tape begins, it sounds as though you had asked some question about who made up the family.

MISS DEY.: You usually ask, "Who is in the house?"

DR. P.: I think I was under the influence of some article I had just read and I asked, "How do you define your family? Who do you think makes up the family?" Actually, we don't have any standard first question.

INT.: You go to the son right off. Why is that? You might have started with the supposed patient.

DR. P.: The supposed patient, when the secretary had made efforts to get information, had been totally uncooperative. I wanted to find out about these people, but I felt I wasn't going to get anything out of her. Anyway, we would tend not to start with the supposed patient, because this would point to her as being the trouble right away. If I had walked in, shoved Mrs. Clapp aside, and said, "I'll take responsibility for this crazy woman here," that would have been disastrous. It would have given them exactly what they wanted, which was to get the old lady off their hands for good.

INT.: It's always interesting to see who the therapist turns to first. Granted that you wouldn't start with the mother, you might have asked the first question of her sister.

DR. P.: I might, but she seemed a little too eager to be my informant. Watching the family from behind the screen, I had the feeling that there was something important going on between the son and the mother and that the sister was somewhat peripheral.

INT.: You head for the mystery right off.

DR. P.: I think we start with the things we don't understand. I didn't understand what was going on between this boy and his mother to make her act that way. And you see, the sister comes right in and takes over. So I shift it back to the boy.

INT.: You ask him how old he is. Did you already know that?

DR. P.: Oh, yes. He'd already given that information to the secretary while I was behind the screen.

INT.: It's curious that you asked him when you already knew it.

DR. P.: He didn't know I knew it.

INT.: You also knew that he was living at home. Were you deliberately putting yourself in a more ignorant position?

DR. P.: I was wondering why, at the age of twenty-four, he was still living with his mother. I suppose I wanted to make the point that this was a somewhat unusual family constellation.

INT.: You're not really getting information, you're giving it.

Dr. P.: I suppose so. Also, the sister had set herself up as the spokesman and was explaining everybody else's feelings. By turning back to the boy, I was saying, "Look, you're a grown man, why are you letting your aunt speak for you?"

Int.: This also brings in the assumption that he is part of what's happened.

Dr. P.: Yes. The boy's air of superiority to his mother, the way he was baiting her as the secretary took the information, suggested that he didn't think he had any share in it. This was something that had happened to his mother and he was suffering unfairly for it. I felt he was involved and I wanted to find out how. I wasn't buying the picture that the family was presenting. Their behavior told me that they wanted me to do business with the sister, worry about the old lady, and ignore the son. What I did was to shut up the sister, ignore the old lady, and talk to the son.

Int.: Whatever the family indicates, you go in the other direction.

Dr. P.: Yes. One of the first things we try to do with a family is to dispel their set idea of what is going on.

Int.: You might have done that more directly. Some therapists will say to a family, "You're all in treatment."

Dr. P.: You can say that to a family and not have it mean much. On occasion I have made the mistake of walking in and telling the family that this is the way I see the problem, but they don't take it very well. Focusing on the person who seems least willing to acknowledge any involvement seems to me a more fruitful way to shatter the picture they present and get at the real one. Here, by bringing in the son, I'm questioning whether the sister, who is all too eager to display her involvement, has any right to it. This also puts me in control rather than the aunt.

Int.: Or than the son, who is defining the situation by staying out of it.

Dr. P.: Or than the mother, who is claiming to be the problem.

Int.: You're also doing what some therapists would call "taking the label off the identified patient." Can you give another example of the way you might start a session?

Dr. P.: One of the largest groups we've seen was a couple with six children. We saw all eight of them together. I remember that we started by questioning the youngest child who could talk, a girl of three or four. This was the clearest way we could demonstrate that whatever the problem was, they were all part of it. We got the child to tell us her concept of what was going wrong. She brought out a lot of information, how her parents were fighting all the time, how her mother was going to work and leaving her fourteen-year-old sister in charge, and how she didn't like this. The problems she brought up were no secret, but the parents had no idea of the extent to which even the youngest members of the family were affected by them.

DR. P. (*to Paul*): Do you work?
PAUL: Yes.
DR. P.: What do you do?
PAUL: Ah, I'm just a warehouse worker out at [*store*].
DR. P.: Why do you say "just"?

INT.: What cued you to pick up that "just"?

DR. P.: This was a very pompous boy, and he felt the need to apologize to me for not being more successful. That told me something about his problems. I expected him to put the blame on his mother for his failures as well as hers, and I wanted to draw him out about his failures first. It was another way of getting him involved as a patient, rather than merely as the son of a patient.

PAUL: Well, it's, ah, substandard as far as I'm concerned in that I've, ah, I'm studying to be an engineer. Electrical engineer.
DR. P.: Are you in school now?
PAUL: No.
DR. P.: When were you last in school?
PAUL: About a year ago.
DR. P.: That's not too temporary then.
PAUL: No.
DR. P.: Do you plan to go back?
MRS. W.: He won't get to go back for (*inaudible phrase*).
PAUL (*overlapping*): Well, I won't be going back for a while, that's . . .
MRS. W.: He won't get to go at all.
MRS. C. (*overlapping*): He needs another year, if he can finish.
DR. P.: What do you mean, he won't get to go at all?
MRS. W.: He doesn't have the money to go.

DR. P.: Uh-huh. (*To Mrs. W.*) Are you working? (*Pause.*)

MRS. W.: (*Shakes head.*)

DR. P.: Have you been?

MRS. W.: No. I've never worked much in my life, that, that's it. I just can't, I'm not trained for anything, to be specifically . . .

DR. P.: Um-hm.

MRS. W.: You have to be trained for something. I tried to do, ah, baby-sitting with [*agency*].

DR. P.: Yeah.

MRS. W.: They'd send me, well, I'd go twenty miles, clear out here by [*street*] . . .

DR. P.: Um-hm.

MRS. W.: . . . and make a dollar and fifty cents. For three hours.

DR. P.: How much were you making?

MRS. W.: Fifty cents an hour.

DR. P.: Fifty cents an hour?

MRS. W.: Yeah, and set three hours in the afternoon. A dollar and fifty cents. You can't make it that way, you know. You can't make a living that way.

DR. P.: You see, Mrs. Willy broke in with something quite rational. She quit her crazy behavior. She had been sitting over in the corner grimacing and making noises until I started attacking her son, and then she came to his defense by saying he couldn't afford to go back to school. Her tone suggested that she was also blaming herself. I didn't know yet how much truth there was to this, but at least she was operating on a level where I could deal with her.

INT.: When you started focusing on the boy's problems, she became sensible.

DR. P.: If I'd started by focusing on her problems, she probably would have gone on being crazy.

INT.: But when she becomes sensible, you talk to her. Is this routine?

DR. P.: Yes. The son and the sister had obviously been rewarding this woman's craziness by paying her all sorts of attention when she was crazy. That's why I refused to talk to her at first. But the first time she said something uncrazy, I rewarded her.

INT.: The way you rewarded her must have been something of a shock. You asked her if she were working. You must have known she couldn't be working.

DR. P.: Yes, I did.

INT.: So again this isn't a question to get information.

DR. P.: It's a directive question. I'm telling her, "We expect you to work; we expect you to function. You may be crazy now, but we have a right to expect certain things of you and so does your son."

INT.: You don't put it, "Why aren't you working?" you assume that she can. There's an implication here that if you treat people as if they were capable of working, they will come up with that.

DR. P.: We think intolerance of psychotic behavior is in itself pretty anti-regressive medicine.

INT.: You go so smoothly here, first asking the son if he is working and then if she is working. The implication is that neither of them is doing as well as he could. It cancels out the difference between them.

DR. P.: You see how nicely she responds. That speech of hers about the baby-sitting is perfectly sensible, perfectly sane. It's what any middle-aged, inexperienced woman would say about the difficulties of getting a job.

DR. P.: Have things been pretty bad as far as money is concerned?

MRS. W. (*tearfully*): Yes.

DR. P.: You don't think they've been (*inaudible phrase*).

MRS. W.: They have. He can't make it. He's got more bills than he can meet.

PAUL: Now frankly, I think, ah, we're probably getting on as well as anyone we know.

MRS. C.: Average working family, you know.

MRS. W.: Now, Paul, why don't you admit the truth?

DR. P.: Your mother is pretty discouraged, isn't she?

INT.: Do you remember the rest of that sentence, "You don't think they've been . . ."?

DR. P.: I think I was trying to get at the facts about the financial situation. This was the first clear-cut, specific problem I could deal with. Mrs. Willy seemed pretty upset about money, and I wanted to find out how realistic she was being.

INT.: You sound so sympathetic when you ask her if things have been bad.

DR. P.: I guess I'm always sympathetic to people who are broke.

INT.: You might have chosen not to show sympathy.

DR. P.: I think I was trying to encourage her. This was the first sensible behavior she had demonstrated since I saw her in the waiting room upstairs. I was probably sitting on the edge of my chair, saying, "Yes, yes," and begging her in every possible way to continue with this nice, sensible behavior.

INT.: The prognosis must have looked good when she came through as well as that.

DR. P.: I was very surprised and very pleased.

INT.: When the others break in to say the finances are just fine, why do you ignore them? Did you think they might be wrong and she might be right?

DR. P.: I didn't know. There were plenty of reassurances that there was no real financial problem. But there must have been something that this woman was perceiving. That's why I said to the son, "Your mother is pretty discouraged." I was saying, "There must be some reality to what your mother says."

INT.: It sounds terribly reasonable to us now, but it's a relatively new premise in the world to assume that when somebody who is crazy says something there must be some reality to it.

DR. P.: I don't think I've ever run into a delusion that on some level wasn't true.

INT.: Until ten years ago, most therapists would have interpreted that statement about money in terms of love or something symbolic like that. You don't say to Mrs. Willy, "Let's see what your preoccupation with money really means."

DR. P.: We tend to accept the idea that there's an underlying reality to psychotic productions. To assume that the symbolism is what is important would be putting the cart before the horse.

INT.: It's part of the crisis framework. You are out to change the reality situation as rapidly as possible.

DR. P.: That's right. If we were taking this woman on as a long-term individual psychotherapy case, or even as a long-term family case, we might spend a lot of time on the symbolism. But this is a crisis we're dealing with. Mrs. Willy is screaming that she doesn't have enough money and her family says she does. I've got to get the facts straight in a hurry if I'm going to convince the family that her security is being threatened in some real way and that this is a real problem in which the whole family is involved.

INT.: You're not only getting the facts straight but also teaching the family what this procedure is about. Your interest in practical matters lays the groundwork for what comes later, inevitably.

DR. P.: With any therapy, you're constantly training people to be the sort of patients you want them to be. You're trying to establish with them what sort of a game this is. I'm telling these people that this is a reality-oriented game and that we're interested in immediate results.

MRS. C.: She's worried about money and bills and she just doesn't seem to (*sighs*) have confidence that Paul can keep things up, that's all, for some reason or another.

MRS. W.: How can he keep things up on the little that he makes? See, he'd have no deductions. He gets about . . .

DR. P. (*overlapping, to Paul*): How much do you make?

PAUL: $2.69 an hour.

DR. P.: $2.69 an hour. How many hours a week do you work?

PAUL: Well, forty, just about guaranteed forty, plus during the summer we get quite a bit of overtime.

DR. P.: That's pretty good.

PAUL: That's not bad.

MRS. W.: Well, he just can't make it, though.

DR. P.: This, this is bound to add up to well over a hundred dollars a, a week.

PAUL: Yeah, it grosses about a hundred, hundred a week.

DR. P.: Yeah.

MRS. W.: But you see, he has no deductions. He has no, ah . . .

DR. P. (*overlapping*): Why not?

MRS. W.: Well, he has no children, see, to—exemptions.

MRS. C.: Well, honey . . .

DR. P.: But you're . . .

MRS. C.: He's got you, he deducted you this year.

DR. P. (*overlapping*): Yeah, if you're the sole support of your mother and your sister . . .

PAUL (*overlapping*): Yeah, she's a deduction.

DR. P.: . . . then you, you have these, you have deductions for yourself and the two . . .

PAUL: Well . . .

MRS. C.: Just one . . .

PAUL: . . . not exactly, my sister has a government . . .

MRS. W. (*tearfully*): She won't be getting that now, I won't be there to sign it.

DR. P.: The thing is, if she's not getting it, and she's living there and you're supporting her, then you can take her as a deduction. Ah . . .

MRS. W.: I won't be there to sign it.

DR. P.: . . . if she's living elsewhere, somebody else will be supporting her. (*Pause.*)

MRS. W.: Now, Paul, you know you're painting a picture different than it is. (*Mrs. C. laughs.*)

DR. P.: Well . . .

INT.: Here I gather you're both clarifying the reality of the situation and doing more.

DR. P.: I think one is always doing "more."

INT.: What are you doing here?

DR. P.: The old lady had started going way out again, so I'm shutting her up and once more focusing on the son. From what they've been saying, he is in charge of the financial situation in the family.

INT.: You were baiting him before. Now you're supporting him in his responsibility as head of the family.

DR. P.: That's true. But in the interest of supporting the mother.

INT.: How are you supporting her?

DR. P.: By pointing out to the son, in the mother's presence, that he is making a reasonable living.

INT.: How does this support her? It contradicts her statement that he can't make it.

DR. P.: "Support" may be the wrong word. I'm reassuring her, telling her that things aren't so bad. But I do this indirectly by talking to the son. To argue her down directly would be futile. As it turned out, my reassurance was pretty futile too, because it wasn't about the real issues.

INT.: What were the real issues?

DR. P.: At this point I didn't know. We found out in the next interview. Mrs. Willy was very concerned about being dependent on her son because she had no way of knowing that he was going to be able to support her. He never made her aware of the financial situation, and he wasn't giving her enough money to run the house or anything to spend on herself. That's why she kept bringing up the deductions. She felt some bitterness at the fact that he was getting her as a deduction while she wasn't getting anything in return.

INT.: So in spite of the fact that the son was doing well, they really didn't live well.

DR. P.: Exactly. As it turned out, Mrs. Willy had been married four times and none of her husbands had ever supported her properly. After she got divorced the last time, she turned the house over to Paul. She had a great weakness for men, and she realized that if she kept the house, some other man would probably come along and take her for a ride. But she got into the same situation with her son that she had been in with the husbands. He had mortgaged the house, taken the money to invest in the stock market, and wouldn't tell her what stocks he had or how well he was doing. He didn't share his profits with her, just used the money to reinvest. He was leading a very meager existence himself, and as far as she knew, he was pouring house and all down the drain.

INT.: Did she know he was playing the stock market?

DR. P.: Oh, yes. But he kept telling her, "This is none of your business, everything is taken care of." He was in a difficult position himself. All the other relatives, including a stepson who was the rightful heir to the house, were terribly bitter that Paul had gotten it. This was one reason why he didn't want anyone to know he was making money on it.

INT.: Was he?

DR. P.: Sure. In that one year, he had made a thousand dollars on five. What made Mrs. Willy's situation worse was not only that Paul kept quiet about his profits, but that the other relatives tried to undermine her faith in Paul's ability to support her, in the hope that she would do something to redivide the estate.

INT.: So when she goes on about being homeless, it's close to the literal reality as she would have to perceive it.

DR. P.: Yes. Later in the interview she starts wailing that the dikes are going to break in Holland, that there'll be mud all over, and that they'll all run naked in the streets. This was pretty literal too. It turned out that one of the big issues between her and Paul was that the washing machine had broken down and neither of them would do anything to fix it. Each insisted it was the other's responsibility. So for many weeks Mrs. Willy was taking the clothes to have them washed by Gloria, her oldest daughter, who lived down the street. Gloria used entirely too much bleach on the clothes and they came out ragged and full of holes. So when Mrs. Willy says, "We're going to run naked in the streets," that's exactly what she means. And when she says, "The dikes are go-. ing to break in Holland and there'll be mud all over," this is her way of saying, "The washing machine has broken down and I can't get anything clean."

MRS. C.: She's just been worked and worried about these bills and that's just the thing, it got to where she just couldn't cope with the problem of financial things and in her mind they are three times worse than they are, see . . .

MRS. W.: That's just not true.

MRS. C.: . . . and that thing is the thing that's done it, it's just, she just feels like there's never enough to go around.

MRS. W.: There isn't. Right now, they're liable to shut our water off because the water hasn't been paid for, and they're liable to shut, I know they'll shut the telephone bill off next month . . .

MRS. C.: Sweetheart, Paul's paid them every month, and he will.

MRS. W.: He won't!

MRS. C.: Paul always will keep paying them.

MRS. W.: His cars are shot and the rear end went out of his, ah, car, the other day. Oh, ah, his car was parked and the windshield blew all to, you know, the heat got in there and just popped the whole back. So there he's got no car.

DR. P. (*to Paul*): You can drive it?

MRS. W.: Huh?

DR. P.: You can drive it, can't you?

MRS. W.: Oh, no, he can't . . .

PAUL (*overlapping*): Yeah, we have transportation.

MRS. W.: He can't drive it . . .

PAUL: As far as that goes, if I need one, I can always buy another one.

DR. P.: That's right.

MRS. W.: Now, Paul!

DR. P.: How's your financial position right now?

PAUL: Well, we get along. You know.

MRS. W.: Now, that is not true!

PAUL: Small savings, ah, about twenty bucks a week builds up, so . . .

MRS. W.: Paul . . .

PAUL: A lot of people don't do that well.

INT.: There's such a sudden flowering of the old lady here. It's conceivable that it's because she felt her point about the deductions was missed.

Dr. P.: I think she may have felt she wasn't getting across to me. I was trying to get at the facts and was being reasonably neutral about whose reality I was going to accept, especially since I didn't understand what was going on yet.

Int.: Is there one single reality you look for?

Dr. P.: We try to avoid imposing our own concept of reality on people. We're looking for points of agreement among their concepts. Somewhere, among all the different perceptions, is enough information so that if it's all out on the table, most of the family will arrive at a consensus.

Int.: Is that why you let the sister take the floor here?

Dr. P.: She was coming in with her reality, and I thought it was worthwhile. She obviously shared Mrs. Willy's fear that Paul would abandon her, which would mean that she would have to take her sister in. She wanted to make it clear to us that Mrs. Willy ought to be put away, so that she could go back home in peace.

Int.: When Mrs. Willy starts wailing about the car, you take her seriously and ask about it. Was the son driving her car?

Dr. P.: No. Both cars were out of commission, and he was driving a motorcycle. She was pretty upset, as it turned out, because the grease from it kept dripping down onto the front porch. She sounds wild and hysterical here, but she is really lodging a legitimate complaint against the son.

Int.: That's a pretty slippery statement the son makes. He doesn't tell you whether the car is in shape to drive, he just says, "I have transportation."

Dr. P.: He's continuing his secretiveness about his financial situation. He's trying to send me the message, "Look, I've got plenty of money, I can buy a car if I want, but let's not go into details."

Int.: There's a very striking thing here, and it happens many times during this interview. Whenever Mrs. Clapp starts to talk about her sister's craziness, Mrs. Willy jumps in, as if on cue, and demonstrates it.

Dr. P.: Isn't it beautiful? Every time the sister opened her mouth, it seemed that Mrs. Willy got crazier. We had a patient who started acting crazy as soon as he got to the hospital. We asked him why he was behaving this way, and he answered, "Isn't that what I'm supposed to do here?" People act very much the way they're expected to, and in this case the relatives wanted this woman to prove to us how crazy she was, so we'd put her away.

INT.: When you talk about families, it's almost as though you are saying, "These people give each other explicit instructions on how to behave."

DR. P.: I think they do. I think people fit whatever role the family expects them to. If they don't fill that role, the family puts such great pressure on them that they fill some other role, such as being a patient, that takes the burden off the family for putting them in the role they couldn't live up to in the first place. Putting the person in the hospital is a way the family absolves itself of guilt for making him sick. This declares to the world that he is incompetent by nature. Even psychiatrists, with their idea that there is something wrong with the basic ego strength of the person who becomes psychotic under pressure, are agreeing with the family on this. But we feel that anyone, given enough pressure, is capable of becoming psychotic.

INT.: This classification of people by ego strength is a way of saying that they all face essentially the same situation and that some can tolerate it and some can't. But obviously they don't face the same situation.

DR. P.: They certainly don't.

DR. P.: Ah, how does, how does it look for you to make the necessary money to be able to go back to school?

PAUL: Well, I don't think I'll be going back to school for a while, unless . . .

MRS. W.: Well . . .

PAUL: . . . something else happens, you know. It's quite distant.

MRS. W.: We're going to lose the home, there.

DR. P.: What's this something else that, ah, you're anticipating happening?

PAUL: Oh, I'm not anticipating, it's possible, that ah, you know, that I might inherit a million dollars, or something like this.

MRS. C. (*laughing*): He doesn't have much hopes of going back.

DR. P.: They took that program off the air.

PAUL: Uh-huh. You know, my mother might become more, ah, independent and decide that she wants to work and stuff like this.

MRS. C.: I think . . .

DR. P.: How do you feel about the fact that she's not working?

MRS. W.: He knows I'll never work.

PAUL: She never has, it's, ah, probably quite an adjustment for her, too, she always, she's seemed to have had a lot of difficulty.

MRS. W.: I just can't work.

DR. P.: Would you like for her to?

MRS. W.: They won't even take my application when I go. Penny's: "You had any experience?" "No." Ward's: "You had any experience?" "No."

DR. P.: Have you been to the State Employment Agency? See what they could work out for you?

MRS. C.: I don't think she could cope with a job at all because she's entirely too nervous and, and too upset about all these things.

DR. P. (*to Mrs. W.*): Do you feel you're too nervous to work?

PAUL: She, ah, she's been to, ah, the local State Board and they always give her housecleaning, or something.

MRS. W.: A cleaning job, twenty miles, and then I got to go way out here and clean one day.

DR. P.: How do you like it?

MRS. W.: Why, I didn't mind the work, but, it's nothin'—just, now, he's having to drive my car, and it's an old thing, the tires are just threadbare, brakes are gone, the windshield's cracked, it won't get a sticker on it, I know, and that's the truth. You can't deny that.

DR. P.: Ah, I'm wondering whether . . .

MRS. W. (*overlapping*): They're trying to paint a picture brighter than it is, I'll tell you the truth. (*Pause.*)

DR. P.: When the son says he can't go back to school unless "something else" happens, I was wondering if he had in mind putting his mother away and selling the house. I didn't know yet that he already had the house and was making money on it.

INT.: When he answers your question about what that "something else" might be, he puts it as something that could never in the world happen. In the next breath he equates this with his mother going out and working. "It's inconceivable that she could work," is what he's saying.

DR. P.: She eventually did go out and work.

INT.: Did you feel that helping her get a job would be the best way to get her on her feet?

DR. P.: Yes. At the same time, the most effective way to say to the family that Mrs. Willy is not necessarily lazy and crazy and incompetent is by talking to her about how she can get a job. This is the second time I've done this.

INT.: Is this typical of the way you operate, to give people some practical task?

DR. P.: Yes. We try to get people to work at whatever seems appropriate to them.

INT.: I take it that your assumption that this woman is capable of working is based on a therapeutic ideology, not on the basis of what she's delivered in the interview so far.

DR. P.: That's true, but you'll notice that every time I introduce this assumption, she immediately starts talking realistically.

INT.: It's a way of helping her to get to a better state of competence, whether she gets a job or not.

DR. P.: Yes. I don't think that her getting a job is as important as whether she cleans her kitchen or not.

INT.: You're really talking about functioning in general. It's not that you believe that people who go to work and earn money are better off than people who don't.

DR. P.: Mrs. Willy was complaining about not having money, so it was logical to think it might help matters if she were able to earn some herself. But you're right. We're taking the stand that functioning is better than not functioning, and the family is taking the stand that you get more rewards if you don't.

INT.: So just as she is sensibly talking to you about how to get a job, the family rushes in to say she's too sick.

DR. P.: Don't forget that we're fighting a battle right now as to whether this woman goes into the hospital or not. It was an unstated battle, and at this point I didn't realize how hard a battle it was, because I didn't know that the resident had already discussed hospitalization with them.

INT.: When you think someone should get a job, do you actively go out and find work for the person?

DR. P.: No. We make telephone calls to vocational rehabilitation services or send the person to the State Employment Agency, but that's all we do right now.

INT.: Do you have access in the community to jobs, or some organization of employers who are willing to cooperate?

DR. P.: No, we haven't investigated that possibility.

INT.: I should think it would be a problem. A woman who has been in an institution and has no experience would find it hard to get a job.

DR. P.: She got one. It was a part-time job as a cleaning woman, but she got it and was very proud of it. It gave her some pin money to buy some things for herself.

INT.: How long after this interview did she get it?

DR. P.: About two months later.

DR. P. (*to Mrs. W.*): How long has it looked this bad to you?

MRS. W.: Well, I guess it's been happening all the time, but I didn't wake up to the fact till a year ago that . . .

DR. P. (*overlapping*): A year ago you started realizing what a terrible situation . . .

MRS. W. (*overlapping*): I woke up, I woke up to the fact that I would have been starved to death now if it hadn't been for Paul . . .

MRS. C.: But you've got Paul.

MRS. W.: . . . because the Welfare here told me they don't put women my age on welfare, now what they do, I don't know. A woman fifty years old can't get a job, I don't know what they do here.

INT.: You don't say to Mrs. Willy, "How long has it *been* bad?" but "How long has it *looked* bad?"

DR. P.: This was the moment at which I decided that Mrs. Willy's perception of the family's financial situation was not totally realistic. I began looking at it as a symptom, whereas before it had been an open question. Now I felt it was important to find out what had taken place to precipitate this symptom.

INT.: Do you typically try to find the provoking situation for a symptom?

DR. P.: Always, if it's a recent symptom that's causing the trouble. Sometimes the symptom isn't a new one, but something has happened to make the family less tolerant of an old symptom. That can be a more difficult situation. The family has been rewarding the patient for having a certain symptom, and all of a sudden it's because of the symptom that he has to go. But Mrs. Willy did have a new symptom, which was her constant distress about how badly off they were. Once we had clarified that, our interest would be to see what change had taken place that had made it necessary for her to act this way.

INT.: You are placing responsibility for the symptom on the whole situation.

DR. P.: Well, she didn't develop it in a vacuum.

INT.: You say that so automatically. It shows what a new generation you belong to. For hundreds of years, when people had a symptom it was thought that something had gone wrong inside them. You assume something entirely different, that a symptom comes about as a way of handling a change.

DR. P.: Exactly. We believe that a symptom develops as a result of some change that produces a family crisis in which there has to be a shift of roles. You could say that Mrs. Willy developed her symptom not only because she had a childhood predisposition toward it which was reinforced by her experience with several husbands who had let her down, but because something had happened in her relationship with Paul that made her begin to doubt his ability or desire to support her.

INT.: How would you describe this in terms of a shift in roles?

DR. P.: Well, the event that led to the shift in this case was the mother's turning the house over to the son. This led each one to have new expectations in regard to the other. The mother, in return for the house, expected the son to be the economically good husband she never had. The son accepted responsibility for the mother as an unfortunate liability that went with the house, but one he was willing to accept as long as she kept house for him and didn't get in his way. The other relatives shared Paul's expectations of his mother. What Paul didn't realize was that in his attempt to play down his financial success so as not to arouse jealousy, he also caused Mrs. Willy to believe that they were about to be destitute. So she went back on her part of the bargain as a message to him that he wasn't keeping up his part by supporting her. The only role she saw that would provide her with security was for her to be crazy, totally helpless, and then everyone would gather around and do all the things for her that needed to be done. The result was that they tried to put her into the hospital. And I don't think she was really against it. She had pretty well given up on the idea that Paul was going to help her, and the hospital, which she had experienced before, was a fairly nice place where meals and clothes were provided and you didn't have to run naked in the streets. What we tried to do, then, was to get Paul to fill certain aspects of the role Mrs. Willy was expecting him to fill. We tried to get him to keep her posted on the financial situation and give her a few dollars a week to spend on herself. He was willing to go along with this, especially after we pointed out that it would cost him money to have her in the hospital, which came as a surprise to him. We got her, in turn, to live up to what he wanted. So it all worked out. But here, at this early date, we didn't have the necessary facts to piece together how Paul was contributing to Mrs. Willy's craziness. It would have been inappropriate to turn suddenly on Paul and say, "What have you done to your mother to make her act like this?" I was just trying to pinpoint it: when did it start, what led up to it?

INT.: You wouldn't, as some people do, start by taking a family history and get the information that way?

DR. P.: I am taking a family history.

INT.: I mean a more formal kind of history.

DR. P.: Sometimes, if we're trying to get to the basic problem and things are confused, we will go back and sift out, one by one, how they met, when they got married, and so on. Or if we can't get people to admit to any problems at all, we will take a formal history, but then it rather becomes a framework within which to watch them interact.

> DR. P.: Well, then I see one thing we can do right off, which is to help you find a job. But, ah, meanwhile, I mean, if you're too nervous today to get a job, maybe you'll feel like getting one tomorrow. Ah, now, what did you come to the hospital for today?

DR. P.: Again the same maneuver, treating Mrs. Willy as if she were perfectly capable of functioning, and expecting it of her.

INT.: When you say "we" will help you find a job, do you mean your outfit?

DR. P.: I meant us and the son and the sister. This statement is for them too. It involves them in our joint effort to help Mrs. Willy go to work.

INT.: Then comes this remarkable statement, addressed to a woman who has just been brought in raving, "If you are too nervous today to get a job, maybe you'll feel like getting one tomorrow."

DR. P.: I was making it clear that we felt her disability was only temporary.

INT.: It's using a framework in an interesting way. Here they are, putting her in a hospital, and within that framework you persistently talk to her as if she came there looking for a job.

DR. P.: Well, that's the way she's acting now. In these five minutes she has changed from a mental patient to a housewife looking for a job.

INT.: Would you say this to any patient, or have you had enough indication that she can be rational?

DR. P.: I think we say this to most patients. We've used this technique with even the most psychotic patients with good results. Of course, it works better with hysterics, and this may be why Mrs. Willy responded to it so well. There was more a hysterical quality to her than a psychotic quality. Her craziness was so much in response to what was going on, and so obviously under her control, that I had the feeling that she was a wild hysteric playing a role.

INT.: You ask, "Why did you come to the hospital today?" Was that to Mrs. Willy?

DR. P.: It was to all of them. I'm trying not to say "you all" since I left the South, but I should have here.

INT.: Is there some reason why you wouldn't ask that question until this far along in the interview?

DR. P.: If I'd asked it at first, I would have been told, "Because Mrs. Willy is crazy," and we wouldn't get anywhere. Now, even though I have agreed that she has a slight symptom, it's a little clearer that she is not as sick as they thought and that they are more involved than they thought.

INT.: Would you use this question as an opening with another kind of family?

DR. P.: With people who aren't this verbal, we might, or when it's not clear who the patient is. In general we avoid it, because it puts us under the handicap of having the problem stated in a prejudiced form from the beginning.

INT.: So when you ask it this far along, it's not for information.

DR. P.: No, it's to make clear that the reasons they thought they had for coming here are not good reasons. She is not now the bag of psychosis they came to deposit.

INT.: It would be very hard for them to say she is, after you have reframed this situation this way.

DR. P.: That's right. We are putting them in a somewhat difficult position. From this point on, it is perfectly all right if Mrs. Willy goes through a whole lot of psychotic behavior, because we have shown that her psychotic behavior is related to the way she is treated.

INT.: Are you always able to get such a good first five minutes?

DR. P.: It's what we work for. It creates a problem too. In one of the few cases that we hospitalized, the patient, who came in with his wife, was doing fine as long as we were in the room structuring him and supporting him, the way we were doing with Mrs. Willy. As soon as we walked out, he started throwing ashtrays, took off all his clothes, and tried to swing from the microphone in the ceiling. His wife refused to take him home and in the hospital he displayed all the symptoms he'd ever had or ever seen. After all, the way to act in a place for crazy people is crazy. It's expected of you. The people in the hospital encourage this without realizing it. They focus on pathology and expect the patients to show it to them. And the patients do.

INT.: Do you feel you lost ground with this man because you put him in the hospital?

DR. P.: I think putting him in the hospital encouraged him to be crazy. On the other hand, he was so frightened of what he might do, on the basis of the perception of the people around him, that he was afraid to go home, and his wife was afraid to have him. The man had become violent once when his wife left him briefly twenty-two years before, and he was in the hospital for three years after that. Since then, he has never been violent. Yet she is constantly expecting him to be, and has subtly reminded him every day for the past twenty years that he was in the hospital for three years because he was uncontrollable and she certainly hopes he doesn't do that again today. This latest crisis occurred when his mother was removed to a nursing home under circumstances which he couldn't prevent but felt very guilty about. The day his mother was taken to the home, he was found wandering around the golf course at two o'clock in the morning, and his wife brought him to the hospital. I think the whole thing would have cleared up very satisfactorily as soon as the mother became settled in the home if it hadn't been that everybody around him kept saying, "Remember what happened twenty years ago, you might get violent again."

INT.: This is such a clear turning point in the interview that I'd like to look at it a little more. It's possible to see therapy in terms of an encounter or conflict between the therapy group and the family group, and hypothesize that out of this struggle comes some kind of change. Here, the relatives have come in with this woman with an inclination to dump her and the inclination of the therapy group is not to have her dumped. Now contact has been made and you have managed to re-frame the situation. There's not nearly as much wrong as they thought, they are involved in it too, and it is probably temporary anyway. Then comes this "Why did you bring her to the hospital?" which makes it hard for them to insist on dumping her. What is unusual about your group is that the conflict between you and the family is so evident. Most therapists don't have a clear crusading purpose the way you do. They can't formulate their goals as neatly as you can, because their goals are to produce a change without articulating just what that is. But all you say is, "We want to keep this woman from going into the hospital." I assume you have some deeper aims in mind, but phrasing it this way at first would give you enormous strength, I should think.

DR. P.: It does, but it's not just a surface action. We can't try to even up responsibilities and work for better functioning if one member of the family is in the hospital weaving baskets and the others are home feeling they have nothing to do with his problem. Keeping people out of the hospital is not just a display of virtuosity, it's basic to our whole approach to treatment.

PAUL: Well, we didn't come here, ah, directly, we went to Dr. Clark, a psychiatrist over on [*street*] . . .

DR. P.: Yeah.

PAUL: . . . and he talked to my mother and my aunt and I for a while, and then he suggested that she be admitted to a hospital for . . .

DR. P.: Um-hm.

PAUL: . . . intensive treatment and, ah, he suggested probably that, since he thought it would take quite some time for my mother to become better, that a state-supported hospital would be, ah, more ideal.

DR. P.: How do you feel about the fact that Dr. Gray and I, ah, think that we can do it otherwise, or would like to give it a try?

MRS. C.: Do it what?

DR. P.: How do you feel about Dr. Gray's feeling and my feeling that we'd like to give it a try keeping her out of the hospital?

MRS. C.: Keeping her *out?*

DR. P.: Yes.

MRS. C.: Well, that would be wonderful, if it's possible.

PAUL: Yeah, that's nice, ah (*Mrs. W. talking in background*), but I was under the impression Dr. Gray wanted to put her in [*state hospital*]. That's, he mentioned that to us, didn't he?

DR. P.: Well, now, let's find out what you want to do.

MRS. C.: Well, we don't want . . .

DR. P. (*simultaneously*): Do you want to put her in [*state hospital*]?

MRS. C.: No! Definitely!

PAUL (*overlapping*): Well, I think the ideal thing would be to, ah, give her a few tranquilizers and let her stay at home and, if that would help her, but I don't, frankly, I don't think that tranquilizers would change her . . .

MRS. C. (*overlapping*): I thought she would probably need these, ah . . .

PAUL: . . . attitude, or anything like that.

MRS. C.: . . . shock treatments, but he says no.

DR. P.: Dr. Gray was the admitting psychiatrist.

INT.: And you were hopefully bringing him in on your side.

DR. P.: I didn't know that he had given them a different opinion.

INT.: Who was Dr. Clark?

DR. P.: The private psychiatrist who told them that the woman needed to be admitted.

INT.: When the son quotes the psychiatrist as saying that it would take some time for his mother to get better, is he implying that private therapy would be too expensive because it would take too long?

DR. P.: He's implying that he doesn't expect her ever to get well and that he wants her put away. As he so delicately puts it, "a state-supported hospital would be more ideal."

INT.: Then you make the statement about keeping her out of the hospital, and they go into a flurry.

DR. P.: I think that was the first indication they'd had of what I was up to. Suddenly the battle was out in the open.

INT.: That's a classic example of social hypocrisy, there. The aunt says, "How wonderful," when she means, "How dreadful," and the son says the ideal thing would be for his mother to stay at home when he has just said the ideal thing would be for her to be committed.

DR. P.: He says it quite sarcastically. He sounds very doubtful about the tranquilizers because she had been going to a day hospital for most of that year and getting various medications that didn't help very much. Of course, I didn't know this at the time.

INT.: And they didn't tell you. But I doubt that you'd have gotten even that ambivalent mixture of "How wonderful it would be, but—" if you had started right out by declaring your intention.

DR. P.: I doubt it too. A lot had happened in these five minutes.

PAUL (*overlapping*): I'd prefer to avoid the hospital, ah (*Mrs. W. trying to break in*), it's possible, ah, apparently it does—see, the psychiatrist, Dr. Clark . . .

DR. P.: I'm a psychiatrist, too.

PAUL: Yeah, well . . .

MRS. C.: (*Inaudible phrase.*) He said definitely she would have to come.

PAUL (*simultaneously*): He directed us here, so there seems to be a conflict.

MRS. W.: Does that mean, ah . . .

DR. P.: No, there's no conflict of opinion, ah, at all about this. We only take patients that everybody feels should be in the hospital. Those are the only ones we bother to, that we even see.

MRS. C.: Um-hm.

DR. P.: They don't, they don't call us about any others.

INT.: What do you mean when you say to them, "Let's find out what you want to do"?

DR. P.: "Let's find out what neurotic reasons you had for wanting to get rid of her." I realized that I couldn't bring the admitting psychiatrist in on my side, so I was shifting my technique. I began to browbeat them into refuting the ugly idea that they wanted her in a state institution.

INT.: And you go on to indicate that it really isn't a conflict at all since you only take people whom everybody else feels should be in the hospital. That's such a nice piece of logic.

DR. P. (*cont.*): Ah, our team consists of me, a social worker, and a nurse.

MRS. W.: You mean that's all there is here or in (*inaudible words*).

DR. P. (*overlapping*): No, in this particular unit. We take as many patients as the, each of the other units of the hospital, we keep them out of the hospital. We do have beds to put people in the hospital if this is necessary.

MRS. C.: Well, that's what Dr., ah, what's his name?

DR. P. (*overlapping*): Ah, for quite some time we have not found it necessary to put anybody in the hospital.

MRS. C.: Well, that sounds wonderful.

DR. P.: And we've managed to get—well, I'll tell you this, that I don't guarantee you any results, of course, but the last patient we had whom we saw last Wednesday, he came in, he was unable to talk, he was shaking all over, and couldn't talk with us at all. On Thursday he was back at work for the first time in two months.

MRS. C.: Wonderful.

DR. P.: And on Saturday, he left with his family to go on a weekend fishing trip. He's doing fine now.

INT.: Do you usually explain your project to people?

DR. P.: Ordinarily we don't. The family may be ambivalent about keeping someone at home, but they don't usually bring it up and we don't usually ask. We don't like to get into an open power struggle with the family over it.

INT.: What happens when you do?

DR. P.: If we win, as we did here, it's all right. But in the cases where we've gotten into a power struggle and didn't win, we've had serious difficulty. We have to present a tremendous aura of confidence and strength to people. If we lose the initial battle over the hospital, we are no longer the strong authority figures they can fall back on and we lose ground.

INT.: Have you worked out any sort of calculated technique for preparing a family not to put the patient in the hospital?

DR. P.: We play it by ear. We've found that the best course is to express no doubt at all, to act absolutely sure of ourselves, but to sympathize with the real difficulties of having the patient at home. Most of the time the families come in desperate and ready to accept whatever the expert recommends. And often the family is delighted to take the person home. But when there has already been experience of hospitalization, or when other authorities have told the family that hospitalization is necessary, as they did here, we have to be particularly persuasive. That's why I went into such detail about the last patient we had.

INT.: It's a nice positive emphasis. So many forms of therapy start by saying, "I had a patient who did well." Usually the framework of the office and the waiting list does this. What was impressive here was the explicitness of your statement. It shows that you've worked with hypnosis. With hypnosis you don't have to persuade the person that he is going to be hypnotized, but you have to persuade him that it's a good possibility.

DR. P.:   I've done some work with hypnosis. But with this kind of therapy, we feel we have to back up our promises. We don't feel we can say, after ten minutes, "You go home and everything will be better." We have to effect some change, or inspire some hope for change, around the family issues. It doesn't have to be a big change; it can be a small one which we make look big.

INT.:   It's like any form of brief therapy. You need to show evidence of a change quickly.

DR. P.:   It's part of crisis work too. When I do long-term therapy in my private practice, there's no need to effect immediate change. I wouldn't succeed if I tried. If people aren't in a crisis, they are not going to listen to an expert tell them how to run their lives. But these families do arrive in a state of crisis, and it's not only that you are expected to do something right away, you've *got* to do something right away or you'll miss your chance.

INT.:   Timing seems always to be important in therapy, even when the therapist has all the time in the world. It's not so much a matter of how quickly you can make a change but of whether you can make it at the right time.

DR. P.:   I think you're right.

INT.:   There's one other aspect of your work which should give you a particular advantage. It comes out in your phrasing: "We only take patients that everybody feels should be in the hospital. Those are the only ones we bother to see." This immediately puts what you are trying to do in a special category, as though keeping the person out of the hospital were some kind of heroic achievement. Then when you go on to say how successful you are, there's less chance that they'll resist you, because you're being successful against odds. This way of putting it could offer an irresistible appeal to some families to join you. One of the things about the psychotic family is that, as villainous as they are, they are so protective. If they see you standing alone against the world, they'll join you to protect you. Your procedure is unique enough to set you against the majority of your profession. If you can get a family to join you in this crusade, they will have to improve because they are part of the crusade.

Dr. P.: We've thought a lot about this question of missionary zeal. At first we used to get very enthusiastic about this new thing we were trying to do, and it was transmitted to the families, with mixed results. We've calmed down a bit now, and we've been wondering how important a factor it is.

Int.: It's not a minor aspect. One thing that seems true of faith healing is that it works best when there's opposition to the faith healer.

Dr. P.: I do think we tend to make people feel that they are part of a scientific experiment of some magnitude which goes against established practice.

mrs. w.: What'd you do to him?

dr. p. (*laughing*): We found out what the devil was going wrong in the family to make him need to get sick. I can see one thing, right now—ah, I think there's a general feeling that if you were well taken care of some place where you didn't have to worry about anything, then the rest of your family could go about their business without having to worry about you.

mrs. c.: But it *isn't* that we *don't* want to have her locked up . . .

dr. p. (*overlapping*): No. No.

mrs. c.: . . . if there's any way to . . .

dr. p. (*simultaneously*): No, what I'm saying is, what . . .

mrs. c.: . . . to make her well so she could come back and be at home, that's what we want.

mrs. w.: Did you hear about . . .

dr. p. (*interrupting, to Mrs. W.*): What I'm saying is that your family is very worried about you . . .

mrs. c.: Well, yes.

mrs. w.: Do you, you don't (*inaudible phrase*).

dr. p. (*overlapping*): . . . and they would like for you to be some place where you were well taken care of.

mrs. w.: You don't have those hot baths and things any more, here, huh?

paul: Well, ah . . .

mrs. c.: Well, we want what's the best . . .

paul (*overlapping*): I know this . . .

mrs. c.: . . . so she can get well and be at home.

INT.: You say, "We found out what the devil was going wrong in the family to make him need to get sick." This is your first statement that it is a family problem. And you phrase it in such a way that they can't resist it. This is probably a brand-new idea to them, but they can't say, "There's nothing wrong with our family," because you're talking about some other family.

DR. P.: I didn't want to alienate them. I was still trying to sell them on our approach. Also, I do go on to their family in the next statement.

INT.: With such an appearance of logic. You say, "Now I can see one thing," as if you were about to finish, "one thing wrong with *your* family." But you don't. Instead, you go into a long "ah" and start talking about how they want to see that Mrs. Willy is well taken care of. They could make the leap and say, "So that's what he thinks is wrong with us," but it's framed so benevolently that they can't be sure.

DR. P.: I may have been hesitating because I wanted to point out some obvious problem and couldn't think of one.

INT.: What you do here seems to be a common technique in therapy. You manage to side with everybody and at the same time keep out of coalitions with individuals. Here you're rephrasing the family's desire to get rid of Mrs. Willy in the same benevolent terms they would use: "They want you to be where you'll be well taken care of." You could have sided with Mrs. Willy against them by saying, "What you really want to do is to get rid of Mrs. Willy," and they would have become antagonistic. Instead, you appear to go along with them in such a way that they have to refute you, but they can't take exception because you are on their side.

DR. P.: Yes. After that they couldn't pressure for hospitalization without making it clear that what they wanted was not to have to worry about her any more.

INT.: And the aunt makes that terrible slip: "It isn't that we don't want to have her locked up."

DR. P.: I was kind enough not to take her up on it. But that effectively put an end to the issue of hospitalization.

DR. P. (*overlapping*): Well, the thing is this, the thing is, we . . .

MRS. W. (*overlapping*): Do they have cells and things where they lock people up here?

DR. P.: We can put you in the hospital . . .

MRS. C. (*overlapping*): See, she has that fear.

DR. P.: We can put you in the hospital if we have to, there are no hot baths, no locked doors.

MRS. W. (*overlapping*): Do they have cells?

DR. P.: No, no cells.

MRS. W.: Thanks.

DR. P.: No cells, the rest of the hospital is just like this. You wear your own clothes, everything's very nice. Ah, the thing is . . .

MRS. W.: I ain't gonna have my own clothes.

DR. P.: . . . we'd like to give it a try of keeping her out of the hospital.

MRS. W.: I ain't gonna have no clothes to wear.

DR. P.: What this is going to involve—of course, it's going to be far, far cheaper, to keep her out of the hospital, our charges are very, very small for our services, the reason being that, ah . . .

MRS. W. (*overlapping*): Do people have to pay it?

DR. P.: . . . we try to encourage people to stay out of the hospital.

MRS. W.: Do, ah, the relatives . . .

DR. P.: The hospital is much too crowded and it turns out people get in the hospital, they stay for months and, ah (*sighs*), ah, it takes a month or so for people to get accustomed to the hospital enough so that they can start getting better. If you keep them out of the hospital, they can start getting better immediately.

MRS. C.: Well, it sounds wonderful.

PAUL: Well, ah . . .

DR. P.: You're skeptical.

PAUL: Well, ah, as far as I'm concerned, ah, it seems to me that Mother will probably worry, you know, all the time, but lately, it's been kind of hard on me and everyone around home . . .

MRS. C.: She gives . . .

PAUL: . . . but she hasn't been able to do anything, ah . . .

MRS. W. (*overlapping*): I don't even cook or anything.

PAUL: . . . take care of the house, ah, the garden or anything like this, and . . .

MRS. W. (*tearfully, overlapping*): He hasn't come home . . .

PAUL (*overlapping*): . . . it's gotten to be quite a burden . . .

MRS. W.: . . . he ain't even eating anything.

PAUL: . . . and I figure if you could get her adjusted to assuming some kind of responsibility, it would help a lot.

MRS. W.: Do the relatives have to pay for them to be in here now-adays? How are they going to pay it and make the expenses?

DR. P.: Well, that's what I'm saying, you're not going to have to go to the hospital.

MRS. C.: Wouldn't you like it that way?

MRS. W. (*overlapping*): These people that are poor, how can they afford to pay for their folks to be in here?

DR. P.: If you're poor enough, you don't have to, but you're not poor enough. You all have got plenty of money.

MRS. C.: Her whole concern is about money, that, that seems to be the whole thing.

MRS. W.: Paul just can't make it, that's all, he just don't have the money.

MRS. C.: He'll be sending you home.

MRS. W.: Oh, my, it's always (*inaudible phrase*).

MRS. C.: Does it?

MRS. W.: (*Inaudible phrase.*)

MRS. C.: No, if there's any way to keep her out and get her well, we want that (*Mrs. W. overlapping, inaudible phrase*) he mentioned [*distant state hospital*], but *that* is *out,* definitely.

INT.: Mrs. Willy was apparently just getting the point that she wasn't going to be locked up.

DR. P.: Well, she didn't know quite what was happening. She wanted to find out whether the hospital had changed since she had been there.

INT.: She was in the same place some years before?

DR. P.: Yes. That didn't come out till later in the interview, but it would be an important fact for us to know. Families who haven't used the hospital before are much easier to deal with, no matter how severe their problems are. In this case, they had experience with hospitals, they expected hospitalization, and this was another reason why I had a hard time selling them on our approach.

INT.: Why did you mention how inexpensive the treatment was going to be? Do you often use this as a selling point?

DR. P.: No. Here I was very anxious to get them to cooperate with us, so I was being pretty direct and a little bit desperate. But most families do react pleasantly when they find out that it's so inexpensive. The most we charge is ten dollars a week. I think they are more willing to use our services if they know this.

INT.: I have the impression that you caught yourself because you found yourself painting too pretty a picture of the hospital.

DR. P.: It's a fact that hospitals are too nice these days. It makes our job that much harder.

DR. P. (*overlapping*): Okay, the first, first step . . .

MRS. W.: Well, I . . .

DR. P.: First step, find out what's going on, because if we can solve the problem that's making her have to act like this, then she'll have it (*inaudible phrase*).

MRS. W. (*overlapping*): I tell you, if you'd go to our house and just looked around, you'd know.

DR. P.: Okay, shall we come out tomorrow?

MRS. W.: You going to come over to visit?

DR. P.: Would you rather that we come out tomorrow to look at your house, or Friday? I think it might be best if, ah, you came in tomorrow morning. (*To Paul.*) What hours do you work?

PAUL: Eh, tomorrow, from nine till, whenever we get off, usually . . .

DR. P.: Okay.

PAUL: . . . from 5:30 to 7:30.

DR. P.: Okay. Can you come in at eight and be a little bit late to work tomorrow morning, then on Friday . . .

MRS. W. (*interrupting*): Oh, he can't do that.

DR. P.: I think it's quite necessary.

PAUL: Possibly my sister could bring her in.

MRS. W.: Well, her battery won't work.

PAUL (*simultaneously*): I have an older sister who lives out that way.

DR. P. (*to Paul*): I think, I think that you're as involved in this as your mother is, at least. I think, I think . . .

MRS. W. (*overlapping*): What do you mean, he's got . . .

PAUL (*overlapping*): You want me to start missing work over it, huh?

MRS. C.: You mean, bring her in here? Is that what you mean?

DR. P.: What I'm saying is, if you're very interested in your mother getting well . . .

MRS. W. (*overlapping*): But he can't stop work . . .

DR. P.: . . . we will ask you to make a few sacrifices for the moment, for the . . .

MRS. W. (*overlapping*): That's all he's ever done, is make sacrifices . . .

DR. P.: Ah . . .

MRS. W.: He can't miss his work.

PAUL (*overlapping*): Oh, I can take off the whole day, it's . . .

DR. P.: Well, I don't think that's necessary, but I think if you can, if you and your mother, and your sister . . .

MRS. W.: Why come in again?

DR. P.: . . . can come in at, ah, eight o'clock in the morning . . .

MRS. C.: Mm. Well . . .

MRS. W.: She can't do that . . .

DR. P.: Well, if you can't come in . . .

MRS. W. (*overlapping*): She's a widow, she has to . . .

DR. P.: . . . bring your mother in at, ah . . .

PAUL: All right, I'll bring her in.

MRS. W.: Why, why in the morning? What's you gonna do then?

DR. P.: Then on Friday, we'll go out to the home and try to arrange it at a time when, ah, this, this—(*Mrs. C. interrupts.*)

INT.: I take it you always make a home visit.

DR. P.: Yes. We feel that we can get more information that way than from several hours in the office.

INT.: You included these visits right from the beginning of the project?

DR. P.: Yes. We're sold on the value of one, though not necessarily more than one. We use the home visit to get a quick assessment of the situation, not usually as the setting of an interview. That's why we try to go out right away, at the beginning. Also, the home visits tie in with our notions of functioning. When we're trying to get someone to clean up a kitchen, we can talk with authority. We know what's in it, where it's messy, what has to be done.

INT.: I should think the fact that people know you're coming out to see their kitchen would put some pressure on them to clean it up.

DR. P.: Sometimes. We told Mrs. Willy during the next session that we wanted her to clean her kitchen, and our impending visit, which was planned for the day after, had some effect. At least Gloria, her daughter, was out there and they were making a stab at the mess.

INT.: Home is admittedly a big feature of this interview. What did you find out about it?

DR. P.: It was a very attractive home, which looked as if it had been well kept until recently. This was a pretty good indication of the duration of her dysfunction. The visit is also a check on the reality of what people tell us. Mrs. Willy insisted the place was hopeless, but it wasn't, not by our standards. It was messy but not unbearably so, and the yard was overgrown, but there was nothing that a little mowing and weeding wouldn't set to rights. On the other hand, she was perfectly right about her clothes. We saw every garment the woman owned and they really were in shreds. She talked about starving, and we found that there actually was very little food in the refrigerator or on the shelves.

INT.: Why did you choose that particular moment to bring up the home visit?

DR. P.: I didn't bring it up, Mrs. Willy did. She said if we came out, we'd see how hopeless things were. So I said, "Okay, we'll be out tomorrow."

INT.: It's such a rapid sequence. Mrs. Willy starts off again about how terrible things are at home, if you could only see, and you take her up on it as if it were a literal invitation to come out. It's such a sudden shift, it sobers her right up. Then you cut off any argument by saying, "Would you rather we came out to your house tomorrow or Friday?" Then you shift again and say that it might be best if the family came in the next morning. You hadn't prepared them for this at all.

DR. P.: That's right. I was working on them to come in. I remember one case where the man refused to come in, so we said, "Well, if you don't want to come in, shall we come out?" and he said, "Oh, no, don't come out." And we said, "All right, then you'll come in?" He said, "No, I won't come in," and we said, "Okay, take your choice, shall we come out to your house or do you want to come in?" And he said, "Okay, I'll be in."

INT.: It's the technique of giving people alternatives that assume the real issue is settled. I notice that you don't bother to deal with the mother's objections but go on working out the matter of the next meeting with the son.

DR. P.: If I'd stopped to listen to her, I wouldn't have gotten the main issue settled, the issue of whether she was going into the hospital or not. The son was the one who would be bringing her in, so he was the one I had to work on.

INT.: He's trying to hand the job to his sister.

DR. P.: That's why I say to him, "You're as involved as your mother." His response is, "Do you want me to start missing work over it?" So I ask him if he's interested in getting his mother well. If he can't miss work, it means he doesn't want his mother to get well.

INT.: You put a lot of pressure on him there.

DR. P.: I'm just trying to settle the routine business we generally get through in the first session.

INT.: You also get in the first direct statement that he's a patient too.

MRS. C.: They want to talk with you tomorrow, is that it, yes, trying to get her started.

MRS. W.: You come out there you'll know, the things are gone (*starting to cry*).

DR. P.: We'll come out.

MRS. C.: Ah . . .

DR. P.: Now this . . .

MRS. C.: Now, I could come in if it wasn't quite so early.

MRS. W. (*overlapping, weeping*): You'll see that, we're gonna starve to death . . .

DR. P.: If it wasn't quite so early, your nephew . . .

MRS. C.: He . . .

DR. P.: . . . would have to take off more work, and I'd rather that he has to take off as little as possible.

MRS. C. (*overlapping*): You could come earlier in the morning than you could in the afternoon, do you mean, Paul? Do you think they'd let you off in the morning, and you go back in the afternoon? I . . .

DR. P.: Well, see, if he came in at nine, at eight . . .

PAUL: I'm sure they'd let me off.

DR. P.: . . . see, you'd be an hour late to work, which I'm sure you could arrange.

MRS. C.: Yeah.

DR. P.: For something like this.

PAUL: Uh-huh.

DR. P.: I'm sure . . .

MRS. W. (*overlapping, crying*): Things didn't used to be like that there . . .

DR. P.: Where?

MRS. C.: Well, now, I . . .

MRS. W.: At home, they didn't used to, it's hard, you couldn't even *believe* it! I mean . . .

MRS. C.: You know what's happening, she can't keep up the house. He works all day and . . .

MRS. W. (*overlapping*): It's *terrible!*

MRS. C.: And then . . .

MRS. W.: I've never *seen* anything like it!

MRS. C.: She can't get the dishes washed and she gets her clothes throwed around and that sort of a scramble of all these things in the house messed up that . . .

MRS. W. (*overlapping*): Why don't you just come out there tomorrow and . . .

MRS. C.: . . . confusion of clothes and dishes . . .

MRS. W.: Paul . . .

MRS. C.: That's right.

DR. P.: We're going to have to be seeing you every day for the next week or so.

MRS. W.: They just can't bring me in, my boy just can't do it, he's got to work, he'll lose his job.

DR. P.: We, we'll arrange it, we'll arrange it.

MRS. C. (*overlapping*): Honey, maybe Gloria can get you in here . . .

MRS. W.: Gloria, she don't have . . .

DR. P.: I don't think it's a matter, Mrs. Willy, of just you coming in, I think it's a matter of you *and* your son coming in.

INT.: Mrs. Willy really starts to go here.

DR. P.: She hadn't been able to get our attention at all. She had to scream pretty loud to get it.

INT.: I thought it might be a reaction to the cold way the sister talks about "getting her started." It's the way you'd talk about getting a patient started in the old days.

DR. P.: That may be. If you notice, it's the sister who takes the cue from Mrs. Willy this time: "She can't keep house, she can't cook."

INT.: It's almost as if they were trying to block you. And the sister is still insisting that there's only one patient, when she says that Gloria could bring Mrs. Willy in. You counter her pretty sharply on that.

DR. P.: I sometimes think our most successful therapeutic maneuver was getting Mrs. Clapp out of the way and back to her home.

MRS. C.: Well, if Paul can't get off every day . . .

MRS. W. (*overlapping*): He—well, now listen . . .

MRS. C.: . . . we could put it in reverse. If I could come one day and he the next, would that help you, Paul?

MRS. W.: Clear from [*sister's town*]?

DR. P. (*to Mrs. C.*): I don't know how you're involved in this.

MRS. W. (*weeping*): I know you don't, there's nothing like it in the city of Denver.

DR. P. (*overlapping*): This is what we want to find out. (*To Mrs. C.*) Look, how do you . . .

MRS. W. (*overlapping*): There's *absolutely* nothing like it!

DR. P.: . . . what's your contacts with your sister?

MRS. C.: She's my sister.

DR. P.: I know, but how often do you see her?

MRS. W.: Why, she's been coming up every little bit.

MRS. C. (*simultaneously*): Well, I've been coming up every, every two weeks, always I come in and see her, on Sundays, I'll come in on Sundays, and there've been a few times that I've come in on Monday afternoon.

DR. P.: Yeah. Yeah.

MRS. C.: And I come in and pick up the clothes . . .

MRS. W. (*overlapping*): I don't know what's going to happen . . .

MRS. C.: . . . and straighten the house because that's the thing that upsets her.

DR. P.: What do you think's going on?

MRS. W. (*screaming*): It's a *terrible* situation that's ever been known in the city of Denver.

MRS. C.: See, she gets hysterical about it.

MRS. W.: It is, you'll admit it, when you're, when you see, it, it just, *happened,* just, I don't know, it's just gotta, everything got out of hand.

MRS. C.: She just got where she felt like she couldn't cope with this financial thing, and . . .

MRS. W.: It ain't that now.

MRS. C.: . . . that's why Paul gave up his, gave up his going back to college and stayed . . .

MRS. W.: (*Inaudible phrase, weeping.*)

MRS. C.: . . . and stayed to, to get this job, see . . .

DR. P.: Here's the Kleenex, Mrs. Willy.

MRS. C.: . . . and to try to stay there. Then . . .

MRS. W.: It's just *inconceivable!*

MRS. C. (*overlapping*): Then, it seemed like that didn't help, see, I mean, even though he meets all the bills, and all that, she just can't seem to realize that he . . .

MRS. W. (*interrupting*): Well, he can't meet 'em.

MRS. C.: . . . that he is taking care of these things . . .

MRS. W.: No, he isn't. You're painting a picture that isn't true.

MRS. C. (*overlapping*): . . . and she gets hysterical about these things. There for a few months now, she was, she would cook his meals, and she would keep things up pretty good, but she's just getting to the point, more and more she just gets so nervous and hysterical about all this that, that she just gets up late lots of times in the morning, she never dresses all day long, she just walks around the house and goes on and I don't know what, all to herself all day, about these bills and things that are piling up in her mind.

MRS. W. (*overlapping*): Well, it's the most *terrible,* I just can't believe it, because . . .

MRS. C.: Because she can't wash the dishes and she doesn't clean the house and she doesn't put the clothes away and she just throws things everywhere and then the house is terrible and then when I can go up and straighten things up, well, when I come back, it's in the same mess, see.

MRS. W. (*overlapping*): She always does what she can.

DR. P. (*to Mrs. C.*): What's your financial situation?

MRS. C.: Well, I'm a widow and I have a [*business*] in my home and that is it, and I just make bills meet.

MRS. W.: She's just barely making it.

INT.: When you ask the sister what her contacts with Mrs. Willy are, it sounds as if this was the point at which you had decided that she shouldn't be a part of this.

DR. P.: I had decided that the sister was probably one of those people who enter the picture after the crisis with the prime function of continuing the crisis and encouraging the symptom. In almost every family where crisis occurs, there seems to be somebody whose job it is to stand there and fan the flames. It is usually somebody who handles the crisis by taking sides in such a way as to make things worse, and then deciding that so-and-so has to go to the hospital. The uncle who came up and told the family that something had to be done about Mrs. Willy played this role, and Mrs. Clapp did too.

INT.: Do you often find that there is some person who has to be taken out of the picture in order to get some progress?

DR. P.: Yes. The new people, who had no real function in the family during healthy periods, come in during the crisis and continue it unwittingly by infantilizing or blaming the patient. You have to push them out of the way to get the patient back to reasonable functioning. Nobody can clean her kitchen if she has her sister standing there telling her she ought to go to bed or to the hospital.

INT.: The idea that there is somebody who is keeping the mess going and should be taken out of the family is such a change from the idea that there is something wrong with the patient and that he should be taken out of the family. Yet the formal process is similar, in getting someone out. Here, how did you know that the sister had no real previous function in the family? You had very little information about her at this point.

DR. P.: I knew that she didn't live with Mrs. Willy and that the contact had been greater during the time of the illness. It was obvious from the sister's attitude that she felt it was her job to come down and help Paul put his mother away.

INT.: That seems to be the alliance. There doesn't seem to be any agreement between the two women about how Paul is failing his mother. The sister doesn't even take a neutral stance such as, "These two aren't getting along."

DR. P.: I don't think she knows what she thinks. She's down here for one purpose, to put her crazy sister away.

INT.: You come right out and ask her what her justification for this is. Why didn't you deal with her by ignoring her, as you did before?

DR. P.: Well, now that I've got the contract to come into therapy established with the family, I'm going after more information. I thought I would try the sister before I narrowed things down to the nuclear pair.

INT.: You're looking forward to dealing with the mother and son?

DR. P.: That was the big, meaty issue. Mrs. Clapp seemed more like hors d'oeuvres.

INT.: She gets right back to how terrible her sister is. Why did you decide to stop her at this point?

DR. P.: She was fanning the flame again and upsetting Mrs. Willy. So I turned her off.

INT.: You wouldn't consider it useful to get all the information you can from a relative if it isn't being given in a productive way?

DR. P.: No, I wouldn't.

INT.: I notice you switch to the subject of her finances. Mrs. Willy says later that the sister paid for a divorce. Did you think the sister was worried that she might have to contribute to the therapy?

DR. P.: I wasn't thinking along those lines, I was just groping. Money seemed to be a topic that everyone enjoyed talking about.

INT.: It does seem the only topic that ever effectively competed with Mrs. Willy.

DR. P. (*overlapping, to Mrs. C.*): Does anybody live with you?
MRS. C.: No, no. I live alone.

MRS. W.: She's just barely . . .

DR. P.: Do you have any children?

MRS. C.: Two grown daughters.

DR. P.: Two grown daughters who are married.

MRS. W.: She's just barely making, in fact, she's, she's come up so much to see me and, I think she's going to lose her home this week, this winter.

MRS. C.: Well, I don't.

MRS. W.: Well, I do.

MRS. C.: I make my bills, I make everything meet, but I don't save any money, let's put it that way.

DR. P.: Who does?

MRS. C.: No, nobody does.

MRS. W.: She paid for a divorce for me and, and she . . .

DR. P. (overlapping): Things don't seem to be getting better for anybody else I know of as far as saving . . .

MRS. C.: It seems like . . .

MRS. W. (loudly): Her house is nice!

MRS. C.: I mean, she tears these things up all day long and throws things around and then the dishes pile up and then that makes her hysterical, the little girl just got to where she couldn't—because she goes on all day long just about that, about these terrible things that are going to happen.

DR. P.: Now, now the girl— (To Paul) What's your sister's name?

PAUL: Mara, the little sister, we have a . . .

MRS. C.: Thirteen.

PAUL: . . . a married sister.

MRS. W. (wailing): She's gone, I'll never see her again!

DR. P.: Tamara?

PAUL: Mara.

DR. P.: Mara?

PAUL: Just Mara.

DR. P. (spelling): M-a-r-a?

PAUL: Right.

DR. P.: That's a pretty name. I've never heard that before.

PAUL: Uh-huh.

MRS. C.: Well, Mara got so she, she would rave like this all day long.

MRS. W.: She would go to the neighbors all day long and stay . . .

MRS. C.: She'd close the blinds, she stays in there all alone, she won't read, she won't do anything, she won't, ah, have the radio, just that terrible going on all day long, all over the house . . .

MRS. W. (*overlapping*): You'll think that they'll lock us both up for the rest of your lives if you ever come out there.

DR. P.: Who?

MRS. C.: This little girl just couldn't stand that.

DR. P.: Who should we lock up?

MRS. C.: So Mara would go over to the neighbor's and stay, all day long with the little girl, she just couldn't stay in the house with her. Well, then Paul had that to face when he comes home.

DR. P.: So now, Mara is staying with your brother.

MRS. W. (*weeping*): She's just down there, but I know Arlene, she's going to send her back on the bus naked.

MRS. C.: No, dear, she won't.

MRS. W.: She will, too!

DR. P.: And is this your brother, or your sister that she's with?

MRS. W.: My brother.

MRS. C.: A brother.

DR. P.: Your brother.

MRS. W.: She ain't gonna put up with her.

DR. P.: Did, ah, your brother know she was coming?

MRS. C.: They were here Sunday and took her.

MRS. W.: Took her.

DR. P.: And took her. Uh-huh.

MRS. C.: He talked with Agnes [*Mrs. W.'s name*].

DR. P.: How did they like the idea?

MRS. C.: They talked, and he sat there and talked with Agnes for about three hours and he . . .

MRS. W. (*overlapping*): Mara is . . .

MRS. C.: . . . and he was shocked to find her in this mental state . . .

MRS. W. (*overlapping*): Well, it ain't only that, he's just *shocked!* (*Sobs.*)

MRS. C.: He says he'll take her back with him and that'll help, because Mara couldn't concentrate on her studies or anything, she just couldn't cope with it, you know.

MRS. W. (*loudly, tearfully*): Two years ago that border, that flower border was cleaned as clean as that table. You couldn't believe it, and tu-, and iris was set in there, on that whole side. Now it's that high with weeds. (*Weeping.*)

DR. P.: Who, who takes care of the, of the grounds?

MRS. W. (*weeping*): Nobody's taking care of it, it's just, just . . .

MRS. C.: Well, the sister comes down and mows it, the girl would mow it, and when Paul has time, they, I mean . . .

MRS. W. (*weeping, overlapping*): It's *terrible,* I just can't believe it, I'm just a *mess!*

DR. P. (*to Mrs. W.*): Where does your older daughter live? (*Pause.*)

MRS. W.: She lives out in [*town*].

DR. P.: Out in [*town*]? Does she live near you?

MRS. C.: Out in [*suburb*].

MRS. W. (*tearfully*): She's (*inaudible words*). She's got her problem start—the battery wouldn't go yesterday . . .

DR. P.: Ah, she's married?

MRS. W.: Yeah, but her, the battery wouldn't go . . .

DR. P.: What does her husband do?

MRS. W.: Well, he's, he's not with her right now . . .

DR. P.: Where is he?

MRS. W.: I don't know.

DR. P.: Are they separated?

MRS. W.: Oh, he just takes out, he gets mad and goes off.

DR. P.: How do you feel when your son-in-law leaves like this?

MRS. W.: They're gonna starve to death, that's what's gonna happen to them.

INT.: This scene is wild. You've been trying to get the information you want, which is what happened to make Mrs. Willy get sick, and they're trying to give you the information they want, which is how badly off she is, and she is carrying on in the background. You seem to be blocking them with a series of factual questions, almost like a questionnaire, except that the questions are completely *non sequitur.* Were you really interested in the answers?

DR. P.: No. I was getting tired of Mrs. Willy screaming in my ear, and I knew that I could get her to quiet down by asking simple questions. I wanted to give my eardrums a rest. But I fouled up on the last one, when I asked, "How do you *feel* when your son-in-law leaves?" I didn't know any better then, but I have since learned that asking people who aren't functioning how they feel usually leads nowhere. It only gets them to act crazier. If you ask about the facts, they are much more apt to be reasonable. We now instruct our secretary, when she takes information from the families, to ask the patient at least one or two questions that are appropriate to him and not to accept the answers that other family members give. I did go in one day and find her desperately asking, "Where do you live?" to a man who was screaming and beating his head against the wall, but in general it works quite well.

INT.: The tone of your voice is so calm and flat here.

DR. P.: We've learned that when people are shouting and things are getting out of hand, a good way to act is to talk very softly and quietly. I'm deliberately using this tone with Mrs. Willy.

INT.: She settles down when you do that?

DR. P.: Yes.

INT.: What's amusing is that in the midst of this dreadful morass, you take time out to ask about the little girl's name.

DR. P.: I was really interested in it. It was an odd name. But also I hadn't heard it right and I wanted to be sure of it.

INT.: This shifts you from the position of expert to one of more equality. They have to tell you the spelling. It's suddenly a more social interchange.

DR. P.: I'm fairly relaxed with families. I have to get some enjoyment.

DR. P.: I've never heard of anybody starving to death.

MRS. W. (*loudly*): Well, you're gonna hear it this time, it's gonna be in the papers!

DR. P.: Well, we've got a social worker, Mr. Flomenhaft, who I think can prevent that from happening.

MRS. W.: No, they told me out there . . .

DR. P.: But they can.

MRS. W.: . . . they wouldn't help me.

DR. P. (*loudly*): Ah . . .

MRS. W.: When are you comin', are you actually mean that you're comin' out there?

DR. P.: Yes, we're coming out.

MRS. W.: When?

DR. P.: Coming out Friday morning. We can't . . .

MRS. W.: What day is this?

DR. P.: This is Wednesday.

MRS. C.: Wednesday, honey.

DR. P.: We can't come out, ah, tomorrow.

MRS. W. (*overlapping*): Just one of you?

DR. P.: No, there'll be three of us. A nurse, a social worker, and me. In fact, you'll meet the nurse and the social worker in a few minutes, they're at a meeting right now.

INT.: This exchange about the starving is a curious one. The mother says they're going to starve to death, and instead of ignoring her, as you've been doing, you call her on the literal truth of what she's saying, as if she could understand how crazy she's being.

DR. P.: I think she can. I'm telling her, "Look, don't talk to me in this exaggerated, flamboyant fashion or I won't understand you." I'm telling her to stop acting crazy.

INT.: In the next line you switch and accept the reality of her statement. You tell her your social worker can keep her from starving.

DR. P.: There I'm telling her that I know that what she's really saying is that she needs security, and that we're there to provide security.

INT.: But you don't put it plainly like that. You use her own language to talk back to her. I think it's that and the rapidness of the succession that get her. She sobers right up and starts asking you about the visit you're going to make.

DR. P.: Yes. How are we going to go about giving her this security?

INT.: It's a sequence of two parts. The first part says to her, "If you present what you say literally, I'm not going to accept it. If you'll agree that we're speaking metaphorically, I'll support you."

DR. P.: You make it sound very involved. I felt I was just ridiculing her a little, trying to bring her back to earth.

INT.: It's not the same as saying, "Stop acting crazy."

DR. P.: No, it isn't. I suppose I am agreeing with the family that the literal presentation of poverty she's making is crazy, but agreeing with her that she's not getting what she needs. We were communicating about this and it didn't have to do with food, or even money, but security?

INT.: What you do is to follow with what the family never does. They say, "I never heard of anyone starving to death," but they never add, "If you start to starve, I'll take care of you." I think that's why you reach her.

MRS. W. (loudly): Well, I'll tell you, I can't tell you how this happened.

DR. P.: Well, let's find out what sort of things you're worried about.

MRS. W. (loudly): That home was nice there, even, ah, even them two years ago, it, ah, you couldn't believe it, I had my clothes closet, up on the shelf I had all my hats and my pocketbooks, my clothes, then I had, ah, just some, ah, you know, old checks and things I had written down there.

DR. P.: Mm-hm. Ah, what size house is it?

MRS. W.: (*Pause.*) There's two bedrooms and a . . .

MRS. C.: Three, you might say. They've made one into a (*inaudible word*).

PAUL (*overlapping*): (*Inaudible words.*)

MRS. W. (*weeping*): I say, I just, I just can't stand it.

DR. P.: How old is, how old is your daughter? Your oldest daughter.

MRS. W.: She's about a year younger than he is.

PAUL: No, the oldest daughter, Mother.

MRS. C.: She's older, honey, Gloria's older, Gloria's older.

DR. P.: How old is Gloria?

PAUL: Thirty-five.

MRS. W. (*overlapping*): Oh, that's right.

DR. P.: Thirty-five?

MRS. W.: I was thinkin' she was . . .

DR. P. (*to Mrs. W.*): Now, how many times have you been married? (*Long pause.*)

MRS. C.: Well, tell him, honey.

MRS. W. (*tearfully*): I don't want to.

MRS. C.: Well, he wants to know, this all helps.

DR. P.: I need to know this. I mean, I know your son's name is different from yours.

MRS. W.: I was married to *his* father. (*Pause.*) We nearly starved to death when, when they was little. We lived 'way down there in the dust bowl down there in the drylands, you know, during those five years, in that awful dust . . .

DR. P.: Where?

MRS. W.: Down at [*town in nearby state*].

DR. P.: Down at [*town in nearby state*].

MRS. W.: You know, where that . . .

DR. P.: No, I'm from Georgia, I've just been here a couple of months.

MRS. W.: Well, you don't know . . .

MRS. C.: It's up near [*town*].

INT.: Did you already know how many times Mrs. Willy had been married?

DR. P.: I only knew that it was several times. I was starting to focus on her now, trying to make some sense out of her confused life.

INT.: Did you suspect that this subject of marriage was so loaded? That was a long pause there, and the tone of her voice when she finally answers is very faint and solemn.

DR. P.: Four marriages and all that trouble, it would make me solemn too. At least I found out that this was one subject that would sober her up.

INT.: I take it you don't mind telling patients something about yourself. If they ask you if you're married, you'll tell them you are.

DR. P.: Yes. We'll sometimes tell stories about our own families or problems we've had with our kids that are similar to theirs. In long-term psychotherapy I don't reveal so much about myself. But with families in a crisis, I think it's necessary to let them know a little more about me, to be more human with them.

INT.: There seems to be a need to hit them right away and develop a quick relationship, and one technique you use is yourself and the knowledge about yourself. Also, I think it's more common for family therapists to respond when asked about themselves.

DR. P.: Yes. But there's one thing I don't do, and that is to get into first names. I think that calling older patients by their first names infantilizes them and, if their children are present, tends to degrade them. I think a professional attitude of mutual respect is far better than a pseudo-friendliness that doesn't exist.

INT.: You don't want to be too condescending with your patients, and at the same time you don't want to be too free and easy, you want to keep a good balance.

DR. P.: I'd say the relationship I try for is similar to the classical doctor-patient relationship. It's not the usual psychotherapy relationship with all the mystery about it.

INT.: That can infantilize the patient. It also puts the therapist on a pedestal, and it's very hard to sit up there, I should think, if you're dealing with a crisis.

DR. P.: In a crisis, I'm serving the family better if I'm in the position of expert, the doctor they come to, rather than some sort of mysterious father image. I'm too much of the authority figure as it is.

INT.: You don't have to add to your authority, the crisis does it for you. You have to keep them from adopting an attitude of helplessness with you. This gets back to the way you use "infantilize." You seem to see it as equivalent to "making a person act helpless."

DR. P.: Yes. When we say we don't want to infantilize somebody, we mean we don't want him to become too dependent on us as father or mother figures.

INT.: Or power figures. So you present yourself as an expert, and at the same time you treat them like equals, and you play with this all the time. Otherwise they won't work for you. They'll hand all the responsibility to you.

DR. P.: It's a delicate balance and one we don't always achieve. A few times we've built up such an enormous transference reaction that it's created problems.

INT.: "Transference" is another word that therapists don't always use the same way. What do you mean by it here?

DR. P.: Usually I mean feelings that are inappropriately transferred from previous relationships, but here I'm thinking more of patients transferring their expectations of an ideal parent upon us.

INT.: Do you see a whole family as having transference in this sense?

DR. P.: Yes, but I'm thinking more of individuals in a family. We've found that there's a great danger in letting any individual family member establish too strong a relationship with any one of us. Since I talk a lot, and I'm the doctor, this tends to come to me more than to the others. I'm the one who has to be most careful about it.

INT.: There are two ways to look at transference, and family work raises some problems about it. One way to see it is that the individual has a set of expectations from the past which he carries into therapy and pins on the therapist. Another way to see it is that the therapist promises more than he means to or can deliver, and the patient takes him dead seriously and hangs him on it. The phenomena seem the same on the surface, and I wondered whether you were thinking of transference in a family setting in terms of this second thing.

DR. P.: I'm sure we do promise a great deal more than we mean to in many ways. Families in crisis are desperate and clutching at straws, and we probably do hold out some straws camouflaged as branches. We don't try to cut into their magical expectations too early, but we do try to clear them away before we let the family go. If they've got magical expectations the first day, all the better, because then we get some hypnotic phenomena and a good placebo. But if we let the attachment get too strong, it does create problems.

MRS. W.: The dust storms are so bad that, that—I bet, you won't believe this, but I got pictures . . .

DR. P: Where did you come from, originally?

MRS. W.: And my baby, I couldn't even see it, on my lap, for the dust storm.

DR. P.: Where did you come from originally?

MRS. W.: [*Name of state.*]

DR. P.: Where in [*state*]?

MRS. W.: Oh, around [*city*].

DR. P.: How old were you when you came out here?

MRS. W.: Eight.

DR. P.: Eight?

MRS. W.: My dad was a good provider and my mother had me dressed real well and all.

DR. P.: What did your father do? Farmer?

MRS. W.: Truck, mostly.

DR. P.: Truck?

MRS. W.: Farm work and farm.

MRS. C.: Farm.

DR. P.: How many children were there?

MRS. W.: Three. Her . . .

DR. P. (*overlapping*): You, your sister . . .

MRS. W.: Bob . . .

DR. P.: . . . and your brother down in, ah, down in [*state*].

MRS. C.: Uh-huh.

MRS. W.: And he's a, a *success!*

DR. P.: You the youngest, oldest?

MRS. W.: Uh-huh. And he's the youngest.

MRS. C.: He's the youngest.

DR. P.: He's the youngest.

MRS. W. (*loudly*): Yes, my brother is a big *success!*

DR. P.: Which of you two is the older?

MRS. C.: Hm?

DR. P.: Which of you is the older?

MRS. C.: Which? (*Laughing.*) Oh, I am.

DR. P.: Oh.

MRS. C.: I'm older, I'm five years older.

DR. P.: Uh-huh. You're five years older?

MRS. C.: Uh-huh.

MRS. W. (*loudly*): Now she's got a nice home and it's well kept and she does it all herself.

DR. P.: Well, now, you have a nice home, too, don't you?

MRS. W.: Oh, no!

DR. P.: Well, you said it used to be nice, so it must be a nice house.

MRS. W.: It ain't any more, it's just—*everything*. I (*starting to cry*).

MRS. C.: It's just messed up and throwed around (*inaudible phrase*).

MRS. W. (*overlapping*): It's *terrible!*

MRS. C.: It isn't, it's the confusion that she can't keep these things up, see.

MRS. W.: Well, it's *terrible,* it's beyond all . . .

DR. P.: How long have things been so bad? I know you say that they've been perfectly terrible for a year, but how long have you been feeling this way about everything, that everything was terrible, you're going to starve and . . .

MRS. W.: Well, the borders was, ah, pretty clean, and the ba-, and the back yard, we used to keep it mowed.

MRS. C. (*overlapping*): Honey, he wants to know, how long since you started worrying? How long since you came to my house and stayed a while?

MRS. W.: Paul's gonna starve, I tell you . . .

MRS. C.: It's been a year, just a year.

DR. P.: Paul will never starve.

MRS. W. (*loudly*): Yes, he will!

DR. P.: Look, I'll feed you, before you starve.

MRS. W.: I bet you would! You want me to come over your house for supper? (*Everybody laughs.*)

DR. P.: Tonight?

MRS. W.: Yeah.

DR. P.: Okay.

MRS. W.: But your wife wouldn't be expecting us.

DR. P.: That's okay. (*Mrs. W. sobs.*) I'm not going to let you starve.

MRS. W. (*tearfully*): I don't believe that. I can't understand it, it's never happened in the city of Denver. Never. People have been drownded, they've been burned up in airplanes, they've been burned up in houses, and hotels, and what, when the hotels burn and all their clothes burn, I don't know what they do, why they don't go out on the street naked.

DR. P.: Ah . . .

MRS. W.: Do you understand that?

DR. P.: Yes, I understand.

INT.: When you ask Mrs. Willy for supper, what are you trying to do?

DR. P.: I said I'd feed her before she starved. But she wasn't starving, and neither was Paul, and we both knew it. So this was a *reductio ad absurdum* that effectively stopped the talk about starving. I was expressing as clearly as possible my faith that Paul, with our help, would provide her with whatever she needed.

INT.: It's the same thing you did before when you said the social worker would take care of her. Again it's in a sequence of two parts. First you say jokingly, "I'll feed you before you starve," meaning, "Don't be crazy." Then you come in without joking and say, "I'm not going to let you starve."

DR. P.: I'm bringing her back to the reality of, "No, of course you're not coming over to my house for dinner, but we're going to take care of you all the same."

INT.: She tests you to make sure you mean it, and then starts going on about the hotels burning down.

DR. P.: I think she was responding genuinely to me, even if she's using that same crazy language. When she says, "It's never happened in the city of Denver," she's really saying, "It's never happened that any-one has promised me this." It's the way someone will weep when he's offered a bit of consolation.

INT.: There's an impressive moment at the end of that speech when she says, "Do you understand that?" and you answer, "Yes, I do." The whole tone of the exchange suggests that you'd really gotten together.

DR. P.: I think we had. She was agreeing with me that we were communicating, that I was beginning to get the message in all this crazy talk.

INT.: She's pretty straightforward. Many psychotics would say, "There's some understanding in China," or something like that. After all the confusion that went before, it must have been a relief for her to come through so well.

DR. P.: It certainly was.

MRS. W.: If you was in a hotel and all the people out, hotel burned, and all your clothes . . .

DR. P.: They wrap themselves up in blankets. (*Pause.*)

MRS. W.: Well, where do they get any more clothes if they're on a trip?

DR. P.: Go down to the Salvation Army.

MRS. W.: Well, they wouldn't have enough for a whole—they charge so darn much nowadays. Did you ever go down there?

INT.: Here's the same sequence again. She asks what people do if they don't have any clothes, and you say, "They wrap themselves up in blankets."

DR. P.: This time we were really joking.

INT.: Then comes the second part, where you're not quite joking. You say that they can go down to the Salvation Army. After all, you've already presented your outfit as a kind of Salvation Army.

DR. P.: You're right. I hadn't thought of that.

INT.: Her responses are mixed, too. She's pulling you down a kind of logical absurd path. She asks where do they get more clothes, but in such a sane way. Then she quibbles with you legalistically but humorously when she says the Salvation Army charges too much.

DR. P.: We were still together. I had cut through this crazy stuff and we were talking through a joke.

DR. P. (*coughs*): Mrs. Willy. Now, let me find out some more about you. How many times have you been married? And when was the last time?

MRS. W.: Well, I married his father when I was nineteen.

DR. P.: You stayed married to him for a long time?

MRS. W. (*low voice*): Twenty years.

DR. P.: What happened? Is he living now?

MRS. W.: Yes, in [*state*].

DR. P.: Is he married again?

MRS. W.: Yes, he married a woman up there.

DR. P.: Did he leave you?

MRS. W.: Huh?

DR. P.: Did he leave you?

MRS. W.: Well, he was workin' up here at a Denver, ah, at this [*hospital*] as a janitor for a hundred a month, and there was five in the family, we couldn't live on that.

DR. P.: Your son's making a hundred a week. And there are just two of you.

MRS. W.: Then. A hundred a month we couldn't live, we couldn't live on a hundred a month.

DR. P.: Okay. But you managed.

MRS. W.: No, we didn't manage.

DR. P.: What happened?

MRS. W.: Well, I had to went to my folks . . .

INT.: You sound so sympathetic to Mrs. Willy, when you're drawing out the details of her hard life. Then you shift back to the present to remind her that her son is making a hundred a week. You're really asking her how she can complain about being so badly off now when things were so much worse then.

DR. P.: For some reason I felt the need to get back to the symptoms at that point. I think it was beginning to be clearer to me that she was reliving the same situation with Paul that she'd been in with his father.

INT.: But that's not what you say to her.

DR. P.: I'm implying that if she's miserable now, it's not a question of money.

INT.: She goes right back to the past again and again you undercut her complaints by saying, "You managed."

DR. P.: That's a reassurance, too.

INT.: You might also have been resisting her ability to pull you along. This woman, when she does go sane, has a very skillful quality of getting someone to feel sorry for her.

DR. P.: You may be right. It's clear I liked her.

DR. P.: Here are Mr. Flomenhaft and Miss DeYoung. Let me ask them to come in. (*Dr. P. goes out.*)

MRS. W.: (*Inaudible phrase.*)

MRS. C.: Well, that's fine.

MRS. W.: It ain't fine.

MRS. C. (*to Paul, low voice*): He's giving her the psychological treatment right now. See what I mean?

MRS. W.: He'll give Paul one, if he comes out there . . .

MRS. C.: No.

MRS. W.: Now, how're you gonna get me up here tomorrow?

MRS. C.: This is the way they talk to them. You're gettin' as good a one right now as we had today.

PAUL: (*Inaudible phrase.*)

DR. P. (*entering with nurse and social worker*): Okay. Now, this is Miss DeYoung and Mr. Flomenhaft.

MISS DEY.: How do you do.

MRS. W.: Hello.

DR. P.: Paul and the sister are getting together here about what treatment Mrs. Willy's going to have. With her overhearing it, of course.

INT.: She gets back at them when she says, "He'll give Paul one, if he comes out there." That's the first remark any of them have made pinning something on Paul. Now, when you bring your team in, is it usual for you to introduce them in the middle of an interview?

DR. P.: No. Ordinarily, two of us will take the family and we won't call the third member of the team in till the end. But in this interview I was alone and I was needing reinforcements. My ears were ringing and I was floundering. This was about as little information as I'd ever gotten out of a family in the first part of an interview.

MISS DEY.: You did look pretty distraught.

DR. P.: I was feeling irritated by the fact that Kal and Carol took so long to get there. There was another reason why I wanted them in. This was the most interestingly psychotic family that we had yet seen, and it was kind of "Come in and see what I caught."

INT.: When a family comes in, how do you decide which two will take them?

DR. P.: As I think I said before, we more or less take turns, with the third member observing. If I'm behind the screen and something comes up about drugs, I'll come in and deal with it. Or if something comes up about social agencies and Kal is there, we'll bring him out.

INT.: When the project was first organized, why did you decide to put this kind of team together?

DR. P.: It's partly the crisis nature of the work. When you have to get things moving quickly, it's helpful to have more than one person working on the case. There are so many immediate decisions: where do we go from here, when's the next appointment, which agency should be contacted. A team like this provides a variety of expertise. Carol has a background in public health, Kal is a social worker, I'm a doctor. We each contribute specific areas of knowledge.

MR. F.: I think another reason why a team was set up is that it's traditional to have a team in a hospital.

INT.: I was thinking that your emphasis would almost require all these different skills, because you go outside the office into the lives of these people in a very practical way.

DR. P.: Yes. Kal and I can't go out to some woman's house and spend a couple of hours cleaning up her kitchen. Her husband would come home and shoot us. Also, Carol's motherliness and her ability to say "Come off it!" with a beatific smile on her face is the sort of thing we can't do. And the way Kal can manipulate social agencies is a joy to behold. His function is very important, because right from the beginning of therapy, we're trying to get the family out of therapy. Anything beyond the acute crisis, we try to hand over to other social agencies.

INT.: This seems to get to the heart of what your goals are. Your group is only trying to deal with the immediate crisis and restore the family to previous functioning.

DR. P.: Our goals are very limited. We don't try to make a family over. There's one exception to this, which we call the House of Cards type of family, in which there never was a real contract between the members to begin with. Mrs. Willy and her son are a good example of this type. Here we helped them write a contract for the first time, so they had something they didn't have before. But in the majority of cases, we just try to get the family back to its previous way of life, no matter how peculiar it might seem to us, and then leave them alone. We're pleased if they want long-term therapy for further change, but that's outside of our project. I sometimes say to people that our most successful case was a married couple, two paranoid schizophrenics, who lived peacefully supporting each other's delusions way out in the country. Every time some neighbor came and built a house too near them, they would move further out. This couple had a child who was five years old when we saw them. They had apparently survived this experience but weren't letting the child go to school. Otherwise, they were doing fine, until the wife's parents tried to get her to take charge of her even more paranoid schizophrenic sister, who was just coming out of the hospital after ten years. Then the wife started having delusions that people were spying on her from airplanes and looking down the chimney. We encouraged the couple to tell the parents that they didn't want the responsibility of the sister, and this relieved the immediate symptom. Then we did something which I think was a therapeutic triumph. We convinced these people to send the little girl to nursery school three days a week. We also got the wife to go and play bingo at the church every Sunday, and finally she was even able to go to the grocery store by herself. But the funny incident that happened at the end of treatment—which took only three visits over a two-week period —was that they finally broke down and allowed Kal and Carol to make a home visit. It was all very polite, except that after it was over, the wife called me up and said, "Your nurse and social worker are very nice people, but would you please tell them to stop circling our house in that helicopter and go home? My husband tells me there is lead in the ceiling so they can't see through even with radar, but I wish you'd get them away because they're upsetting me and I can't hang out my clothes." So I said I'd keep them away from her house and we never heard any more about it. I thought it was a good sign that instead of the enemy airplanes circling the house, there was now only a helicopter with a friendly nurse and a social worker. A year later, they were still paranoid about us but not about anybody else. And if the little girl can continue to be exposed to the outside world, she may survive. So we're willing to count this as one of our successes.

INT.: It's unusual to hear a therapist take this position. Some family therapists feel that if they haven't broadened life for each individual in the family, they've failed.

DR. P.: The family pattern here is almost as sick now as it was before, but that wasn't the problem the family came to us for. The problem was that this pattern was being threatened. We felt that our job was to remove that threat, not threaten it even further. We get into trouble when we try to change completely family patterns that wouldn't suit us but which other families manage to live with quite well.

INT.: Do you feel that your intervention has any long-range effect in helping a family cope better?

DR. P.: We hope that the crisis will be a turning point, and that with our help and the help of the other agencies we refer them to, they will achieve a better level of functioning. But if another crisis arises, we expect to see them again.

INT.: Do you find that this second crisis is easier to deal with?

DR. P.: If they've had a good experience with us, it's usually much easier. We can often handle it with a couple of telephone calls.

INT.: The criticism most often aimed at brief methods is that they may produce changes but these changes are superficial and don't last. Now, some pretty good evidence is accumulating to support the idea that a family changes more if the therapist gets in and makes a change and gets out than if he keeps the family in weekly treatment over a long period. But in most therapy of this sort the patient will come in for a recharge after a certain period of time. There will be a recess and the patient will come in again because of some new problem. Do you find this sort of thing happening?

DR. P.: We do. We hope there won't be future crises that the family can't handle, but if there are, we make it clear that we want to be called. What we don't like is when families come in for a touch of magic from us without having any acute problems. And we get concerned when there are severe or recurrent crises. We try to make a new or better referral then.

INT.: You don't on your own initiative ever bring people in and start them again for a few sessions and then let them go?

DR. P.: No, though on occasion we have seen danger signals in a family during a follow-up interview, and would have liked to spend some time doing preventive work. But as things are now, we limit ourselves to being an acute service and leave less pressing matters to the community agencies. We're finding that subsequent contact with us may stir up a lot of old problems. We even avoid follow-up by the team in cases where the family was overly dependent on us before. We work so briefly that we tend to remind people of the crisis, not the resolution.

DR. P.: Miss DeYoung is a nurse here and Mr. Flomenhaft's a social worker. Now this is Mrs. Willy, who, ah, has been telling me that she's convinced she's going to starve, ah . . .

MRS. W. (*overlapping*): I, I am.

DR. P.: This is her son, Paul Gibson.

MRS. W.: I'm gonna starve to death, too.

DR. P.: And Paul is working and making about a hundred dollars a week and, ah . . .

MRS. W.: No, he is bringing home about sixty, he's starving to death, too. (*Weeping.*) Look how thin he is.

DR. P.: And this is Mrs. Willy's sister, Mrs., ah . . .

MRS. C.: Clapp.

DR. P.: Clapp.

MRS. W.: Believe it or not, her home's nice in [*town*], she's got a nice home there.

DR. P.: I know she does.

MRS. W.: Well, you won't believe it when you come out to my house, but it's true.

MISS DeY.: Where do you live?

MRS. W.: In [*town*].

MISS DeY.: Um-hm.

DR. P.: What I suggested was that, ah, Paul bring his mother in tomorrow at eight, ah, since he's got to get on to work, and . . .

MRS. W. (*overlapping*): Couldn't you just skip that and just come out there Friday?

DR. P.: And then we'll be out there Friday. No, we can't skip it.

MRS. W.: Well, he might get fired.

MRS. C. (*simultaneously*): One day's work.

DR. P.: No, he's not going to get fired.

MRS. W.: Well, he just as well get fired now as any time because he can't make it out there to work the rest of the winter in that old car of mine.

DR. P.: Bet he can.

MRS. W.: Brakes are gone, the windshield's got a chip in it, he can't get it, ah, sticker on it . . .

DR. P. (*overlapping*): Now you were telling me something a minute ago, Mrs. Willy, you were telling me how many times you were married. You were married to Paul's father for twenty years, then, he wasn't making enough money to support all of you, so you went back to your parents and he went to [*state*] and he's married again and you apparently married again to somebody. You've been married three times?

MRS. W.: And then, ah, he died, ah, he died, ah, up here at, ah . . .

PAUL: [*Name of hospital.*]

MRS. W.: [*Name of hospital*], a heart, ah, heart attack.

INT.: Why did you start off by telling your team that Mrs. Willy was afraid she was going to starve?

DR. P.: That was what Mrs. Willy had mostly been talking about. I was saying, "Here is Mrs. Willy and this is her delusion. And this is her son Paul and he assures me there's no reality to it."

INT.: When you get to the marriages, is that to them or to her?

DR. P.: To them, partly. I was trying to share with them the meager information that I had. But I mainly wanted to make it clear to Mrs. Willy that I knew that this business of her marriages was very significant to her and I wanted to get back to it.

INT. (*to Miss DeY.*): You come in here too, to ask where Mrs. Willy lives. Was this merely to acknowledge her, or did you have a practical reason?

MISS DEY.: She had just been talking about our coming out to see her, so I was asking her address. It was practical.

INT. (*to Dr. P.*): Is it usual for you to summarize your impression of the situation for the people who have just come in?

DR. P.: Yes, if we don't start together. Sometimes it's helpful for one of us to summarize in the middle of an interview just for our own benefit. I'll say, "I'm a little confused, but this is the way it looks to me. Correct me if you see it differently."

MR. F.: There was one funny time you did this, went into a long rationale for what was going wrong in the family, and the father blurted out, "I disagree!"

DR. P.: Well, I could be wrong, and it helps to get their reaction.

INT.: Do you sometimes carry on a conversation with the other team member in the presence of the family?

DR. P.: Sure. We'll go into long asides, first telling them, "If you don't mind, we want to talk together about some points that puzzle us." Then we'll go on for about fifteen minutes to clarify issues for them, or simply to demonstrate communication. Or we'll stop in the middle of an interview and keep the family waiting while we go out and compare notes. Or sometimes one of us will say, "I'm not getting anywhere, I give up," and hand the interview over to the other team member till he gets revived.

INT.: Do you ever clown around in front of the family, to break the tension, or change the mood, or for some other reason?

DR. P.: We don't clown, exactly, but we do tease people sometimes. One time Carol and I decided we would show the family what they sounded like, so we repeated a bit of dialogue they had just gone through. Another time, a woman was brought in to us supported by several people. She couldn't walk or talk; you had to lean your ear right between her teeth to get what she was saying. I was responding to her by talking very softly and gently to her and for some reason this annoyed Kal.

MR. F.: I didn't feel we could get anywhere as long as she was controlling the situation with her symptom, so I started talking to her much louder than I usually do, as if I were hard of hearing. Every time she whispered something, I would shout, "I can't hear you, I wish you would speak up, what's that you say, you're saying something about you're going to speak up, is that it?" Finally she yelled, "Will you please quit telling me to speak up!"

INT.: One interesting question is who a therapist tends to side with, the man, the woman, the child, the patient. A single therapist can easily become the victim of his own preferences, and it must be an advantage to be working with a team from this point of view.

DR. P.: I think that my greatest weakness as a family therapist is my tendency to look upon the patient as invariably the victim. In evening up the responsibility, I weigh too heavily on the relatives or the spouse and let the patient off. But with three of us, if I'm fingering someone too hard, one of the others will instinctively come in to right the balance. That's also why we try to see the family as a system. We get into trouble when we pick on an individual.

INT.: Having more than one therapist in the room certainly gives you flexibility. You can drop out of character, or shift from the family to yourselves, or take turns, or whatever you fancy.

DR. P.: I think we all appreciate the freedom it gives us.

DR. P.: Is he [*second husband*] the father of your youngest daughter?

MRS. W.: Little girl. Uh-huh.

DR. P.: Your little girl. And the little girl left yesterday to go to [*nearby state*] to stay with her uncle . . .

MRS. W. (*overlapping*): Yeah, but they ain't, they ain't gonna keep her . . .

DR. P.: . . . with Mrs. Willy's and Mrs. Clapp's brother.

MRS. W.: . . . they, they'll send her back.

DR. P.: This is the thirteen-year-old daughter, Mara. (*To Mrs. W.*) And then, after your second husband died, you married again.

MRS. W.: Yeah.

DR. P.: Uh-huh, and was that Mr. Willy?

MRS. W.: No . . .

PAUL: No. Mr. Willy was the second.

MRS. W. (*overlapping*): Mr. Willy was, ah . . .

DR. P.: Mr. Willy was the second.

MRS. W.: Uh-huh.

DR. P.: And then the third . . .

MRS. W.: I got my name back.

DR. P.: Yeah, and you, and your third husband, you were divorced . . .

MRS. W. (*overlapping*): I married Mr. Larrabee, and then, that didn't last very long.

DR. P.: And then did you marry again after that?

MRS. W.: No.

DR. P.: So you've just had three husbands?

MRS. C.: Four.

DR. P.: Four. (*Pause.*) Yeah.

MRS. W.: But things weren't like this then.

DR. P. (*interrupting*): But when was the last, when did you leave your last husband, your fourth husband?

MRS. W.: November, wasn't it?

MRS. C.: Well, really, last year, about in August, honey, a year ago.

DR. P.: What happened there? Was this Mr. Larrabee?

MRS. W. (*tearfully*): It's just un—inbelievable.

DR. P.: What happened with Mr. Larrabee?

PAUL: Well, she divorced him, ah, once, after—how long did you live with him the first time? Several years, I think.

MRS. C.: No, she was married two years, altogether.

PAUL: Yeah, two years.

MRS. W.: No . . .

MRS. C.: They were divorced twice in one, in two years.

PAUL: And then, ah, I don't know if he divorced her or she divorced him.

MRS. C.: He divorced her the first time, she divorced him the last time.

PAUL (*overlapping*): But, ah, they went back together for a very short period of time and then . . .

MRS. C.: Well, nine, ten days, they were just together for ten days.

DR. P. (*interrupting, to Mrs. W.*): Well, you haven't really been without a husband except just the last year, for any length of time.

MRS. W.: Well, I guess so.

DR. P.: Well, this must be very hard on a woman who has been used to having a, a husband around, doing without one for a year.

MRS. W.: We're gonna, we're gonna be throwed out in the street.

DR. P.: Oh, now, we're going, not going to let that happen. (*Mrs. W. trying to talk.*) I told you to come to my house for dinner tonight, now, let's not worry about that, but, ah, for the last year, you've been without a husband, have you ever been without a husband for that long before?

MRS. C.: (*Pause.*) No.

MRS. W.: Well, now, I remem-, yes, when Jerry died, I was . . .

MRS. C.: Two years, honey.

MRS. W.: Longer than that.

MRS. C.: Yes, she was two, two years there before she remarried.

DR. P.: How did you do during those two years? Did you find it hard? Did you worry a lot?

MRS. W.: I always kept the bills up.

DR. P.: Uh-huh. Were you working then?

MRS. W.: No, I had, ah, some Social Security and . . .

MRS. C.: Social Security and Veterans, so she didn't have to work then.

DR. P.: Uh-huh.

MRS. C.: She had approximately, what was it, three or four hundred a month coming in, and then she lost it all when she got married, and that's where it seemed to go.

DR. P.: How long were you married to Mr. Larrabee?

MRS. W.: Oh, about two years.

DR. P.: Now, now, what about the third husband?

MRS. C.: That was Ed.

DR. P.: That was who?

MRS. C.: Ed.

MRS. W. (*tearfully*): I don't want to talk about it.

MRS. C.: Tell him, tell him about Ed, honey.

MRS. W.: Well, there's no use . . .

MRS. C.: See . . .

MRS. W.: . . . he couldn't be, he couldn't under-, ah, I could, I could tell you about Paul, but if you didn't see him, you wouldn't know one thing about him, would you?

DR. P.: That's right, that's why we need to see him, too.

MRS. W. (*overlapping*): So what's the use of me trying to tell you?

DR. P.: Well, I just want to find out, you know, what happened, what went wrong.

INT.: I gather that all through this long interrogation you're trying to get at what led up to the crisis.

DR. P.: Yes. I got one clue when Mrs. Willy spoke of her life with her first husband in such a way that I felt she was confusing him with her son. Another clue was that she seemed to have to have a man around, because she apparently couldn't tolerate being unmarried for any length of time.

INT.: It's certainly a chaotic history. But she comes in very clearly. She even corrects her sister from time to time.

DR. P.: As long as I'm focusing her on matters of fact, she does pretty well.

MRS. C.: Well, it seemed like from the time after she had had this money coming in there for two years and then she married this guy, this Ed, and for some reason or other, he swayed her, she didn't want to get married, she even, she says she even, cried going to the, to, ah, to get married because she felt like that wasn't what she would do, should do, but after she had been married just a few days it dawned on her, she had, especially when the first checks didn't come in, what she had done, and he was very worthless, he didn't work, he didn't do anything, he was supposed to be some kind of mechanic, and it seems as though all he actually married her for was because he thought she had all this money coming in, and this home that he would eventually get, he, he was just a rounder.

DR. P.: How long did this last?

MRS. C.: Well . . .

MRS. W.: He was a rounder.

MRS. C.: Well, he was gone more times than he was there. He was just in and out, weeks at a time, and in and out, when he saw that there was no money coming in, that was a different story then, and so, the time went on for a year but actually they weren't living together in that time, very little, just (*inaudible phrase*).

MRS. W.: Uh, ah, you know when they had those floods there in Holland and, ah, washed away all the people's homes, you know, and the ocean come in on them . . .

DR. P.: They were all insured.

MRS. W.: In Holland?

DR. P.: Now . . .

MRS. W.: How'd the people build homes in the mud puddles?

DR. P.: They were all insured, all insured. (*Pause.*) (*To Paul*) Do you appreciate how your mother has gone through an entire lifetime of never having anybody that she could rely on to support her? Do you see this pattern?

PAUL: Ah, I don't understand your sentence.

MRS. C.: Well . . .

PAUL: Do I appreciate the fact that my mother has never had to work for a living?

DR. P.: No, do you appreciate the fact that she's never had anybody to support her, and she's never had the security of knowing that she had a man who was going to be bringing in a paycheck that was going to be adequate to meet the bills each week?

INT.: "They're all insured," is another of your crazy-talk responses. You jump from the husbands to the people in Holland, and you go to as literal an extreme as she does, except in the opposite way.

DR. P.: She didn't want to talk about the third husband. I did. So I was trying to ridicule her a little, dismiss all this nonsense.

INT.: Again, you don't just ridicule her. You pick up her real meaning by saying the people are insured. You're telling her, "You have more security than you think."

DR. P.: Well, underneath the absurd talk she's saying, "I'm helpless," and I'm saying, "No you're not."

INT.: Why did you turn to the son here? This is the first time you've suggested that, whatever is wrong, he might be contributing to it.

DR. P.: I was finally letting him know that in this discussion of the marriages we were really talking about him and not the husbands. He was another insurance policy. I was seeing this pattern of looking for security a little more clearly.

INT.: When you see such a pattern, and you share what you see with the family, do you feel that this knowledge is going to help them improve?

DR. P.: I didn't feel that sharing this observation with the son was going to produce any magical changes, but I wanted him to know that he was included in what Mrs. Willy was talking about.

INT.: So it really wasn't to give him understanding, but to shift some responsibility onto him.

DR. P.: Yes. But without confronting him directly and getting into a power struggle. I still didn't know in what way Paul had failed to provide his mother with security, but I suspected that this was part of the problem, and I wanted to alert him to the fact that I suspected it.

INT.: So often, when you get an interpretation like that, it looks as if you're providing understanding, and yet it has so many other functions too. You could presumably not share this information at all. When you begin to sense a pattern or a trend, you could store it up in your mind and go on to the particular action prescription you think is going to help. Would you ever do that?

DR. P.: I think storing it up would have been a mistake because at some point I would have had to burst forth with everything and take him by surprise. Then I would have a fight on my hands.

INT.: By isolating the mother's experiences with men as a pattern, you avoid blaming the son. It's not him, it's the whole pattern she has lived through, of which he is a part.

DR. P.: Yes. I'm not saying he's a bad son, I'm saying that his mother has a need which has arisen from certain experiences in the past and which now places a certain responsibility on him. He can't very well argue with me.

INT.: What he does is to twist it and say, "What you mean is that my mother has never had to go out and work for her living in her life."

DR. P.: Which was a very good technique. And which I then counter.

INT.: It's a tricky exchange. You are defending her behavior because it is determined by her past. Then he says, "No, she's just lazy." But his position is weak because it contradicts the position he's been taking, which is that she's crazy. He can't have it both ways.

DR. P.: Actually, when he says she's lazy, there's just as much reality to his perception as there is to mine. The only difficulty is that his perception of reality wouldn't work in establishing a future relationship between him and his mother because it's a blaming thing.

INT.: In other words, it isn't a question of what is so, it's a question of what can be engineered to go somewhere else.

DR. P.: That's right. A relationship depends on an immense amount of cooperation; it can't be worked out through mutual blame.

INT.: If you can get them jointly to blame the circumstances of her past, it would be better.

DR. P.: Right. If they can scapegoat the past, or the "pattern," rather than blame each other, then they can go on.

INT.: I suspect that's the reason for all the fascination with the past in the development of psychiatry.

DR. P.: Well, there has to be another step beyond blaming the past. I had one patient who had had several years of intensive psychotherapy and he said, "Isn't it a shame that I don't work and support my family and that they are on the verge of starvation, but you see I had this relationship with my father."

INT.: That's really using the language against you.

MRS. C.: Only Jerry, Jerry did.

PAUL: Ah . . .

DR. P.: Now this was her husband who . . .

MRS. C.: The second husband.

PAUL: The second one.

MRS. W.: That died at the [name of hospital].

DR. P.: Yeah. Okay.

PAUL: Yeah, I, ah, I am sympathetic to her, when she doesn't have security, she, ah . . .

MRS. W. (*overlapping*): Thank God he died, he's out in his grave.

DR. P.: Yeah. You haven't got much right now, either, do you?

PAUL: Well, I don't know, it's . . .

DR. P.: Except yourself.

PAUL: I'm as secure as, ah . . .

DR. P.: Okay.

PAUL: . . . I want to be.

MRS. W. (*tearfully*): You're most secure, more secure, insecure than you've ever been. The day you was born, if I'd just set you out on the doorstep and said, "There's the world, there," that's how secure . . .

DR. P.: He can take care of himself pretty well, can't he?

MRS. W.: No.

DR. P.: No? Can't he?

PAUL: I think so.

MRS. W.: I don't. He knows better, he's just trying to put up a front.

INT.: The son finally comes around to agreeing with you about his mother's insecurity. Then you move rapidly to his own insecurity.

DR. P.: I wanted to support him. He had agreed with my point, so I was giving him a bonus.

INT.: You were also shifting the symptom again. "You feel insecure too."

DR. P.: I was pointing out that it applied to both of them. His mother wasn't providing him with much security either.

INT.: The son is courteously agreeing with you while somewhat reluctant to accept that.

DR. P.: I still wanted to avoid blaming him. I could have said, "You're a bad guy, you're not being good to your mother." But again it wouldn't have led anywhere.

INT.: When the mother comes in to agree with you about her son's insecurity, you switch again and say, "He can take care of himself."

DR. P.: Well, I have to defend him in his independence from his mother.

INT.: It's a complicated sequence.

DR. P. (*to Paul*): Look, what's happened here in the last few months to make the situation get so bad about your mother's fear that somebody's not going to be around to support her? Are you, are you threatening to leave her?

MRS. W. (*overlapping*): He may be called to the Army any day.

PAUL: Well, ah . . .

MRS. W.: He's eligible, you see. While he was in school . . .

PAUL: I don't know, she seems to, ah, feel real upset any time I go on a date or anything like this.

DR. P.: Oh, so you're afraid that he's going to get married and leave you.

MRS. W.: Well, he could go to the Army any time.

DR. P. (*to Paul*): You thinking about getting married?

PAUL: No.

MRS. W.: Well, he may be drafted.

PAUL: It's a possibility, but not right away.

MRS. W.: I don't think he will ever get married.

DR. P.: Well, do you want him to?

PAUL: As far as being drafted, ah, when she was at [*hospital*], they, ah, changed my rating to 3-A, or something like that.

MRS. W.: Then, see, that was that year.

PAUL: Well, it's still 3-A.

DR. P.: You get the same rating. (*To Mrs. W.*) Now, how did you happen to go to [*hospital*] last year?

INT.: Why did you ask the son if he was threatening to leave?

DR. P.: This was a straightforward question because I was sure at this point that this was what he was planning to do. It still hadn't been established that he had any real responsibility for his mother, so I was suggesting, "If you are preparing to leave her, this is having a great deal of effect on her and we'd better consider whether this is the wisest move for you to make right now."

INT.: Did this turn out to be true, that he was planning to leave?

DR. P.: Actually no.

INT.: You still get in the point that he has some responsibility for her. And you do this just after his mother has said, "No matter what circumstance I would put you in, you'd still be insecure." He would have to react against that.

DR. P.: It had already been established that he was capable of providing his mother with the security the other men hadn't been able to give her. So I'm asking him, "Why don't you take care of her?"

INT.: It's quite a pressure on him to take the position of the strong one. Then you get to the question of whether he's thinking of getting married. Why didn't you pick up the mother's statement that she doesn't think he ever will?

DR. P.: Because she was denying it, and I didn't feel that she was willing to admit her fears about it at that time. I noted that as something to come back to. I still felt it was a possibility.

MISS DEY.: I also think that the previous hospitalization was something you wanted to get at.

DR. P.: That's right.

MRS. W.: Well, I went up to [*sister's town*] and, ah, my sister's, ah, doctor gave me some shots, which didn't do me one bit of good. Paul had to pay fifty dollars out there.

DR. P.: What sort of shots were they?

MRS. C.: Nerves, just a (*inaudible phrase*).

MRS. W. (*overlapping*): Just shots, they didn't do me a bit of good.

PAUL: I don't know, must have . . .

MRS. W. (*overlapping*): Whenever you doctors think a shot in the—of medicine, is gonna help somebody that's upset, you're mistaken. And, ah, anyway, then the washin' machine went out and he had to pay seventy-five dollars to get the darn thing fixed, now it don't work, the water just, just drips. Then his car . . .

DR. P.: Look . . .

MRS. W.: . . . four new tires for his car . . .

DR. P.: Mrs. Willy, what happened about your going to—look, he's making a good living—what happened about your going to [*hospital*]? How did this come about that you went there?

MRS. W.: Well, the doctor up at [*sister's town*] recommended it. You know.

DR. P.: How long were you there?

MRS. W.: Well, I, he hauled me out there every day last winter from November clear till spring and . . .

DR. P.: How long were you in the hospital?

PAUL: She was an outpatient.

MRS. W. (*overlapping*): Well, I was a, ah, outpatient.

PAUL: We'd take her out there in the morning when they were there.

MRS. W. (*overlapping*): They don't keep hardly anybody there any length of time, they kick them out.

PAUL: Then my older sister would pick her up in the afternoon and bring her home.

MR. F.: Is that spring of this year?

MRS. C.: Yes. Last fall and this spring.

DR. P.: Hm.

MRS. C.: But they really didn't seem to give her any help.

MRS. W. (*overlapping*): It's just a treadmill, it's just like a mouse goin' around a . . .

MRS. C. (*overlapping*): She went in on her own, see, we let her go in on her own, and she was . . .

MRS. W. (*overlapping*): You would just go and then come home, and go and come home, and go and come home, and mill up and down the halls and . . .

MISS DEY.: What section of the hospital, what, ah (*inaudible words*).

MRS. W.: [*Name of county.*]

MISS DEY.: [*Name of county.*]

DR. P.: Here I was getting at the facts about Mrs. Willy's previous hospitalization. This was the first time I'd heard about it.

INT. (*to Miss DeY.*): Why did you ask her what section of the hospital she'd been in?

MISS DEY.: Because I'd been working at that hospital last year.

INT.: I take it she had been a day patient there.

MISS DEY.: Yes. I thought I might know some of the people who had worked with her, in which case I could contact them to get some quick information about her instead of waiting for the written report. One of the things we try to do right off is to get all the information we can from a current or past agency that has worked with the patient or the family. For instance, if some medication has been helpful, we like to know about it, because Frank might want to prescribe it again.

DR. P.: How would you feel if I gave you some tranquilizers? Would you take them?

MRS. W.: Well, I could take them but they wouldn't make me go to sleep.

DR. P.: Well, maybe not, but would you take them?

MRS. W.: Oh, yes.

PAUL: Yeah, she'd take 'em home if you give them to her.

MRS. W. (*overlapping*): Won't do any good. I haven't slept for a year or two.

DR. P. (*to Paul*): You sound kind of discouraged.

MRS. C.: Well, it's been awfully hard on him.

PAUL (*overlapping*): Well, you, you, ah, have heard her carry on, if you will.

DR. P.: Yeah.

PAUL: This starts about five in the morning when I get up, and when I come home it's the same thing, so, ah, it kinda gets on my nerves.

MRS. W.: He don't get any rest day or night.

DR. P.: You need tranquilizers, too?

PAUL: What?

DR. P.: You need tranquilizers, too?

PAUL (*laughing*): I probably could have some.

INT.: Why did you bring up the question of medication at this point?

DR. P.: I was wondering what sort of cooperation I was going to get from her after she had expressed doubts about previous medication.

INT.: Do you give medication of some kind routinely?

DR. P.: We give some sort of medication to the patient in about three-fourths of our cases. Or maybe some to the family and none to the patient.

INT.: Is this partly for psychological reasons, to make them feel they are getting a proper doctoring?

DR. P.: We've had relatives call us and say, "How long are you going to keep on with this talking before you get around to the treatment?" So we do sometimes give drugs, simply to make the family feel that something's being done. But usually we give them because we feel that they are indicated. I do believe that drugs work. And in this case I think they did help. Mrs. Willy had been saying that shots weren't any good, so I wanted to be sure that she would take tranquilizers. If she wouldn't take drugs, I knew we would be in for trouble.

INT.: In what way?

DR. P.: I felt that they would have a hard time handling her at home without some degree of sedation.

INT.: Hadn't they been putting up with her fairly well?

DR. P.: Well, coming to the hospital is a sort of an end point. The family comes in expecting to get immediate relief from the problem of having somebody crazy. If you don't take the patient off their hands, you've got to produce some kind of result within twenty-four hours. I felt that drugs would produce sufficient results in this woman, even if we didn't do anything in psychotherapy in that first hour.

INT.: So the medication is as much for the family as it is for her.

DR. P.: In a way, yes.

INT.: You do a curious thing here. The mother says she hasn't slept for a year, and instead of sympathizing with her, you say to the son, "You sound kind of discouraged." Was this deliberate?

DR. P.: Oh, yes. I wasn't going to reward that comment of hers because it was a crazy comment. I also wanted to show the son that we knew it would be a hardship on him to have her at home instead of at the hospital.

INT.: Then you go on to ask if he needs tranquilizers too. Did you genuinely feel he might?

DR. P.: Yes, but I'm also telling her, "You're not the only patient."

INT.: Do you often prescribe medication to other members of the family as a way of suggesting this?

DR. P.: Oh, yes. As an indication that we know they're hurting too.

INT.: What is unusual about this part of the interview is the way you continually shift perspective from the mother to the son. She's insecure, he's insecure; she's got problems, he's got problems.

DR. P.: I'm trying to focus on the relationship between them.

INT.: But not in a direct way. If you told them they were both part of what's wrong, they could ignore you or disagree. But by playing first one, then the other, you tease out their involvement, and at the same time keep them even.

DR. P.: You may be right. But this is more of an instinctive underpinning than anything I do formally.

MRS. W. (*loudly*): I tell you what he needs . . .

DR. P. (*to Paul*): I can sympathize. (*To Mrs. W.*) What does he need?

MRS. W.: Well, yeah, eh, did you ever have an operation? You never had an operation?

DR. P.: Yeah, I've had an operation.

MRS. W.: They put you to sleep?

DR. P.: Um-hm.

MRS. W.: Didn't know a thing?

DR. P.: Right.

MRS. W.: Well, if you doctors could invent some kind of medicine, you know, give people a shot like that, put 'em to sleep, you just keep on sleepin', never wake up . . .

DR. P.: Do you want to kill yourself?

MRS. W.: Be out of their troubles, then.

DR. P.: Do you want to kill yourself?

MRS. W.: I couldn't if I wanted to, now how would you kill yourself?

DR. P.: It's not very easy, is it?

MRS. W.: No, it isn't. (*Laughing.*) You take a knife and stick your-self a little bit, it hurts. Just a teeny bit, it hurts.

DR. P.: That's right, all you'd end up doing would be make yourself kind of sick.

MRS. W.: I saw patients out there at the hospital, they slashed their wrists with a razor blade, a little teeny cut along there. It's a long ways from killing yourself.

DR. P.: It sure is. (*Pause.*)

MRS. W.: It's a long ways.

INT.: Is it routine with you to handle talk about suicide in this way?

DR. P.: We talk about suicide very freely. If somebody says anything that sounds like a suicide threat, we'll confront him with it right off.

INT.: Do you think you got a true answer, when Mrs. Willy says she doesn't want to kill herself?

DR. P.: I think I got a true answer, yes. She was expressing what sounded like suicidal thoughts, so I asked her about them and she gave me the assurance that she didn't want to commit suicide, that it was repugnant to her. She even implied that it was my idea, not hers, that she would even think about it. So I let it go at that.

INT.: But you find it best to bring it up this directly if there's any hint at all.

DR. P.: Yes. If you react to a suicide threat with alarm, or by shying away from it, you convey to the patient that you are afraid of it, and this may make him doubt himself, doubt his control over it. But by talking with him about it openly, rationally and calmly, you re-affirm his hope that he has control over it. That's why we always try to put it as something he *wants* to do, not as something he may not be able to resist.

INT.: You pick up the control aspect.

DR. P.: Yes. We say, "It does appear that you might attempt suicide because you want to so badly. Let's see what we can do to make you *not* want to."

INT.: Have you had many problems with suicidal patients since the project began?

DR. P.: We had one suicide that really threw us, and since then we have done a lot of things differently. This was a woman who had been totally nonfunctioning and getting tranquilizers from multiple sources. She'd been hospitalized for most of the past eight years and had never made any improvement. She came to us after she was discharged from her last hospital as untreatable. We took her off drugs and made the greatest effort we've ever made. She began to function a little and her husband seemed satisfied. Then, ten days after we had started to see them, the husband suddenly decided that he was leaving her. We had no inkling that he was thinking of this, and neither did she. When he told her, she beat herself up in his presence and stabbed herself in the back of the neck with a knife, severing the spinal cord. She died three days later. It was apparently an accident; she hadn't wanted to kill herself, just to scare him into staying. Hopefully, if the husband had told us beforehand what was on his mind, we could have averted the tragedy. Anyway, this shook us up very badly and since then we don't press people too hard. We're more alert to signs telling us the family can't take it, and we're more careful to leave sources of dependency, like the drugs, temporarily intact.

INT.: Do you ever use hospitalization for suicide prevention?

DR. P.: We're willing to hospitalize any suicidal case we can't handle on an outpatient basis, though this doesn't happen very often. Our experience so far has borne out our conviction that hospitalization isn't always the way to prevent suicide. We've had two cases of people who made serious suicide attempts, or threatened to. One was a young man who couldn't live with his mother and couldn't live without her. He had tried to get married several times, and each time the marriage broke up. He had also been in several hospitals, but he couldn't get away from his mother that way either. So he kept making bizarre suicide attempts in front of her, which she both encouraged and condemned. The other case was a domineering woman who had a weak little husband and three husky sons. When her health failed and the four males began to rebel against her, she used suicide attempts to try to control them. Both patients stayed suicidal and both families were unbending, so we hospitalized them at another hospital for long-term treatment. But the woman made a suicide attempt in the hospital; in fact, she ran through several hospitals before she got electroshock treatment, which finally helped her. The man made a suicide pact with another man in the hospital; he killed the friend but not himself, and is now under maximum security.

INT.: I should think a major question for you would be the amount of risk you're willing to take with this kind of project.

DR. P.: We don't feel we're taking too much risk now, but we'd like to take even less. We're working on a prognostic scale on which to score the families, to try to make our successes and failures more predictable. We're examining various factors, adding new ones as we go, hoping we can tell more quickly who is going to stay out of the hospital, who is going to return to the status quo, and who is going to be a suicide risk. All of this is still fairly tentative and needs much more investigation, but there are a few factors that seem to hold up. Most of these factors are just clues to the family's willingness to be involved and to see the symptom as a family problem, because our success is dependent on that. Whether someone goes into the hospital or not depends on whether they've been there before and how often. This applies mostly to psychiatric hospitalization, but an excessive use of general hospitals is an indication that there may be a pattern of the family using the hospital as an escape from problems. We're also finding that it's a good sign for a return to the status quo if some member of the extended family is involved in the crisis.

INT.: Why is that?

DR. P.: Well, if the family falls apart on its own, we feel this means that it's pretty unstable. If it falls apart when the mother-in-law is visiting, that is a different matter. The analogy I use is that if a house collapses of its own weight, it's probably weaker structurally than a house that collapses under the weight of a falling meteorite.

INT.: Like a mother-in-law.

DR. P.: Exactly. We hope we will eventually be able not only to predict outcome but even to score the prediction. If we know the chances of success with a case are slim, we'll be more alerted to suicide. But it's still too early to be sure about these factors.

MRS. C.: When she was at my house she was so upset, see, this, ah, there had been this interval when this fourth husband, after they'd been, ah, separated all this time, and she was at that time trying to make ends meet, see, and the son was in his, in his college, so it was all her then, too, she'd babysit and did housework and a little work in, ah [hospital], but there was just not enough money to make the rounds, and I think she got frightened and afraid that, that, ah, she just wasn't gonna make it.

MRS. W.: Well, I knew I couldn't.

MRS. C.: So this, this fourth husband had always been poundin' at her to come back to him, anyhow, so she did, on the spur of the moment. (*Sighs.*) She went back to him and that lasted ten days, because he was very rough and mean and tried to beat her and a lot of things in that ten days, and I was on a trip, and when I come back from the trip she called me that morning to come and get her, that he was going to kill her or lock her up. Now that was it. I went down and got her and I brought her to [*Mrs. C.'s town*] and I kept her for two months.

MRS. W.: No, he wasn't gonna lock me up, because he didn't want to pay the bill.

MRS. C. (*overlapping*): And this husband would keep comin' out there and threaten her and all this and that. He was a very high-tempered, wild sort of a fellow and, ah, our doctor had given her these treatments for these . . .

MRS. W. (*overlapping*): Said I had a demon and he could cast it out.

MRS. C.: He gave her the injections . . .

DR. P.: Sounds kind of crazy.

MRS. C.: . . . for nerves. Well, he was, really, I mean the man was just wild. (*Sighs.*) I don't know what was the matter with him.

DR. P.: What do you think the problem is right now? I mean, something is apparently happening to make your sister . . .

MRS. C. (*overlapping*): Well, well, you see . . .

DR. P.: . . . make you feel, make the two of you feel, and Dr. Clark feel, that, ah, she should come into the hospital today.

MRS. C.: Well, Dr. Clark told us that she should come right on in, we had no thought, I thought if we took her out there . . .

DR. P. (*overlapping*): Yeah, well, what, what, what, ah . . .

MRS. W. (*overlapping*): I told 'em they couldn't afford no, how could they afford to pay Dr. Clark?

DR. P.: Okay. What made you decide to bring her to see Dr. Clark?

MRS. C.: Well, when my brother come up from [*nearby state*] and he came and saw her like that, she was raving and carrying on there and just, just simply wild . . .

DR. P.: Well, is she any different from the way she's been for the last year?

MRS. C. (*overlapping*): He was shocked to see her. But he hadn't seen her and he was shocked.

DR. P. (*overlapping*): Well, do you feel that she is any different from the—has she been getting gradually worse?

MRS. C. (*overlapping*): Yes, all through, all through July and month of August she was getting much worse. 'Cause I could go up there on Sundays and we'd take a ride and there would be times she would be real calm and we'd go on a picnic and, and everything was all right, only she'd keep going back to this starving and all that.

DR. P. (*to Mrs. W.*): I wonder if it had anything to do with your daughter being at home during the day rather than in school. Was this hard on you? (*Pause.*)

MRS. W. (*tearfully*): It's killin' me to see her like she is, the worse child in the block, oh, I can't understand how things got so out of hand.

DR. P.: They have gotten out of hand, haven't they? Things have really gotten out of hand.

MRS. W. (*overlapping*): It didn't seem, when Jerry was there he had a nice little flower box there in front of the porch on this side, and a nice one here, and it fell over and this one fell over, and the water frost got in 'em and, and they, ah, busted open, you know, from the drain.

DR. P.: Well, we'll come out Friday and see.

MRS. C. (*overlapping*): It just seemed like that through, through July and August she began getting more worked up about these bills (*inaudible phrase*) insecure.

MRS. W. (*overlapping, loudly*): When you come out there you'll wring your hands and you'll say well, God, I, I couldn't solve it, not God couldn't solve it.

INT.: I take it you're again trying to get at the precipitating factor for Mrs. Willy's symptom. Did you feel that the little girl's being at home during the summer could be it?

DR. P.: I didn't know. I was groping. But the fact that the family got her out of the house to relieve the situation suggested that it was at this point that they perceived there was a problem. I was trying to jog their minds back to that time.

INT.: All through this part you keep asking the family what brought them in, and it's apparent that you haven't got a satisfactory answer yet. Could you be more clear about what sort of thing you're after, not necessarily with this family, but in general?

DR. P.: Until a symptom makes such good sense that the events leading up to the crisis, and the crisis, and the symptoms, and the decision to come to the hospital, all fit together like a beautifully composed short story, we continue looking. This is what we feel we've got to have before we can decide how to handle the case and what specific recommendations to make. The story we've developed here is that of a woman who desperately needs security, who needs some man to take care of her financially. We've got a son who by his story is doing this, but by her story is not. We still don't know why she looks to this son for security or why he's living at home. And we don't know the part the sister is playing in all this. The story still has holes in it.

INT.: It's obvious that the family isn't thinking of the problem of Mrs. Willy as a beautifully written short story. When you ask them why they're there, they say, "Because she's crazy."

DR. P.: I don't expect them to share my premises.

INT.: Not all therapists share your premises either.

DR. P.: They're the logical outcome of the idea that symptoms make sense.

INT.: But not everybody operates on the assumption that you can't do effective therapy until you understand them. It hasn't been established that there's any connection between what's wrong and what you do to fix it. There are many methods that ignore causal factors and still seem to work.

DR. P.: We feel more confident about moving in and starting to make recommendations if we can all arrive at some agreement about what the situation is. The way we work is to give out, right away, specific directives, so that people have something objective and practical to do. So we try to find out as quickly as possible what the family problems are, in order to decide what kind of action will be most useful in solving them. In most of our cases, we have had no trouble figuring out the short story. And ending it differently.

MR. F.: There was one case we had some question about and didn't all agree about what was going on. The husband was out of work and depressed and the wife was acting terribly nice about it. She'd say, "Everything'll be all right, honey," and present herself as a tower of love and support. It just didn't ring right, but we couldn't find any way in which she was contributing to his depression.

INT.: Did you get him over his symptom?

DR. P.: Yes, and he went back to work. It was a very successful case, really. Many important changes were set in motion. But we never quite understood it.

MR. F.: I often wonder if we don't make people feel better even though we may be completely wrong about what's happening.

DR. P.: Kal may be right. As long as we get a short story that satisfies us, perhaps it doesn't matter if it's the right one.

INT.: Since therapy is often a matter of engineering what you want to have happen, you can equally well say you write the story you want people to read.

DR. P.: That may well be. Just the same, I think we feel a lot better about what we're doing and where we're going if we can first build up a meaningful picture of what's going on with the family. In this interview, unfortunately, I'm not succeeding in building up much of a picture at all. It wasn't until the second interview that the facts about the house came out and we began to see what the arrangement between Mrs. Willy and her son was and why it was breaking down.

INT.: You may have had trouble getting the facts, but you've managed to get in quite a bit of therapy.

DR. P.: Well, we are working rather acutely and we do feel the need to use therapeutically at any given point in time whatever comes up, rather than waiting and holding it, hatching it, nurturing it. So if we get some interpretation that seems appropriate, we go ahead and make it, even though we haven't gathered all the information. The fact that the interpretation may turn out to be inappropriate at a later date doesn't seem to matter.

DR. P.: Mrs. Willy, let's talk for a minute about the financial situation. (*To Paul*) You're making over a hundred dollars a week.

MRS. W. (*overlapping*): Paul's puttin' up a big front, now.

PAUL: Yeah, that's the gross. By the time I get done, ah, union dues, ah, income tax, all this, it's about eighty and then, like I said, I save twenty of it, so all I get . . .

DR. P. (*overlapping*): You save twenty of it?

MRS. W.: Tries to . . .

DR. P.: For what?

PAUL: Well, just to have it.

MRS. W.: They'll take it.

DR. P. (*simultaneously*): Okay. How much do you have saved?

PAUL: Oh, I don't know, it's around four . . .

MRS. W. (*loudly*): They'll come and take—I owe Dr. Cooper fifty dollars for fixin' my teeth that I can't pay. (*Dr. P. and Paul talking, inaudible exchange.*) And the collectors are gonna come in . . .

DR. P. (*overlapping, to Paul*): Do you have any particular outstanding bills?

MRS. W.: 'Cause I just can't pay that fifty dollars.

MRS. C.: Just the house.

PAUL: Just the house payment, that's the only one, that's the only regular big one.

DR. P.: So there's absolutely no reason for your mother to worry about money.

MRS. W. (*tearfully*): That's not true.

DR. P.: I think that things are . . .

PAUL (*simultaneously*): Well, I wouldn't worry.

MRS. W. (*loudly*): I owe Dr. Cooper fifty dollars . . .

MISS DEY. (*to Mrs. W.*): Now listen, you have to listen.

DR. P. (*simultaneously*): Just a second, just a second. Your son has told me what the financial situation is. He's got money in the bank, he's got enough money to pay the bills, and he's got money coming in. This is about as much as you could ever ask for. You're in good financial shape. Your son is going to take care of all that. Now then, I don't think this is the thing you are saying, at all, that your son's not making enough money. I think what you're saying is that you're afraid your son's going to go off and leave you.

MRS. W.: Dr. Cooper is, ah, he's waited two years.

DR. P.: Mrs., Mrs. Willy, Dr. Cooper can wait two more years.

MRS. W.: He won't. He's gonna put it in a collector's hands . . .

DR. P. (*overlapping*): What's he going to do, well, put it in a collector's hands, let's not worry about that.

MRS. W. (*overlapping*): After two years.

DR. P.: Your son can take care of it, anyway.

MRS. W. (*overlapping*): He needs it and I feel bad, I'd rather have my tooth . . .

DR. P.: How much do you owe Dr. Cooper?

MISS DEY.: Never mind that, you've got to listen, it's very important.

PAUL: I don't know, I think it's about fifty or sixty bucks.

INT.: I notice Carol comes in twice here to keep Mrs. Willy quiet. Is that her usual function with a patient who is upset?

DR. P.: It was this time. Carol was sitting right next to Mrs. Willy, hovering over her, trying to focus her attention, and being somewhat motherly. She was conveying to me, "I'll take care of her and you go on doing what you're trying to do." I remember the relief I felt at being able to turn the control of Mrs. Willy over to her.

MR. F.: I think Carol and I sat on either side of Mrs. Willy.

INT.: Do you position yourselves strategically?

MR. F.: Quite often we try to get in between the members of the family, to separate them. If we're seeing a couple, that means they have to look at each other.

MISS DEY.: We like to sit so that we can see each other too. We try to communicate as we go along, to keep in touch.

> DR. P. (*to Mrs. W.*): Okay. Look, it's a very small amount compared to what, what you've got. Look, let's talk about this, ah, it's not the money, your son's got the money and he's making money, we're not worried about this, I told you if you, if you start to starve, come over to the house, we'll feed you, don't worry about that. Ah, now then, I think what you're worried about is that your son is going to leave you.
>
> MRS. W.: Well, he may be drafted.
>
> MRS. C.: She worries about that a lot.
>
> DR. P. (*overlapping*): I don't think you worry about his being drafted, now he cannot be drafted, he's in a category where he cannot be drafted.
>
> MRS. W.: Why? He isn't in school.
>
> DR. P.: He can't be drafted because he has to support you. So he cannot be drafted. He is not going to be drafted. Okay? Will you believe me? Now, then, how else could he leave you? He says you're scared when he dates anybody, for fear that he's going to get married and go off and leave you.
>
> MRS. W.: He won't get married, I know that. I ain't the least worried about that.
>
> DR. P.: This is the only thing you tell us that you're not worried about, which makes me think that this is the one thing you are worried about. (*Laughing.*)
>
> MRS. W.: No, if a girl were to marry him . . .
>
> MRS. C.: Knowing Paul, she isn't worried about that, I don't think. He never dated through high school and college.
>
> MRS. W.: He's not so—that kid's smart, he, ah, you can't believe it, but he's smart, you know, you have to be smart to go four years to college.
>
> DR. P.: Uh-huh. Okay.

MRS. W.: It's hard to believe.

DR. P.: Not only is he smart, but he's got a good job and he's making good money. (*To Paul*) What do you think she's worried about? How do you think she . . .

PAUL (*overlapping*): I think just about everything.

DR. P.: How do you think she thinks you're going to leave her?

PAUL: Oh, I'm not, I, I wouldn't want to analyze it and say that that is her problem, because, ah, she's always (*inaudible phrase*), she's been that way for a long time.

DR. P. (*overlapping*): I'm not saying that's the only problem, the thing is that . . .

MRS. W. (*overlapping*): I'm not (*inaudible phrase*), how are these clothes gonna last me the rest of my life?

PAUL: I wouldn't want to say that my leaving was her big problem, frankly.

MRS. W.: Now the store's not gonna give me any.

MRS. C. (*simultaneously*): I don't think she's afraid of that.

MR. F.: What's that?

MRS. W.: The store, you gonna walk up to the store they ain't gonna give you any clothes.

PAUL: She's always had the same basic attitude . . .

MR. F.: Well, let's, let's listen to Paul.

PAUL: . . . for probably her whole life.

DR. P.: I'm trying to narrow it down here. I got the money thing out of the way. And it can't be the draft. Then I go on to the one explanation that's left for why Mrs. Willy is afraid that her son is going to leave her.

INT.: Did you get any evidence that he really was thinking about getting married?

DR. P.: No. Everybody agrees that this is the last thing this boy is going to do. And I think they were right. He was quite asexual.

INT.: Was part of his motivation for staying in this situation that it saved him from the draft?

DR. P.: I don't think so. I think he made a deal with his mother that in return for the house he would give up all else and so took vows of poverty, chastity, and obedience.

MISS DEY.: I remember he wore a ring on his wedding finger. When we mentioned it, he switched it to his right hand.

DR. P.: He was a peculiar boy. I didn't feel I should pass judgment on his life, though he certainly got his kicks in a different way from the way I get mine. But he did have some feeling that this was not the culturally accepted role for him and that he was sacrificing himself to be his mother's keeper.

INT.: Sometimes you find that a wife or mother like this will go to pieces as a way of holding somebody else together. As she began to pull herself together, did he begin to fall apart?

DR. P.: No, he didn't. We had some concern about whether he would allow his mother to get well. But he did, and encouraged it.

INT.: At any rate, you allow them to convince you that getting married isn't the problem.

DR. P.: Yes. I was as much in the dark as ever. Kal was the one who started to notice the hints Mrs. Willy was dropping about the clothes. And, of course, the major issue was not that Paul was threatening to leave her but that he was not supporting her properly. I missed her allusion to it here. I even missed Kal's effort to pick it up.

DR. P. (*to Paul*): What do you think would be the best thing for your mother?

PAUL (*laughing*): Oh, I haven't any idea.

DR. P.: What do you think?

PAUL: I really don't.

MRS. C.: Well, I, I couldn't tell you, I, I had thought that maybe she needed some kind of, ah, of these shots, because I, I thought that's what she needed, maybe it was a nervous condition, see . . .

DR. P. (*overlapping*): That would help temporarily, but I think she'd go right back to the same state.

MRS. C.: . . . a terrible nervous condition but, now I don't know, see . . .

MR. F.: Now you don't know . . .

MRS. C.: Well, I mean the doctor out here in the hall said she definitely didn't need shots, so I have to go along with that. I just thought that it was a terrible nervous cond-, condition, that had been brought up through the years of not always having security and, and she just sort of couldn't cope with it like the rest of us can.

INT. (*to Mr. F.*): Who were you talking to when you said, "Now you don't know"?

MR. F.: The sister. I think I was trying to say, "Since you don't really know, why don't you keep quiet?" That voice of hers was affecting me too.

INT.: All the same, she's the only one who is giving you any facts.

DR. P.: Sure. We're trying to manage her, but we don't want to silence her completely. She's the only informant we've got. People like this woman, who aren't so involved as the principals, can see the overall picture better, even though they sometimes drive you out of your mind. And at least she's starting to cooperate with us and give us some real information, instead of cueing Mrs. Willy off onto some more of her crazy talk.

DR. P. (*interrupting Mrs. C.*): Okay, okay, okay, she needs security, how's she going to get it? She can't get it by marrying one more man after another.

MRS. C.: No. No, no.

DR. P.: She's tried that. (*To Mrs. W.*) How are you going to get some security? What would give you security? What about a job?

MRS. W.: I can't get a job. (*Crying.*) This is all the dress I got!

MRS. C.: Sweetheart!

DR. P.: If you got a job, you could buy all sorts of new dresses.

MRS. W.: I can't get there, I have no car.

DR. P.: Paul can take you.

MRS. W.: He's got to go to work.

MRS. C. (*overlapping*): I think if she had some money coming in . . .

DR. P.: Mr. Flomenhaft's got a car, he can take you.

MRS. W.: Now, why do you say foolish things like that?

DR. P.: He can take you down to get a job and you could, once you find your way, you can go on the bus. (*Pause.*) How would you like to get a job?

MRS. W. (*overlapping*): I tried that cleaning, and I'd go out and clean for a lady on one day and then she'd say, well, I'd work myself nearly to death cleaning her house and then she'd want, ah, somebody to be there on Friday, they all want, they think there's a lot of Fridays in a week, you know.

DR. P.: Everybody wants a maid, wants somebody to do the cleaning on Fridays.

MRS. W.: Yeah. (*Pause.*)

MRS. C.: It does seem to me like that she lost that security when she lost this money. She had never worked before, she'd always just done housework. And that was it.

MRS. W. (*overlapping*): Well, I thought that was it, I thought as long as I could write a check, that was security . . .

MRS. C.: That was it, and then when she remarried . . .

MRS. W. (*overlapping*): . . . but I woke up to the fact that there was a lot more to it than that.

MRS. C.: . . . that, that seemed to be the beginning of it, she begin to see she hadn't, didn't have this money coming in and since she had never worked, only done her own housework through the years, it, it seemed like then these checks weren't coming in . . .

DR. P.: Mm-hm.

MRS. C.: . . . see, and now even though Paul is making the living, somehow or other she feels like that that's coming to Paul is not coming to her, and she worries because she doesn't want Paul to have to, it's, a lot of it's pride. She doesn't want Paul to have to take care of her and support her.

MRS. W. (*overlapping*): It's not pride.

MRS. C.: I know that.

MRS. W.: If I had my way, you know what'd happen?

DR. P.: What?

MRS. W.: It'd take a—well, it just couldn't be done, that's all.

DR. P.: What? What would you like to see happen?

MRS. W.: You know when they built the May Company up there, how deep they dug?

DR. P.: How deep?

MRS. W.: Well, pretty deep, you know, was you here?

DR. P.: No, I wasn't here, I've been here two months. What would you like to see happen?

MRS. W.: Just like my whole house to sink down and be covered up like that and, ah . . . (*Starting to cry.*)

DR. P.: I don't think you mean that. I think you want some security.

MRS. C.: That's it. When she came to my house she went to bed in the daytime, to cover up.

DR. P. (*overlapping*): And I think you're having to face up to the fact that some of this security has got to come from you.

INT.: Your tone changes here. It sounds more forceful, more determined. I get the feeling that you're shifting gears, changing over from getting information to the stage where you decide what you're going to do.

DR. P.: I wasn't aware of this here, but we do tend to bear down toward the end of the interview. People are screaming, wanting someone to go into the hospital, and we've got to accomplish something, no matter how small.

MRS. W.: Alice is gonna lose her home, this year.

MRS. C. (*simultaneously*): (*Inaudible phrase.*)

DR. P.: Aw, she's not going to lose her home.

MRS. W.: Yes, she is.

DR. P.: No, she's not.

MRS. W.: Yes, she is too.

MRS. C. (*overlapping*): See, she would go to bed in the daytime to cover up and I—and maybe she'd go to bed just the minute she'd swallowed her supper, and git in bed and cover up, because she seemed to want to hide, and she'd say, "I just want to hide from it all," see?

MR. F.: I gather, I just walked in here, you know, that, that something has happened lately that you feel that either Paul is not going to be able to continue to support you . . .

MRS. W.: I know he won't . . .

MR. F.: But . . .

MRS. W.: (*Inaudible phrase.*)

DR. P.: You're saying it has to do with the draft, but I don't think this is it because Paul's pretty secure as far as the draft is concerned. (*Mrs. W. talking in background.*) (*To Paul*) Have you thought about joining the Service?

PAUL: Oh, sure.

MRS. W.: He'd like to, he wishes now he'd a joined when he got outa college and . . .

DR. P. (*overlapping*): Have you thought about running out on this situation?

MRS. W.: . . . get outa this mess.

PAUL: No, not lately.

DR. P.: You haven't?

PAUL: Ah, I don't think there is anyone else that would handle it as well as I do and who could . . .

DR. P.: Okay. I think you get some gratification out of handling it as well as you do.

PAUL: I'd rather it wasn't existing, actually, but, ah . . .

DR. P.: Okay.

PAUL: I wouldn't run out on it.

DR. P.: Okay. I think that we all know that.

MRS. W. (*overlapping*): He's gonna be *put* out on it.

DR. P.: We want to make your mother more self-supporting, in one way or another, more secure.

MRS. W. (*tearfully*): I can't understand it, it's just, you know, it's just of all the people in the world, why does it happen to me?

PAUL (*overlapping*): I wouldn't mind her just being dependent as much as her constantly worrying and talking about it all the time.

MRS. C.: Just pacin' the ground, you know.

INT.: You're finally confronting the son, asking him right out what he has done or is thinking of doing that has put his mother in such a state.

DR. P.: I've really been dealing with him for quite a while, but it's been in bits and pieces, because the mother is pretty distracted, and the sister is too, and the son sort of deflects it. What I was trying to do was to con him into giving me some glimmer of what I suspected, which was that yes, he was thinking of running out.

INT.: But you couldn't con it out of him.

DR. P.: Because he really wasn't thinking of running out.

INT.: At least you got the negative side into the picture, to reassure the mother. She's voicing doubts again.

DR. P.: She was feeling that he was doing too much, sacrificing his own life to stay with her. She couldn't believe he was going to be able to keep it up. And she probably felt guilty too. After all, she gave Paul the house as a bribe to stay with her.

INT.: Was there an element of testing in her craziness? To see whether, if she made it really impossible for him, he would still stay?

DR. P.: The boy was clearly not going to put up with his mother being crazy. But he was quite happy to put up with her as long as she cooked his meals and kept his house straight. This kept him from having to go out and be a heterosexual, and it enabled him to be a better husband to his mother than his father, and to gain power through the use of money.

INT.: That's why you say he's getting some gratification out of the situation.

DR. P.: I think the whole problem was that they hadn't worked out a contract and her efforts to convey to him what she expected in return for the house had failed.

INT.: All through this interview, but here particularly, you have a way of talking to the other family members about Mrs. Willy as though she weren't there.

DR. P.: It's usually to let her know that when she talks in this hysterical way I don't approve of her. All the same, I would always be careful not to give the family the impression that by ignoring her I am agreeing with them that she is the patient. I do here to some extent, but that is after it has been established that she is not as crazy as they think and that they are part of it too. Once we have reached a commitment about the proper way of approaching this, I can go ahead and admit that she's acting crazy and deal with the other family members about the reality of her craziness.

INT.: I'm thinking more in general about the technique of dealing with one person by speaking to someone else. It's like playing billiards, where you aim for one ball in order to hit another.

DR. P.: I think we do that all the time.

INT.: People can't very well counter you when you address them that way. It's one of the merits of family therapy.

PAUL: There's no—and she, she should be able to function as, as a housekeeper, or something, around the house, there.

MRS. C.: It is hard on Paul. When he comes home to everything in a mess, the morning dishes still there . . .

MRS. W. (loudly): He don't eat, that boy don't eat, you know what he eats?

DR. P.: What?

MRS. W. (wailing): Maybe a few, couple a eggs in the morning, no lunch, he comes home and he don't have any supper.

DR. P.: He can afford it, if he wants to.

MRS. W.: And workin' in that [store] warehouse.

MRS. C. (overlapping): He comes home for supper, but she can't, she won't have it ready, see.

MRS. W.: He's just, he's just skin and bones.

MR. F.: What do you, why don't you . . .

MRS. C. (overlapping): She just can't seem to get in there and do that.

MR. F.: . . . why don't you cook him the meal?

MRS. C.: Now she did that all until the last two months, she did that.

MR. F.: What stopped that?

DR. P. (to Mrs. W.): Why can't you cook him a meal? Like you think he ought to eat? (*Pause.*) I think you ought to start cooking every meal.

MRS. W. (*overlapping*): I'm alive, and that's all.

MR. F.: Well, why don't you go out and cook him up a meal?

DR. P.: Well . . .

MISS DEY.: And start kicking.

INT.: It's clear that the cooking is what you've decided you're all going to zero in on. How did you signal for this?

DR. P.: She wasn't cooking. And a woman should cook. Everybody knows that.

INT.: You came up with this spontaneously?

DR. P.: It wasn't quite as simple as that. But everybody was agreeing that one of the big problems was that she wasn't cooking Paul's supper. We knew now that Paul wasn't going to leave, and if he wasn't going to leave, how were they going to work things out while he was there?

INT.: When the son says she isn't functioning as a good housekeeper, that cues you off?

DR. P.: Yes. Paul was saying, "If only she would keep house for me, I could put up with everything else." If she would only cook his supper that night, we would have a lever for the next day's interview. We were still looking for that lever. That little change that would start everything moving.

INT.: And you all know you're looking for that lever before the end of the session.

DR. P.: Yes. The two women were saying that Paul had nothing to eat, so when Kal suggested that Mrs. Willy should cook the meal, I thought it was a good idea and jumped in too, and Carol followed us.

INT.: It's interesting, the way you go about getting this woman to cook. It's a triple assault.

DR. P.: That's right.

INT.: You don't see it as a problem of how to manage this woman into cooking, but how to pressure her into it.

DR. P.: There are two ways of going about it. One is to cut off all side issues that would prevent her from cooking. We'll say, "What is it that keeps you from cooking?" and she'll say, "The pans are dirty," and we'll say, "We'll come out and help you wash the pans." Or we'll use a direct frontal assault, as we did here. Though it's usually a combination of the two.

INT.: But you would never, for example, get together with her by sympathizing with her about how bad a cook she was?

DR. P.: Never. We just tell people straight out what they have to do. The other way might work in a week, but we have to have results by the next day. We borrow a page from military psychiatry: "If you're tired and can't work, we'll give you a hot meal and a good night's sleep and expect you to go to work tomorrow." This is basic, the expectation of function.

MR. F.: She could spend ten years on the couch, finding out why she couldn't cook.

INT.: Another device you use, as I understand it, is to go right into somebody's house and put the mop in her hand.

DR. P.: Yes. A few days later, Carol was standing over Mrs. Willy while she mopped her kitchen floor.

INT.: How far do you go in coercing people?

DR. P.: Pretty far sometimes. We had a school phobia case, a fourteen-year-old girl who refused to go to school. Carol went out, tried to get her dressed, struggled with her, and finally called for reinforcements. So Kal and I joined her, dumped the girl in the car and sent her off to school.

MISS DEY.: After that, the family was able to take over and get her to school themselves.

INT.: I should think that part of your success is that you make yourselves a little bit disagreeable.

DR. P.: Oh, yes. We've had people call us and say that if we'd just leave them alone and stop picking at all these fine points, they'd do whatever we said. There was one woman who phoned us to say, "Okay, I will go back to my sink if you'll just get this visiting nurse out of my house."

INT.: One of the functions of working this way would be to pull the family together against the team that steps in.

MR. F.: Well, when someone comes for help, the whole relationship means "There's something wrong with me." So we try to get them to want to say, "Let's agree that I don't need you."

INT.: There's another factor in this direct assault, that if you push people too far, they'll go halfway.

DR. P.: That's possible.

INT.: There's something else about it too. It's not really so direct. When you started this interview, you suggested that Mrs. Willy might go to work and everybody said, "How can she, she's crazy!" All this time you've been working to make her seem less crazy and to implicate the son, and you never push her to take responsibility without pushing him first. Once you got him to acknowledge that he wasn't going to leave her, then you could move in and say, "All right, Mrs. Willy, you cook."

DR. P.: It's the process of negotiating a contract. We've gotten into trouble every time we've focused on only one person and tried to make him change his way of operating without getting the other person to make a move too. We have to be able to say to Mrs. Willy, "Since Paul is willing to stay home and have the burden of you, why don't you cook him a meal?"

INT.: When you say this, you're also telling the rest of the family that they can act differently with her.

DR. P.: Yes. We are relieving them of the burden of making concessions to her craziness.

INT.: It's putting the environment to work. You're the experts, and when you refuse to make concessions to her, it invites them to follow suit. But from then on, it isn't so much that she's going to cook because you say so, but because they say so.

DR. P.: There's another aspect. When these families come in, they are in a state of crisis, and it's a lot easier to make direct suggestions and have them followed than if they come in when there is no crisis. We had two cases of girls who were arrested for shoplifting. In one case, the shoplifting was part of a crisis, and we cleared it up by working with it on that basis. But in the other case, the girl was supporting her family by shoplifting because she didn't want her husband to go to work, she liked him at home with her. She had been picked up for this, and the judge let her off because she said, "I've got this fear that I'm going to kill my child." So he sent her down to the hospital, and she was sent on to us. When we investigated, we found everything peaceful at home, no crisis, no believability to the announcement about killing her child, nothing. What we did was to discount the symptom and tell her husband to go to work, which, with sufficient prodding from the authorities, he did. We treated it not as a crisis in their relationship but as a matter to be settled between them and their parole officers.

INT.: You seem to be suggesting that direct pressure is only useful when there's a crisis. I would question that. A kind of mystique has developed that a psychiatric patient should never be told what to do, but there's tremendous advantage in doing just that, not only in crisis situations but in chronic situations too.

DR. P.: We've found it works in our situation. After all, we did get Mrs. Willy to cook.

INT.: That night?

DR. P.: No, but the next one.

INT.: This interview travels from the point where you invite Mrs. Willy to come to supper to the point where you tell her to cook supper at home.

DR. P.: We feel that talking about cooking is a better way of dealing with someone's helplessness than talking to her about her helplessness.

INT.: That seems to sum up your approach. One could call you the kitchen-sink school of psychiatry. But it's not quite a real kitchen sink.

DR. P.: We do tend to use things like the kitchen sink as symbols of functioning, but I wouldn't like our method to be characterized that way.

MRS. C.: We've tried to talk to her to have his meal and keep the house up, it seemed like this thing just worries her so, she just mills around all day in the house and everything gets (*inaudible phrase*).

DR. P. (*overlapping*): You know, she has just about convinced the two of you that she's helpless, and she's not.

MRS. C. (*laughing*): Well, maybe you're right, there, I think it's . . .

DR. P.: She's not helpless at all.

INT.: What's your evidence for saying that Mrs. Willy is not helpless?

DR. P.: Anybody who can keep this many people in that degree of turmoil for that amount of time is not helpless.

INT.: But you don't direct this speech to her. You talk to the others. You tell them, "She's convinced the two of you that she's helpless." It's again that method of accusing somebody in a way he can't counter because you're not talking to him.

DR. P.: I'm not accusing her, I'm appreciating her. When I say that she has convinced them, the implication is that this is an effect that she is trying to produce, that she has effectively produced.

INT.: You put them in a bind. Either they stop letting her get away with it or they have to admit that they're being conned.

DR. P.: This is placing responsibility on her, too, for making them feel this way.

INT.: And on them for buying it. You distribute the responsibility.

DR. P.: That's right.

INT.: It's a very complicated comment when you stop to think about it. If she's helpless, she couldn't convince anybody.

DR. P.: That's what I want them to see.

MRS. C.: I, I've got a silly feeling that if she had a pay check coming in every week and she could see that pay check and it's made out in her name, that that would satisfy her (*inaudible words*).

MRS. W. (*overlapping*): If I had a billion dollars in greenbacks (*inaudible phrase*) my whole clothes closet, or a house full, it wouldn't help me one bit. It might help you, but it wouldn't help me.

DR. P.: Why wouldn't it help you?

MRS. W.: Might not help you, either.

DR. P.: Why wouldn't it help you?

MRS. W.: Because it just wouldn't help.

DR. P.: It wouldn't be enough?

MRS. W.: Well, it just ain't what's needed. (*Laughs.*)

DR. P.: What's needed? I think what you're telling me is you need a man. A man you can rely on. A man who's going to take care of you.

MRS. W.: No, they're just like a stick to me, they're just walkin' around like a—jack in the box. (*Everybody laughs.*)

INT.: The whole group seems to breaking up over this.

DR. P.: I think we all appreciated her sense of humor. For her to put over a point as indirectly as that and have everybody get it was pretty effective.

INT.: You must have welcomed this as another indication that she wasn't really so crazy.

DR. P.: Yes. It showed that she had a lot of control over what she said and did.

INT.: Why did you turn here and go in the other direction? You stop telling Mrs. Willy what you think she needs and ask her instead what she'd like.

DR. P.: I'm still bargaining for them. Paul has told me what he expects of her, so now I'm trying to find out what she expects of him. I'm trying to find out what aspect of a man she wants him to provide, since as far as I could see she didn't need one for money. Well, she tells me what aspect of a man she *doesn't* need.

> MRS. C.: (*Laughing, inaudible words.*)
> DR. P.: What?
> MRS. C. (*laughing*): The last two were such (*laughing*) mistakes. I don't think she'd want another.
> DR. P. (*to Mrs. W.*): You've had bad luck with them, I know.
> MRS. C.: She did take care of the money and all the bills all the time Jerry was in the hospital sick with this heart trouble and, and she felt authority, she felt like she could handle the money and pay these bills, even though these checks were coming in, and now that she has to, to lean on Paul, it seems to have . . .

INT.: The sister has swung around here. She's swung from her astonishment that her sister isn't going into the hospital to an appreciation of how well she has handled a very hard life.

DR. P.: Yes. When she came in, she was on Paul's side. Now she's on her sister's side. She's saying, "My sister hasn't done so badly; she's had a lot of trouble and she's coped with it. If something is going wrong, it must be in the way Paul is treating her." This is the first admission we've had from anybody that Mrs. Willy isn't so crazy.

INT.: Of all the people in the interview, the sister is the person who has changed her attitude the most.

DR. P.: One thing we've noticed repeatedly is that the extended family member, the one least involved in the family, is the one who is in the best position to change. And who, by changing, can effect a change in everybody else. This is why we focus so much on the extended family.

INT.: Do you try to see everyone or only those persons who come in with the patient?

DR. P.: Everyone that we can get hold of, everyone that we feel plays any kind of part in the family.

MRS. W.: See, I had a little girl that had cirrhosis of the liver. Died, eleven years old.

MR. F.: When was that?

MRS. W.: Oh, here a few years ago.

MRS. C.: Four, four years.

DR. P.: Was this between Gloria and Paul?

MRS. C.: No, just four years ago.

PAUL: She was the youngest.

MRS. C.: She died after Jerry. She died right, a year after Jerry died . . .

PAUL: She . . .

MRS. C.: . . . one year after her husband died and he . . .

PAUL (*overlapping*): She was the youngest child by the first husband.

MRS. C.: . . . that was a terrible shock to her.

DR. P.: The youngest child by the first husband.

PAUL: And she was the second from the bottom, as far as age goes.

MRS. W.: Anyway, she died. I was at the hospital most of the time with her for four years, off and on. (*Long pause.*)

DR. P. (*to Mrs. W.*): What do you enjoy? What do you like to do? I know you like to have your house looking good, but what else do you like to do?

INT.: Why does Mrs. Willy suddenly come in with that story about the child?

DR. P.: I think she was reacting to what her sister was saying about how well she had done. She wanted to display another instance in which she had struggled with a difficult time and done well.

INT.: She's talking with a lot of real, not crazy, feeling.

DR. P.: I don't think I was very sympathetic to her, though I was pleased to see her functioning so well.

INT.: I gather you're not interested in helping her explore her feelings about the child who died.

DR. P.: No. I didn't want to get into a long grief reaction.

INT.: Is that why you cut her off?

DR. P.: She cut herself off. There was quite a pause between the end of that story and where I came in.

INT.: All through the interview you've been asking about the bad things that have happened to her, but here you ask, "What do you enjoy?"

DR. P.: This is a technique I use quite often when someone is depressed.

INT.: Then you shift from "What do you enjoy?" to suggesting that she enjoys housework. You go from what she *likes* to what she likes to *do*. When it doesn't follow logically.

DR. P.: It is just another way of saying, "We expect you to have your house clean. We know you're going to be functioning from this point on."

INT.: It's hypnotic technique again. You take it for granted that she's going to work; it's just a question of what kind of work.

MRS. C.: She's a wonderful cook. When she, when she has lovely salads and things like that . . .

MRS. W. (*overlapping*): No, I'm not either. I used to make chocolate pies, you know, with frosting on them . . .

MRS. C.: She loves flowers . . .

MRS. W.: . . . cream pies, and . . .

MRS. C.: . . . she had beautiful roses in the back, she was proud of them.

MRS. W.: I did, oh, my gosh!

MRS. C.: Now the roses are all up in weeds and that bothers her.

MRS. W. (*wailing*): Weeds, weeds, weeds, weeds! Hundreds of trees growin' up, it's gonna, the neighbors are going to . . .

DR. P.: Why don't you go and mow them?

MRS. W.: I can't, they're, they're, beyond, beyond, ah, control.

DR. P. (*to Paul*): What are your plans this weekend?

PAUL: Pardon?

DR. P.: What are your plans this weekend?

MRS. W.: He works.

PAUL: I work.

MRS. C.: He has no weekends.

PAUL: Except for Monday and Wednesday.

DR. P.: You work every day except Monday and Wednesday. Okay. What are your plans Monday?

PAUL: Oh, I don't know.

DR. P.: Okay. Why don't you and your mother get out in the yard and clean the thing up?

MRS. W.: Beyond control.

DR. P.: Aw, I don't believe it. We'll see it on Friday. If it's beyond control, we'll pass judgment on it and say so.

MRS. W.: Oh, I know it is. It's just the weeds, they're growin' up, the edges are growin', and by next summer, it's gonna be that tall, and then it's gonna be up to . . .

DR. P. (*overlapping, to Paul*): Would you like a chocolate pie?

PAUL: Not especially.

MR. F.: What would you like your mother to cook?

DR. P.: What would you like for your mother to cook for you?

PAUL (*laughing*): Oh, I don't know, whatever we have, chicken . . .

MRS. W. (*overlapping*): He'd like to have a good meal once more in his life.

MR. F.: What's a good meal?

MISS DEY.: He wants chicken.

DR. P. (*simultaneously*): Look, what I'm saying is this—chicken, he wants chicken.

MRS. C.: If it's up to Paul, it's baked duck. (*Laughing.*) He used to bring the baked duck home. (*Laughs.*)

INT.: When you direct Paul and his mother to clean up the yard, I take it this is again finding something specific they can do.

DR. P.: Yes. Something they can do together this time. The sister was saying that Mrs. Willy was the one who had handled the yard up till then, and by putting Paul in charge we were making a change from the way things had been. But I think in every interview we try to point out some relatively small, practical thing the other family members can do to help. As I said before, it's got to be a mutual proposition, even if it's just a face-saving device. I'll say to a husband, "Okay, if you go to work and bring home a pay check and quit running around with women and quit drinking, your wife will cook lamb chops for you once a week."

INT.: It's this bargaining again.

DR. P.: That's right. Since we weren't clear about whose responsibility the yard was, we said, "You do it together." Otherwise we might have handed the task to Paul alone.

INT.: How successful were you in getting them to clean up the house and yard?

DR. P.: The day after the second interview, we went out, and Gloria, the oldest daughter, had done some work about the house and was out mowing the lawn. We told her to leave it till Paul came home. He got the yard done by the following Monday.

INT.: Why was Gloria there mowing the lawn?

DR. P.: She was invited to. Mrs. Willy wanted things to look nice for our visit. All the same, when we got there Mrs. Willy was walking around wringing her hands and saying that it was all hopeless. So we simplified her task. We focused first on the kitchen floor, then on this, then on that, until she finally got the place cleaned up.

INT.: You went step by step with the housecleaning?

MISS DEY.: No, we'd just say generally, "Clean the kitchen," and she'd know what to do. We'd check with her each day to make sure she had done what we expected her to do, or go out and stand there till she did it. It took us several days to get her to mop the kitchen floor, but as soon as she did that, she got through all the rest.

INT.: And you kept on pressuring Paul to do his share?

DR. P.: Yes. To weed the yard, get the washing machine fixed, get his motorcycle off the porch. With other families, later on, we became quite sophisticated and subtle. We'd go through entire schedules with some of them.

INT.: How do you decide on what practical tasks to give your families?

DR. P.: It depends on the kind of things they say they haven't been doing. With one woman, it was picking up a pile of dirty laundry and moving it to the laundry room.

INT.: What do you do when you have somebody whose trouble can't be pinned down to a matter of mopping the kitchen floor?

DR. P.: We don't usually deal with kitchen floors with nonpsychotic women. When people are able to handle the daily aspects of their lives, there isn't the problem of getting them to function, and we tend to deal more in abstract ideas. But we still feel that if we can take the abstract and reduce it to something concrete, to some practical gesture, we're ahead of the game. One case we had was a nurse who was married to a very hard-driving, successful man and had managed to keep up with him. He would call her on the phone and say, "I've got a live one here, come on down and we'll have martinis for lunch." And she'd come down and join him in this salesman-like world and it was a great relationship, until she became physically ill and had four operations in a year. Then she began demanding that he stay home with her and give her a little support. She'd say, "I can't keep up with you," and he'd say, "I don't care, if you want to be with me, you've got to join me." Finally she called him and said, "If you don't get me to a psychiatrist, I'm going to kill myself." And he said, "Look, I'm busy right now, I'm closing a big deal, I won't be home tonight, we'll talk about it tomorrow." So she made the suicide attempt. We saw these two people together and we were dealing with abstractions the whole time. The only practical suggestions that were made came from them. One suggestion the husband made was that she take a job in his office, which she had done before. And she did, and they've made a pretty good adjustment. But I don't think we assigned any other tasks.

MISS DEY.: We suggested that they go out and have sex under the trees. This was because they told us that the times during their marriage when they felt most free and happy was when they would go off to their summer cabin, and when they felt like it, they would run off to the woods and "have sex under the trees." So we took their happy reminiscence and based a practical suggestion on it, to try and bring out the strengths in the marriage.

DR. P.: We don't like to impose a task if we can get people to come up with one themselves. If the situation is a relatively healthy one, as it was here, they usually do.

MR. F.: I think it also makes a difference that most of our patients come from a lower-income population. It's easier to reach a task-oriented outlook with people in that group.

INT.: That isn't always true. The more educated people are, the more often this sort of approach works, because it's so simple. They can't handle you by it. People come in expecting a lot of psychiatric gobbledygook, and you tell them to perform some ordinary task.

DR. P.: We've had a few people come in and say, "What kind of therapy is this? I thought you were supposed to lie down on the couch and talk." They are quite surprised. But I agree with Kal, this approach is often resented by upper-middle-class families.

INT.: Your kind of therapy also has the advantage of not threatening to expose people. You're not going to drag all the skeletons out of people's closets.

DR. P.: That's true. We have been careful about secrets, for fear that we'd dig up more trouble than we could deal with in a few interviews. We're trying to separate secrets that are known, or should be, but are being denied, from those that should be kept secret. We feel we can't move frozen relationships so long as there is something embarrassing which everyone knows about but can't face, so we try to get it looked at. There is also the kind of secretiveness that looks trivial but which actually amounts to a block in communication, such as Paul's hiding his financial setup. On the other hand, we don't see much advantage in having everybody shout out the details of past affairs.

MISS DEY.: I think that what impresses us most is the amount of confrontation families are able to take. They're not as fragile as you'd think.

> DR. P.: Look, what I'm trying to say is this—anybody who is treated like a helpless child is going to act like one. Now somewhere along the line your mother has started telling everybody she's a helpless child and she can't do anything, she can't take care of anything, and all the world's going to fall in on top of her, and you've begun to believe it. As far as her own health is concerned.
>
> PAUL (*overlapping*): Oh, no, I, I usually get up. I say, "Would you mind fixin' my breakfast?" And lately she hasn't been fixin' my breakfast. But when she did fix my breakfast—couple eggs, no salt, no pepper, burnt . . .
>
> MRS. C.: That's just in the last . . .
>
> PAUL: . . . so I'd rather fix my own breakfast.
>
> DR. P.: That's just been in the last couple of months.
>
> MRS. C.: Yeah. Um-hm.
>
> DR. P. (*to Mrs. W.*): Can you fix his eggs? (*Pause.*)
>
> MRS. C.: She just . . .
>
> DR. P.: Well, that's a silly question, of course you can fix his eggs.
>
> MRS. C.: See, she does start these things, but she walks away and lets them burn up. I mean, she just forgets about them.

INT.: Again you make the point that if Mrs. Willy is helpless, it's because they treat her as if she were helpless.

DR. P.: As I said before, we put the responsibility on the people around the patient. This is also the most effective way to put pressure on the patient.

INT.: By this point in the interview, the son and the sister are not treating Mrs. Willy as if she were helpless. The sister is talking about how well she cooks, and the son is complaining about how his breakfast is being fixed, not that his mother is crazy. This is a major shift.

DR. P.: We've gotten down to the real issues.

INT.: Like burning the eggs. I'm wondering why you wouldn't bring up the idea that she might be burning the eggs because she was angry at Paul. Why you wouldn't go into the feelings behind it.

DR. P.: Because, whether she is angry or not, this is something she has control over. Carol once said to a patient, "We don't care how you feel, you still have to clean the kitchen." Exploring Mrs. Willy's feelings is not going to make her stop burning the breakfast. Making her aware that this is something she can choose not to do, and making the person she's cooking the breakfast for aware of this too, is going to make her stop it.

INT.: You wouldn't feel, as some therapists might, that if you tell her that burning the breakfast is a way of being mean to him, she'll feel so guilty that she'll stop?

DR. P.: I think that would be a little complicated and abstract. We'd have to get her agreement on that motivation and work through the whole thing.

INT.: I notice that you felt you'd made a mistake here, where you corrected yourself about fixing the eggs.

DR. P.: I did make a mistake. We're not asking her opinion about whether she can fix his eggs. We're assuming she can.

INT.: You would have preferred a phrasing of *"Will* you fix his eggs?"

DR. P.: Yes. But by making a mistake and covering it that way, I think I made the point more effectively than if I'd said it right to begin with.

MISS DEY.: Well, tomorrow morning before you come in . . .

MRS. W.: Well, I don't see how Paul can miss work.

DR. P.: Look, let Paul worry about that, he can miss work tomorrow morning.

MRS. W.: Can't, can you, Paul?

DR. P.: Sure he can.

PAUL: I'll just call 'em up, they'll probably give me the whole day off.

MRS. W.: Well, what are they gonna do for a man?

PAUL: (*Inaudible phrase.*)

DR. P.: Let them worry about that, you're worried about everybody else's problems, even people in Holland, and that's a long way away.

MRS. C.: Well, that's where her mother was born.

DR. P.: Yeah, but she's not there now, so let's, let's not worry about Holland, or let's not worry about his problems.

MRS. W. (*overlapping*): Thank God she died before she was throwed on the street.

DR. P.: Now, nobody's been throwed on the street.

MRS. W.: And she had a beautiful little home. And she kept it up real nice till she was aged seventy-six years old.

DR. P.: Look, can your daughter come in tomorrow, too?

PAUL: She can . . .

MRS. C. (*simultaneously*): That is a problem.

MRS. W.: No, she has three babies and she . . .

DR. P.: She can bring them, too.

MRS. W.: She's got to get some of them in school and . . .

DR. P.: She can bring the three babies, we'd like to see her, too.

MRS. C. (*low voice*): I don't think she'd come . . .

PAUL: Would you like to have her come?

MISS DEY.: Yes.

DR. P.: Yes.

MRS. W.: I don't think she can come.

PAUL (*overlapping*): Well, we can request it.

MRS. C.: You're going to find part of the trouble there, a very hysterical, nervous woman.

MRS. W.: Well, why wouldn't she be?

MRS. C.: She upsets her, when, when she has her problems and brings them home to her, and she carries on and goes on about her family and her problems with this terrible, hysterical (*sighs*) tone of voice and then she's all upset for days and days about it.

DR. P. (*overlapping, to Paul*): Is she just like your mother, thinking the world's going to come to an end the next minute?

PAUL: No, ah, she's pretty optimistic, but she just . . .

MRS. W.: She's more optimistic than she's got a right to be.

PAUL (*overlapping*): She's, she's kind of, ah, ah, I don't know, you know, she talks in either a loud voice or screams or . . .

MRS. C.: Nervous.

PAUL: Very nervous.

MR. F.: Does she make you nervous?

MRS. C.: Yes.

DR. P.: You know, it's a wonder you've stayed as long as you have.

MRS. C.: And she goes on then for days about their problems, how they are, the daughter brings these problems home to her and she shouldn't mention them but she does . . .

PAUL: I know, she's not like Mother at all, she, ah, seems to lack any control when it comes to talking like this, you know.

INT.: It's amazing to hear the son now defining his mother as a person who has some control over herself.

DR. P.: I think he may be reacting to the new evaluation of his mother that has come out during the interview.

INT.: Was Paul right in saying that Gloria was less controlled than his mother?

DR. P.: Well, she was continually reinforcing her mother's belief that the dikes were going to break in on her. Mrs. Willy would say, "Maybe if I could get things cleaned up, the house would look a little better," and Gloria would say, "No, it won't." And she'd say, "Paul is going to starve," and Gloria would say, "He probably will." By constantly undercutting him, she was expressing her anger at her mother for turning the house over to Paul.

INT.: Did you work with this daughter?

DR. P.: We tried to get her to come in, but she wouldn't. So we concentrated on extruding her. There was another boy, Wayne, who was Mr. Larrabee's son by a previous marriage. He was the rightful heir to the house and he had been heard to say that he was so mad at Paul that he was going to kill him. He was a very psychopathic boy. We never saw him, but the opinion of everybody in the family seemed to support this. There was some realistic basis for Mrs. Willy to believe that Wayne would make some effort to hurt or incapacitate Paul. We never saw the uncle who came and took the little girl away, but his primary concern was that she shouldn't be around because Paul wasn't strong enough to handle the situation. All these relatives were trying in one way or another to undermine Mrs. Willy's belief in Paul's ability to support her, and they were all coming in and out of the house as if it were a railway station. One of our first maneuvers was to get them all out of the picture as soon as possible.

INT.: How did you do that with Gloria? She lived just down the street.

DR. P.: We got them to fix the washing machine, so that Gloria didn't have to do Mrs. Willy's laundry. And we pointed out to Gloria that her dismal outlook was making things worse for her mother and that it would be better if she'd stay away. We sent Mrs. Clapp back home to her shop, and the little girl didn't return till a couple of months later. So we reduced this chaotic house of cards down to the duo, which we then worked with quite successfully.

INT.: How did things turn out?

MR. F.: Very well. I met Mrs. Willy in the supermarket the other day and she was so pleasant and attractive you wouldn't know she was the same lady. She has a part-time job and is doing nicely. Paul hasn't gone back to school but is thinking about it. He's been offered a better job and may take that instead. What was nice was that Paul bought a Volkswagen, which Mrs. Willy just loved, and they've been traveling all over the state in it since.

DR. P.: Okay. Well, look, ah, can you give some information to our secretary real quick before she gets away?

MRS. C.: Yeah.

DR. P.: And, ah, yeah, and I will give you some medicine for you to take . . .

MRS. W.: Do you know where to come at, ah, Friday morning?

MISS DEY.: We'll find out tomorrow.

DR. P.: We'll find out tomorrow, and you and your son and hopefully, your daughter, will come in at eight o'clock in the morning and see us.

MRS. W.: Now, what if we don't make it, what if he can't get off, would you . . .

MISS DEY.: He'll get off, and you'll make it.

DR. P.: He'll get off, you'll make it. If there's any difficulty about anything, call us on extension 506.

PAUL: All right.

DR. P.: 399—

MISS DEY.: 1211.

DR. P.: 1211. (*To Mrs. W.*) Now, we'll give you some pills. (*Leaves room.*)

PAUL.: 399—

MISS DEY.: 1211. Extension 506.

PAUL: That's Dr. who?

MISS DEY.: Dr. Frank Pittman.

PAUL: Pittman.

MISS DEY.: My name is Miss DeYoung. (*Spelling*) D-E-Y-O-U-N-G, capital Y-O-U-N-G. And he's Mr. Flomenhaft.

PAUL: Oh, all right.

MISS DEY.: Ah, and if there's any difficulty, this evening or . . .

PAUL: All right, we'll be in. Ah, where do you want us to come?

MISS DEY.: Right here.

PAUL: The same, ah . . .

MISS DEY.: Yeah. (*Voices fading away, tape recording ends.*)

INT. (*to Miss DeY.*): When you begin that "Tomorrow morning before you come in," what were you planning to tell them?

MISS DEY.: I was going to say to Mrs. Willy, "Tomorrow morning, before you come in, fix Paul's breakfast."

INT.: And this got lost in the shuffle?

DR. P.: I guess my impatience to end the interview was pretty evident in that I was cutting Carol off. I shouldn't have, because Carol was pursuing something very important, which was to settle the issue that Mrs. Willy should cook a meal.

INT.: You would ideally aim to settle at least one issue that first interview?

DR. P.: Yes. I think I assumed that the matter of the cooking was settled, and it certainly wasn't. If we were doing the case again, I would try to get a clear-cut agreement on that.

INT.: Did you check about the breakfast the next day?

DR. P.: Yes, and she hadn't cooked it.

INT.: Did you take this as discouraging?

DR. P.: We took it as a little bit discouraging and were a great deal more specific about what she was to do the day after, which was to clean the kitchen floor and cook Paul's breakfast too. And she did. Of course, one important issue that we did settle in the first interview was the matter of the pills. Before they left, I made sure Mrs. Willy knew she had to take them.

INT.: And did she?

DR. P.: Yes. That was the first thing we checked on the next day. We also got her to admit that she had had a good night's sleep. We feel we have to obtain some evidence of improvement during the first twenty-four hours.

INT.: What would you have done if she hadn't taken the pills?

DR. P.: We would have asked for a very clear-cut understanding about why she hadn't, particularly whether some other member of the family had been standing in her way.

INT.: Is it also that you want evidence that they have followed through on a directive of yours?

DR. P.: Oh, yes. But since the only thing we really insisted on in the interview was the pills, we had to establish not only that she had taken them but that she had allowed herself to feel better.

INT.: You put in the assumption that if she feels better it's because she is willing to feel better, not because she has taken the pills.

DR. P.: That's right. We made it clear that it's still something she controls.

INT.: I'm beginning at this point to notice a fairly clear structure to this interview, and I'd like to know if this is the sequence you generally follow. First comes the confrontation when your group wants to keep the patient out and the family wants to put her in, and you pull that switch that makes it very difficult for them to press for hospitalization. Then you get them committed to coming into therapy as a family. Then you start exploring the issues that are involved. Finally you move in to make specific recommendations.

DR. P.: I think you're right. In all our initial interviews, the first thing we try to do is to dispel the family's idea of what the problem is, the idea that "So-and-so is crazy and has to come to the hospital and the rest of us are not involved but we suffer a lot as a result of it." And this first five minutes are the most important part of the interview. Then we go on and convince the family of the value of our approach in such a way that they are prevented from doing anything else. Then we get information. And in the last part of the interview, we make it clear what we expect of everybody for the next twenty-four hours. We don't deliberately divide the interviews that way, but this is a pattern they roughly follow. Of course it varies. We didn't get as much information in this interview as we generally do.

INT.: I take it you usually provide the family with a little more rationale for moving into the last stage than you did here.

DR. P.: Yes. We're usually much more explicit about the picture as we see it.

INT.: You couldn't be explicit here, because you didn't understand it.

DR. P.: That doesn't mean we couldn't *tell* them we understand it. Or at least tell them what we do understand. I'm surprised at how inexplicit we were. The next day, we gave them a very clear outline of the way we saw the thing.

INT.: If you're not getting the information you want, do you sometimes take a break and then meet again?

DR. P.: If we don't have a good moment to start closing, we may say, "Look, we don't understand this yet, so you get together and talk about it and we'll get together and talk about it, and we'll meet back in half an hour and compare notes." If we do this, we usually explain how the picture looks to us so far and ask them to work on it. But here it was getting late and I was tired. We also thought we understood what was going on a little better than we did.

INT.: In any case, I take it that when Paul told you he wasn't going to leave, this gave you sufficient assurance to move to the stage where you give specific directives and start to close.

DR. P.: Yes. We hadn't filled all the holes in the picture but we were pretty clear and we were moving in the right direction.

INT.: Before ending, you give them a name and number to call in case anything comes up during the night. Is this routine?

DR. P.: Yes. We tell the family that we are available any time they need us. We're offering an alternative to hospitalization, and the idea is that since the hospital is available to a patient twenty-four hours a day, we should be available too.

INT.: How long did you see this family?

DR. P.: They came in eight times over a six-week period. At the end of that time they were doing so well that we didn't refer them. Instead, we asked them to call us if they needed us.

INT.: Is it usual for you to see people this long?

DR. P.: This was longer than usual. We saw them intensively during the first week, and after that mostly when Paul was off work, Mondays and Wednesdays.

MISS DEY.: I made home visits on two Saturdays.

INT.: How do you decide when to terminate?

DR. P.: I usually say that it's when they no longer present the symptoms that brought them to the emergency room. But we take care to spell this out to people from the beginning, so that they won't expect a long-term arrangement.

INT.: You make it clear that you're a limited service and that they have to start pulling their own weight.

DR. P.: Yes. We make a referral if treatment seems to be dragging on too long. We explain to them that we'll still be available in emergencies and that we will cooperate in any way we can with the source we're referring them to.

INT.: Do you have any problem in educating referral agencies in the approach you use, so that they won't work at cross purposes with you out of some different treatment ideology?

DR. P.: Our experience with the people in these agencies is that they are very receptive to us. We see them as vital to the success of our work and extend ourselves to them, and they are very cooperative as a result. They may see what we do as a different kind of therapy than what they're used to, but I think that the fact that it's not mysterious, that it is practical and even simple, makes it very appealing to them. Also, part of our hope in educating these agencies is to make community resources more available to people who are in trouble, so that they won't automatically think the hospital is the only answer.

INT.: Part of your fight against hospital addiction is to train the social agencies that could take the hospital's place.

DR. P.: That's right. For the most part, people who work with outpatients are not accustomed to handling psychotics, or if they do see them, it's generally in a hospital setting. As a result, if a patient acts crazy or threatens suicide, they get frightened and call the hospital. Very often a person gets sent to the hospital because of that kind of anxiety, not because this is what ought to be done.

INT.: You feel that some of the difficulty lies in the community services that feed the hospital.

DR. P.: Yes. And the hospital can't survive without patients, so there's no advantage to them in keeping people out. We now have a well-functioning emergency service. The admitting psychiatrists are beginning to sort out some of the people who don't need hospitalization and to provide short-term treatment for some individuals as an alternative. As a result, we're getting tougher cases now, which delights us.

INT.: At least you're having some impact on the hospital community.

DR. P.: A little. But what we do goes against established practice and is far from being accepted. One difficulty we face comes from certain aspects of psychiatric theory. I teach residents and medical students that a doctor is very limited in what he can do. Most of what he can effectively accomplish is to remove stresses and manipulate certain aspects of reality, then let the body's own innate defenses take care of the healing process. This applies to surgery, to psychiatry, to anything in medicine. It's certainly possible to try to reinforce the body's ability to handle stress, but this is difficult and not often effective. Psychiatry, under the influence of psychoanalysis, has gotten into the habit of thinking that this is the only thing of value. I'm not questioning the theory, but I feel that we need to develop new, more practical techniques which concentrate not so much on changing people as on changing the situations they are in, so that they have room to grow and develop on their own.

INT.: You seem to have changed the situation here. In this hour and a half, the relationships that came in the door have been totally realigned. The mother and son are now acting as equals in a friendly bargaining situation, and the sister has become a sympathetic bystander.

DR. P.: You're right. It's possible that everything we did from then on was only reinforcing this basic change.

Bibliography

This selection of articles and books on marriage and family therapy emphasizes therapy more than diagnosis or research.

Ackerman, N. W.: "A Dynamic Frame for the Clinical Approach to Family Conflict," in Ackerman, N. W., Beatman, F. L., and Sherman, S. N., eds.: *Exploring the Base for Family Therapy.* New York: Family Service Association of America, 1961.

Ackerman, N. W.: "Emergence of Family Psychotherapy on the Present Scene," in Stein, M. I., ed.: *Contemporary Psychotherapies.* Glencoe, Ill.: Free Press, 1961.

Ackerman, N. W.: "Family-focused Therapy of Schizophrenia," in Scher, S. C., and Davis, H. R., eds.: *The Out-Patient Treatment of Schizophrenia.* New York: Grune & Stratton, 1960.

Ackerman, N. W.: "Family Psychotherapy and Psychoanalysis: Implications of Difference." *Family Process,* 1 (1962), 30–43.

Ackerman, N. W.: *The Psychodynamics of Family Life.* New York: Basic Books, 1958.

Ackerman, N. W.: "Toward an Integrative Therapy of the Family." *American Journal of Psychiatry,* 114 (1958), 727–733.

Ackerman, N. W.: *Treating the Troubled Family.* New York: Basic Books, 1966.

Ackerman, N. W., and Behrens, M. L.: "The Family Group and Family Therapy: The Practical Application of Family Diagnosis," in Masserman, J. H., and Moreno, J. L., eds.: *Progress in Psychotherapy,* Vol. 3. New York: Grune & Stratton, 1959.

Alexander, I. E.: "Family Therapy." *Marriage and Family Living,* 25 (1963), 146–154.

Appel, E., Goodwin, H. M., Wood, H. P., and Askren, E. L.: "Training in Psychotherapy; the Use of Marriage Counseling in a University Teaching Clinic." *American Journal of Psychiatry,* 117 (1961), 709–711.

Arlen, M. S.: "Conjoint Therapy and the Corrective Emotional Experience." *Family Process,* 5 (1966), 91–104.

Arnold, A.: "The Implications of Two-Person and Three-Person Relationships for Family Psychotherapy." *Journal of Health and Human Behavior,* 3 (1962), 94–97.

Bannister, K., and Pincus, L.: *Shared Phantasy in Marital Problems: Therapy in a Four-Person Relationship.* London: Tavistock Institute of Human Relations, 1965.

Bardill, D.: "Family Therapy in an Army Mental Hygiene Clinic." *Social Casework*, 44 (1963), 452–457.

Basamania, B. W.: "The Emotional Life of the Family: Inferences for Social Casework." *American Journal of Orthopsychiatry*, 31 (1961), 74–86.

Beatman, F.: "The Training and Preparation of Workers for Family-Group Treatment." *Social Casework*, 45 (1964), 202–208.

Becker, J.: "Good Premorbid Schizophrenic Wives and Their Husbands." *Family Process*, 2 (1963), 34–51.

Beecher, W., and Beecher, M.: "Re-Structuring Mistaken Family Relationships." *Journal of Individual Psychology*, 13 (1957), 176–181.

Bell, J. E.: "Contrasting Approaches in Marital Counseling." *Family Process*, 6 (1967), 16–26.

Bell, J. E.: "The Family Group Therapist: An Agent of Change." *International Journal of Group Psychotherapy*, 14 (1964), 72–83.

Bell, J. E.: *Family Group Therapy*. Public Health Monograph No. 64, U. S. Department of Health, Education, and Welfare, 1961.

Bell, J. E.: "Recent Advances in Family Group Therapy." *Journal of Child Psychology and Psychiatry*, 3 (1962), 1–15.

Bell, J. E.: "A Theoretical Position for Family Group Therapy." *Family Process*, 2 (1963), 1–14.

Belmont, L. P., and Jasnow, A.: "The Utilization of Co-therapists and of Group Therapy Techniques in a Family Oriented Approach to a Disturbed Child." *International Journal of Group Psychotherapy*, 11 (1961), 319–328.

Blinder, M. G., Colman, A. D., Curry, A. E., and Kessler, D. R.: "MCFT: Simultaneous Treatment of Several Families." *American Journal of Psychotherapy*, 19 (1965), 559–569.

Boszormenyi-Nagy, I., and Framo, J. L., eds.: *Intensive Family Therapy: Theoretical and Practical Aspects*. New York: Harper and Row, 1965.

Boszormenyi-Nagy, I.: "Intensive Family Therapy as Process," in Boszormenyi-Nagy, I., and Framo, J. L., eds.: *Intensive Family Therapy: Theoretical and Practical Aspects*. New York: Harper and Row, 1965.

Boverman, M., and Adams, J. R.: "Collaboration of Psychiatrist and Clergyman: A Case Report." *Family Process*, 3 (1964), 251–272.

Bowen, M.: "Family Psychotherapy." *American Journal of Orthopsychiatry*, 31 (1961), 40–60.

Bowen, M.: "Family Psychotherapy with Schizophrenia in the Hospital and in Private practice," in Boszormenyi-Nagy, I., and Framo, J. L., eds.: *Intensive Family Therapy*. New York: Harper and Row, 1965.

Bowen, M.: "The Use of Family Theory in Clinical Practice." *Comprehensive Psychiatry*, 7 (1967), 345–374.

Brodey, W. M., and Hayden, M.: "The Intrateam Reactions: Their Relation to the Conflicts of the Family in Treatment." *American Journal of Orthopsychiatry*, 27 (1957), 349–355.

Brody, S.: "Simultaneous Psychotherapy of Married Couples," in Masserman, J. H., ed.: *Current Psychiatric Therapies*, 1 (1961), 139–144.

Carek, D. J., and Watson, A. S.: "Treatment of a Family Involved in Fratricide." *Archives of General Psychiatry*, 11 (1964), 533–543.

Carroll, E. J.: "Family Therapy—Some Observations and Comparisons." *Family Process*, 3 (1964), 178–185.

Carroll, E. J.: "Treatment of the Family as a Unit." *Pennsylvania Medical Journal*, 63 (1960), 56–62.

Carroll, E. J., Cambor, C. G., Leopold, J. V., Miller, M. D., and Reis, W. J.: "Psychotherapy of Marital Couples." *Family Process*, 2 (1963), 25–33.

Charny, I. W.: "Integrated Individual and Family Therapy." *Family Process*, 5 (1967), 179–198.

Charny, I. W.: "Family Interviews in Redefining a 'Sick' Child's Role in the Family Problem." *Psychological Reports,* 10 (1962), 577–578.

Clower, C. G., and Brody, L.: "Conjoint Family Therapy in Outpatient Practice." *American Journal of Psychotherapy,* 18 (1964), 670–677.

Cooper, S.: "New Trends in Work with Parents: Progress or Change." *Social Casework,* 42 (1961), 342–347.

Curry, A. E.: "The Family Therapy Situation as a System." *Family Process,* 5 (1967), 131–141.

Curry, A. E.: "Therapeutic Management of Multiple Family Groups." *International Journal of Group Psychotherapy,* 15 (1965), 90–96.

Cutter, A. V., and Hallowitz, D.: "Diagnosis and Treatment of the Family Unit with Respect to the Character-Disordered Youngster." *Journal of the American Academy of Child Psychiatry,* 1 (1962), 605–618.

Cutter, A. V., and Hallowitz, D.: "Different Approaches to Treatment of the Child and the Parents." *American Journal of Orthopsychiatry,* 32 (1962), 152–158.

Davies, Q., Ellenson, G., and Young, R.: "Therapy with a Group of Families in a Psychiatric Day Center." *American Journal of Orthopsychiatry,* 36 (1966), 134–147.

Elkin, M.: "Short-Contact Counseling in a Conciliation Court." *Social Casework,* 43 (1962), 184–190.

Erickson, M.: "The Identification of a Secure Reality," *Family Process,* 1 (1962), 294–303.

Feldman, M. J.: "Privacy and Conjoint Family Therapy." *Family Process,* 6 (1967), 1–9.

Fisch, R.: "Home Visits in a Private Psychiatric Practice." *Family Process,* 3 (1964), 114–126.

Fleck, S.: "Psychotherapy of Families of Hospitalized Patients," in Masserman, J. H., ed.: *Current Psychiatric Therapies.* New York: Grune & Stratton, 1963.

Framo, J. L.: "Rationale and Techniques of Intensive Family Therapy," in Boszormenyi-Nagy, I., and Framo, J. L., eds.: *Intensive Family Therapy.* New York: Harper and Row, 1965.

Framo, J. L.: "The Theory of the Technique of Family Treatment of Schizophrenia." *Family Process,* 1 (1962), 119–131.

Freeman, V. J.: "Differentiation of 'Unity' Family Therapy Approaches Prominent in the United States." *International Journal of Social Psychiatry,* Special Edition 2 (1964), 35–46.

Freeman, V. S., Klein, A. F., Riehman, L. M., Lukoff, I. F., and Heiseg, V. E.: "Family Group Counseling as Differentiated from Other Family Therapies." *International Journal of Group Psychotherapy,* 13 (1963), 167–175.

Friedman, A. S.: "Family Therapy as Conducted in the Home." *Family Process,* 1 (1962), 132–140.

Friedman, A. S.: "The Incomplete Family in Family Therapy." *Family Process,* 2 (1963), 288–301.

Friedman, A. S., Boszormenyi-Nagy, I., Jungreis, J. E., Lincoln, G., Mitchell, H. E., Sonne, J. C., Speck, R. V., and Spivack, G.: *Psychotherapy for the Whole Family.* New York: Spring Publishers, 1965.

Friedman, A. S.: "The 'Well' Sibling in the 'Sick' Family: A Contradiction." *International Journal of Social Psychiatry,* Special Edition 2 (1964), 47–53.

Fry, W. F.: "The Marital Context of an Anxiety Syndrome." *Family Process,* 1 (1962), 245–252.

Gehrke, S., and Kirschenbaum, M.: "Survival Patterns in Family Conjoint Therapy." *Family Process,* 6 (1967), 67–80.

Gehrke, S., and Moxom, J.: "Diagnostic Classifications and Treatment Techniques in Marriage Counseling." *Family Process,* 1 (1962), 253–264.

Geist, J., and Gerber, N. M.: "Joint Interviewing: A Treatment Technique with Marital Partners." *Social Casework,* 41 (1960), 76–83.

Glower, C. G., and Brody, L.: "Conjoint Family Therapy in Outpatient Practice." *American Journal of Psychotherapy,* 18 (1964), 670–677.

Gomberg, M. R.: "Family Oriented Treatment of Marital Problems." *Social Casework,* 37 (1956), 3–10.

Goolishian, H. A.: "A Brief Psychotherapy Program for Disturbed Adolescents." *American Journal of Orthopsychiatry,* 32 (1962), 142–148.

Goolishian, H. A., McDanald, E. G., MacGregor, R., Ritchie, A. M., Serrano, A. C., and Schuster, F. P.: *Multiple Impact Therapy with Families.* New York: McGraw-Hill, 1961.

Gralnick, A.: "Conjoint Family Therapy: Its Role in Rehabilitation of the In-patient and Family." *Journal of Nervous and Mental Diseases,* 136 (1963), 500–506.

Gralnick, A.: "The Family in Psychotherapy," in Masserman, J. H., ed.: *Science and Psychoanalysis, Vol. 2: Individual and Family Dynamics.* New York: Grune & Stratton, 1959.

Gralnick, A.: "Family Psychotherapy: General and Specific Considerations." *American Journal of Orthopsychiatry,* 32 (1962), 515–526.

Green, R.: "Collaborative and Conjoint Therapy Combined." *Family Process,* 3 (1964), 80–98.

Greenberg, I. M., Glick, I. D., Match, S., and Riback, S. S.: "Family Therapy: Indications and Rationale." *Archives of General Psychiatry,* 10 (1964), 7–25.

Grosser, G. S., and Paul, N. L.: "Ethical Issues in Family Group Therapy." *American Journal of Orthopsychiatry,* 34 (1964), 875–884.

Guerney, B., and Guerney, L. F.: "Choices in Initiating Family Therapy." *Psychotherapy,* 1 (1964), 119–123.

Gullerud, E. N., and Harlan, V. L.: "Four-Way Joint Interviewing in Marital Counseling." *Social Casework,* 43 (1962), 532–537.

Haley, J.: "Marriage Therapy." *Archives of General Psychiatry,* 8 (1963), 213–234.

Haley, J.: *Strategies of Psychotherapy.* New York: Grune & Stratton, 1963.

Haley, J.: "Whither Family Therapy." *Family Process,* 1 (1962), 69–100.

Hallowitz, D., and Cutter, A. V.: "The Family Unit Approach in Therapy: Uses, Process and Dynamics." *Casework Papers.* New York: Family Service Association of America, 1961.

Hallowitz, D.: "Family Unit Treatment of Character-Disordered Youngsters." *Social Work Practice.* New York: Columbia University Press, 1963.

Hallowitz, D., Clement, R. G., and Cutter, A. V.: "The Treatment Process with Both Parents Together." *American Journal of Orthopsychiatry,* 27 (1957), 587–601.

Handlon, J. H., and Parloff, M. B.: "The Treatment of Patient and Family as a Group: Is It Group Psychotherapy?" *International Journal of Group Psychotherapy,* 12 (1962), 132–141.

Harms, E.: "A Socio-Genetic Concept of Family Therapy," *Acta Psychothera-peutica.* 12 (1964), 53–60.

Hoffman, L., and Kantor, R. E.: "Brechtian Theater as a Model for Conjoint Family Therapy." *Family Process,* 5 (1966), 218–229.

Jackson, D. D.: "Family Interaction, Family Homeostasis, and Some Implications for Conjoint Family Psychotherapy," in Masserman, J. H., ed.: *Science and Psychoanalysis, Vol. 2: Individual and Familial Dynamics.* New York: Grune & Stratton, 1959.

Jackson, D. D., and Satir, V.: "A Review of Psychiatric Developments in Family Diagnosis and Family Therapy," in Ackerman, N. W., Beatman, F. L., and Sherman, S. N., eds.: *Exploring the Base for Family Therapy.* New York: Family Service Association of America, 1961.

Jackson, D. D., and Weakland, J. H.: "Conjoint Family Therapy: Some Considerations on Theory, Technique and Results." *Psychiatry,* 24 (1961), 30–45.

Jackson, D. D., and Weakland, J. H.: "Schizophrenic Symptoms and Family Interaction." *Archives of General Psychiatry,* 1 (1959), 618–621.

Jolesch, M.: "Casework Treatment of Young Married Couples." *Social Casework,* 43 (1962), 245–251.

Kaffman, M.: "Family Diagnosis and Therapy in Child Emotional Pathology." *Family Process,* 4 (1965), 241–258.

Kaffman, M.: "Short Term Family Therapy." *Family Process,* 2 (1963), 216–234.

Kantor, R. E., and Hoffman, L.: "Brechtian Theater as a Model for Conjoint Family Therapy." *Family Process,* 5 (1966), 218–229.

Kempler, W.: "Experiential Family Therapy," *International Journal of Group Psychotherapy,* 15 (1965), 57–71.

Kohl, R. N.: "Pathologic Reactions of Marital Partners to Improvement of Patients." *American Journal of Psychiatry,* 118 (1962), 1036–1041.

Kwiatkowska, H.: "Family Art Therapy." *Family Process,* 6 (1967), 37–55.

Landes, J., and Winter, W.: "A New Strategy for Treating Disintegrating Families." *Family Process,* 5 (1966), 1–20.

Laqueur, H. P., and LaBurt, H. A.: "Family Organization on a Modern State Hospital Ward." *Mental Hygiene,* 48 (1964), 544–551.

Laqueur, H. P., LaBurt, H. A., and Morong, E.: "Multiple Family Therapy," in Masserman, J. H., ed.: *Current Psychiatric Therapies, IV.* New York: Grune & Stratton, 1964.

Laqueur, H. P., LaBurt, H. A., and Morong, E.: "Multiple Family Therapy: Further Developments." *International Journal of Social Psychiatry,* Special Edition 2 (1964), 70–80.

Lehrman, N. S.: "The Joint Interview: An Aid to Psychotherapy and Family Stability." *American Journal of Psychotherapy,* 17 (1963), 83–94.

Leichter, E., and Shulman, G.: "The Family Interview as an Integrative Device in Group Therapy with Families." *International Journal of Group Psychotherapy,* 13 (1963), 335–345.

Leslie, G. R.: "Conjoint Therapy in Marriage Counseling." *Journal of Marriage and the Family,* 26 (1964), 65–71.

Leveton, A.: "Family Therapy as the Treatment of Choice." *Medical Bulletin, U. S. Army Europe,* 21 (1964), 76–79.

Liebermann, L. P.: "Joint Interview Technique—An Experiment in Group Psychotherapy." *British Journal of Medical Psychology,* 30 (1957), 202–207.

Lindberg, D. R., and Wosmek, A. W.: "The Use of Family Sessions in Foster Home Care." *Social Casework,* 44 (1963), 137–141.

MacGregor, R.: "Multiple Impact Psychotherapy with Families." *Family Process,* 1 (1962), 15–29.

Machotka, P., Pittman, F. S., and Flomenhaft, K.: "Incest as a Family Affair." *Family Process,* 6 (1967), 98–116.

Markowitz, I.: "Family Therapy in a Child Guidance Clinic." *Psychiatric Quarterly,* 40 (1966), 308–319.

Martin, F., and Knight, J.: "Joint Interviews as Part of Intake Procedure in a Child Psychiatric Clinic." *Journal of Child Psychology and Psychiatry,* 3 (1962), 17–26.

Messer, A.: "Family Treatment of a School Phobic Child." *Archives of General Psychiatry,* 11 (1964), 548–555.

Midelfort, C. F.: *The Family in Psychotherapy*. New York: McGraw-Hill, 1957.

Midelfort, C. F.: "Use of Members of the Family in Treatment of Schizophrenia." *Family Process*, 1 (1962), 114–118.

Miller, D., and Westman, J. C.: "Family Teamwork and Psychotherapy." *Family Process*, 5 (1966), 49–59.

Minuchin, S.: "Conflict Resolution Family Therapy." *Psychiatry*, 28 (1965), 278–286.

Minuchin, S.: "Family Structure, Family Language, and the Puzzled Therapist." *American Journal of Orthopsychiatry*, 34 (1964), 347–348.

Minuchin, S., Auerswald, E., King, C., and Rabinowitz, C.: "The Study and Treatment of Families that Produce Multiple Acting-Out Boys." *American Journal of Orthopsychiatry*, 34 (1964), 125–134.

Mitchell, C.: "A Casework Approach to Disturbed Families," in Ackerman, N. W., Beatman, F. L., and Sherman, S. N., eds.: *Exploring the Base for Family Therapy*. New York: Family Service Association of America, 1961.

Mitchell, C.: "The Use of Family Sessions in the Diagnosis and Treatment of Disturbances in Children." *Social Casework*, 41 (1960), 283–290.

Osberg, J. W.: "Initial Impressions of the Use of Short-Term Family Group Conferences." *Family Process*, 1 (1962), 236–244.

Parloff, M. B.: "The Family in Psychotherapy." *Archives of General Psychiatry*, 4 (1961), 445–451.

Pattison, E. M.: "Treatment of Alcoholic Families with Nurse Home Visits." *Family Process*, 4 (1965), 75–94.

Patton, J. D., Bradley, J. D., and Hornowski, M. J.: "Collaborative Treatment of Marital Partners." *North Carolina Medical Journal*, 19 (1958), 523–528.

Paul, N. L., and Grosser, G. H.: "Family Resistance to Change in Schizophrenic Patients." *Family Process*, 3 (1964), 377–401.

Pollak, O.: "Issues in Family Diagnosis and Family Therapy." *Journal of Marriage and the Family*, 26 (1964), 279–287.

Pollack, O., and Brieland, D.: "The Midwest Seminar on Family Diagnosis and Treatment." *Social Casework*, 42 (1961), 319–324.

Pittman, F. S., Flomenhaft, K., DeYoung, C., Kaplan, D., and Langsley, D. G.: "Crisis Family Therapy," in Masserman, J. H., ed.: *Current Psychiatric Therapies*. New York: Grune & Stratton, 1966.

Pittman, F. S., Langsley, D. G., Kaplan, D., DeYoung, C., and Flomenhaft, K.: "Family therapy as an Alternative to Hospitalization." *APA Psychiatric Research Reports*, 20 (1966), 188–195.

Rabiner, E. L., Molinski, H., and Gralnick, A.: "Conjoint Family Therapy in the Inpatient Setting." *American Journal of Psychotherapy*, 16 (1962), 618–631.

Ravich, R. A.: "Short-Term Intensive Treatment of Marital Discord." *Voices*, 2 (1966), 42–48.

Reding, G. R., and Ennis, B.: "Treatment of the Couple by a Couple." *British Journal of Medical Psychology*, 37 (1964), 325–330.

Reidy, J. J.: "An Approach to Family-Centered Treatment in a State Institution." *American Journal of Orthopsychiatry*, 32 (1962), 133–141.

Ritchie, A.: "Multiple Impact Therapy, an Experiment." *Social Work*, 5 (1960), 16–21.

Rubinstein, D.: "Family Therapy," in Masserman, J. H., ed.: *Progress in Neurology and Psychiatry*, Vol. 18. New York: Grune & Stratton, 1963.

Safer, D. J.: "Family Therapy for Children with Behavior Disorders." *Family Process*, 5 (1967), 243–255.

Sager, C. J.: "The Development of Marriage Therapy: An Historical Review." *American Journal of Orthopsychiatry*, 36 (1966), 458–468.

Sager, C. J.: "Transference in Conjoint Treatment of Married Couples." *Archives of General Psychiatry,* 16 (1967), 185–193.

Sager, C. J.: "The Treatment of Married Couples," in Arieti, S., ed., *American Handbook of Psychiatry.* New York: Basic Books, 1959.

Satir, V.: *Conjoint Family Therapy.* Palo Alto: Science & Behavior Books, 1964.

Satir, V.: "The Family as a Treatment Unit." *Confin. Psychiatry,* 8 (1965), 37–42.

Satir, V.: "The Quest for Survival: A Training Program for Family Diagnosis and Treatment." *Acta Psychotherapeutica,* 2 (1963), 33–38.

Schaffer, L., Wynne, L. C., Day, J., Ryckoff, I. M., and Halperin, A.: "On the Nature and Sources of the Psychiatrist's Experience with the Family of the Schizophrenic." *Psychiatry,* 25 (1962), 32–45.

Scheflen, A. E.: *Stream and Structure of Communicational Behavior.* Philadelphia: Eastern Pennsylvania Psychiatric Institute of Behavioral Studies, Monograph No. 1, 1965.

Scherz, F. H.: "Multiple-Client Interviewing: Treatment Implications." *Social Casework,* 43 (1962), 120–125.

Schuster, F. P.: "Summary Description of Multiple Impact Psychotherapy." *Texas Reports on Biology and Medicine,* 17 (1959), 426–430.

Serrano, A. C., and Wilson, N. S.: "Family Therapy in the Treatment of the Brain Damaged Child." *Diseases of the Nervous System,* 24 (1963), 732–735.

Shellow, R. S., Brown, B. S., and Osberg, J. W.: "Family Group Therapy in Retrospect: Four Years and Sixty Families." *Family Process,* 2 (1963), 52–67.

Shereshefsky, P. M.: "Family Unit Treatment in Child Guidance." *Social Casework,* 8 (1963), 63–70.

Sherman, M. H., Ackerman, N. W., Sherman, S. N., and Mitchell, C.: "Non-Verbal Cues and Reenactment of Conflict in Family Therapy." *Family Process,* 4 (1965), 133–162.

Sherman, S. N.: "The Sociopsychological Character of Family-Group Treatment." *Social Casework,* 45 (1964), 195–201.

Siporin, M.: "Family-Centered Casework in a Psychiatric Setting." *Social Casework,* 37 (1956), 167–174.

Sonne, J. C., and Lincoln, G.: "Heterosexual Co-Therapy Team Experiences During Family Therapy." *Family Process,* 4 (1965), 177–197.

Sonne, J. C., Speck, R. V., and Jungreis, J. E.: "The Absent-Member Maneuver as a Resistance in Family Therapy of Schizophrenia." *Family Process,* 1 (1962), 44–62.

Speck, R. V.: "The Home Setting for Family Treatment." *International Journal of Social Psychiatry,* Special Edition 2 (1964), 47–53.

Speck, R. V.: "Family Therapy in the Home." *Journal of Marriage and the Family,* 26 (1964), 72–76.

Thomas, A.: "Simultaneous Psychotherapy with Marital Partners." *American Journal of Psychotherapy,* 10 (1956), 716–727.

Thoman, G.: "Family Therapy—Help for Troubled Families." *Public Affairs Pamphlet No. 356.* New York, February, 1964.

Warkentin, J.: "Psychotherapy with Couples and Families." *Journal of the Medical Association, Georgia,* 49 (1960), 569–570.

Warkentin, J., and Whitaker, C.: "Serial Impasses in Marriage." *Psychiatric Research Report 20.* American Psychiatric Association, 1966.

Watson, A. S.: "The Conjoint Psychotherapy of Marriage Partners." *American Journal of Orthopsychiatry,* 33 (1963), 912–923.

Whitaker, C. A.: "Psychotherapy with Couples." *American Journal of Psychotherapy,* 12 (1958), 18–23.

Whitaker, C. A., Felder, R. E., and Warkentin, J.: "Countertransference in the

Family Treatment of Schizophrenia," in Boszormenyi-Nagy, I., and Framo, J. L., eds.: *Intensive Family Therapy*. New York: Harper and Row, 1965.

Wyatt, G. L., and Herzan, H. M.: "Therapy with Stuttering Children and Their Mothers." *American Journal of Orthopsychiatry*, 32 (1962), 645–659.

Wynne, L. C.: "Some Indications and Contraindications for Exploratory Family Therapy," in Boszormenyi-Nagy, I., and Framo, J. L., eds.: *Intensive Family Therapy*. New York: Harper and Row, 1965.

Wynne, L. C.: "The Study of Intrafamilial Alignments and Splits in Exploratory Family Therapy," in Ackerman, N. W., Beatman, F. L., and Sherman, S. N., eds.: *Exploring the Base for Family Therapy*. New York: Family Service Association of America, 1961.

Zierer, E., Sternberg, D., Finn, R., and Farmer, M.: "Family Creative Analysis: Its Role in Treatment." *Bulletin of Art Therapy*, 5 (1966), 87–104.

Zuk, G. H.: "The Go-Between Process in Family Therapy." *Family Process*, 5 (1967), 162–178.

Zuk, G. H.: "Preliminary Study of the Go-Between Process in Family Therapy," in *Proceedings*, 73rd Annual Convention of the American Psychological Association, Chicago, 1965.

Zuk, G. H., and Boszormenyi-Nagy, I.: *Family Therapy and Disturbed Families*. Palo Alto: Science and Behavior Books, 1966.

Zuk, G. H., and Rubinstein, D.: "A Review of Concepts in the Study and Treatment of Families of Schizophrenics," in Boszormenyi-Nagy, I., and Framo, J. L., eds.: *Intensive Family Therapy*. New York: Harper and Row, 1965.